LA VOZ LATINA

La Voz Latina

Contemporary Plays and Performance Pieces by Latinas

Edited by

ELIZABETH C. RAMÍREZ
AND CATHERINE CASIANO

UNIVERSITY OF ILLINOIS PRESS
Urbana, Chicago, and Springfield

First Illinois paperback, 2021

1 2 3 4 5 C P 5 4 3 2 1
♾ This book is printed on acid-free paper.

The Library of Congress cataloged the cloth edition as follows:
La voz Latina : contemporary plays and performance pieces by Latinas / edited by Elizabeth C. Ramírez and Catherine Casiano.
p. cm.
ISBN-13: 978-0-252-03622-4 (hardcover : alk. paper)
ISBN-10: 0-252-03622-0 (hardcover : alk. paper)
1. American drama—Hispanic American authors.
2. American drama—Women authors.
3. Dramatists, American—21st century—Interviews.
4. Hispanic American women authors—Interviews.
I. Ramírez, Elizabeth C. II. Casiano, Catherine.
PS508.H57V69 2011
812'.609928708968—dc22 2010046896

PAPERBACK ISBN 978-0-252-08598-7

To our lasting memory of our dear friend, Oscar G. Brockett,

and to our parents,

Margarita C. and Pedro F. Ramírez

and Theresa R. and Victor L. Casiano, M.D.,

and to

Elizabeth R. Casiano, M.D., Jason Cruz, J.D.,

and especially Pedro C. Ramírez, M.F.A., theatre manager,

Guadalupe Cultural Arts Center,

and Diego, our great performer and true inspiration.

CONTENTS

Acknowledgments ix

Introduction: Latinas Take the Stage 1

I. **CREATING A PERFORMANCE VOICE: THEMES OF FAMILY, RELIGION, AND COMMUNITY** 25

1. Milcha Sanchez-Scott's *Roosters* 31

2. Cherríe Moraga's *Waiting for Da God* 68

II. **CHICANAS AND CHICANO TEATRO: STAGING IDENTITY** 87

3. Diane Rodriguez's *The Path to Divadom, Or How to Make Fat-free Tamales in G Minor* 93

4. Yareli Arizmendi's *Who Buys Your Shoes?* 103

III. **LA INDÍGENA/THE INDIGENOUS: STAGING MYTH** 119

5. Celia Herrera Rodríguez's *Cositas Quebradas: Performance Codex* 125

6. The Colorado Sisters' *Chicomoztoc: Mimixcoa—Cloud Serpent* 140

IV. **"RACE MATTERS"** 165

7. Josefina Báez's *Dominicanish* 171

8. Evelina Fernández's *Luminarias* 188

V. **WHERE IS HOME AND HOW DO WE GET THERE?** 237

9. Carmen Peláez's *El Postre de Estrada Palma* and *My Cuba* 239

10. Carmen Rivera's *La Gringa* 254

11. Migdalia Cruz's *Another Part of the House* 305

VI. **COMMENTARY ON LATINA THEATRE IN THE UNITED STATES** 357

12. Contributions by Women of Color —Kathy Perkins 359

13. NoPassport: Dreaming the Americas —Caridad Svich 362

ACKNOWLEDGMENTS

We want to express our deepest gratitude to all of the theatre artists who have contributed to this book. These women inspired us with their generous and unwavering support and patience during the long development phase of this project. *¡Mil gracias y fuertes abrazos a nuestras hermanas teatristas!*

Many colleagues have expressed great interest and eager anticipation for the completion of our work, and we remain indebted to them. We could not have completed this book without the wisdom and advice of certain outstanding figures in our lives. Judy Lee Oliva, an award-winning Chickasaw playwright, was once a student and has become a colleague *en el teatro de la indígena y siempre será nuestra hermana.* Mary Miller, executive director, Curriculum and Support, Edgewood Independent School District, is perhaps the most insightful administrator who understands why every child deserves an arts education. Kathy Perkins continues to be our toughest critic and greatest colleague, *y siempre* part of our sisterhood. Jorge Huerta is perhaps the greatest mentor, and he and his wife and life partner Ginger have a special place in our hearts. Above all, Oscar Brockett will always be the most significant because of his encouragement to write our own history and because he brought us to Joan Catapano, and while we mourn losing Brock, his spirit and laughter will outlast all of us.

We would also like to express a very special thanks to Dean Reynaldo Anaya Valencia, professor of law at St. Mary's University School of Law, who read our manuscript with an entirely different eye than the perspective from our colleagues in performance studies. Professor Valencia provided us with his unique insight on race and gender discrimination, given his work on the Supreme Court of Texas Task Force on Gender Fairness and many years of teaching in the area of race and racism in U.S. law and gender discrimination, as well as many years of experience and numerous publications. To all of these mentors and colleagues, we extend our appreciation for all of their help and encouragement through many, many years.

We are grateful for the assistance of Mario C. Ramírez with photo selection and photo editing. Our editors at the University of Illinois Press have been so careful to safeguard our work, and their attention to the many special details is greatly appreciated. Above all, we are indebted to Joan Catapano for her unwavering belief in our project, sustained also by invaluable reviewers who provided us with significant commentary and suggestions that helped to steer our course.

Finally, we could not have completed this project without the love and support of our families. *Mil gracias* to Pedro F. and Margarita C. Ramírez, Theresa R. and Victor L. Casiano, Elizabeth II, Jason, Pedro for his genius in every aspect of performance, and our youngest performance voice, Don Diego.

INTRODUCTION
Latinas Take the Stage

In surveying the Latina/Latino theatre movement in the United States, M. Teresa Marrero observes that "since the 1960s, a significant amount of ground has been gained by Latina and Latino performers and playwrights: a ground they have fought for in the political and cultural arts arenas. A reading of the development of Chicano/Latino theater offers an oppositional dynamic, an impetus towards the interruption of the stereotype. The energy of this rethinking has been largely *women's*. Indeed, it is Latina women who now lead the Latino theater into the new millennium" (original emphasis).[1] Certainly, at the end of the first decade of the new century, it is evident that the momentum of Latinas contributing to the annals of the stage continues. In effect, this compelling voice remains at the very forefront of Latina/Latino theatre in the United States, making an impact on the U.S. stage. Because of the importance of this creative voice, that is, *la voz Latina,* the primary goal of this project is to broaden its audience.

This book serves as a "document of a key period in Latina performance history" by a select group of female playwrights from 1980 to the present, working in very distinct forms, styles, themes, and genres. Through this diversity we encounter "the rich multiplicity of cultural subject positions and artistic expressions encompassed by the term 'Latina.'" Contrary to the magical realism stereotype of Latina/Latino drama or to "the perception that politically engaged work among Latina/Latino artists must take the form of social realism and its Brechtian-inflected adaptations," this compilation of work "shows that Latinas are not content to be limited to these forms" generally associated with Latinas/Latinos.[2]

We began editing this collection of plays and performance pieces in 2000. In the intervening decade we have encountered numerous life-altering experiences that have impacted completing this book. Catherine followed her passion for helping the Latina/Latino community by pursuing a career in law and began working to defend and protect the constitutional rights of indigent clients whose voices are continually silenced by local governments, corporate businesses, or even an abusive spouse. Elizabeth left higher education in order to reconnect with educating K through 12th-grade children and their teachers through the fine arts, survived health crises, and became a caregiver to elderly parents while still working professionally as a dramaturg and holding a full-time job. Along the way, we have maintained one strong motivating force to complete this endeavor, namely, the desire to bring the growing body of performance work by Latinas to theatre practitioners, researchers, and the widest possible audience. Elizabeth introduced her niece, Catherine, to performance at an early age. Elizabeth's immersion in theatre as a scholar and practitioner instilled a love for playgoing and performance in many of her family members, particularly Catherine, who in turn, spent many years assisting Elizabeth with research and special performance projects. Over the years, Elizabeth and Catherine attended countless theatrical performances, both together and separately, and the question raised over and over again for both was "where is the Latina voice?" Elizabeth had been heavily involved in the Chicano movement when she attended UCLA and had gone on to found and direct the Chicano Theatre Program at California State University, Sacramento, and Catherine was heavily involved in Latina/Latino issues throughout her time working toward her degrees in higher education, but it became clear that a compilation of plays written by Latinas was necessary to fill a void and ensure that those important Latina and Latino voices were heard by others. Since our own lives have always been connected through performance, this project has been the ideal in terms of bringing critical voices for the stage by Latinas to others. Even more so, the women who have contributed to this collection have been unwavering in their support of this project, and we remain indebted to them.

Through select works and playwrights, these Latinas can serve as representatives from varying backgrounds that both set them apart from others as well as show shared common experiences. Collectively, these women's roots represent great diversity. We learn about indigenous cultures as well as about urban Latinas and Latinos, and by representing distinct Latina/Latino cultures, great depth is added to the field. Since most of the plays were unpublished, this collection makes a significant contribution to the field. The plays themselves are distinct in focus, structure, and interest. A further distinction lies in the fact that all of the playwrights are also theatre practitioners in either academic or professional settings or both.

Why These Voices/¿Y Estas Voces?

Beginning with a list of names of playwrights we already knew, we were confident that we could obtain permissions for ten plays or performance pieces in order to fill a book. We wanted to showcase samples of works by women who were already recognized for their writing, and we wanted to show the great variety in the type of work that has been written, from short monologues to full-length, multicharacter plays. Because production history was an integral part of the project, we also wanted to be sure that each entry we used had a stage life. Some playwrights on our initial list could readily contribute and others simply could not do so at the time. Of those who were willing to participate, some had works that were too long for inclusion or their offered play had never been produced and therefore had no production history. Even so, our collection began to take shape with the abundance of works that did fit our criteria.

We soon arrive at a group of playtexts that offered the kinds of voices we were hoping for that could represent *la voz latina*. The intent of this collection from the onset was to give already known and new playwrights alike an opportunity to let our audience know about new and different work as well as to revisit some of the works that have had viable lives on the U.S. stage. In order to accomplish this task, we knew that between the two of us we would be able to obtain works from a core group of women we already knew and, based on those initial agreements, we felt confident that we could also approach others we wanted to include. In addition, we wanted to show a variety in terms of cultural roots and place of family origin.

We continued to review incoming entries since we always intended to begin with one volume, with the expectation that others would follow. With this forward-looking plan, we expected that at a later date we would be able to include entries like the exciting original ensemble work by Teatro Luna, the "Latina/Hispana" ensemble, founded in Chicago, Illinois, in 2000, whom we met when they were performing at the Guadalupe Cultural Arts Center's theatre in San Antonio, Texas, expressing great interest in being a part of this or future projects on the work of Latinas; possibly the work by the newly formed Teatro de la Colectiva de Mujeres, a theatre company of Latina immigrant women day laborers creating original work through the auspices of El Teatro Jornalero! (ETJ!), a theatre company based in San Francisco and made up entirely of Latin American immigrant workers; and certainly the work of the highly prolific and acclaimed Caridad Svich, who has become a significant force in Latina/Latino theatre for far more than her expansive body of dramatic work, as the founder of NoPassport, an unincorporated theatre alliance and press devoted to expression and advocacy for crosscultural diversity and difference in the arts. Thus, not withstanding noticeable omissions, especially in the wake of more new playwrights emerging since we first began this collection, our expectation remains that these and other women's work not included here will appear in future collections.

In the case of Caridad Svich, because her work with NoPassport has been so influential both nationally and internationally, we invited her to submit a nondramatic piece expressing her view on the state of Latinas in theatre, which she generously accepted. In the same vein, for the purpose of an even more diverse perspective, we asked Kathy A. Perkins to share her comments on the same topic, given the groundbreaking collection, *Contemporary Plays by Women of Color: An Anthology*, she coedited with Roberta Uno, and her ever-expanding work in the field and outstanding voice on the topic of women of color.[3]

And Where Is Fornes?/¿Y Donde Está la Fornes?

We had always intended to begin with a work by Maria Irene Fornes, who represented for us perhaps the most influential figure of the 1980s on Latina playwrights. We remain grateful to Morgan Jenness, Fornes's agent at the time, for all of her efforts in attempting to secure the rights for one of the works that Irene and Elizabeth had planned on for this collection, yet it was soon evident that negotiating for rights to Irene's work was completely out of both Irene's and Morgan's hands and was more problematic than first expected. Nevertheless, not to be discouraged, we arrived at a way to keep Fornes at the forefront of our collection.

Knowing that her spirit would be with us throughout, we held on to the fact that Irene had been enthusiastic about the project from the onset.[4] We both knew that it was Irene's will to be a part of this project. Thus, given the complicated circumstances, we determined that the already extant wealth of publications by her and about her were readily accessible. In our view, it became our responsibility to take the next step of showcasing outstanding playwrights who had been influenced by her as our starting point. Thus, as a tribute to Fornes, we are fortunate to be able to begin with two major figures in Latina theatre, Milcha Sanchez-Scott and Cherríe Moraga, and we close with the work of Migdalia Cruz and a commentary by Caridad Svich. In their own words, our entries on these dramatists show the significance of Irene in their career.

About the Voices in This Book/Sobre las Voces en Este Libro

Several of the playwrights represented here have already amassed a great body of critical reviews, and numerous studies have been published about them and their work. In this book, by gathering both new and sustained voices, we highlight the growth and development in the field of Latina dramatic literature. The women are also practitioners as well as playwrights, and, when available, we provide full booking and production rights information for each piece or a means to be able to contact them for that information. Many selections in this volume stem from women who have assumed the dual role of playwright and actor. Diane Rodriguez, the Colorado Sisters, Josefina Báez, Celia Herrera Rodríguez, Evelina Fernández, and Carmen Peláez are all performance artists, and their spoken words have been driven by a necessity of staging what they consider a critical voice. Toward that end, we felt that the anthology would be of interest to producing organizations, both for mounting new productions or for booking those meant to be performed by the writers/performers themselves. On the whole, the work presented here will add to an ever-growing market comprised of both those within this Latina group and a more widespread audience also interested in this culture.

This collection of performance work meets a socioanthropological need, improving our understanding of Latinas'/Latinos' influence on the broader U.S. culture. This compilation also imparts insight into Latina/Latino culture and community. By examining select playtexts, their production history, and information about their creators, we can view particular cultural values, beliefs, and aspirations of this group. Thus, this anthology contributes to an understanding of the cultural contributions of Latinas/Latinos to U.S. and world culture. The intended audience for this collection includes scholars in theatre and performance history, English, ethnic studies, American studies, women's studies, anthropology, cultural studies, world history, and those interested in expanding cultural expression and exploration. We anticipate the greatest interest to be in Chicana/

Chicano and Latina/Latino studies. In higher education and among researchers and professionals in the field, making performance works available broadens the repertoire, increases resources for teaching, and allows for the development of new courses in multiculturalism and diversity in the curriculum. In addition, the ever-growing Latina/Latino presence in the United States widens the appeal for the valuable contributions of Latinas/Latinos, both for U.S. audiences and for audiences abroad who are interested in this aspect of U.S. history.

We asked playwrights to contribute a playtext of their choice that would make it possible for others to know more about them and their current work. Some submitted several works, allowing us to choose the one that fit our purposes best. We created a biographical questionnaire for the dramatists, which allowed them to submit firsthand, original accounts of their unique experiences. We relied on the playwrights' responses for information for "The Playwright/La Dramaturga" and "Production History" sections. The responses from the playwrights in the "Artistic Vision" sections appear here entirely in their own words, except for minor editorial adjustments, such as agreement or updating information. Those written responses constitute a unique contribution of this book, giving fascinating insight into the playwrights' artistic vision.

In some cases, circumstances required us to rely more heavily on already-published biographical materials or other materials furnished by the playwrights for the purposes of completing the information on the playwright and the production history for the playtext. Some playwrights were interviewed long distance, others wrote their responses to the questionnaire between other projects, and still others took ownership of their chapter in order to convey directly their point of view. Throughout the process, the willingness of these women to contribute, and their determination to doing so while living out their busy lives, were driven by their overall desire to broaden the Latina voice for others, an opportunity that surmounted all of the obstacles along the way.

We provide an excellent sample of *la voz latina contemporanea,* that is, the contemporary Latina voice. This entire endeavor has resulted from our own goal of expanding the repertoire of women's performance and dramatic expression. In the late 1980s, Elizabeth had begun to undertake dramaturgical work at numerous venues, including the American Repertory Theater, Trinity Rep, and Arizona Theatre Company, among others. In all of these producing organizations there was an expressed desire to bring diversity and the Latina/Latino voice to their audiences. Yet, despite an earnest interest from administrators, production teams, and company members among others, to bring this kind of fare to the stage, it seemed generally accepted that there simply were no plays by Latinas or Latinos, and the fare of choice became Shakespeare or other classics à la "multicultural casting," or "color-blind casting," as it was often described.[5]

When we both engaged in dramaturgical work at the Oregon Shakespeare Festival (OSF) in the late 1990s, we encountered interest in the Latina/Latino experience. Yet, despite good intentions, people generally accepted that there simply were no plays by Latinas or Latinos, rather than committing to developing such projects. OSF's solution was to rework one of the classics in modern Spanish theatre, a work by Federico García Lorca. Despite the refreshing approach to *Blood Wedding* by the director, Jim Edmondson, in which Vilma Silva, one of the rising Latina/Latino actors at the time, was brought in to accompany company members for the season, for those of us who were Latinas/Latinos, García Lorca's work was as far removed from the Latina/Latino experience as his Spanish motherland was to Oregon or to the rest of the United States.

Nevertheless, there was an interesting turn of events as production commenced. During the process of casting and developing the production, it was clear that character development, use of language, and an overall depiction of the milieu that García Lorca presented was of enormous interest to the company. This development was important because the OSF, one of the most recognized regional stages in the United States, known for its focus on Shakespeare and the classics, was beginning to make important strides in connecting to the Latina/Latino culture. Language, dress, customs, and other aspects of this connection to a Spanish life soon came under discussion, and the entire production became immersed in a fascinating layering of many cultures, which resulted in an exciting production. For us, witnessing the enthusiasm of the company and audiences alike was exhilarating, yet the company's lack of familiarity with new playtexts by Latinas and Latinos was still disconcerting.

Thus, we committed to this project, which has subsequently led us on a long journey of bringing sample works by already prominent artists, by those who persevere in honing their craft and creative expression despite the struggle of finding venues for their work, and by those completely new voices that are making an impact on the U.S. stage. For us too, our own work and interests made it a necessary exploration that exclusively centered on women. Throughout our development of this collection, we respected and resolved to uphold the evident singularity of each woman as we determined the playtexts we would use. The result was that each playtext contributes its own individual perspective, and in many cases, the format of the chapters may vary as well. Just as we sustained our firm belief that the individuality of each playwright's words would stand out above all of the materials we had gathered, we became satisfied that we could maintain the integrity of the anthology despite the stylistic differences among chapters. For us, the dissimilarity conveyed the value of difference within a group that had long suffered from stereotyping and marginality.

New Spaces for New Audiences/ Nuevos Espacios Para Nuevas Audiencias

As the United States was undertaking a new census in 2010, we knew that the Hispanic population in the United States had undergone tremendous growth since the 2000 U.S. Census. The census then profoundly illuminated the changing U.S. demographics with regard to Latinas/Latinos. According to *The Hispanic Population: Census 2000 Brief*, out of 281.4 million residents reported in the 2000 census (excluding the Commonwealth of Puerto Rico and the U.S. Island Areas), 35.3 million, or 12.5 percent, were Hispanic, of which 7.3 percent were Mexicans, 1.2 percent Puerto Ricans, 0.4 percent Cubans, and 3.6 percent were "other Hispanics."[6]

The 2000 census data forecast a new picture of the nation. In a 2001 article titled "Mexican-Americans: Forging a New Vision of America's Melting Pot," Gregory Rodriguez honed in on the largest of the Latina/Latino populations: "Mexicans are by far today's biggest immigrant group," and "as such, they are the most likely to leave a prominent imprint on the culture." He added that "as political and economic power continues to shift westward, Mexican-Americans will increasingly inject this mestizo vision onto American culture." In Rodriguez's follow-up piece two months later, titled "150 Years Later, Latinos Finally Hit the Mainstream," he emphasized the widespread effect on the country of this growing population in the United States, citing that the "massive contemporary Latin American immigration, combined with the emergence of a Latino middle class, have forced both political and commercial marketers to rethink their approach to a group on the verge of becoming the nation's largest minority."[7]

Clearly, these outstanding numbers were presenting a new picture of the nation, showing both a firm presence as well as continual growth.[8] By May 2008, when the U.S. Census Bureau released its report for 2007, the U.S. Hispanic population had surpassed 45 million, thus becoming 15 percent of the total population.[9] According to the U.S. Census Bureau report released in August 2008, "the nation will be more racially and ethnically diverse," and "the Hispanic population is projected to nearly triple, from 46.7 million to 132.8 million during the 2008–2050 period."[10] These national and state estimates by race, Hispanic origin, sex, and age also showed that the Hispanic population exceeded 500,000 in 16 states, again remaining the largest minority group in the United States and the fastest-growing minority group between July 1, 2006, and July 1, 2007.[11] By the time the nation celebrated Hispanic Heritage Month in September 2009, the U.S. Census Bureau showed further growth, with an estimated Hispanic population of 46.9 million, or 15.4 percent, in addition to the approximately 4 million residents of Puerto Rico.[12]

As Henry G. Cisneros declares, in his overview of the role of Latinos in the future of the United States, "the Latino population is now so large, its trajectory of growth so rapid, its contrast in relative age to that of the general population so stark, that it will not be possible for the United States to advance without substantial, and so far unimagined, gains in the economic, educational, and productive attributes of the nation's Latino community." He further reports that "Latinos are such a rapidly growing part of the population that they will increasingly influence every measure of national performance. The Census Bureau's mid-range estimates for 2050 assert that the nation's Latino population will grow by 63 million people or a stunning 48 percent of total U.S. growth, and that Latinos will constitute 25 percent of the U.S. population in 2050." Latinas/Latinos currently account for about half the nation's population growth, as Leobardo F. Estrada points out, and the United States will "undergo a Hispanic transformation over the next fifty years." As Estrada notes, "the life cycle of every Latino has demographic implications," and "these demographic factors add up to forces that will have a profound impact on social change and shape the future of the United States."

As such, "the power of demographic change is reflected in the Hispanic population," and "the future of U.S. and Hispanic growth is inextricably intertwined."[13]

In this vein, Nicolás Kanellos assesses the historical significance of this presence. He writes: "The story of Latinos in the United States begins slowly and, over the centuries since the early 1500s, gathers a momentum and pervasiveness that continues to this day," adding that "with a population of one in four Americans of Latino blood and background now on the horizon, it is a story that can no longer be ignored." These deeply seated Latina/Latino roots indeed comprise much of what we define as *American,* and the cultural contributions of this group "add to and transform the American Dream," as Kanellos points out. In Kanellos's assessment, "Latinos have the potential to become the brokers for transnational and transcultural business, education, media, entertainment, sport, arts, etc.," but "this vision is not exclusionary." Even more broadly, he adds: "Non-Latinos who overcome any prejudices and short-sightedness have the same potential, once they become bilingual and bicultural and learn to operate within Latino cultures at home and abroad. Latino success will be measured in how many non-Latinos become part of this new national/transnational dynamic."[14]

The impact of this changing demographic on performance is great. As Joe García writes in "La Gran Oportunidad/Up for Grabs/The Hispanic Opportunity," "the Latino wave, as it has been called, is the single most important element of the recent demographic and sociological change in the United States." In her "Making the Next Generation Our Greatest Resource," Sarita E. Brown writes that "the nation must see Latinos for what we are: a vital portion of the American population, with cultural contributions that are becoming more deeply embedded in the American fabric every day." In fact, she adds, "the future of the Latino community and that of the country as a whole are interwoven." Thus, as Tara Bracco points out in a 2007 forum report, in this climate, "theatres, like other businesses, need to respond to change and not merely hide their heads in the sand hoping traditional operating procedures will carry them through." She continues: "Teresa Eyring, executive director of TCG [Theatre Communications Group], comfortably uses 'innovation' to describe the vision needed to adapt to the current cultural climate. Theatres, according to Eyring, are at 'an exciting but terrifying moment in our history because the way people engage with creativity and content is changing and will continue to change.' With a shifting consumer market, some theatres have already responded with new strategies and ideas, while others are just beginning to think about innovation."[15]

To this end, among other changes, "imaginative uses of spaces are allowing theatres to reach their communities in new ways," and "theatres are exploring how their spaces are relevant to their communities." As Bracco points out, "innovative spaces also offer additional opportunities to deepen relationships with audiences and create new avenues of connections . . . theatres are reinventing their identities and their ties to their communities." In the words of Luis Castro, director of arts development at Time Warner, "the audience and community are changing, and what's important is that what's on the stage reflects and speaks to those different communities."[16]

Differences among Latinas/Latinos/¡Que Viva la Diferencia!

Given the demographics for Latinas/Latinos in the United States, as Sergio Muñoz Bata observes, there is a vastly "diverse community formed by people coming from different countries and with very heterogeneous views and interests," and, as such, their contributions are distinct. Robert Suro discusses the differences among Latinas/Latinos in the "American landscape." As Suro writes, "One of the key distinctions that Latinos draw among themselves is by country of origin. Mexicans think of themselves as different from Salvadorans, Dominicans see themselves as different from Cubans, etc. And, this sense of difference is as widespread among the American born whose connections to a country of origin might be quite distant, as they are among the recently arrived."[17]

The term *Latino* appeared on the census form for the first time in 2000, along with a note that the terms *Hispanic* and *Latino* could be used "interchangeably to reflect the new terminology" in the standards that were to be implemented by January 1, 2003.[18] People who marked "other Spanish/Hispanic/Latino" were given additional space to write their specific Hispanic origins, such as Salvadoran or Dominican. As the data indicate, there are differences within the Latina/Latino group, and those very distinctions reveal the importance of the contributions that all of the individual playwrights make to this book. The growing numbers of Latinas/Latinos in the United States make it vital that the individual contributions of each be understood, and it is by seeing their similarities and differences that we can accomplish this.

As Marisa Trevino notes, according to the 2000 census figures there were 17.1 million Latinas in the United States, and although "each woman is categorized as Latina, they don't share the same ethnic background." Thus, as Roberto Suro observes about the significant increase in the Latina/Latino population, "We are well past the start of a new era in American history, an era in which Latinos will play an ever larger role. The size and the growth of the Hispanic population guarantee that. But, the manner of growth, immigration, and high standing, ensures that it won't be just one role and that the emergence of multiple roles will not be a linear or predictable process. Instead, Latinos will be engines of change, changes in their own identities, changes in the ways they relate to the rest of society and changes in the ways that society relates to them. The outcomes may be unknowable, but they will be important to all Americans."[19]

In this context we have persevered in making the diverse work by Latinas available. *La Voz Latina* presents English and bilingual playtexts that aim to inform others about this remarkable group in the United States. This anthology is distinguished by its variety in form and content. Through the creative expression found in this compilation, we examine the work of eleven playwrights who are also theatre practitioners to varying degrees. Of the twentysome Latina origins found in the United States, this first volume features Cuban, Puerto Rican, Chicana, and Dominican voices, as well as those whose origins are a blend of more than one background, with the expectation of including additional voices and worldviews in future volumes.

The Essential Criticism/Sobre la Crítica

The contribution of Latinas to the U.S. stage is significant. The following overview of the critical books that have helped define the field of Latina theatre shows that, despite the scarcity of such books, as one commentator on this anthology has written, *La Voz Latina* is "significant in the Latina canon as it takes its place alongside the too few others dedicated to the work of the Latina playwright." This book, along with others on the subject at hand, "give insight into the culture and counterculture, acculturation, and counteracculturation of the history of the Latina in today's America."[20]

As already noted, the extant literature in the field is limited, but important critical studies have contributed to defining the field of Latina/Latino theatre. Precursors to *La Voz Latina* include three collections of plays by Chicanas/Chicanos published in the 1970s. *Actos,* by Luis Valdez and El Teatro Campesino (ETC, farmworkers' theater), is mentioned here in light of the critical study Yolanda Broyles-González has written, *El Teatro Campesino: Theater in the Chicano Movement.* Broyles-González analyzes the role of women in the work of the company, noting that "within the vast body of critical writings on El Teatro Campesino, critics have overlooked the history of women's participation," in which "women have constituted a distinct force within the Teatro Campesino and, by extension, within the history of Chicana/o theater." Given the collective nature of this theatre ensemble, it is appropriate to include *Actos* in this discussion, for, as Broyles-González points out, "the creative process drew from the vision of all Teatro Campesino members."[21]

Following stage lives that began in 1965, nine short pieces were published in *Actos* in 1971, with introductory notes by Luis Valdez on the subject of "Chicano theater." In writing about Valdez in *Latina Performance,* Alicia Arrizón says: "Valdez is commonly termed the 'father' of Chicano theater; his approach profoundly affected Latino theater traditions in the U.S. and elsewhere." According to Jorge Huerta, as "the undisputed leader of the Chicano Theatre Movement," Valdez and his fellow Teatro Campesino members "were looked up to as role models by the younger, emerging teatristas (theatre workers)," and *Actos* did much to build the repertoire of the early *teatros* who were inexperienced in performance techniques but were intent on bringing community audiences their message about social change.[22]

Actos is comprised of nine dramatic pieces and two short essays, namely, "Notes on Chicano Theater," and "The Actos." In the latter two articles, Valdez defines Chicano theatre and describes the "acto" form. An acto is a dramatic sketch, created collectively, with a very specific intent, as described by Valdez, to: "inspire the audience to social action. Illuminate specific points about social problems. Satirize the opposition. Show or hint at a solution. Express what people are feeling." As Huerta points out, "the Teatro Campesino's *actos* became the standard model for these young troupes because the *acto* form is easily emulated and adaptable to any socio-political motive or situation," adding that "anyone with a cause can collectively create an *acto,* but the cause is essential." As the leading director and playwright, and as founder of ETC, Valdez "inspired a national movement of theatre troupes dedicated to the exposure of socio-political problems within the Chicano communities of the United States."[23]

While there were other *teatros* in operation during the 1970s, El Teatro Campesino was the most well-known, due largely to its national and international presence. In 1968 it garnered an Obie, the Off-Broadway award sponsored by the *Village Voice* and equivalent to the Broadway Tony Award. Nevertheless, with regard to Chicana/Chicano theatre, prior to the 1980s, as Yvonne Yarbro-Bejarano writes, "most texts constructed a male subject through notions of class, 'racial,' and cultural identity that reinscribed tacit cultural definitions of masculinity and femininity within the heterosexual structure of the family." She adds: "While not unique to Chicano theatre, the representation of the male subject and of 'woman' as Other was accomplished through discourses of class, sexual, 'racial,' and cultural difference that were culture-specific." In the case of Valdez, as Alicia Arrizón points out, although Valdez's "revolutionary concepts were crucial to the development of Chicano theater, his vision tended to marginalize women."[24] Fortunately, the tide soon changed, and it was not long before a Chicana dramatist was published.

In 1972, the work of Estela Portillo Trambley, the first Chicana playwright to gain recognition within the Chicano cultural movement, was first published in *El Espejo—The Mirror: Selected Chicano Literature. The Day of the Swallows* was the only full-length playtext in the collection of twenty-nine pieces. Jorge Huerta writes that Portillo Trambley, the first Chicana to win the prestigious Quinto Sol literary prize, "is regarded by most Chicana/o critics and scholars as the woman who inspired and opened the doors for all the Chicana writers that followed her."[25]

After 1972, her work continued to be anthologized and was eventually collected in a book of Portillo Trambley's own. When it was reanthologized in 1976 with seven other plays, *Day of the Swallows* was the only work by a woman in *Contemporary Chicano Theatre.* Her *Sun Images* was published in a special-issue journal in 1979, and in 1983 Portillo Trambley published her own collection of four plays as *"Sor Juana" and Other Plays.*[26] Even after her death in 1998, this prolific writer, whose published work also includes poetry, short stories, and novels, remains an important voice in the annals of Latina theatre history.

Significant headway in disseminating Latina voices was not made until the publication of *On New Ground: Contemporary Hispanic-American Plays* in 1987, and *Shattering the Myth: Plays by Hispanic Women* in 1992.[27] Both of these collections were enormously useful for those of us developing new courses in universities on Chicana/Chicano, Latina/Latino, and multicultural theatre and performance. Apart from individually published plays and works acquired directly from producing groups and playwrights, and the scant live productions of the plays, these two books were among the few texts that allowed for further reading on the subject of Latina/Latino performance.

Three of the six plays editor M. Elizabeth Osborn selected for *On New Ground* were by women: Lynne Alvarez, Maria Irene Fornes, and Milcha Sanchez-Scott. Probably owing mostly to its Theatre Communications Group (TCG) distribution, the book became a mainstay in academic courses, and José Rivera's *The House of Ramon Iglesias* and Milcha Sanchez-Scott's *Roosters* have enjoyed perhaps the greatest stage life. *Roosters* reappeared in an acting edition by Samuel French, and the teleplay was aired nationally as part of the *American Playhouse* series in 1986. The play has gone on to receive even greater exposure with perhaps the widest distribution coming from its publication in *American Theatre* magazine. Our "About the Play/Sobre la Obra"section on *Roosters* details further information about its striking longevity.

Six years after *On New Ground* was published, *Shattering the Myth* appeared, playing a long-awaited critical role in introducing plays by Latinas, perhaps most important in academic settings, where plays found their way onto required reading lists. Selected by Denise Chávez and edited by Linda Feyder, the six plays in the collection were written between 1986 and 1991, with some having had a stage life and others a reading. Central to these works was the "problematic relationship Hispanic women have to their inherited customs," as Feyder explains in her introduction, questioning deeply rooted traditions in their culture while also "reinterpret[ing] the inherited customs for a new identity in their present bicultural existence." As the editor notes, "Their plays, indeed, shatter myths and, in so doing, are creating a broader, freer space for women's identity and cultural development."[28]

Before another collection of Latina/Latino plays was published, we were fortunate to find important entries in Kathy Perkins's and Roberta Uno's award-winning and highly acclaimed *Contemporary Plays by Women of Color*, the first anthology to show the far-reaching diversity on the U.S. stage with their eighteen entries, which included five plays by Latinas. The volume introduced many readers to names that were new to them, including Marga Gomez, Evelina Fernández, and the Colorado Sisters, as well as the more recognizable dramatists, Migdalia Cruz and Cherríe Moraga.

In her review of the book, Judith Williams comments on the fact that, "although multiculturalism may have had its vogue, the problems that it revealed have not disappeared." In Williams's insightful view, *Contemporary Plays* "creates an implicit dialogue among playwrights of color, revealing their 'wounds,' the diverse space they occupy, and their knowledge of how issues of race and ethnicity are always complicated by gender." Indeed, she found it to contain "a balanced selection of plays by African American, Asian American, Native American, and Latina women." As Uno explains in her portion of the introduction, she and Perkins "were struck by the recurrence of certain themes: violence against women, response to media and historical stereotypical images, identity formation, the impact of poverty on individuals, families, and communities; the relationship of woman to her body, the relationship of women to each other, the response of a given community to crisis." For Uno and Perkins, the plays presented "varying approaches to playmaking, including solo performance and collective creation," and the compilation remains a significant contribution to the field.[29] Besides introducing new plays and playwrights to a wide readership, the volume includes a useful appendix of published plays by women of color, which furthers audience awareness about the work of women of color for the stage.

With regard to criticism, one of the most influential critical studies of Latina performance and theatre has been Alicia Arrizón's *Latina Performance: Traversing the*

Stage (1999)}. Unlike those literary critics who analyze the written text, Arrizón has a remarkable grasp of performance. Firmly situated in contemporary cultural and performance studies, and the interchange of race and ethnicity with gender and sexuality, her interdisciplinary approach has made a significant contribution to the field. Arrizón has numerous publications on the subject of Latinas, and her work has received critical acclaim. As Gwendolyn Alker points out in her review, with *Latina Performance,* Arrizón "creates one of the first book-length studies that interrogates the connections between Latina identity and the emergence of a Latino/a performance aesthetic in the United States during the twentieth century."[30]

In his own review of Arrizón's critical study, Jorge Huerta notes its significance as a "valuable addition to the growing number of books that discuss, analyze, and appreciate Latino theatre and performance in the United States," and "one of the few books that centers on women in Latina/o performance and theatre." Huerta compliments Arrizón on "bring[ing] the performance pieces to life while adding a critical analysis," thus giving "visual authority" to the monologues "with vivid descriptions and intelligent commentary." Reviewer Christopher Joseph Mitchell comments on the study's concern "with 'border crossings,'—not simply in the physical sense of migration from south to north, but in the multiple engagements Latinas face in an Anglo-, phallo-, and hetero-centric society that enforces assimilation at every turn." Thus, Mitchell adds, "in Arrizón's analysis, Latinas in the theatre arts historically have found it necessary to confront these borders head-on in the process of constructing their performative identities," and with this book, "Arrizón provides a significant foray into that arena in order to meet the goal of 'expand[ing] the possibilities of Latina theatre and performance studies.'"[31]

The year 2000 ushered in several new publications of both plays and criticism. Perhaps the most extensive anthology to appear, and the one with the most impact, was *Latinas on Stage,* edited by Alicia Arrizón and Lillian Manzor. With an article by Elizabeth also included, this long-awaited collection of plays and performance texts, interviews with playwrights, and criticism on a wide range of topics related to Latina performance was enormously helpful in furthering the field, especially in Latina studies and women's studies. Encompassing theatrical voices from the early 1900s to the last decade of the century, this work has played an important role in showing the diversity of the Latina voice for the stage. In their attempt to "define, in practice and theory, a Latina theatrical aesthetics in the United States," the editors' goal was to "construct a space in which Latina playwrights, performance artists, and directors" could "enter into dialogue with performance theorists and historians."[32]

At the time *Latinas on Stage* appeared, publication by Latinas was scant, and the book made it possible to advance research in the field, teaching about the subject, and dissemination of the work. As Patricia Ybarra writes in her review, "The critical essays vary widely in subject matter and theoretical approach. Together, they expand the focus of the anthology to include a more pointed consideration of representations of Latinas, and particularly the materiality of the performed Latina body on stage." *Latinas on Stage* has certainly been, as Ybarra had projected, "a great asset to Latina/o Studies and theatre scholars."[33]

Also published in 2000, *Puro Teatro: A Latina Anthology,* edited by Alberto Sandoval-Sánchez and Nancy Saporta Sternbach, contains one-act and full-length plays, collaborative works, performance pieces, and *testimonios,* or "short autobiographical statements," focusing on such topics as race, gender, class, sexual identity, and the empowerment of an educated class of women. With many of these works previously unpublished, the editors provide brief introductions to situate them, showcasing how "Latinas working in the Theater have moved from their marginal positions backstage to become the central protagonists of an emerging, hybrid, multicultural art form."[34]

In *Stages of Life: Transcultural Performance and Identity in U.S. Latina Theater,* published the following year, Sandoval-Sánchez and Saporta Sternbach offer a critical analysis that they describe as an "[attempt] to address the transcultural dynamics of a politics of representation, identity, and location."[35] Chapters include "Staging the Discourses of Home in U.S. Latina Theater," "Setting the Stage: Un Teatro de Mujeres," and "The Performance of Their Lives: A Hybrid Genre for Transcultural Identities," and the book contains bibliographies of Latina playwrights and critical works.

Three other publications from 2000 shine attention on the work by Latinas (and Latinos): *Out of the Fringe: Contemporary Latina/Latino Theatre and Performance,* edited by Caridad Svich and María Teresa Marrero, is a collection of ten plays, six by women; Jorge Huerta's critical study, *Chicano Drama: Performance, Society and Myth,* analyzes the work by Chicanas/Chicanos from 1979 to 1999; in Elizabeth C. Ramírez's *Chicanas/Latinas in American Theatre: A History of Performance,* an investigation of these women on the U.S. stage from pre-Columbian beginnings to the present, we find that women played an important part within this history.[36] The last book chronicles Latinas in performance from pre-Columbian beginnings through the 1980s. This history reveals an important body of work, showing that until the 1970s, Latinas' contribution to the stage was primarily through the area of performance, with scant evidence of plays written by them. However, the 1980s ushered in an influx of Latina playwrights who began to make their mark in the annals of U.S. and world theatre. Today, *la voz latina* continues to prosper through dramatic expression, and we hope that the present book will shed further light on its continuing growth. Latinas have attained an acknowledged prominence in U.S. theatre in various areas of performance, and this volume of works for the stage, devoted entirely to this group, fulfills the kind of attention their voices deserve.

Theatre as Community: Family, Friends, and Theatre/ Teatro Como Comunidad: La Familia, la Amistad, y el Teatro

Vicki Ruiz has written that "sustaining community space can be as important as finding it."[37] The playwrights in this book show how they have drawn from their own families and friends in their surrounding communities in order to tell us their stories. Sometimes filled with humor and often serious in tone, the characters they create are truthful depictions of their view of the world in which they live. Through these plays we are introduced to and often reacquainted with characters we may have known about previously, such as fathers, mothers, family, and friends in the neighborhood, but they are no longer presented as one-dimensional stereotypical figures. They are now shown from the cultural and ethnic perspectives these women bring to the stage.

Often these playwrights transcend the connection that they have to their community by crossing national and international borders. Just as Vicki Ruiz notes that "through poetry, short stories, and novels, Latina writers engender region in ways that are instructive for historians," so too we find dramatic expression revealing similar kinds of "physical landscape and mestiza soul." Dramatic work also enables "narratives as born of conquest and shaped by globalization, past, present, and foreseeable future." Many of our entries help shape Latina history through the same kind of recounting that Ruiz delineates in the historical accounts she studies, "in which a fuller recounting of Latina history" emerges through "locating gendered ethnoracial identities within matrices of place as landscape and metaphor, of migration and settlement, and of political space," along with other means.[38]

Through the physical space that theatre allows, we find the shaping of community. Yet, disjunctures and the dysfunctional also occur. Finding themselves displaced from their homelands and their people, encountering racism and loss, we learn how women have revisioned myths in reclaiming their heritage, faced oppression, appropriated new myths, and essentially found a voice through theatre. But perhaps the most challenging factor in the entire scheme of things is that of finding a playing space and an audience to hear the work. While we encounter cases where establishing a theatre community continues to be challenging, even in these cases, women have forged new directions for themselves through the power of representation that theatre offers.[39] Fortunately, most of the creators of these new stage personages have effectively arrived at claiming performance space through the bonds they have formed with theatre communities that support their work. Along with the support of families and friends and surroundings, these women have affiliated with professional theatre artists, companies, and producing organizations that have played a major role in introducing their work to many different audiences, nurturing them as artists, and sustaining them along the way. We discover how they are situated within the theatre community in which they work, a community that has sustained them in cultivating an expression of self through performance. They have brought their work to already established audiences as well as drawn in new audiences of their work.

The Term *Latina* and Other Notes/ ¿Y Quien Es una Latina? Y Otras Anotaciones

There are several terms used in the United States for people with origins in Spanish-speaking countries. While the individual playwrights may use one term or another when they are speaking about themselves and their culture and heritage, we want to clarify our rationale for the terms we have selected for our discussion. According to the Office of Management and Budget (OMB), in a 1997 document titled "Revisions to the Standards for the Classification of Federal Data on Race and Ethnicity," "the term 'Hispanic' refers to persons who trace their origin or descent to Mexico, Puerto Rico, Cuba, Central and South America, and other Spanish cultures." In addition, the OMB specified that the term should be *Hispanic* or *Latino,* and in fact the two terms are often used interchangeably. *Hispanic* was a term that non-Hispanics used in earlier decades (mainly during the Nixon administration) to describe the collective group rather than the particular groups within that whole. Within these groups, some speak Spanish fluently, others have either learned the language in school or have no familiarity with it at all. Of all these groups, including Cuban Americans, Puerto Ricans, and others, the most populous is Chicanas/Chicanos, referring to those individuals from Mexican heritage that reside in the United States, and even in this group, the conservative term *Mexican American* is often used. Generally, however, the term *Latina/Latino* remains perhaps the most often used term for the enormous number of women and men descended from Spanish-speaking groups now residing in the United States.[40]

While the term *Latina/Latino* is generally reserved for those descendants of Latin American parents born or living in the United States, it may also be applied to direct immigrants from Spain, Mexico, Central America, and South America. In *From Out of the Shadows: Mexican Women in Twentieth-Century America,* Vicki L. Ruiz writes that the term "Latina emphasizes a common bond with all women of Latin American origin in the United States, a politicized Pan American identity," and in that spirit, we too embrace that term.[41] With regard to gender, Spanish nouns are either masculine or feminine, which causes exclusion of one or the other when the terms are used, very much like the use of the masculine plural "men" in the English language, which has not historically included women. The slash, as in *Latina/Latino,* is used here and elsewhere to make Spanish terms gender inclusive. Except in cases where direct quotations from sources make particular use of certain terms, "Latina" is used here for women, "Latino" for men, and "Latina/Latino" for both.

In addition, as a rule, we use accents and the tilde (ñ) where the Spanish requires them; however, accents and the tilde are omitted when these markings are not used by authors in print and in quotations and other printed matter in which accents or specific markings were not used.

The term *actor* now often refers to both females and males, and thus, except for quoted material, we designate male or female as appropriate, although the term *actor* alone is preferred.

Our spelling of *theatre* must also be mentioned here. While some professionals use *theater* to refer to the physical structure in which a performance occurs and *theatre* for everything else applied to performance, as practitioners it is our practice to use *theatre* for all aspects of production. However, in some chapters the featured playwrights use one term or another, and in some cases, physical buildings or companies have designated a specific spelling for that term, and we have abided by their own use of the term.

With regard to the terms used for the dramatic work itself, in our apparatus we generally use the term *playtext* instead of *play* due to the difficulty in identifying or distinguishing a performance piece from the traditional term for a stage work, namely, a *play.* Nevertheless, while our preferred term for these works is *playtext,* often the artists themselves use one or another as they prefer, and we have retained their usage when it appears in their own writing.

Although there are many words to identify the people who write dramatic material, our preferences and training as well as our exchanges with these women have led us to use the term *playwright* throughout to emphasize the craft of writing, since the writers chosen for this anthology are the creators of the work being presented. The direct Spanish translation of a female *playwright* is *dramaturga,* and because we both work as dramaturgs, we particularly wanted to use this word alongside the English because *dramaturga* calls attention to the valuable role that this person holds in the theatre. Just as we function as the "holder of the script" and work toward comprehending the world of the play, and work with a production team to realize the playwright's intent, this parallel in terminology drew attention to the creator of the play.

In the playtexts, there is variety among the playwrights in how they treat Spanish and English (using or not using italics for Spanish), and we retain the playwrights' preferences; however, in our apparatus, we italicize Spanish words and phrases (except proper nouns). In addition, the nature of our correspondence, conversations, and the world in which we operate brought us back again and again to the duality of language in our work and how we speak and often how we think, and using both English and Spanish in our subheads throughout this book seemed an appropriate way to pay homage to our long lineage of Spanish-speaking ancestry and brought to prominence the bond that we held with the playwrights we worked with in this collection.

The Structure of the Book/La Estructura de Este Libro

The eleven playtexts are organized into five parts and followed by a commentary part. Each of the five parts delineates the ethnic and cultural roots of the artists that serve as the framework in which their works are situated, and each part opens with an introduction that frames the playtexts that follow within the larger historical or genealogical narrative.

In part 1, "Creating a Performance Voice: Themes of Family, Religion, and Community," both Milcha Sanchez-Scott's *Roosters* and Cherríe Moraga's *Waiting for Da God* allow for discussion about one of the central themes in Latina/Latino theatre, namely, *la familia* and how Latinas function within that unit. Layered upon family dominance in their lives is the part that religion plays. Hand in hand with both of these concepts, we witness how daughters, as central figures, experience love, family, and community. Faced with denial and abandonment, faithful women emerge as true saviors rather than "waiting for da God," who never comes. Even more so, perhaps the greatest sources for conflict stem from the disruptive breaches that occur both within their own immediate familial community and by outside forces.

In part 2, "Chicano Teatro and Chicanas: Staging Identity," the framework of the Chicano Movement provides the context for understanding why and how Chicanas have been driven to appropriate the stage in order to give voice to their ideas. Diane

Rodríguez recognizes that *The Path to Divadom, Or How to Make Fat-free Tamales in G Minor* lies within her grasp, altering cultural traditions and enacting social change along the way. In the same vein, the "many voices" of Yareli Arizmendi reveal, as in the playtext title, "who buys your shoes." These two dramatists exemplify how a Chicana can undertake anything she sets out to do, from directing to acting, to producing, to spearheading special projects that serve as vehicles for political and sociological expression. Through these theatre practitioners we also delve into the evolution of Chicano teatro, which has resulted in Chicana's present-day dramatic expression.

In part 3, "La Indígena/The Indigenous: Staging Myth," both through Celia Herrera Rodríguez's artist's canvas and the stage, in *Cositas Quebradas: Performance Codex,* and through Elvira and Hortencia Colorado's re-creating myths in *Chicomoztoc: Mimixcoa—Cloud Serpent,* we investigate the indigenous connections that have shaped contemporary Latinas, whether through language, identity, blood, or other factors. Part 4 illustrates how "race matters" through the role of "dando palabra" (spoken word) in Josefina Báez's *Dominicanish,* and Evelina Fernández's *Luminaria* sheds light on "race, gender, and the professional woman." Part 5 culminates in a discussion revolved around the centrality of home and how we get there, with an exploration of Carmen Peláez's *El Postre de Estrada Palma* and *My Cuba,* two short pieces centered on going back to Cuba and the memory of homeland, a young woman's return to Puerto Rico in Carmen Rivera's *La Gringa,* and the complexity of desire in Migdalia Cruz's *Another Park of the House.*

In part 6 we follow the collection with commentaries by women who have made a difference in terms of women's voices for the stage, with Kathy Perkins's essay, "Contributions by Women of Color" and Caridad Svich's "NoPassport: Dreaming the Americas." Perkins and Svich bring us to the present with their assessment of the state of Latina performance on the U.S. stage.

Within the individual entries, while we have strived for uniformity throughout, as we have already pointed out, each playtext entry will not be quite like another in almost every case.

The entry for each playwright consists of five main sections. The first is a brief biography of the dramatist, under the heading "The Playwright/La Dramaturga." Apart from minor points of clarification and understanding, the playwrights' responses in those sections are reproduced largely as they were received, following our wish to remain true to our goal of this book being "in her own words." In the next section of each chapter, "About the Play/Sobre la Obra," we include a concise analysis of the playtext based on our own reading, supplying additional criticism and the playwright's commentary when available. In "Artistic Vision/Punto de Vista Artístico," we reproduce the dramatists' responses to a questionnaire about their work. We based a nine-question questionnaire on the kinds of questions we felt would result in compelling testimony from the playwrights about their background, their creative process, and what readers would want to know about them. A "Production History/Palabras Dramatúrgicas" section on the playtext itself is followed by contact information for readers wishing to contact the playwright or query production rights.

The final section for each playwright is the playtext itself, reproduced as closely as possible to the playwright's original vision. We carefully reviewed the manuscripts we received, queried the playwrights when there were questions or clarifications needed, and researched unusual names, places, and other details that would aid the reader in grasping the world of the play. Because most of the playtexts have not been previously published, we feel it is critical that each written work appears as the playwright intended it. Josefina Báez's playtext, for example, resembles as closely as possible the typography and spacing of her original manuscript. Finally, we have added notes to assist readers of *La Voz Latina* where needed, and the following list explains abbreviations used in some of the plays:

C	center stage
D	downstage
DC	downstage center
DR	downstage right
OS	offstage
SL	stage left
SR	stage right
U	upstage
UL	upstage left
UR	upstage right

The Playtexts/Los Proyectos

The first playtext that appears in *La Voz Latina* is what Jorge Huerta has called "the most produced Chicana/Chicano play during the 1980s." Sanchez-Scott's full-length, multi-character play, *Roosters,* frames a varied range of performance pieces, with examples of solo voices in traditional monologue and spoken word by contemporary artists between newer and longer works at the end.[42] The playwright brings to the stage a multiplicity of cultures that comprise her ethnicity along with the use of poetry and magical realism, two styles long associated with the Latina/Latino tradition.

The second playtext, on the other hand, is a new work for the stage. Cherríe Moraga is one of the most recognized Latina writers of the day, and with this publication of *Waiting for Da God,* her literary accomplishments continue to expand to creative expression for the stage. As Alicia Arrizón writes, "Moraga's impact on Latina theater is by now almost literally legendary."[43] Here Moraga introduces us to a character that appears as a central figure in one of her latest dramatic works, *The Mathematics of Love,* giving us insight into her creative process of bringing a character to life.

The subsequent playwrights represented fall into place for us, and we end with longer works that illustrate how varied the work of many of these playwrights has become, either due to being nurtured and sustained through collaborations with some of our most distinguished regional stages or because they have been driven to seek or create their own venues in order to ensure that their voices would not be silenced. In addition, through the playwrights' own words, we are able to discover how these women have been able to give life to their work under extraordinary circumstances.

There is little reason to doubt that the Latinas whose work appears in this collection will endure as productive contributors to world theatre. Furthermore, these women are also known for their work beyond writing for the stage. While some of these playtexts may be available elsewhere, they have not been compiled within a theatrical history that highlights their particular significance. In our view, this volume is a springboard for theatre practitioners and others to broaden their scope in terms of world theatre. These representative plays serve to introduce—in some cases to reintroduce—and to disseminate this vital work in theatre, and it is up to theatre practitioners and those who study theatre to reach beyond this volume to the ever-growing body of work by these women.

We now turn to the playwrights and the playtexts themselves.

Notes

1. M. Teresa Marrero, "From El Teatro Campesino to the Gay 1990s: Transformations and Fragments in the Evolution in Chicano/a to Latina/o Theater and Performance Art," in *The State of Latino Theater in the United States: Hybridity, Transculturation, and Identity,* ed. Luis A. Ramos-García, (New York: Routledge, 2002), 61.

2. Comments from anonymous reviewers for the University of Illinois Press.

3. Kathy A. Perkins and Roberta Uno, eds., *Contemporary Plays by Women of Color: An Anthology* (New York: Routledge, 1996).

4. Maria Irene Fornes, interview by the editors, 1997–98, University of Oregon, Eugene, Oregon.

5. See Kate Taylor, "Multicultural Stages in a Small Oregon Town," *New York Times,* August 15, 2009, available at http://www.nytimes.com/2009/08/15/theater/15oregon.html, accessed November 6, 2010; Robert Brustein, *Letters to a Young Actor: A Universal Guide to Performance* (New York: Basic Books, 2005), 81–84; and Sharon Jensen, "The Non-Traditional Casting Project," National Endowment for the Arts, available at www.nea.gov/resources/accessibility/ntcp.html, accessed November 6, 2010.

6. U.S. Census Bureau, *The Hispanic Population: Census 2000 Brief,* (Washington, D.C.: U.S. Department of Commerce, May 2001, C2KBR/01-3, available at http://www.census.gov/prod/2001pubs/c2kbr01–3.pdf, accessed September 1, 2010. See also: "Census Bureau Release Population Estimates by Race, Hispanic Origin and Age for States and Counties," *U.S. Census Bureau News,* August 4, 2006, available at http://www.census.gov/Press-Release/www/releases/archives/population/012496.html, accessed August 15, 2008. In the census 2000 reporting, "people of Spanish/Hispanic/Latino origin could identify as Mexican, Puerto Rican, Cuban, or other Spanish/Hispanic/Latino." See U.S. Census Bureau, *Hispanic Population* (2000).

7. Gregory Rodriguez, "Mexican-Americans: Forging a New Vision of America's Melting Pot," This Week in Review, *New York Times,* February 11, 2001, sec. 4:1, 4. Gregory Rodriguez, "150 Years Later, Latinos Finally Hit the Mainstream," This Week in Review, *New York Times,* April 15, 2001, 4.

8. "Hispanic Heritage Month 2007: Sept. 15–Oct. 15," Facts for Features, *U.S. Census Bureau News,* July 16, 2007; Randal C. Archibold, Steve Friess, Carolyn Marshall, and Gretchen Ruethling, "The Immigration Debate: The Overview, Immigrants Take to U.S. Streets in Show of Strength," *New York Times,* Sept. 15, 2007, A18; Hernán Rozemberg, "1 in 5 To Be Immigrant? Study: By 2050, 19 Percent of U.S. Will Have Immigrated Here," *San Antonio Express-News,* February 12, 2008, 1A; and Jeorge Zarazua, "U.S. Hispanic Population May Become More Like Texas," *San Antonio Express-News,* August 14, 2008, 8B.

9. "U.S. Hispanic Population Surpasses 45 Million Now 15 Percent of Total," *U.S. Census Bureau News,* May 1, 2008, 1–4.

10. "An Older and More Diverse Nation by Midcentury," *U.S. Census Bureau News,* August 14, 2008, 1.

11. Patrick Healy, "Democrats Reach Out to Hispanic Voters," *New York Times,* September 10, 2007; Jeorge Zarazua, "Births Fuel Boom in Hispanic Population," *San Antonio Express-News,* October 24, 2008, 1A.

12. "ACS Demographic and Housing Estimates: 2008," *American Community Survey* (Washington, D.C.: U.S. Department of Commerce, 2008); "Facts for Features: Hispanic Heritage Month 2009: Sept. 15–Oct. 15," *U.S. Census Bureau News,* July 16, 2009, 1.

13. Henry G. Cisneros, "An Overview: Latinos and the Nation's Future," in *Latinos and the Nation's Future,* ed. Henry G. Cisneros with John Rosales (Houston: Arte Público Press, 2009), 4. Leobardo F. Estrada, "The Raw Numbers: Population Projections and the Power of Hispanic Demographic Change," in *Latinos and the Nation's Future,* 153.

14. Nicholás Kanellos, "The Latino Presence: Some Historical Background," in *Latinos and the Nation's Future,* 15, 24–25, 25.

15. Joe García, "La Gran Oportunidad/Up for Grabs/The Hispanic Opportunity," in *Latinos and the Nation's Future,* 103. Sarita E. Brown, "Making the Next Generation Our Greatest Resource," in *Latinos and the Nation's Future,* 86. Tara Bracco, "The Innovation Imperative: TCG's Fall Forum Zeroes in on How Theatres Bring New Ideas to Life," Special Report from Theatre Communications Group Fall Forum 2007, *American Theatre* 25, no. 6 (July/August 2008): 36–37.

16. Bracco, 41. Castro quoted in ibid., 40.

17. Sergio Muñoz Bata, "Latino Progress and U.S. Foreign Policy," in *Latinos and the Nation's Future,* 143.

18. U.S. Census Bureau, *Hispanic Population.*

Roberto Suro, "Latino Numbers and Social Trends: Implications for the Future," in *Latinos and the Nation's Future,* 160.

19. Marisa Trevino, "Latina Playwrights Probe Collision of Cultures," *Women's E News* (November 23, 2006): 2, also at http://www.womensenews.org, accessed November 8, 2010. Suro, 166.

20. Reader's report, University of Illinois Press.

21. Luiz Valdez and El Teatro Campesino, *Actos* (San Juan Bautista, Calif.: Menyah Productions, 1971). Yolanda Broyles-González, *El Teatro Campesino: Theater in the Chicano Movement* (Austin: University of Texas Press, 1994), 134–35, 131.

22. Alicia Arrizón, *Latina Performance: Traversing the Stage* (Bloomington: Indiana University Press, 1999), 26. Jorge Huerta, *Chicano Drama: Performance, Society and Myth* (Cambridge: Cambridge University Press, 2000), 3.

23. Valdez, *Actos,* 6; Huerta, 26–27, 3, 26.

24. Yvonne Yarbro-Bejarano, "The Female Subject in Chicano Theatre: Sexuality, 'Race,'

and Class," in *Performing Feminisms: Feminist Critical Theory and Theatre,* ed. Sue-Ellen Case (Baltimore, Md.: Johns Hopkins University Press, 1990), 134. Arrizón, 26.

25. Estela Portillo Trambley, *The Day of the Swallows,* in *El Espejo—The Mirror: Selected Chicano Literature* (Berkeley, Calif.: Quinto Sol, 1972), ed. Octavio Ignacio Romano-V. and Herminio Ríos C., 150–93. Huerta, 20.

26. Estela Portillo Trambley, *The Day of the Swallows,* in *Contemporary Chicano Theatre* (Notre Dame, Ind.: University of Notre Dame Press, 1976), ed. Roberto J. Garza, 205–45. Estela Portillo Trambley, "Sun Images," in "Nuevos Pasos: Chicano and Puerto Rican Drama," ed. Nicolás Kanellos and Jorge A. Huerta, special issue, *Revista chicano-riqueña* 7, no. 1 (Winter 1979): 19–42. Estela Portillo Trambley, *"Sor Juana" and Other Plays* (Ypsilanti, Mich.: Bilingual Press, 1983).

27. M. Elizabeth Osborn, ed., *On New Ground: Contemporary Hispanic-American Plays* (New York: Theatre Communications Group, 1987). Denise Chávez, comp., and Linda Feyder, ed., *Shattering the Myth: Plays by Hispanic Women* (Houston: Arte Público Press, 1992).

28. Chávez and Feyder, 5.

29. Judith Williams, review of *Contemporary Plays by Women of Color,* ed. Kathy A. Perkins and Roberta Uno, *Theatre Journal* 50, no. 1 (1998): 138–39. Perkins and Uno, 10. Williams, 139. Perkins and Uno, 10.

30. Gwendolyn Alker, review of *Latina Performance: Traversing the Stage,* by Alicia Arrizón, *Dance Research Journal* 33, no. 1 (Summer 2001): 107–9.

31. Jorge Huerta, review of *Latina Performance: Traversing the Stage,* by Alicia Arrizón, *Theatre Journal* 52, no. 1 (March 2000): 141–42. Christopher Joseph Mitchell, review of *Latina Performance: Traversing the Stage,* by Alicia Arrizón, *National Women's Studies Journal* 13, no. 2 (Summer 2001): 169–75.

32. Alicia Arrizón and Lillian Manzor, eds., *Latinas on Stage* (Berkeley, Calif.: Third Woman Press, 2000), 10, 13.

33. Patricia Ybarra, review of *Latinas on Stage,* by Alicia Arrizón and Lillian Manzor, eds., *Theatre Journal,* 3, no. 5 (December 2001): 668–70.

34. Alberto Sandoval-Sánchez and Nancy Saporta Sternbach, *Puro Teatro: A Latina Anthology* (Tucson: University of Arizona Press, 2000), xi.

35. Alberto Sandoval-Sánchez and Nancy Saporta Sternbach, *Stages of Life: Transcultural Performance and Identity in U.S. Latina Theater* (Tucson: University of Arizona Press, 2001), 9.

36. Caridad Svich and María Teresa Marrero, eds., *Out of the Fringe: Contemporary Latina/Latino Theatre and Performance* (New York: Theatre Communications Group, 2000). Elizabeth C. Ramírez, *Chicanas/Latinas in American Theatre: A History of Performance* (Bloomington: Indiana University Press, 2000), 105.

37. Vicki Ruiz, "Claiming Public Space at Work, Church, and Neighborhood," in *Las Obreras: Chicana Politics of Work and Family,* ed. Vicki Ruiz (Los Angeles: UCLA Chicano Studies Research Center, 2000), 31.

38. Vicki L. Ruiz, intro., in *Memories and Migrations: Mapping Boricua and Chicana Histories,* ed. Vicki L. Ruiz and John R. Chávez (Urbana: University of Illinois Press, 2008), 3, 7.

39. See Debra J. Blake, "The Power of Representation: History, Memory, and the Cultural Refiguring of La Malinche's Lineage," in *Chicana Sexuality and Gender: Cultural Refiguring in Literature, Oral History, and Art* (Durham, N.C.: Duke University Press, 2008), 13–69.

40. Office of Management and Budget, "Revisions to the Standards for the Classification of Federal Data on Race and Ethnicity," Federal Register Notice, October 30, 1997; available at http://www.whitehouse.gov/omb/fedreg_1997standards, accessed November 7, 2010. *The Oxford Encyclopedia of Latinos and Latinas in the United States,* ed. Suzanne Oboler and Deena J. González (New York: Oxford University Press, 2005), provides further information and various entries on the use of these terms. See the introduction, xix–xx, and see the "Latinos" and "Latino Identities and Ethnicities" entries for detailed definitions of various terms used to name and define this population.

41. Vicki L. Ruiz, *From Out of the Shadows: Mexican Women in Twentieth-Century America* (Oxford: Oxford University Press, 1998), xiv.

42. Huerta, *Chicano Drama,* 107. Paraphrase of comments by an unidentified reviewer of an earlier draft of this book for the University of Illinois Press.

43. Arrizón, 167.

PART I

Creating a Performance Voice

Themes of Family, Religion, and Community

The golden age of Spanish drama, between 1580 and 1680, coincided with Spain's entry into the New World. This tradition continued in Mexico, bringing both amateur and professional theatrical activity to the New World. George C. D. Odell, in his *Annals of the New York Stage,* mentions that the *conquistadores* gave the first Spanish-language dramatic performances in what became the United States.[1] Professional Spanish-language acting companies arrived in the United States from Mexico before the nineteenth century, providing us with a lasting theatrical tradition.[2] Touring circuits were established alongside the U.S.-Mexican border in Texas, New Mexico, and as far north as San Francisco in California. On the East Coast, New York and Tampa became the centers of Latina/Latino theatre, with touring companies coming from Spain, Cuba, Mexico, and Argentina. The tradition died out in the 1930s, when the Great Depression caused the decline of most acting companies.

Besides the professional touring, resident, and combination companies that established themselves in the United States, other popular forms of theatrical activity were also found in the Southwest and on the East Coast. In the Southwest, the *carpas* (tent shows) became just as popular as they were on the English-language stage, offering comedy through stock characters that fast became favorites for a hungry audience in the far reaches of the country that generally had little other fare, especially at affordable rates. Another popular form, the *tandas de variedad* (variety shows) of the 1920s that persisted into the 1950s, provided another alternative to the English-language vaudeville circuit for Latinas/Latinos. When the Latina/Latino community in the Chicago area was virtually decimated with the mass deportation of Mexicans and "Mexican Americans" during the Depression, theatrical activity was sustained by Puerto Ricans who had migrated to the Midwest in the 1940s with the help of church groups and mutual-aid societies, similar to the traditions that Mexicans had begun previously.[3]

In New York City, the large Puerto Rican migration that began in the late 1930s and boomed in the late 1940s and 1950s heightened demand for variety shows over traditional plays and musicals.[4] Although there is evidence that some traditional theatre reappeared in Latina/Latino communities in New York and Chicago, for the most part activity had ceased. Besides the Depression, only in the mid-1950s did theatre reappear in Latina/Latino communities in New York and Chicago. Besides the Depression, economic and political factors, namely, the Spanish Civil War and World War II, contributed to the collapse of Latina/Latino theatre throughout the country. The popularity of films and the coming of television hastened the end of the popular forms in the 1950s. While evidence of some manner of theatrical expression in limited fashion could still be found in Latina/Latino communities, in comparison to its former popularity it had entered what amounted to an extended intermission. Yet, this vast and varied theatrical activity led to the establishment of cultural centers in the United States that still exist, and in the 1960s Spanish-language dramatic activity once again came into prominence.

The political turmoil of the 1960s greatly impacted the growth of contemporary Latina/Latino theatrical expression. In *Latina Legacies: Identity, Biography, and Community,* Vicki L. Ruíz and Virginia Sánchez Korrol write about the effect of the civil rights movement of the 1960s and 1970s, galvanizing Latinas/Latinos into a political force: "As part of the global student movements, Mexican and Puerto Rican youth created a myriad of organizations to address continuing problems of discrimination, particularly in education and political representation." As these historians point out, "bursting with cultural pride, some students dreamed of revolution, others of social reform," hand in hand with an impetus on art and writing, and encouraging Latinas in feminist studies, all contributing to an ideal setting for *la voz latina.*[5]

The growth of Latina/Latino theatre that developed through the 1980s resulted in highly diversified artistic expression that continues to make a significant contribution to U.S. theatre. Within this development, the Latina performance voice continues to bring distinctive cultural themes that are at once shared and distinct. Given the distinct Latina/Latino populations on each side of the country, with the eastern part of the United States historically different from the borderlands of the Southwest, we still find common themes, especially when we examine the three largest Latina/Latino groups, namely, Puerto Rican, Chicana/Chicano, and Cuban.[6] With numerous topics that these groups may share, three particularly dominant cultural themes are found in *la voz latina,* namely, values, beliefs, and aspirations as they revolve around *la familia*/the family, religion, and community.

Through the work of Milcha Sanchez-Scott and Cherríe Moraga we can begin to discover how playwrights apply these prevalent ideas. In both *Roosters* and *Waiting for Da God,* Sanchez-Scott and Moraga, respectively, address the dominance of the family as the center of their universe. In Latina/Latino culture, the family is the nucleus, generally with the mother as the main caregiver and the father as the recognized head of the household, although with the mother wielding enormous power "behind the scenes," as

Denis Lynn Daly Heyck describes these roles in her collection of written work by Latinos and Latinas in the United States, *Barrios and Borderlands.*[7] However, it is not surprising that these two playtexts present family situations that counter traditional roles.

Conflict makes good drama, and situating the family at the heart of the story occurs again and again. Jorge Huerta emphasizes the conflicting nature of the family in his *Chicano Drama.* As he explains, all of the plays he included in that book are about families, "the vast majority of which would be termed dysfunctional," and "not because all Mechicano families are as dysfunctional as the characters and situations in these plays, but because they make much better drama or comedy." He adds: "Each playwright expresses her/himself differently, of course, but these writers are all conscious of the fact that happy families do not make good drama. It is the dysfunctional family that fascinates us and the most evil characters that draw our attention and our ire. Perhaps it is human nature to be more interested in the villain than the heroine, even if that villain is a product of your own community."[8]

Clearly, the changing nature of the father's role in the family is of enormous concern today, with his authority diminishing more and more both in the family and in the greater society and culture. Yet, as Heyck points out, even though the Latina/Latino family is "under great pressure today—generational, cultural, and economic—still it represents the most basic source of cultural values" for Latinas/Latinos in the United States, serving as a major source of strength. In effect, life in the United States for Latinas/Latinos "sharpens points of conflict and convergence between traditional and changing family and gender roles and expectations."[9]

Luis Ricardo Fraga and Sharon A. Navarro cite the important work that Maxine Baca Zinn has done on the changing nature of Chicanas in the family: "In her article, 'Chicanas: Power and Control in the Domestic Sphere,' Baca Zinn reexamines Chicanas within the family to show that 'they have had great influence on Chicana survival in an Anglo-dominated society.' It is the mother's role within the family that helps preserve its stability and its source as a 'refuge and protection from an oppressed society.'"[10]

Here we find one mother who has had to take over the role of both father and mother with her husband shut away in prison, whereas the other is shut away in a mind and body lost to senile dementia and old age. In both settings, the family unit has been ruptured, and only the daughters are capable of holding it together, one by appropriating the power of traditional religion and the other by relying on her own spirituality when her absent brother fails to fulfill the traditional leadership role and sustenance expected of him.[11]

Hand in hand with the importance of the family, religion for Latinas/Latinos is an integral part of life. Although largely Catholic, they can be of other Christian denominations and are often found to hold deeply rooted traditions and practices that reflect great spiritualism and deep faith. Fraga and Navarro point out that "in *Borderlands/La Frontera* (1987), Gloria Anzaldúa delineates the importance of spirituality as part of the mestiza consciousness, further enriching the understanding of Chicana feminism," and Vicki Ruiz brings up the important role that community plays within the values and beliefs of the family, reminding us that "Chicana feminism also represents a commitment to community." Just as Donna R. Gabaccia and Vicki L. Ruiz describe the work of social historians, who "rely on the building blocks of race, class, and gender" when they explore "the creation of communities—whether rooted in place, culture, or interests," Sanchez-Scott and Moraga also provide us with settings in which "community building" occurs.[12]

The communities in which our playwrights immerse us show unity and support along with difficulty and strife. More profoundly, we witness the breakdown of family and religion within the community in which the characters of the dramas reside. The power of these two dramatists is found in the approach to the writing, with Sanchez-Scott expressing herself through magical realism and captivating poetry, and Moraga through the continual exploration of feminist narrative that she brings to the stage.

Notes

An earlier version of a portion of this introduction first appeared in Elizabeth C. Ramírez, "Playwrights," in *The Oxford Encyclopedia of Latinos and Latinas in the United States*, ed. Suzanne Oboler and Deena J. González (New York: Oxford University Press, 2005), 391–96, and is reprinted here by permission of Oxford University Press, Inc.

1. George C. D. Odell, *Annals of the New York Stage* (New York: Columbia University Press, 1927), 15 vols.
2. See Elizabeth C. Ramírez, *Footlights across the Border: A History of Spanish-Language Professional Theatre on the Texas Stage* (New York: Peter Lang, 1990); and Elizabeth C. Ramírez, "Homeland/Sin Fronteras to Borderlands" and "The Critical Role of the Mexican Revolution and Its Impact on the American Stage," *Chicanas/Latinas in American Theatre: A History of Performance* (Bloomington: Indiana University Press, 2000), 10–48.
3. Joanne Pottlitzer, *A Report to the Ford Foundation: Hispanic Theater in the United States and Puerto Rico* (New York: Ford Foundation, 1988), 11; see also Frank De Varona, *Latino Literacy: The Complete Guide to Our Hispanic History and Culture* (New York: Henry Holt, 1996), 129–31; Juan Gonzalez, *Harvest of Empire: A History of Latinos in* America (New York: Penguin Books, 2000), 81–90; Vicki L. Ruiz, *From Out of the Shadows: Mexican Women in Twentieth-Century America* (Oxford: Oxford University Press, 1998), 86–89; Suzanne Oboler and Deena J. González, in *Oxford Encyclopedia of Latinos and Latinas in the United States*, 1:318–20.
4. Pottlitzer, 10.
5. Vicki L. Ruiz and Virginia Sánchez Korrol, *Latina Legacies: Identity, Biography, and Community* (New York: Oxford University Press, 2005), 15.
6. Denis Lynn Daly Heyck, *Barrios and Borderlands: Cultures of Latinos and Latinas in the United States* (New York: Routledge, 1994), 2.
7. Ibid., 18.
8. Jorge Huerta, *Chicano Drama: Performance, Society and Myth* (Cambridge: Cambridge University Press, 2000), 10.
9. Heyck, 20.

10. Luis Ricardo Fraga and Sharon A. Navarro, "Latinas in Latino Politics," in *Latino Politics: Identity, Mobilization, and Representation* (Charlottesville: University of Virginia Press, 2007), 187–88.

11. Heyck, 19. See also Peggy Levitt, "Two Nations under God: Latino Religious Life in the United States," in, *Latinos: Remaking America,* ed. Marcelo M. Suárez-Orozco and Mariela M. Páez (Berkeley: University of California Press, 2002), 150–64.

12. Fraga and Navarro, 188; see also Sarah Ramirez, "Borders, Feminism, and Spirituality: Movements in Chicana Aesthetic Revisioning," in *Decolonial Voices: Chicana and Chicano Cultural Studies in the 21st Century,* ed. Arturo J. Aldama and Naomi H. Quiñonez (Bloomington: Indiana University Press, 2002), 223–42. Ruiz, *From Out of the Shadows,* 125; Donna R. Gabaccia and Vicki L. Ruiz, *American Dreaming, Global Realities: Rethinking U.S. Immigration History* (Urbana: University of Illinois Press, 2006), 5.

CHAPTER 1

The "Most Produced Chicana/o Play" of the Late 1980s

Milcha Sanchez-Scott's *Roosters* (1987)

Milcha Sanchez-Scott, by permission of the playwright. Photographer unknown.

The Playwright/La Dramaturga

Sanchez-Scott, born in Bali in 1955, has been described as Chicana rather than Latina, although her mother was Indonesian, Chinese, and Dutch, and her father was Colombian, though partly raised in Mexico; her parents met in Indonesia.[1] Even through working with her as the dramaturg on one of her new plays we find that everything about her very being is Chicana; in M. Elizabeth Osborn's *On New Ground,* the playwright tells us that although she has always been classified as a Chicana writer, only "part of me is. But a larger part is not. My roots are in South America."[2] Nevertheless, her prominence in the Chicana repertoire has become so embedded now that it is difficult to separate her from that group.

In *Chicano Drama,* Jorge Huerta introduces Sanchez-Scott as "one of the more visible playwrights who have written plays that affirm the Mechicana/os spirituality," noting that *Roosters* was "the most produced Chicana/o play during the late 1980s." While we recognize that she does not call herself a Chicana, as Jorge Huerta explains, "she has captured the essence of the Chicano spirit in several of her plays and became the second Latina playwright (writing about Chicana/os) to gain prominence after Estela Portillo-Trambley." In a note he explains that he uses the term *Latina* since "she is not really of Mexican descent," reminding us that Maria Irene Fornes was "the first truly prominent Latina playwright."[3]

In this chapter's "Artistic Vision/Punto de Vista Artístico" section, Sanchez-Scott tells us the significance of Fornes for her. In M. Elizabeth Osborn's collection *On New Ground: Contemporary Hispanic-American Plays,* Sanchez-Scott writes about how she came to work with Fornes. The playwright had been hired as an actor by Susan Loewenberg of L.A. Theatre Works to act in a project at the women's prison in Chino, California. Sanchez-Scott says "Susan was at a TCG (Theatre Communications Group) conference with Max Ferra (Artistic Director of INTAR [International Arts Relations]), and gave him the script [for a combined production of *Dog Lady* and *Cuban Swimmer*]. He called the very next day—he was crazy about the plays. INTAR invited me to join Irene Fornes' workshop for that year, 1984–85. . . . That year was the best thing that ever happened to me. . . . I met some extraordinary Hispanic writers. And I felt more accepted."[4]

Her first play, *Latina,* premiered in 1980 at L.A. Theatre Works, garnering seven Drama-Logue Awards.[5] Her subsequent one-act plays, *Dog Lady* and *The Cuban Swimmer,* written in 1982, were produced by INTAR in 1984 and selected for Theatre Communications Group's Plays in Process series. In his review, Herbert Mitgang singled out the sets designed by Ming Cho Lee: "Through the artistic techniques of perspective, suggestion and just plain legerdemain, the two one-acters in INTAR's 22-foot stage on West 42d Street make you believe that you're watching a wide-angle spectacle at the Winter Garden." He further observed: "In both plays, Hispanic-Americans use athletic skills to propel themselves into the mainstream of middle-class life in this country. It's a traditional theme. The basic plot was advanced long ago in such plays as Clifford Odets's 'Golden Boy,' and since then, in scores of films, books and movies, members of ethnic groups have moved out of the slums."[6]

Also contributing to her widespread renown was the appearance of *Dog Lady* in *Best Plays of 1986.* Another work, *Evening Star,* was first produced by Theatre for a New Audience in New York City (1988), under the direction of Paul Zimet.[7] Sanchez-Scott also garnered numerous awards, including the Vesta, given each year to a West Coast female artist, and she won Le Compte du Noüy Foundation Award, given to "a young writer with a unique voice," and in 1987, she won the First Level Award for American playwrights from the Rockefeller Foundation. Given this growing body of work and the widespread interest in this playwright, it was expected that she would continue to build her impressive profile. While other works have been produced, one stands out above the rest.

About the Play/Sobre la Obra

Roosters was first produced by INTAR and the New York Shakespeare Festival in 1987. *Roosters* has been produced by an unusually wide range of venues, including both Latina/Latino and non-Latina/Latino theatres, and college and university theatre departments both inside and outside the United States.[8] Credit for its vast visibility can perhaps be most attributed to the fact that this play was actually the first play about Chicanas/Chicanos. As Jorge Huerta reminds us, "When it premiered, *Roosters* was the first Chicano play to be seen in New York since *Zoot Suit* (1979), impressing the non-Latino critics as magical realism, with its human dancers portraying fighting cocks and its climactic Ascension, a miracle. Critics have also interpreted *Roosters* as magical realism because of the heightened language, a poetic interpretation of the way working-class Chicanos speak."[9]

In Mel Gussow's highly favorable review of this first production of *Roosters,* he wrote: "With cockfighting as the background, the play inevitably indulges itself in symbolism, but Ms. Sanchez-Scott has a natural theatrical talent and an ability to ensnare an audience in a tale—both comic and poignant—of domestic emotional violence."[10] In that same year, M. Elizabeth Osborn's groundbreaking anthology, *On New Ground,* included this play among only six works. Sanchez-Scott reveals about the origin of the play that "*Roosters* began when a friend, Jerry Garcia, showed me a picture of relatives of his, Mexican-Americans. The woman was this *homely,* plump little thing, and the man looked like Warren Beatty. He was a rooster trainer; he'd been in and out of jail on drug charges, robbery. She was looking up at him like he was heaven on earth. During one of Irene's exercises in the lab these faces came to my mind." Of the play, which she wrote during her year in New York, she says, "it's my tearing-away-from-home play," adding: "When I finished it I remember distinctly feeling how separate I was from my parents, that I was really my own person."[11] *On New Ground* included commentary from the playwright as well as biographical information and a production history of *Roosters,* thus further acquainting audiences to its up-and-coming new playwright. Numerous productions of this work followed, in a wide range of venues, including regional stages, colleges, and cultural arts centers, throughout the United States and abroad.

In 1988, *Roosters* premiered at the Los Angeles Theatre Center, widening its audiences even more. As evidenced by two reviews appearing in the *Los Angeles Times,* the full production, under the direction of Jose Luis Valenzuela, was a success. Don Shirley wrote: "'Roosters' is something of a hard-kicking flyer itself," drawing from the words of the play. He added: "Playwright Milcha Sanchez-Scott kicks machismo around the stage until it hasn't a leg to stand on. Her play also flies, in the sense of ascending. Her language leaps from earthbound conversation into flights of poetic fantasy, and her imagery soars—literally so, at the end of the play, when a character levitates." Janice Arkatov, in her *Los Angeles Times* review, quotes Sanchez-Scott as being influenced by the "magical realism" found in South American authors: "it's very natural for me, because those are my roots. . . . It's a way with language and a heightened reality."[12] Also in 1988, an acting edition of *Roosters* was published by Dramatists Play Service Inc., and in 1995 an American Playhouse Theatrical Film and WMG presentation in association with Olmos Productions of a KCET Theatrical Production appeared under limited release, starring Edward James Olmos, Sonia Braga, and Maria Conchita Alonso under the direction of Robert M. Young.

Unquestionably, this play's outstanding stage life and the additional screen life enabled Sanchez-Scott's dramatic voice to reach a large audience. In *Chicano Drama,* Jorge Huerta provides an excellent analysis of *Roosters,* which he calls a "modern miracle play." *Roosters* brought much attention to the playwright and her works." But perhaps its widest visibility came when it was published in *American Theatre* (September 1987) under the auspices of Theatre Communications Group, making *Roosters* the first play about

Chicanas/Chicanos to appear in this widely distributed magazine. Even more exposure occurred with its inclusion in Oscar G. Brockett's *Plays for the Theatre,* beginning with the sixth edition in 1996.[13] In addition, his accompanying *The Essential Theatre* has an analysis of the play, with some editions including production illustrations and some mention of costume elements.

In the ninth edition of *The Essential Theatre,* now coedited by Brockett and Robert J. Ball, the editors mention the distinctive style of Latina/Latino playwrights in Sanchez-Scott's play: "The atmosphere, shifting easily between realism and fantasy, is characteristic of Latino 'magic realism.'" With the father's return setting the action into motion, utilizing both comic and serious tones, the climactic moment comes when the young daughter enables a miracle that virtually halts bloodshed between father and son, bringing the ruptured family unit to a communal whole, as the final tableau illustrates. In the words of Brockett and Ball, "overall, *Roosters* is a powerful play that has much to say about machismo, women, love, and psychological need in a male-dominated Latino culture."[14]

In her lengthy study on Sanchez-Scott, Rachel Chipman Waite also comments on the distinct style found in *Roosters,* noting this work as the play in which "Sanchez-Scott most vividly dramatizes the struggle between a character's faith in a mysterious world beyond reality and the reality of daily existence; the struggle between 'magic' and 'realism.'" She adds: "The angel-girl Angela is deeply connected to her strange world of saints and angels, which in turn brings this world to life for the audience. With the angel image so prevalent throughout the play, *Roosters* makes the most in depth examination of the underlying mysterious and unexplainable elements of our daily existence."[15]

Sanchez-Scott's work vividly drew from the many traditions of her culture and from her Roman Catholic education and upbringing. She also infused her work with imaginative language and interesting themes and ideas to draw new and multifaceted characters that represented her Latina and Latino world. Plays by Sanchez-Scott have been performed nationally and internationally, and we are fortunate to be able to include an example of her work in this collection.[16]

We can now turn to Sanchez-Scott's own comments about her work, which provide her reflections today about her entire experience in the theatre.

Artistic Vision/Punto de Vista Artístico

ECR & CRC: Briefly describe your theatre experience.[17]

MSS: I worked for several years in acting when I studied with Peggy Fury, who is a very well-known teacher here in Los Angeles. I studied acting with her. I studied in college and high school and I went a couple of summers to the Pasadena Playhouse, to the La Jolla Playhouse. There was a children's theatre that we did one summer at La Jolla. God, there is so much, and it is all scattered. There is also the Cambridge Repertory Company in Boston. I studied at Harvard, some theatre courses. There were some theatre courses there that had to do with acting, Stanislavski, the whole thing. I was married and my husband went to Harvard Law and Business School, and I was there and I worked in Widener Library, and I worked at the Cambridge Rep Company, and I took a couple of courses. It was in the late '70s.

ECR & CRC: How did you decide to write and/or perform?

MSS: All of my experiences in Boston were just in theatre, and when we finished, we came to Los Angeles. I went to tryout for a play called *Savages* at the Mark Taper Forum, and I got a part in that play. It was a big hit, and I got an agent and then I got all those parts in television which I didn't like to do. Then I met Susan [Loewenberg] and Doris Baizley, mainly, and they worked in a group called Artists in Prisons and Other Places, and that's when I was also working at the domestic agency, 'cause I was going out for acting parts, and at domestic agencies they would let me off to go to auditions and if I got a part, then I could work that and come back to work.[18] That's when I got all the material for *Latina,* and I just had enough of acting. It was just sit around, hurry up and wait, and that's just what it was, for these parts of the sister of the *cholo* gang leader who got shot or the girlfriend of the gang leader who got shot. It was all about gangs and stuff like that, and it was just very depressing, so that's when I started writing. That's how I started my writing career, and I think you know where it went from there.

ECR & CRC: Why do you write what you do?

MSS: I don't know if I know how to write anything else. I mean, the magical part, I know now where I get it—that's from my whole background, being in Colombia, being in Mexico, all that magical realism is from there, and that's how my mind always worked, even when I was a little kid writing in school, writing essays, they would go in that direction, and so, I guess I don't know how to write any other way. I think I'm a one-note writer.

ECR & CRC: Who do you write for and what audience are you trying to reach?

MSS: A lot of people, actually, because a lot of people come into my mind when I'm picturing my play in my head, and I'm thinking that I want young people to be inspired, I want old people to laugh, and now I'm writing a lot for middle-aged women. I wonder why that is. It's really for a Latin audience, the more I think about it, but it's not the Latin audience that is from Mexico, necessarily, but those of us that grew up here. That's why Texas was always such a dream for me, why I felt like I had my audience there, because there were all these kids that were Latin that were growing up American Latin. I came here at, I think a very significant age—thirteen—the beginning of my teenage years, and I think that that was very important because that is when you want to be like all those people around you, and you are discovering yourself, and I was discovering my Americanism, the American part of me. We first came to La Jolla because my father had a job at the University of California. I went to the school there, called Bishop's School, which was for girls only at that time. It has since become for boys as well, and there is this famous killer, Andrew Anaton or something, who killed the famous dress designer, Versace, and he went to that school.[19] My father was doing experiments with agriculture for the university.

ECR & CRC: What message, if any, are you trying to convey to your audience with this work and/or with all of your work?

MSS: I think that I am trying to send a message of acceptance for everybody. I mean, we're human. I know that sounds basic. I can't divide it further than that. I guess it's whatever *you're* getting from it too, and there are so many messages. There's the belief in magic, there is the spirituality to it. There's a kind of a "life is tough" for adults. Let's be easy on them. Let's be more accepting of ourselves, and just like a history of people that work in the fields in this country. There are just amazing, amazing people that come to this country doing a lot of—there are criminals coming—but by far, most people come to this country from Latin America, and they're so hard working. There was just such a thing, I think in the '50s. I remember also in the '40s there were these caricatures that they used to make in plaster of the Mexican in the sombrero leaning against the cactus, sleeping. It's like this joke that goes around that says 'What did Jesus say to the Mexicans before he left?' 'Don't do a thing until I come back.' *Como si fueramos flojos* (As though we were lazy). It's just the opposite—I mean I've never seen such industrious people. It just makes me so glad inside when I see Latin Americans getting ahead in this country, when there is a whole middle class of Latin Americans. Of course, there is no middle class in Mexico or Colombia. I mean in South America the middle class is very, very, very, very thin, but here you can just see it in people, that they can buy things for their kids, and there are shops and medicines and the most wonderful things can happen when people have a chance.

ECR & CRC: Who or what has been your major influence?

MSS: I think I would have to say first of all, because I started writing so young, they were the English writers. [Elizabeth Barrett] Browning, *Jane Eyre,* and then the Latin American writers. Of course, [Gabriel García] Márquez. And [Eugene] O'Neill, my ultimate favorite. I still reread those plays. They are just so brilliant and beautiful.

ECR & CRC: What has been your biggest and/or most difficult struggle/challenge in life, in completing a play or getting it produced, etc.?

MSS: In completing it. I never had a problem of getting it produced, but I did have so many problems in completing it. They were never good enough for me, especially the endings. I'd get lost in them. I literally go on a trip and I get lost in them, and then I change everything the next day. It's just so that I've learned to now let it be what it wants to be. Instead of trying to manipulate it. I tried to manipulate it sometimes too much, and then, it always goes where it wants to go anyway. So I say, why even bother. It's just going to do what it wants to do. You can't control it.

ECR & CRC: If you studied with Maria Irene Fornes, is there any commentary you wish to add about her impact on your work?

MSS: It was with INTAR, in 1985 or something like that. I wasn't interested in playwriting at all until I was already out of college. The thing about Maria Fornes to me was that she let you be what you wanted to be. She didn't try to tell you no, this is right, or this is wrong. When the play was completed, she gave suggestions, ideas of what she thought, you know: "You don't really need that scene there" or it usually had to do with eliminating things. But what I found, for her—I was always used to these writing classes where people would critique your work. You would read it and they would critique it, and you were just like your play had pony legs that were quivering and people were kicking at it—she never allowed any critiquing. It was completely written. Then it was okay, but in the beginning of your reading scenes to each other, she didn't want anybody saying anything—good, bad, or indifferent. And in that kind of atmosphere, I think writers can define themselves. They can go and hang themselves and then find out you were up the wrong—this isn't the way I'm supposed to be. You found it out for yourself. I guess that's how I felt about her, the strongness. She let me be who I was, and that sounds like nothing but it's a big, big thing for teaching, a really big thing.

ECR & CRC: Can you offer any words of advice to aspiring playwrights/performers/directors/audiences?

MSS: It seems that if you want it, it's there. Really, it's there. You just have to try to be as good as you can be, and then the more you really take yourself to task, think, reflect, a lot of reflection, a lot of internal stuff. I just see sometimes a lot of playwrights—that things are so facile, but then they are not saying anything. It's not O'Neill. It's not rich and layered. It should be like great chocolate, and in order for that to happen you really do have to spend a lot of time looking and reading. Reading is the biggest thing I could recommend to anybody for an actor, for a writer, read every spare moment you have. Read everybody. Just read—also the audiences—read!

Production History/Palabras Dramatúrgicas

Roosters was originally produced in New York City by INTAR Hispanic American Arts Center (Max Ferrá, artistic director; Dennis Ferguson-Acosta, managing director)and the New York Shakespeare Festival (Joseph Papp, producer) on March 11, 1987. It was directed by Jackson Phippin, with set design by Loy Arcenas, lighting design by John Gisondi, and costume design by C. L. Hundley. The sound design was by Janet Kalas, the fight direction by Nels Hennum, the dialect consultant was Tim Monich, and the stage manager was Michele Steckler. The cast was as follows: Gallo—Joaquim De Almeida; Hector—Joanathan Del Arco; Angela—Sara Erde; Juana—Suzanne Costallos; Chata—Ilka Tanya Payan; and Adan—Albert Farrar.

Contact Information

Stock and amateur production rights to *Roosters* are controlled exclusively by the Dramatist Play Service, Inc., 440 Park Avenue South, New York, NY 10016. Address all other rights inquiries to George Lane, c/o William Morris Agency, Inc., 1350 Avenue of the Americas, New York, NY 100019.

The playwright may be contacted through the editors.

ROOSTERS

Characters

Gallo
Zapata
Hector
Angela
Juana
Chata
Adan
Shadow #1
Shadow #2
San Juan

Time

The present.

Place

The Southwest.

ACT ONE

Scene 1

Stage and house are dark. Slowly a narrow pinspot of light comes up. We hear footsteps. Enter Gallo, a very, very handsome man in his forties. He is wearing a cheap dark suit, with a white open-neck shirt. He carries a suitcase. He puts the suitcase down. He faces the audience.

GALLO: Lord Eagle, Lord Hawk, sainted ones, spirits and winds, Santa Maria Aurora of the Dawn . . . I want no resentment, I want no rancor. . . . I had an old red Cuban hen. She was squirrel-tailed and sort of slab-sided and you wouldn't have given her a second look. But she was a queen. She could be thrown with any cock and you would get a hard-kicking stag every time. I had a vision, of a hard-kicking flyer, the ultimate bird. The Filipinos were the ones with the pedigree Bolinas, the high flyers, but they had no real kick. To see those birds fighting in the air like dark avenging angels . . . well like my father use to say, "Son nobles . . . finos. . . ." I figured to mate that old red Cuban. This particular Filipino had the best. A dark burgundy flyer named MacArthur. He wouldn't sell. I began borrowing MacArthur at night, bringing him back before dawn, no one the wiser, but one morning the Filipino's son caught me. He pulled out his blade. I pulled out mine. I was faster. I went up on manslaughter. . . . They never caught on . . . thought I was in the henhouse trying to steal their stags. . . . It took time—refining, inbreeding, cross-breeding, brother to sister, mother to son, adding power, rapid attack . . . but I think we got him. (*Gallo stands still for* *a beat, checks his watch, takes off his jacket and faces C. A slow, howling drumbeat begins. As it gradually goes higher in pitch and excitement mounts, we see narrow beams of light, the first light of dawn, filtering through chicken wire. The light reveals a heap of chicken feathers which turns out to be an actor/dancer who represents the rooster Zapata. Zapata stretches his wings, then his neck, to greet the light. He stands and struts proudly, puffs his chest and crows his salutation to the sun. Gallo stalks Zapata, as drums follow their movements.*) Ya, ya, mi lindo . . . yeah, baby . . . you're a beauty, a real beauty. Now let's see whatcha got. (*He pulls out a switchblade stiletto. It gleams in the light as he tosses it from hand to hand.*) Come on baby boy. Show Daddy whatcha got. (*Gallo lunges at Zapata. Zapata parries with his beak and wings. This becomes a slow, rhythmic fight-dance. Gallo grabs Zapata by his comb, bending his head backwards until he is forced to sit. Gallo stands behind Zapata, straddling him. With one hand Gallo holds Zapata's comb, with the other he holds the knife next to Zapata's neck.*) Oh yeah, you like to fight? Huh? You gonna kill for me baby boy? Huh? (*Gallo sticks the tip of the knife into Zapata. The rooster squawks in pain.*) Sssh! Baby boy, you gotta learn. Daddy's gotta teach you. (*Gallo sticks it to Zapata again. This time the rooster snaps back in anger.*) That's right beauty . . . Now you got it . . . Come on, come. (*Gallo waves his knife and hand close to Zapata's face. The rooster's head and eyes follow.*) Oh yeah . . . that's it baby, take it! Take it! (*Suddenly Zapata attacks, drawing blood. Gallo's body contracts in orgasmic pleasure/pain. Loudly.*) Ay precioso! . . . Mi lindo . . . You like that, eh? Taste good, huh? (*Gallo waves the gleaming knife in a slow hypnotic movement which calms the rooster.*) Take my blood, honey . . . I'm in you now . . . Morales blood, the blood of kings . . . and you're my rooster . . . a Morales rooster. (*He slowly backs away from the rooster. He picks up his suitcase, still pointing the knife at Zapata.*) Kill. You're my son. Make me proud. (*Gallo exits. Zapata puffs his chest and struts U. Lights go up a little on UL area as the rooster goes into the chicken-wire henhouse. He preens and scratches. Enter Hector, a young man of about twenty. He is very handsome. He wears gray sweatpants and no shirt. On his forehead is a sweatband. His hair and body are dripping wet. He has been running. Now he is panting as he leans on the henhouse looking at Zapata.*)

HECTOR: I saw what you did to those chicks. Don't look at me like you have a mind, or a soul, or feelings. You kill your young . . . and we are so proud of your horrible animal vigor . . . But you are my inheritance . . . Abuelo's gift to me . . . to get me out. Oh, Abuelo, Grandfather . . . You should have left me your courage, your sweet pacific strength. (*A ray of light hits DR. In a semi-shadow, we see a miniature cemetery, with small white headstones and white crosses. We see the profile of a young angel/girl with wings and a pale dress. Angela is kneeling next to a bare desert tree with low scratchy branches. She has a Buster Brown haircut and a low tough voice. She is fifteen, but looks twelve.*)

ANGELA: (*Loudly.*)
Angel of God
My Guardian Dear

To whom God's love
Commits me here
Ever this day be
At my side
To light and guard
To rule and guide
Amen.

Scene 2

As the light changes we hear the clapping of women making tortillas. (*Angela's paper wings get caught in a tree branch.*) "Aw, shit!" (*She exits.*)

Lights come up full. Center is a faded wood-frame house, with a porch that is bare except for a table and a few chairs. The house sits in the middle of a desert agricultural valley somewhere in the Southwest. Everything is sparse. There is a feeling of blue skies and space. One might see off on the horizon tall Nopales or Century cactus. Juana, a thin, wornout-looking woman of thirty-five, comes out of the house. She is wearing a faded housedress. She goes to mid-yard, faces front and stares out.

JUANA: It's dry. Bone dry. There's a fire in the mountains . . . up near Jacinto Pass. (*The clapping stops for a beat, then continues. Juana starts to go back into the house, then stops. She sniffs the air, sniffs again, and again.*) Tres Rosas . . . I smell Tres Rosas. (*She hugs her body and rocks.*) Tres Rosas . . . Ay, St. Anthony let him come home . . . Let him be back. (*The clapping stops. Chata enters from the house. She is a fleshy woman of forty, who gives new meaning to the word blowsy. She has the lumpy face of a hard boozer. She walks with a slight limp. She wears a black kimono, on the back of which is embroidered in red a dragon and the words "Korea, U.S.S. Perkins, 7th Fleet." A cigarette hangs from her lips. She carries a bowl containing balls of tortilla dough.*) I smell Tres Rosas . . . The brilliantine for his hair . . . He musta been here. Why did he go?

CHATA: Men are shit.

JUANA: Where could he be?

CHATA: First day out of jail! My brother never comes home first day. You should know that. Gotta sniff around . . . gotta get use to things. See his friends.

JUANA: Sí, that's right . . . He just gotta get used to things. I'll feel better when I see him . . . I gotta keep busy.

CHATA: You been busy all morning.

JUANA: I want him to feel good, be proud of us . . . You hear anything when you come in yesterday?

CHATA: Who's gonna know anything at the Trailways bus station?

JUANA: You ain't heard anything?

CHATA: Juanita, he knows what he's doing. If there was gonna be any trouble he'd know. Ay, mujer, he's just an old warrior coming home.

JUANA: Ain't that old.

CHATA: For a fighting man, he's getting up there. (*Juana slaps tortillas. Chata watches her.*) Who taught you to make tortillas?

JUANA: I don't remember. I never make 'em. Kids don't ask.

CHATA: Look at this. You call this a tortilla? Have some pride. Show him you're a woman.

JUANA: Chata, you've been here one day, and you already—

CHATA: Ah, you people don't know what it is to eat fresh handmade tortillas. My grandmother Hortensia, the one they used to call "La India Condenada" . . . she would start making them at five o'clock in the morning. So the men would have something to eat when they went into the fields. Hijo! She was tough . . . Use to break her own horses . . . and her own men. Every day at five o'clock she would wake me up. "Buenos pinchi días," she would say. I was twelve or thirteen years old, still in braids . . ."Press your hands into the dough," "Con fuerza," "Put your stamp on it." One day I woke up, tú sabes, con la sangre. "Ah! So you're a woman now. Got your cycle like the moon. Soon you'll want a man, well this is what you do. When you see the one you want, you roll the tortilla on the inside of your thigh and then you give it to him nice and warm. Be sure you give it to him and nobody else." Well, I been rolling tortillas on my thighs, on my nalgas, and God only knows where else, but I've been giving my tortillas to the wrong men . . . and that's been the problem with my life. First there was Emilio. I gave him my first tortilla. Ay Mamacita, he use to say, these are delicious. Aye, he was handsome, a real lady-killer! After he did me the favor he didn't have the cojones to stick around . . . took my TV set too. They're all shit . . . the Samoan bartender, what was his name . . .

JUANA: Nicky, Big Nicky.

CHATA: The guy from Pep Boys—

JUANA: Chata, you really think he'll be back?

CHATA: His son's first time in the pit? With "the" rooster? A real Morales rooster? Honey, he'll be back. Stop worrying.

JUANA: Let's put these on the griddle. Angela, Hector . . . breakfast.

Scene 3

Angela slides out from under the house, wearing her wings. She carries a white box which contains her cardboard tombstones, paper and crayons, a writing tablet and a pen. She too sniffs the air. She runs to the little cemetery and looks up, as Hector appears at the window behind her.

ANGELA: Tres Rosas . . . Did you hear? Sweet Jesus, Abuelo, Queen of Heaven, all the Saints, all the Angels. It is true. It is certain. He is coming, coming to stay forever and ever. Amen.

HECTOR: Don't count on it!

ANGELA: (*To Heaven*) Protect me from those of little faith and substance.

HECTOR: I'm warning you. You're just going to be disappointed.

ANGELA: (*To Heaven*) Guard me against the enemies of my soul.

HECTOR: Your butt's getting bigger and bigger!

ANGELA: And keep me from falling in with low companions.

HECTOR: Listen, little hummingbird woman, you gotta be tough, and grown-up today. (*Angela digs up her collection can and two dolls. Both dolls are dressed in nuns' habits. One, the St. Lucy doll, has round sunglasses. She turns a box over to make a little tea table on which she places a doll's teapot and cups.*)

ANGELA: As an act of faith and to celebrate her father's homecoming, Miss Angela Ester Morales will have a tea party.

HECTOR: No more tea parties.

ANGELA: Dancing in attendance will be that charming martyr St. Lucy.

HECTOR: He will not be impressed.

ANGELA: Due to the loss of her eyes and the sensitivity of her alabaster skin, St. Lucy will sit in the shade. (*She sits St. Lucy in the shade and picks up the other doll.*)

HECTOR: Who's that?

ANGELA: St. Teresa of Avigon, you will sit over here.[20] (*She seats St. Teresa doll.*)

HECTOR: Just don't let him con you Angela.

ANGELA: (*Pouring pretend tea*) One lump or two, St. Lucy? St. Teresa has hyperglycemia, and only takes cream in her tea. Isn't that right St. Teresa?

HECTOR: He's not like Abuelo. (*Angela animates the dolls like puppets and uses two different voices as St. Lucy and St. Teresa.*)

ANGELA: (*As St. Teresa*) Shouldn't we wait for St. Luke?

HECTOR: Stop hiding. You can't be a little girl forever.

ANGELA: (*As St. Lucy*) St. Luke! St. Luke! How that man got into Heaven I'll never know. That story about putting peas in his boots and offering the discomfort up to God is pure bunk. I happen to know he boiled the peas first.

HECTOR: I don't want you hurt. It's time to grow up.

ANGELA: (*As St. Teresa*) St. Lucy! I can only think that it is the loss of your eyes that makes you so disagreeable. Kindly remember that we have all suffered to be saints.

HECTOR: Are you listening to me, Angie?

ANGELA: (*As St. Lucy*) Easy for you to say! They took my eyes because I wouldn't put out! They put them on a plate. A dirty, chipped one, thank you very much indeed! To this day no true effort has been made to find them.

HECTOR: Excuse me! . . . Excuse me, St. Teresa, St. Lucy, I just thought I should tell you . . . a little secret . . . your hostess, Miss Angela Ester Morales, lies in her little, white, chaste, narrow bed, underneath the crucifix, and masturbates.

ANGELA: Heretic! Liar!

HECTOR: Poor Jesus, up there on the cross, right over her bed, his head tilted down. He sees everything.

ANGELA: Lies! Horrible lies!

HECTOR: Poor saint of the month, watching from the night table.

ANGELA: I hate you! I hate you! Horrible, horrible Hector.

JUANA: (*From offstage*) Breakfast! (*Hector leaves the window. Angela sits on the ground writing on a tombstone.*)

ANGELA: (*Lettering tombstone*) Here lies Horrible Hector Morales. Died at age twenty, in great agony, for tormenting his little sister.

JUANA: (*Offstage*) You kids . . . breakfast!

HECTOR: (*Pops up at window*) Just be yourself. A normal sex-crazed fifteen-year-old girl with a big gigantic enormous butt. (*He exits.*)

ANGELA: (*To Heaven*)

Send me to Alaska
Let me be frozen
Send me a contraction
A shrinking antidote
Make me little again
Please make my legs
Like tiny pink Vienna sausages
Give me back my little butt.

(*Juana and Chata bring breakfast out on the porch and set it on the table.*)

JUANA: Angie! Hector! We ain't got all day. (*Angela goes to the breakfast table with the St. Lucy doll and the collection can.*) And take your wings off before you sit at the table. Ain't you kids got any manners? (*Angela removes her wings, sits down, bows her head in prayer. Chata stares at St. Lucy. St. Lucy stares at Chata. Juana shoos flies and stares at the distant fire.*) I hope he's on this side of the fire.

CHATA: That doll's staring at me.

ANGELA: She loves you. (*Lights fade on the women, come up on the henhouse. Adan, a young man of twenty, is talking to Zapata—now a real rooster, not the actor/dancer—and preparing his feed.*)

ADAN: Hola Zapata . . . ya mi lindo . . . mi bonito. En inglés. Tengo que hablar en English . . . pinchi English . . . ¿verdad Zapata? En Español más romántico pero Hector say I must learned di English. (*Zapata starts squawking.*) ¿Qué te pasa? Orita vas a comer.

(*Hector enters.*)

HECTOR: English, Adan . . . English.

ADAN: No English . . . pinchi English.

HECTOR: Good morning, Adan.

ADAN: A que la fregada! . . . Okay this morning in the fields, I talk English pero this afternoon for fight I talk puro Español.

HECTOR: Good morning, Adan.

ADAN: Sí, sí, good morning, muy fine . . . Hector el Filipino he say . . . (*He moves away from Zapata, so bird will not hear him.*) He say to tell you que Zapata no win. Porque Filipino bird fight more y your bird first fight y your first fight y you not no ex . . . ex . . .

HECTOR: Experience.

ADAN: Sí eso, he say you sell bird to him y no fight . . . He say is not true Morales bird porque Gallo not here. El Filipino say if you fight bird . . . bird dead. If bird still alive after Filipino bird beat him . . . Bird still dead porque nobody pay money for bird that lose.

HECTOR: But if he wins, everybody wants him.

ADAN: I say, ay di poor Hector. His abuelo leave him bird. He can no sell. El Filipino say, "Good!" Inside, in my heart I am laughing so hard porque he not know Gallo gonna be here. We win, we make much money.

HECTOR: It's my bird, I have to do it myself.

ADAN: You tonto! You stupido! You mulo! Like donkey . . . He help you, he the king . . . he you papa. For him all birds fight.

HECTOR: No!

ADAN: Why? Why for you do this? You no even like bird. Zapata he knows this, he feel this thing in his heart. You just want money to go from the fields, to go to the other side of the mountains . . . to go looking . . . to go looking for what? On the other side is only more stupid people like us.

HECTOR: How could you think I just wanted money? I want him to see me.

ADAN: Sorry . . . I am sorry my friend . . . I know . . . I stay with you y we win vas a ver! Okay Zapata! We win y ésta noche estamos tomando Coors, Ripple, Lucky Lager, unas Buds, Johnny Walkers, oh sí, y las beautiful señoritas. (*He gives Zapata his food.*) Eat Zapata! Be strong.

HECTOR: I almost forgot, look what I have for you . . . fresh, warm homemade tortillas.

ADAN: Oh, how nice.

HECTOR: Yes, how nice. Aunt Chata made them.

ADAN: Oh, much nice.

HECTOR: Today she woke up at five o'clock, spit a green booger the size of a small frog into a wad of Kleenex. She wrapped her soiled black "7th Fleet" kimono around her loose, flaccid, tortured, stretch-marked body and put her fat-toed, corned yellow hooves into a pair of pink satin slippers. She slap-padded over to the sink where she opened her hippo lips and looked into the mirror. She looked sad. I looked at those lips . . . those lips that had wrapped themselves warmly and lovingly around the cocks of a million campesinos, around thousands upon thousands of mexicanos, salvadoreños, guatemaltecos. For the tide of brown men that flooded the fields of this country, she was there with her open hippo whore's lips, saying "Bienvenidos," "Welcome," "Hola," "Howdy." Those legendary lips, Adan.

ADAN: Yes . . . muy yes.

HECTOR: What a woman, what a comfort. Up and down the state in her beat-up station wagon. A '56 Chevy with wood panels on the sides, in the back a sad, abused mattress. She followed the brown army of pickers through tomatoes, green beans, zucchinis, summer squash, winter squash, oranges, and finally Castroville, the artichoke capital of the world, where her career was stopped by the fists of a sun-crazed compañero. The ingratitude broke her heart.

ADAN: Oh my gooseness!

HECTOR: She was a river to her people, she should be rewarded, honored. No justice in the world.

ADAN: Pinchi world. (*He and Hector look to mountains.*) You look mountains. In my country I look mountains to come here. I am here and everybody still look mountains.

HECTOR: I want to fly right over them.

ADAN: No, my friend, we are here, we belong . . . la tierra.

JUANA: (*From offstage*) Hector, I ain't calling you again. (*Light up on the porch. Juana and Chata are sitting at the table. Angela is sitting on the steps. She has her wings back on. St. Lucy and the collection can are by her side. She is writing on her tablet.*) Oh Gallo, what's keeping you?

CHATA: Men are shit! That's all. And it's Saturday. When do they get drunk? When do they lose their money? When do they shoot each other? Saturdays, that's when the shit hits the fan. (*Enter Hector and Adan with Zapata in a traveling carrier.*)

JUANA: It's because I'm so plain.

HECTOR: We're better off without him.

CHATA: Buenos días, Adan. Un cafecito?

ADAN: Ah, Good morning, Mrs. Chata, no gracias, ah good morning, Mrs. Morales y Miss Angelita. (*Angela sticks out her donation can. Adan automatically drops coins in.*)

JUANA: Angela!

ADAN: No, is good, is for the poor. Miss Angela, she good lady . . . eh, girl. (*He pats Angela on the head.*)

JUANA: Why don't you leave the bird, so your father can see him when he gets home.

HECTOR: He's my bird. He can see it later.

JUANA: I can't believe you would do this to your own father. Birds are his life . . . and he's so proud of you.

HECTOR: This is news. How would he know, he hasn't seen me in years.

JUANA: It isn't his fault.

HECTOR: It never is.

JUANA: Your father is with us all the time, he got his eye on us, he knows everything we're doing.

ANGELA: Everything!

JUANA: I brag about you kids in my letters . . . His friends they tell him what a smart boy you are . . . that you're good-looking like him . . . He's proud . . . "A real Morales," that's what he says.

HECTOR: And did he call me a winner? A champ? A prince? And did you tell him I was in the fields?

ANGELA: What did he say about me, Mama?

HECTOR: Nothing, you're a girl and a retard. What possible use could he have for you? Grow up!

CHATA: No, you grow up. (*Angela buries herself in Chata's lap.*)

JUANA: Hector, please, Hector, for me.

HECTOR: No, Mother. Not even for you.

JUANA: You give him a chance.

HECTOR: What chance did he give us? Fighting his birds, in and out of trouble. He was never here for us, never a card, a little present for Angela. He forgot us.

JUANA: You don't understand him. He's different.

HECTOR: Just make it clear to him. Abuelo left the bird to me, not to him, to me.

JUANA: Me, me, me. You gonna choke on this me, me. Okay, okay, I'm not going to put my nose in the bird business. I just ask you for me, for Angie, be nice to him.

HECTOR: As long as we all understand the "bird business," I'll be nice to him even if it kills me, Mother.

JUANA: Now you're feeling sorry for yourself. Just eat. You can feel sorry for yourself later.

HECTOR: Why didn't I think of that. I'll eat now and feel sorry for myself later.

JUANA: Now, you kids gotta be nice and clean, your papa don't like dirty people.

CHATA: Me too, I hate dirty people.

JUANA: Angie, you take a bath.

HECTOR: Oh, Angela, how . . . how long has it been since you and water came together? (*Angela hits him.*) Oww!

JUANA: You put on a nice clean dress, and I don't wanna see you wearing no dirty wings.

HECTOR: Right, Angie, put on the clean ones.

JUANA: You say "please" and "excuse me" . . . and you watch your table manners . . . I don't want to see any pigs at my table.

HECTOR: (*Making pig noises*) What a delicious breakfast! Cold eggs, sunny-side up. How cheery! How uplifting! Hmm, hmmm! (*He turns so Angela can see him. He picks up the eggs with his hands and stuffs them in his mouth.*) Look, Angela, refried beans in a delicate pool of congealed fat. (*Still making pig noises, he picks up gobs of beans, stuffs them into his mouth.*)

CHATA: A que la fregada! Hector, stop playing with your food. You're making us sick.

JUANA: (*Looking at watch*) 7:20, you got ten minutes before work. (*Hector drums his fingers on the table.*)

HECTOR: Nine minutes . . . I will now put on the same old smelly, shit-encrusted boots, I will walk to the fields. The scent of cow dung and rotting vegetation will fill the air. I will wait with the same group of beaten-down, pathetic men . . . taking their last piss against a tree, dropping hard warm turds in the bushes. All adding to this fertile whore of a valley. At 7:30 that yellow mechanical grasshopper, the Deerfield tractor, will belch and move. At this exact moment, our foreman, John Knipe, will open his pig-sucking mouth, exposing his yellow, pointy, plaque-infested teeth. He yells, "Start picking, boys." The daily war begins . . . the intimidation of violent growth

. . . the expanding melons and squashes, the hardiness of potatoes, the waxy purple succulence of eggplant, the potency of ripening tomatoes. All so smug, so rich, so ready to burst with sheer generosity and exuberance. They mock me . . . I hear them . . . "Hey Hector," they say, "show us whatcha got," and "Yo Hector we got bacteria out here more productive than you." . . . I look to the ground. Slugs, snails, worms slithering in the earth with such ferocious hunger they devour their own tails, flies oozing out larvae, aphids, bees, gnats, caterpillars their prolification only slightly dampened by our sprays. We still find eggsacks hiding, ready to burst forth. Their teeming life, their lust, is shameful . . . Well it's time . . . Bye, Ma. (*He exits.*)

JUANA: (*Yelling*) Hector! You gotta do something about your attitude. (*To herself.*) Try to see the bright side. (*Juana and Chata exit into the house, leaving Angela on the porch steps. Adan runs up to her.*)

ADAN: Psst! Miss Angelita! . . . di . . . di cartas?

ANGELA: Oh, the letters . . . that will be one dollar.

ADAN: One dollar! Adan very poor man . . . (*Angela sticks the donation can out and shakes it. Adan reaches into his pockets and drops coins into the can.*) Oh, sí, you are very good. (*Angela puts on glasses and pulls out a letter.*)

ANGELA: (*Reading letter*) "Adored Señora Acosta: The impulses of my heart are such that they encourage even the most cautious man to commit indiscretion. My soul is carried to the extreme with the love that only you could inspire. Please know that I feel a true passion for your incomparable beauty and goodness. I tremulously send this declaration and anxiously await the result. Your devoted slave, Adan."

ADAN: (*Sighing*) Ay, que beautiful.

ANGELA: "P.S. With due respect, Señora, if your husband should be home, do not turn on the porch light."

ADAN: Ah, thank you . . . thank you very much. (*Adan hurriedly exits. Angela gathers her St. Lucy doll and her donation can, and exits quickly. Chata enters from the home wearing "colorful" street clothes. She looks around, then swiftly exits. Hector enters, picks up Zapata, hurries off. The stage darkens, as if smoke from the distant fire has covered the sun. Drum howls are heard. In the distance we hear a rooster crow and sounds of excited chickens as the henhouse comes to life. Gallo appears.*)

GALLO: Easy hens, shshsh! My beauties. (*He puts his suitcase down, cups his hands to his mouth, and yells to the house.*) Juana! Juana! Juana! (*Juana opens the door.*) How many times, in the fever of homesickness, have I written out that name on prison walls, on bits of paper, on the skin of my arms . . . Let me look at you . . . my enduring rock, my anchor made from the hard parts of the earth—minerals, rocks, bits of glass, ground shells, the brittle bones of dead animals.

JUANA: I never seen you so pale, so thin . . .

GALLO: I'm home to rest, to fatten up, to breathe, to mend, to you.

JUANA: How long? How long will you stay?

GALLO: Here. Here is where I'll put my chair . . . I will sit here basking in the sun, like a fat old iguana catching flies, and watching my grandchildren replant the little cemetery with the bones of tiny sparrows. Here. Here I will build the walks for my champions. Morales roosters. The brave and gallant red Cubans, the hard and high-kicking Irish Warhorses, the spirited high-flying Bolinas.

JUANA: Don't say nothing you don't mean . . . you really gonna stay?

GALLO: (*Gently*) Here. Here is where I'll plant a garden of herbs. Blessed laurel to cure fright, wild marjoram for the agony of lovesickness, cempauchie flowers for the grief of loneliness. (*Gallo gently kisses Juana, picks her up and carries her into the house. The door slams shut. Angela enters, her wings drooping behind her. She trips over Gallo's suitcase. She examines it. She smells it.*)

ANGELA: Tres Rosas! (*Angela looks at the house. She sits on the suitcase, crosses her arms over her chest as if she were ready to wait an eternity. The shadows of two strangers fall on her.*) What do you want?

SHADOW #1: Nobody's home to you, rancor.

SHADOW #2: Just go in, tell him we got something for him.

ANGELA: Nobody's home to you, resentment.

SHADOW #1: Who are you supposed to be?

ANGELA: (*Holding St. Lucy doll*)
I am the angel of this yard
I am the angel of this door
I am the angel of light
I am the angel who shouts
I am the angel who thunders.

SHADOW #1: She is pure crazy.

SHADOW #2: Don't play with it, it's serious.

ANGELA:
You are the shadow of resentment
You are the shadow of rancor
I am the angel of acid saliva
I will spit on you.

SHADOW #1: There's time.

SHADOW #2: Yeah, later. (*Angela spits. The shadows leave. Angela crosses her hands over her chest and looks to Heaven.*)

ANGELA: Holy Father . . . Listen, you don't want him, you want me. Please take me, claim me, launch me and I will be your shooting star woman. I will be your comet woman. I will be your morning-star woman.

Scene 4

Lights become brighter. Angela exits under the house. The door opens. Gallo comes out in T-shirt and pants and goes to his suitcase. Juana comes to the door in slip and tight robe.

GALLO: I never sent him to the fields.

JUANA: I know.

GALLO: I never said for you to put him there.

JUANA: No, you never said . . .

GALLO: Then why is my son in the fields? (*They look at each other. Gallo looks away.*) Don't look at me. I see it in your eyes. You blame me. Just like the old man.

JUANA: Abuelo never said a word against you.

GALLO: I never let him down with the birds, nobody could match me. They were the best.

JUANA: He knew that . . .

GALLO: So, he left the bird to Hector.

JUANA: He wanted him out of the fields. We didn't know when you would be out or maybe something would happen to you.

GALLO: He let the boy into the fields, that was his sin. He allowed a Morales into the fields.

JUANA: He was old, tired, heartbroken.

GALLO: Heartbroken, he wasn't a woman to be heartbroken.

JUANA: His only son was in jail.

GALLO: Yes, we know that, the whole valley knows that. You . . . what did you do? Didn't you lay out your hard, succulent, bitch's teat at the breakfast table? So he would have the strength to stand behind a hoe, with his back bent and his eyes on the mud for ten hours a day.

JUANA: Hard work never killed anybody.

GALLO: Ay, mujer! Can't you think what you've done, you bowed his head down.

JUANA: What was I suppose to do? There ain't no other work here. I can't see anything wrong with it for a little while.

GALLO: The difference between them and us, is we never put a foot into the fields. We stayed independent—we worked for nobody. They have to respect us, to respect our roosters. (*Hector and Adan enter. They are both very dirty. Hector has Zapata, in his carrier. Adan has a carrier containing a second rooster. Gallo and Hector stare at each other.*) Well . . . you are taller. This offshoot . . . this little bud has grown.

HECTOR: Yeah, well . . . that must be why you seem . . . smaller.

GALLO: Un abrazo!

HECTOR: I'm dirty. I'm sweaty.

GALLO: I see that.

HECTOR: I'm afraid I smell of the fields.

GALLO: Yes.

HECTOR: Of cheap abundant peon labor . . . the scent would gag you.

GALLO: It's going to kill you.

HECTOR: Mama says hard work never killed anyone . . . isn't that right, Mother?

JUANA: It's only for a little while. Your papa thinks that—

GALLO: I'll tell him what I think. Now what about those tamales you promised me?

JUANA: Ah sí, con permiso . . . I got some work in the kitchen.

ADAN: Oh sí, Mrs. Juana, los tamales . . . que rico.

JUANA: (*Smiling at Adan*) I hope they're the kind you like. (*She exits into house.*)

GALLO: Hijo, you always take the bird with you into the fields?

HECTOR: No, not always.

GALLO: This bird has to look like he's got secrets . . . no one but us should be familiar with him.

HECTOR: This is Adan.

ADAN: Es un honor, Mr. El Gallo. (*Angela sticks her head out from under the house. Adan and Gallo shake hands and greet each other.*)

GALLO: (*Referring to Zapata*) Let him out . . . he needs a bigger carrier . . . he's a flyer.

ADAN: Como Filipino birds?

GALLO: Yes but this baby boy he's got a surprise. He's got a kick.

ADAN: Like Cuban bird?

GALLO: He'll fight in the air, he'll fight on the ground. You can put spurs or razors on that kick and he'll cut any bird to ribbons. You can put money on that.

ADAN: Hijo! Señor . . . how you know? He never fight. Maybe he only kick in cage.

GALLO: I know because I'm his papa . . . (*Pointing to the other carrier.*) That your bird?

ADAN: Sí, pero no good . . . no fight. San Juan, he run away.

GALLO: I'll make him fight. Just let him out.

ADAN: Mr. El Gallo, you give this pendejo bird too much honor. Gracias Señor, pero this poor bird, he no can fight.

GALLO: Is it the bird, or you who will not fight?

HECTOR: The bird is too young. He doesn't want him to fight.

GALLO: I've never seen a bird that won't fight, but there are men who are cowards.

HECTOR: He is not a coward.

ADAN: This is true, pero I am not El Gallo. In my country all men who love di rooster know Mr. El Gallo. They tell of di famoso Día de los Muertos fight in Jacinto Park.

GALLO: Ah, you heard about that fight. You remember that fight, Hector?

HECTOR: No.

GALLO: First time you saw a real cockfight . . . Abuelo took you . . . How could you forget your first cockfight? (*To Adan.*) Go on, take your bird out. I'll make him fight. (*Gallo takes a drink from a bottle, then blows on San Juan. As he does this, lights go down almost to black. Pinspot comes up C. as other lights come up to a dark red. During this process, we hear Gallo's voice—"Ready," then a few beats later "Pit!" On this cue two dancer/roosters jump into the pinspot. This rooster dance is savage. The dancers wear razors on their feet. The Zapata dancer jumps very high. The poor San Juan dancer stays close to the ground. Throughout the dance, we hear drums and foot-stomping. At every hit, there is a big drum pound. During the fight, Hector appears on the porch.*)

HECTOR: (*To himself*) It was in Jacinto Park . . . the crowd was a monster, made up of individual human beings stuck together by sweat and spittle. Their gaping mouths let out screams, curses, and foul gases, masticating, smacking, eager for the kill. You stood up. The monster roared. Quasimoto, your bird, in one hand. You lifted him high, "Pit!" went the call. "Pit!" roared the monster. And you threw him into the ring . . . soaring with the blades on his heels flashing I heard the mighty rage of his wings and my heart soared with him. He was a whirlwind flashing and slashing like a dark avenging angel then like some distant rainbow star exploding he was hit. The monster crowd inhaled, sucking back their hopes . . . in that vacuum he was pulled down. My heart went down the same dark shaft, my brains slammed against the earth's hard crust . . . my eyes clouded . . . my arteries gushed . . . my lungs collapsed. "Get up," said Abuelo, "up here with me, and you will see a miracle." You, Father, picked up Quasimoto, a lifeless pile of bloody feathers, holding his head oh so gently, you closed your eyes, and like a great wave receding, you drew a breath that came from deep within your ocean floor. I heard the stones rumble, the mountains shift, the topsoil move, and as your breath slammed on the beaches, Quasimoto sputtered back to life. Oh Papi, breathe on me. (*Angela appears and stands behind her brother. Her wings are spread very far out. Drums and stomping crescendo as Zapata brutally kills San Juan. Blackout.*)

ACT TWO

Scene 1

Early afternoon. The table is set up in the middle of the yard in a festive way, with tablecloth, flowers, a bowl of peaches, and bottles of whisky and wine. Gallo is in the henhouse with Adan. Hector is in the bathroom, Juana and Chata are in the kitchen. Angela is by the little cemetery writing on a tombstone.

ANGELA: Here lies Angela Ester Morales died of acute neglect. Although she is mourned by many, she goes to a far, far, better place, where they have better food. (*Angela slides under the house as Juana comes out wearing a fresh housedress and carrying a steaming pot.*)

JUANA: (*Yelling*) Hector! Angela! You kids wash up, it's time to eat. (*Juana hurries back into the house, almost knocking Chata down as she comes out with a tray of tortillas. She [Chata] is heavily made up, wearing tight clothes, dangling earrings, high-heeled shoes. A cigarette dangles from her mouth.*)

CHATA: Why are you eating out here?

JUANA: He wants it. Says he don't wanta hide in the house.

CHATA: Begging for trouble.

JUANA: What can I do, he's the *man.* (*She goes into the house.*)

CHATA: Ah, they're all shit! Just want trouble. Soup's on! (*Chata pours herself a quick shot of whiskey, shoots it down and makes a face. Juana comes out with another pot.*)

JUANA: You better tell 'em that the food's ready. (*Chata goes to henhouse.*) Hector!

HECTOR: (*Coming out on porch*) What?

JUANA: It's time to eat . . . you look real nice honey. Makes me proud to have your papa see you all dressed up.

HECTOR: Okay. Okay. Don't make a big deal about it. I just don't want him to think—

JUANA: I just feel so happy—

HECTOR: I just don't want him to think—

JUANA: Hijito! You love your papa . . . don't you?

HECTOR: Mother!

JUANA: I know you a little mad at him . . . pero when he comes home it's like the sun when it—

HECTOR: Shshshsh! (*Chata, Gallo, and Adan come out of the henhouse.*)

GALLO: We have to sharpen and polish those spurs. I want them to flash.

JUANA: (*To Gallo*) The food's ready . . . we fixed what you like . . . mole, rice, frijolitos . . . tamales.

GALLO: Tamales estilo Jalisco!

CHATA: (*Looking Hector over*) Ay Papi que rico estás! (*Hector quickly sits down.*) Honey! You gonna have to beat all them women off with a stick, when they see you and that rooster tonight.

ADAN: No worry, Hector, I be there . . . down you mujeres, women leave de Mr. Hector and me alone . . . Ay Mama! (*He has a giggling fit.*)

GALLO: (*Kissing Juana*) It's wonderful to be in love . . . to be touched by the noble fever.

CHATA: Ah, you're better off with a touch of typhoid.

JUANA: I . . . gracias al Señor que . . . my whole family is here. (*She looks around. She yells.*)

JUANA: Angela! Angie!

HECTOR: Mom!

JUANA: Where is she? Where is your sister?

HECTOR: Talking to the saints! I don't know. (*Juana gets up, goes to the spot where Angela slides under the house, gets down on her hands and knees and yells.*)

JUANA: Angela! Angela! You leave them saints alone. You hear me! (*As everybody looks at Juana, Angela comes from behind the house and tiptoes toward the henhouse. Hector is the only one to see her. Using hand signals, she pleads to him to be quiet. Juana peers under the house.*) Angie! Honey . . . your mama worked for days to fix this food and now it's getting cold. (*To Gallo.*) You should see how sweet she looks when she's all dressed up. (*To under the house.*) You ain't got no manners . . . ain't even said hello to your father. (*To Gallo.*) She prays a lot . . . and she's got real pretty eyes.

CHATA: (*To Gallo*) She's sorta . . . the bashful type . . . you know.

JUANA: (*To Gallo*) And she ain't spoiled.

CHATA: (*Taking a drink*) Nah, all them kids smell like that.

JUANA: (*To under the house*) Angie!

GALLO: Juana leave her alone.

JUANA: Okay. Angie, I'm gonna ignore you, 'cause you spoiled my day, this day that

I been looking forward to for years and years and now you making me look like a bad mama, what's your papa gonna think of us.

GALLO: Juana, she'll come out when she's ready. (*Juana goes back to the table.*)

CHATA: Maybe was them roosters fighting got her scared.

ADAN: Poor San Juan.

GALLO: Adan, drink up and I'll see you get one of our famous Champion Morales birds.

HECTOR: What famous Champion Morales birds?

GALLO: The ones I paid for dearly, the ones I came home to raise. . isn't that right mi amor?

JUANA: Yes . . . you see honey your papa's gonna stay home . . . raise birds . . . I think Abuelo would want that.

GALLO: And after they see our bird tonight . . . see first I want them to think it's just you and the bird up there. And the bets are down, I'll take over and they're gonna know we got roosters. A toast . . . (*As Gallo stands up, everybody raises a glass, except Hector. Angela tiptoes from the henhouse carrying Zapata. She goes behind and under the house. Only Hector sees her.*) To the finest fighting cocks ever to be seen. (*He slides bottle to Hector.*)

HECTOR: (*Sliding the bottle back*) No. (*Pause.*)

GALLO: Too good to drink with your old man.

HECTOR: I only drink with people I trust.

CHATA: Me . . . I drink with anybody. Maybe that's my problem.

GALLO: I am your father.

CHATA: I like it better when I drink alone. Ya meet a better class of people that way.

HECTOR: But it's my bird. Abuelo left it to me.

GALLO: Abuelo was my father, and you are my son. I see no problem. Now let's eat.

HECTOR: Mother!

JUANA: Let's eat, honey, and we can talk about it later.

ADAN: Ay the mole muy delicious . . . the mole muy rico . . . the mole muy beautiful y Mrs. Juana. Today, you look beautiful, like the mole.

GALLO: Hm, sabroso, exquisite.

JUANA: I bet you been in plenty of fancy places got better food than this.

GALLO: This is home cooking, I know that your hands made it . . . These . . . these are the hands of a beautiful woman . . .

HECTOR: Ha! Bullshit.

GALLO: We say your mother is beautiful and you call it bullshit? I find that very disrespectful.

JUANA: Hijo, you're right . . . it's just the way people talk, I know I ain't beautiful.

ADAN: Sí, muy beautiful.

GALLO: Ya ves! . . . If your son doesn't have the eyes, the soul, the imagination to see it . . . it's his loss.

HECTOR: That's right. I just can't seem to stretch my imagination that far.

GALLO: This is an insult to your mother.

HECTOR: It's the truth. That is a plain, tired, worn-out woman.

GALLO: Shut up.

HECTOR: The hands of a beautiful woman! Those aren't hands, they're claws because she has to scratch for her living.

JUANA: Please, Hector, let him say what he wants . . . I know I ain't beautiful. It don't go to my head.

HECTOR: But it goes to your heart which is worse. Did he ever really take care of you? Did he ever go out and work to put food on the table, to buy you a dress? All he has is words, and he throws a few cheap words to you and you come to life. Don't you have any pride?

GALLO: Your mother has great courage to trust and believe in me.

HECTOR: Stupidity!

GALLO: You know nothing!

HECTOR: You don't seem to realize that it is my rooster. And that after the fight, depending on the outcomes, I will sell him or eat him. I have made a deal with the Filipinos.

JUANA: Ay Hector! You've spoiled everything. All this food . . . I worked so hard . . . for this day.

GALLO: You're not selling anything to anybody. This is nothing to joke about.

HECTOR: I don't want to spend my life training chickens to be better killers. And I don't want to spend my whole life in this valley. Mother, Aunt Chata, excuse me.

CHATA: Ah? . . . O sí hijo pase . . . sometimes Hector can be a real gentleman. (*Hector starts to leave.*)

GALLO: Son! . . . You have no courage, no juice . . . you are a disgrace to me.

JUANA: Ay, Gallo don't say that to him.

HECTOR: Do you think I care what you think . . . Father.

JUANA: Hijo no . . . for me just once for me. I don't wanna be alone no more.

HECTOR: What about me? You have me, you'll always have me, I'll work, I've always worked, I can take care of you. I won't leave you.

JUANA: It ain't the same, honey.

HECTOR: Yeah . . . He comes first for you, he will always come first.

GALLO: If you sell that bird, it will be over your dead body.

HECTOR: You can't stop me. (*Exit Hector. Chata takes a plate of food and bowl of peaches to the under-the-house area and tries to tempt Angela out.*)

GALLO: He doesn't seem to realize . . . coward . . . too bad. (*Gallo goes to the henhouse. Juana starts to follow him.*)

JUANA: Talk to him . . . he's a good boy . . . if you just talk . . . (*Seeing Adan still eating.*) Is it good? You really like it?

ADAN: Hm! Sabroso!

CHATA: Come on Angie . . . it's real good. (*Gallo returns running.*)

GALLO: He's gone . . . the bird is gone . . .

ADAN: Yo no see nada, nada.

JUANA: He'll bring it back, he's a good boy. He's just a little upset . . . you know.

GALLO: Nobody fools with my roosters. Not even this over-petted, over-pampered viper you spawned. Go and pray to your Dark Virgin. You know what I'm capable of.

(*Exit Gallo. Adan stops eating and tries to comfort Juana as she puts her head down on the table and cries.*)

ADAN: No cry, no cry Mrs. Juana. Di women cry y Adan, he not know what to do. (*Juana cries louder.*) Ay Mrs. Juana, for sure di flowers will die . . . di trees will be torn from di ground, freshness will leave di morning, softness will leave di night . . . (*Juana's cries increase.*) Ay Dios! (*From his pocket, he brings out the letter Angela wrote for him. He crosses himself.*) "Mrs. di Juana . . ." (*Reading with great difficulty.*) "Di . . . impulses . . . of my . . . heart . . . are such . . ." (*Throwing letter aside.*) A que la fregada! Mrs. Juana, Adan have mucho amor for you. My heart break to see you cry. I will not a breathe. When you no cry then I will breathe. (*Adan takes a big breath and holds it. Slowly Juana stops crying and lifts her head. Adan, suffering some discomfort, continues to hold his breath.*)

JUANA: I been dreaming. Nothing's gonna change. I gotta face facts. (*Adan let his breath out in a great whoosh. Angela pops out from under the house and takes a peach from Chata's hand. She stares at the peach with great intensity.*)

CHATA: Angie, ain't it nice to have the family all together again?

ANGELA: There is no pit in this peach. It is hollow. Instead of the pit, there is a whole little world, a little blue-green-crystal-clear ocean, with little schools of tiny darting silver fish. On a tiny rock sits a mermaid with little teenie-weenie kinky yellow hair. A tiny sun is being pulled across a little china-blue sky by teenie-weenie white horses with itty-bitty wings. There is an island with tiny palm trees and tiny thatched hut. Next to the hut stand a tiny man and woman. She is wearing flowers and leaves. He is wearing one single leaf. On their heads are little bitty halos. In their arms is a little bitsy baby. He isn't wearing anything.

CHATA: Let me see . . . (*Looking at peach.*) I can't see dick!

(*Blackout.*)

Scene 2

Later in the afternoon. Chata sits on the porch steps, her legs spread out, fanning herself. Juana sits on a straight-back chair, her hands folded on her lap. She rocks herself softly. She watches Angela, who is sitting on the ground drawing circles in the dirt, humming softly in time to her circles. The circles get deeper and deeper.

CHATA: It's hot . . . I am waiting for a cool breeze . . .

ANGELA: Uh ha uh ha uh ha uh haa.

CHATA: Aire fresco . . . come on cool breeze, come right over here.

ANGELA: Uh ha uh ha uh haa.

CHATA: Women! We're always waiting. (*Angela hums for a beat, then there is silence for a beat.*)

JUANA: It's because I'm so plain.

CHATA: Ah, you just work too much.

JUANA: Plainness runs in my family. My mother was plain, my grandmother was plain, my great-grandmother—

CHATA: It was the hard times . . . the hard work that did it.

JUANA: My Aunt Chona was the plainest.

CHATA: I don't remember her.

JUANA: The one with the crossed eyes and the little mustache.

CHATA: Ay, Juanita, that woman had a beautiful soul, sewing those little tiny outfits for the statues of the saints. That woman was a saint.

JUANA: She's the one told on you that time you was drinking beer with them sailors at the cockfight.

CHATA: Disgusting old bitch! (*Angela hums for a beat as she continues drawing circles.*)

JUANA: I get up at six, I brush my teeth, no creams, no lotions, what they gonna do for me? I work that's all. I take care of people and I work. People look at me, they know that's all I do. I ain't got no secrets. No hidden gardens. I keep busy that's what I do. Don't stop, that's what I say to myself. Don't stop, 'cause you're not pretty enough, exciting enough, smart enough to just stand there.

ANGELA: Mama, I don't wanna be plain.

CHATA: Honey, you're too colorful to be plain.

ANGELA: Yeah, that's what I thought.

CHATA: Your mama forgets . . . those years when her heart was filled with wild dreams when she use to weave little white star jasmine vines in her hair and drive all the men crazy.

JUANA: It ain't true . . . she was the one always getting me in trouble.

CHATA: I wasn't the one they called Juanita la Morenita Sabrosita.

JUANA: Oh, Chata. We was young girls together . . . in the summer, at Jacinto Park . . . cockfights, fistfights, the music. At night we would jump out of our bedroom windows in our party dresses. With our good shoes in one hand, our hearts in the other, we ran barefoot through the wet grass, above us all the stars twinkling go, go, go.

CHATA: Nothing could stop us . . . we had such a short time being girls.

JUANA: Now, all I am is an old hag.

CHATA: It ain't true.

JUANA: Sí, it's true enough. I carry burdens. I hang sheets. I scrub, I gather, I pick up, "Here sit down," "I'll wash it," "Here's fifty cents," "Have my chair," "Take my coat," "Here's a piece of my own live flesh"!

CHATA: Es la menopause, that's what it is. You getting it early. I knew this woman once, use to pull out her hair.

JUANA: I don't care. I don't want any stories, I don't care what happens to Fulano Mangano . . . I just wanna stand still, I wanna be interesting, exciting enough to stand still.

CHATA: Ay, mujer!

JUANA: And I want to look like I got secrets.

CHATA: Juana!

JUANA: Don't call me Juana. Juana is a mule's name.

CHATA: Ah, you're crazy! That new gray hen, the kids named her Juana. See, they think of you.

JUANA: A gray hen! An old gray hen, that's all I am. An old gray hen in a family of roosters. No more! I want feathers, I wanna strut, too. I wanna crow.

ANGELA: Mama!

JUANA: Don't! Don't call me Mama. I am not Mama . . . I am . . . I am that movie star, that famous dancer and heartbreaker "Morenita Sabrosita" . . . and now if my fans will excuse me I'm gonna take a bath in champagne, eat cherry bonbons and paint my toenails. (*She goes into house.*)

CHATA: (*To Juana*) We got champagne? (*Chata goes into the house as Angela goes to the little cemetery and puts up a new tombstone.*)

ANGELA: (*Printing on tombstone*) Here lies Juana Morales. Beloved Wife of El Gallo, Blessed Mother to Angela and Horrible Hector. Died of acute identity crisis sustained during la menopause.

Scene 3

Lights go down, as Angela sits on her box/table at the little cemetery. The long shadows of men fall on Angela and the cemetery.

SHADOW #1: There's that spooky kid. You go brother.

SHADOW #2: Ah, it's just a weird kid. Hey! You! Kid! (*Angela does not acknowledge them.*)

SHADOW #1: Call her "Angel."

SHADOW #2: Hey, Angel. (*Angela looks up.*)

SHADOW #1: See what I mean.

SHADOW #2: Listen kid, tell your old man, we got business to discuss.

SHADOW #1: Yeah, and you make sure he gets the message.

ANGELA: My old man, my Holy Father, my all-powerful Father, sees no problems. If there are problems, I am the angel of this yard. I am the comet. I am the whirlwind. I am the shooting stars. Feel my vibrance.

SHADOW #1: I feel it, right behind my ears, like . . .
like . . .

ANGELA: Locust wings.

SHADOW #1: Let's get outta here.

SHADOW #2: Tell Gallo some pals dropped by to settle an old score.

SHADOW #1: Come on!

SHADOW #2: (*Voice trailing off*) Hey! That kid don't scare me, see.

SHADOW #1: (*Voice trailing off*) I'm telling ya, my ears hurt.

(*Exit shadows. Lights go back up. Angela folds her hands in prayer.*)

ANGELA: Holy father, please help me, I feel the illumination, the fever of grace slipping away. I need to know that you are with me, that you take an interest in my concerns. Send me a little demonstration, a sign. Any sign . . . I don't care. Stigmata, visions, voices, send an angel, burn a bush . . . I am attracted to levitation . . . but you choose . . . I'll just lay here and wait. (*Angela lies down on the ground waiting. After a few beats Hector enters. He slowly walks up to Angela and looks down on her for a beat.*)

HECTOR: What are you doing?

ANGELA: (*Sitting up*) Ohhh . . . you're no sign.

HECTOR: What is going on?

ANGELA: Weird, shady men came here looking for Gallo. Two of them. They were not polite.

HECTOR: I see . . . So your reaction is to lay stretched out on the dirt instead of going into the house.

ANGELA: Hector, please, I am scared . . . I wanted a sign. (*Hector sits down next to Angela.*)

HECTOR: Hey, you're the shooting-star woman, you can't be scared.

ANGELA: I am scared. Really scared. If I grow up will I still be scared? Are grown-ups scared?

HECTOR: Always scared, trembling . . . cowering . . . this . . . this second, now . . . this planet that we are sitting on is wobbling precariously on its lightning path around the sun and every second the sun is exploding . . . stars are shooting at us from deep distant space, comets zoom around us, meteor rocks are being hurled through distances we measure in light . . . this very earth which we call our home, our mother, has catastrophic moods, she keeps moving mountains, receding like an overburdened beast trying to shake off . . . Life is violent.

ANGELA: You're scared about the fight . . . huh?

HECTOR: No. Whatever happens, Papi will still only care about the rooster. That's his son, that's who gets it all.

ANGELA: Maybe if we gave him the rooster he'd stay here and be happy.

HECTOR: He has to stay for us not the rooster . . . Angela . . . you . . . you were great taking the rooster.

ANGELA: He kept killing the little chicks. How could he do that, Hector? He's their papa.

HECTOR: Training. Look Angela, you're the angel of this yard. You keep a close guard on that rooster. Don't let anyone near him . . . promise me.

ANGELA: Yes.

HECTOR: That's a real promise now. No crossed fingers behind your back.

ANGELA: I promise already. (*She spreads her hands out in front of her, then kisses the tip of her thumb.*) May God strike me dumb, make me a plain whiny person and take away my gift of faith. Forever and ever, throughout my mortal years on earth, and throughout the everlasting fires of hell. Amen. Satisfied?

HECTOR: Yes.

ANGELA: Gee, maybe I should have given myself a little leeway, a little room for error. (*Chata enters from the house with a bottle and glass.*)

HECTOR: Too late now. Can't take it back.

CHATA: Oh, oh, look who's here. Angie, your mama needs some cheering up, a nice hug, an angel's kiss, maybe a little song.

ANGELA: Litany to the Virgin. That's her favorite. (*She exits.*)

CHATA: Men are shit. Pure shit.

HECTOR: And you're still drinking.

CHATA: Stay outta my drinking. You hurt your mama, Hector.

HECTOR: Too bad.

CHATA: Ay Dios, what a man he is now.

HECTOR: Yeah, well what about you? Didn't you break Abuelo's heart when you became a whore?

CHATA: They called me the encyclopedia of love. You want to turn a few pages? Your Aunt Chata could show you a few things.

HECTOR: You're disgusting.

CHATA: Is that what fascinates you, honey? Is that why I always find you peeping at me, mirrors at the keyhole, your eyeballs in the cracks, spying when I'm sleeping, smelling my kimono.

HECTOR: You're drunk.

CHATA: I ain't drunk, honey.

HECTOR: You drink too much. It's not . . . good for you . . . it makes you ugly.

CHATA: Ain't none of your business. Don't tell me what to do Hector.

HECTOR: I have to, it's for your own good.

CHATA: You got nothing to say about it, you ain't my man, and you ain't your mama's man. The sooner you learn that the better . . . take your bird, leave it, eat or sell it, but get out of here. (*Hector stands alone in the yard, as Chata goes to the door. She turns. They look at each other.*) What you hanging around here for? Go on! Get out! It ain't your home anymore. (*Chata takes a broom and shoos Hector from the yard.*) Shoo! Shoo! You don't belong here, it ain't your place anymore.

HECTOR: Stop it, stop it, stop it. (*Hector goes to the outside boundary of the yard, where he falls to his knees and buries his face in his hands, as Chata comes slowly up behind him.*)

CHATA: I feel like I'm tearing my own flesh from my bones . . . He's back. Honey, we got too many roosters in this yard.

HECTOR: Did you sleep with my father? Did he yearn for you as you slept in your little white, chaste, narrow bed? Did he steal you when you were dreaming?

CHATA: (*Embracing him*) Shshsh . . .

HECTOR: I'm not like him.

CHATA: You're just like him, so handsome you make my teeth ache.

HECTOR: Whore, mother, sister, saint-woman, moon-woman, give me the shelter of your darkness, fold me like a fan and take me into your stillness, submerge me beneath the mysteries, baptize me, bear me up, give me life, breathe on me. (*Chata enfolds him as the lights fade. We hear Angela reciting the litany.*)

ANGELA: (*Offstage*) She is the Gate of Heaven, the Mystical Rose, the Flower of Consolation, the Fire of Transcendence, and the Queen of Love.

Scene 4

Lights come up to indicate that time has passed. Angela is alone in the yard. She sniffs the air.

ANGELA: Tres Rosas! (*Angela slides under the house as Gallo enters. He sees a brief flash of Angela from the corner of his eye. He walks slowly into the yard. He stops by the little cemetery and reads the tombstones. He feels the urge for a drink. He goes to the table and has a shot. He sits.*)

GALLO: Acute neglect? . . . uh-huh . . . I thought I felt a little spirit, slight, delicate . . . yes I feel it. A little tenderness . . . a little greenness . . . (*Examining the ground.*) What's this? Tracks . . . little tiny paws . . . there . . . (*Following tracks.*) and there . . . (*Gallo pretends to be following tracks to the porch. Then with one great leap he jumps in the opposite direction, surprising the hell out of Angela, and pulls her from under the house by her heels.*) Ah, ha!

ANGELA: Shit! Hey! You're ripping my wings! You shithead! Put me down! Don't touch me! (*Gallo puts Angela down, throws his hands up to indicate he won't touch her. They stand and stare at each other. Angela goes to the little cemetery, never taking her eyes off Gallo. They continue to stare for a beat, then Angela looks up to Heaven, slapping her hands together in prayer.*) There is a person here trying to con me, but I don't con that easy.

GALLO: (*Slapping his hands in prayer*) There is a person here who swallows saints but defecates devils.

ANGELA: (*To Heaven*) He comes here smelling of rosas using sweet oily words . . . it's phony, it's obnoxious, it's obscene . . . I wanna throw up.

GALLO: I came here to see my baby, my little angel, my little woman of the shooting stars, my light delicate splendorous daughter. But she is as light, as delicate, as splendid as an angel's fart.

ANGELA: Angels do not fart. They do not have a digestive system. That's why they can all scrunch together on the head of a pin.

GALLO: Oh, . . . I only come with my love—

ANGELA: (*Interrupting*) You only came with words . . . well, where were these words on my birthday, Christmas, my saint's day? Where's my Easter outfit, my trip to Disneyland, the orthodontist . . . You owe me.

GALLO: Sweet Jesus . . . What a monster! I owe you . . . but Angela! Angela! Angela! How many times have I written that name on prison walls. On bits of paper, on the skin of my arms.

ANGELA: (*To Heaven*) He's hopeless! You write everybody's name on your arms.

GALLO: Women like to know that they're on your flesh.

ANGELA: I am not a woman. I'm your baby daughter. You said so yourself.

GALLO: I'm afraid . . . fathers to daughters . . . that's so delicate. I don't know . . . what to do . . . help me Angela. How do I know what to do?

ANGELA: Instinct! Ain't ya got no instinct? Don't you feel anything?

GALLO: (*Moving closer to Angela*) When you were a little baby, you were a miracle of tiny fingers and toes and dimples and you had a soft spot on the top of your head.

ANGELA: I still have it, see.

GALLO: I wanted to take you into my arms and crush you against my chest so that I could keep you forever and nobody, and nothing, could ever, ever hurt you because you would be safe . . . my little offshoot, my little bud, my little flower growing inside my chest.

ANGELA: Papi . . .

GALLO: Sí, sí, hijita. Your papi's here.

ANGELA: And Papi these men come all the—

GALLO: (*Holding Angela*) Shshsh . . it's nothing, nothing and you thought I forgot about you . . . well it just hurt too much, do you understand?

ANGELA: You had to pull down some hard time and the only way to survive was to cut off all feelings and become an animal just like the rest of them.

GALLO: Well, something like that. Honey you know what I wish—

ANGELA: Papa, did the lights really go down when they put the people in the electric chair?

GALLO: Angela, what a . . . Honey you know what I wish—

ANGELA: Did they force you to make license plates? Hector and I would look real close at the one that started with a G. We thought you made them. "What craftsmanship!" Hector used to say.

GALLO: Don't you have any normal interests?

ANGELA: Like what?

GALLO: Like swimming . . . you know what I wish? That we could take a trip and see the ocean together.

ANGELA: I've never seen the ocean. When?

GALLO: Just you and me. Laying on our bellies, feeding the seagulls, riding the waves.

ANGELA: I can't swim.

GALLO: I will teach you, that's what fathers are for—

ANGELA: (*To Heaven*) Angels and saints did you hear? My father's going to teach me to swim!

GALLO: Now Angela, I didn't promise.

ANGELA: But you said—

GALLO: I want to but I have to hurry and fix things. I have to find Hector, talk to him and find that rooster fast before Hector sells him. Honey, you pray to St. Anthony, your prayers are powerful . . . unless . . . St. Anthony, he listens to you?

ANGELA: (*Crossing her fingers*) Hey, we're like that.

GALLO: Ask St. Anthony, Angela . . . then we can go to the ocean.

ANGELA: Truly Papi? Just you and me? And will you stay with us forever and ever?

GALLO: Wild horses couldn't drag me away.

ANGELA: Close your eyes. Tony! Tony! Look around, Zapata's lost and can't be found. (*She goes under the house, gets Zapata, and gives him to Gallo.*) I found him Papi, he was—

GALLO: Ya lindo, ya. (*To bird.*) Papa's got you now. Angela you keep quiet now honey, this is our secret.

ANGELA: What about Hector?

GALLO: I'm going to talk to Hector now. You go inside and get all dressed up. So I can be proud of my girl. I'll pick you up after the fight. (*He exits.*)

ANGELA: Your girl! (*Singing.*) We are going to the ocean, we are going to the sea, we are going to the ocean to see what we can see . . . (*Angela goes into the house. We hear cha-cha music.*)

CHATA: (*Offstage*) One, two . . . not like that . . . I'm getting tired . . . what time's Zorro on?

JUANA: No, no . . . Just one more. (*Singing.*) Cha, cha, cha, que rico, . . . cha, cha, cha . . . Ay, I could do it all night.

(*Enter Gallo running, breathing hard. He has Zapata's carrier. He goes to the door and yells.*)

GALLO: Juana! Juana! (*Juana and Chata come to the door.*) I need money . . . and my stuff. I gotta leave . . . something's come up . . . Do you hear me? I need money now.

JUANA: I hear ya . . . you ain't even been here a day and already you're gone . . . nothing's going to change with you . . . nothing. I was having fun, dancing, remembering old times, do you know how long—

GALLO: I don't have time for this, just give me the money.

JUANA: I ain't got any!

CHATA: I got some. (*She goes in the house.*)

GALLO: The Filipino, somebody told him about the bird. Oh, ya, ya my little hen, don't you ruffle those pretty feathers, I'll be back.

JUANA: No, you always gonna be running.

GALLO: If it was just me, I'd stay. You know that, Juana? You know I'd stay, but I got the bird to think of, gotta hide him, breed him good, soon as I get some good stags I'll come home . . . this is just a little setback. (*Chata returns with suitcase and money.*)

JUANA: You know how long it's been since I went dancing?

CHATA: Here, you're gonna need this. (*Gives him the suitcase.*) And this is all the cash I got. (*Angela enters as Gallo counts the money. She is dressed in a red strapless dress made tight by large visible safety pins, high heels, and a great deal of heavy makeup and jewelry. The effect is one of a young girl dressed like a tart for a costume party. She carries a suitcase, purse and her donation can.*)

GALLO: Is this all you got?

ANGELA: (*Shaking the can*) Don't worry Papa, I got my donation-can money. (*They all stare at her for a beat.*)

JUANA AND CHATA: Angela?!!

JUANA: Angie, you got on your mama's old party dress.

CHATA: Yeah, and all my jewelry . . . where you going?

ANGELA: Papa, didn't you hear me? I have money. (*She shakes the can.*)

GALLO: Oh honey, don't you look pretty . . . now you got a little bit too much lipstick on, let your mama wipe some off.

ANGELA: Are we leaving now?

JUANA: Gallo!

GALLO: Shshsh Juana . . . Angela, I gotta talk to your mama for a few minutes. You go in the house and I'll come and get you.

ANGELA: Are you sure?

GALLO: Don't you trust me, Angie?

CHATA: Come on Angie, I'll show you how to draw eyebrows. First you draw a straight line across your forehead and then spit on your finger and rub out the middle. Let's go in and try it.

ANGELA: Really, Aunt Chata, I'm not a child, you don't have to patronize me.

CHATA: Okay, I'll give you the lowdown on blow-jobs. (*Angela and Chata exit into the house.*) Now, don't tell your mama . . .

GALLO: Juana, keep her in the house until I leave.

JUANA: You promised to take her with you?

GALLO: I had to get the bird. I said I would take her to the ocean.

JUANA: Ay bruto! How could you do it?

GALLO: How was I to know this would happen . . . and Juanita, it hurts me to say this but that kid is crazy . . .

JUANA: No, no, Señor, she is not crazy and I ain't gonna let you call her crazy. She got the spirit they broke in me. I ain't gonna let it happen to her.

GALLO: Shshsh! Don't get so excited. It isn't important.

JUANA: It's important . . . it's her spirit, her soul and you ain't gonna stomp on it . . . you hear me. (*Adan enters running.*)

ADAN: Mr. El Gallo . . . bad men! Mucho bad, y mucho ugly. Looking for you y Zapata. All ober they look for you . . . You leave Mr. El Gallo. You go far away. I take you. I go for my truck.

GALLO: You are a good friend Adan, and my new partner.

ADAN: Oh, thank you Mr. El Gallo. I am proud. But is better I come back here to Mrs. Juana y Hector.

JUANA: Thank you, Adan.

GALLO: We better hurry.

ADAN: Sí, sí, I come back with truck. (*He exits. Juana goes into the house. Hector enters as Gallo starts to pack his suitcase.*)

HECTOR: (*Seeing Zapata*) You must have really sold her a bill of goods to get Zapata.

GALLO: Look, there's trouble . . . the Filipino send you?

HECTOR: No, how could you think I would work for him, but I came to get Zapata.

GALLO: You're the one told him about the bird.

HECTOR: Yes. I made a deal with the Filipino. He'll leave you alone if I give him the rooster.

GALLO: That's a lie and you fell for it.

HECTOR: No, he is an honorable man, we were here unprotected for seven years and he never bothered us. It's his bird, Papi.

GALLO: No, I paid seven years of my life for this baby.

HECTOR: And he lost his son. It's the right thing to do. (*A truck horn is heard. Angela comes out of the house with her suitcase, Juana and Chata follow after her.*)

ANGELA: Papa? Are we leaving now, Papa?

JUANA: Angie! No!

HECTOR: So that's it . . . Angela, get back in the house.

ANGELA: I'm going with him, Hector.

HECTOR: Get back in the house, nobody's going anywhere.

ANGELA: No! I don't have to listen to you anymore. You're not my father.

JUANA: Angie . . . he's not going to the ocean . . . he can't take you. (*We hear the sound of Adan's truck. The horn is heard as Gallo starts backing away, picking up Zapata's carrier.*)

ANGELA: Papi, wait for me! Papa, you promised.

GALLO: You're all grown up now, you don't need your old man.

CHATA: Hector! (*Gallo turns, tries to run out. Angela grabs him, knocking Zapata's carrier out of his hand. Hector picks up the carrier.*)

ANGELA: No Papa, we need you and Mama needs you, we've been waiting and waiting, you can't leave, you promised.

JUANA: They'll kill you Gallo!

GALLO: (*Throwing Angela off.*) Stop sucking off me. I got nothing for you.

ANGELA: (*Beating her fists on the ground.*) No, no, Papa! You promised me! . . . Oh, Hector . . . No, no, I promised Hector. (*Drums begin as punctuation of the pounding of Angela's fists on the ground. Lights change. A special on Angela and another on Gallo and Hector come up, as shadows appear. Angela sees shadows.*) Ah . . . Holy Father, Abuelo.

GALLO: (*To Hector*) Give me that bird.

ANGELA: Saints, Angels, Mama.

JUANA: (*Trying to pick up Angela*) Come on Angie, get up.

GALLO: (*To Hector*) What do you want?

HECTOR: You, alive, Papi.

CHATA: Careful, Hector.

ANGELA: I've lost my faith. I am splintered.

GALLO: (*Imitating Hector*) You Papi . . . Give me life . . . Make me a man. (*He whips out *his stiletto.*) This is how you become a man. (*The drums get louder. We hear howling.*) Come on baby boy, show Daddy whatcha got.

JUANA: Are you crazy! That's your son!

ANGELA: I am cast down! Exiled! (*Gallo stalks Hector as drums follow their movements.*)

JUANA: Oh, Gallo, you're killing your own children.

CHATA: Move Hector, don't think, move!

GALLO: Oh yeah, mi lindo, you like to fight . . . eh?

JUANA: No, stop them! Please, please stop this.

ANGELA: Fallen from the light, condemned to the mud, to the shadows.

GALLO: You gotta learn baby boy.

CHATA: Look at him Hector. He's getting old, his hand is shaking . . . take the knife! Stay down old warrior. Stay down.

ANGELA: Alone and diminished. This loneliness is unendurable.

JUANA: Hector!

HECTOR: Do I have it? Is this what you want me to be . . .

ANGELA: (*Looking to Heaven*)

My brains are slammed against the earth's hard crust
My eyes are clouded
My arteries gush
My lungs collapsed.

HECTOR: (*Letting go of Gallo*) No! I am your son. (*Drums and cries stop.*)

ANGELA: Holy Father, Abuelo, Hector, breathe on me. (*Celestial sound as a white narrow shaft of light falls on Angela. She levitates, her wings spreading. Only Chata and Juana see this.*)

HECTOR: (*Taking a deep breath*) Oh sweet air! (*He gets the rooster and sees Angela.*) Angela!

ADAN: (*Rushing in*) I am here, I have truck . . . (*Seeing Angela, he crosses himself.*) Ay Dios. (*He kneels.*)

JUANA: (*At Gallo's side*) Gallo look!

GALLO: Did you see the hands on that kid, just like steel, never seen finer hands . . . (*Seeing Angela.*) Sweet Jesus, my beautiful monster. (*He crosses himself.*)

CHATA: No, it ain't true.

HECTOR: (*Standing before Angela holding the rooster*) Oh sweet hummingbird woman, shooting star, my comet, you are launched.

ANGELA: Abuelo, Queen of Heaven, All the Saints, All the Angels. It is true, I am back. I am restored. I am . . . Hector, take me with you.

HECTOR: Everywhere . . . Over the mountains, up to the stars.

ANGELA: To the very edge.

ADAN: Hector! Angelita! You take Adan. (*He goes to Angela.*)

CHATA: (*Looking at Angela*) Shit happens . . . been happening all my life, that's all I know.

JUANA: (*Holding Gallo like the Pieta*) We seen it Gallo, with our own eyes.

ANGELA: (*To Hector and Adan*) And I want my doorstep heaped with floral offerings . . . and (*Hector, Adan and Angela freeze. Chata removes the flower from her hair and holds it in her hand, trying to decide what to do. She freezes.*)

GALLO: Ay Juanita, I had a vision of a hard-kicking flyer . . . (*He yawns.*) the ultimate bird, noble, fino. (*He falls asleep. Juana looks at Gallo, smiles, then looks out half-smiling.*)

(*End of play.*)

Notes

The quotation in the title is by Jorge Huerta, *Chicano Drama: Performance, Society and Myth* (Cambridge: Cambridge University Press, 2000), 107.

1. Biographical information is courtesy of the playwright. Also, Elizabeth C. Ramírez served as dramaturg for the Arizona Theatre Company's premiere of Sanchez-Scott's *The Old Matador* (1995), and the playwright discussed her work with Ramírez. See also Elizabeth C. Ramírez, *Chicanas/Latinas in American Theatre: A History of Performance* (Bloomington: Indiana University Press, 2000), 101–2, 104, 110–15, 125, 144, 147.

2. Milcha Sanchez-Scott, *Roosters*, in M. Elizabeth Osborn, ed. *On New Ground: Contemporary Hispanic-American Plays* (New York: Theatre Communications Group, 1987), 246.

3. Huerta, 107.

4. Sanchez-Scott, 246.

5. See Alicia Arrizón, *Latina Performance: Traversing the Stage* (Bloomington: Indiana University Press, 1999), 102–15 for more on *Latina.*

6. Herbert Mitgang, review of *Dog Lady* and *Swimmer*, by Milcha Sanchez-Scott, *New York Times*, May 10, 1984.

7. Ramon Delgado, ed., *Best Short Plays of 1986* (New York: Applause Books, 1986). *Evening Star* is published by *Dramatists Play Service* (New York, 1989).

8. Huerta, 113–18; Jorge Huerta, "Looking for the Magic: Chicanos in the Mainstream," in *Negotiating Performance: Gender, Sexuality, and Theatricality in Latin/o America*, ed. Diana Taylor and Juan Villegas (Durham, N.C.: Duke University Press, 1994), 42–43; Huerta, *Chicano Drama*, 107.

9. Huerta, *Chicano Drama*, 113.

10. Mel Gussow, "Stage: 'Roosters' at INTAR" (review of *Roosters*, by Milcha Sanchez-Scott), March 24, 1987.

11. Sanchez-Scott, 246.

12. Don Shirley, "Stage Review: Machismo Plucked Bare as 'Roosters' Takes Flight," *Los Angeles Times* (Calendar, 6; Entertainment Desk, June 21, 1988). Janice Arkatov, "Playwright Enters World of Cockfighting in Roosters," *Los Angeles Times* (Calendar, 6; Entertainment Desk, June 15, 1988).

13. Huerta, *Chicano Drama*, 107. Oscar G. Brockett, *Plays for the Theatre* (Fort Worth, Tex.: Holt, Rinehart and Winston, 1996).

14. Oscar G. Brocket and Robert J. Ball, *The Essential Theatre*, 9th ed. (Boston: Thompson Wadsworth, 2006), 240.

15. Rachel Chipman Waite, M.A. thesis, "Milcha Sanchez-Scott: An Emerging Latina Voice," University of Oregon, 1993, 102. The thesis, for which Elizabeth C. Ramírez served as the faculty advisor, followed a stage production by Waite of *Roosters,* also supervised by Ramírez.

16. See above about Elizabeth C. Ramírez serving as dramaturg for the premiere of Sanchez-Scott's *The Old Matador,* which informs the discussion of this playwright in this chapter.

17. Playwright's responses to editors' biographical questionnaire via telephone interview, August 19, 2007.

18. Doris Baizley is a founding member of L.A. Theatre Works (originally Artists in Prison) and has been a resident playwright at the Mark Taper Forum for seven years.

19. The notorious murderer of the fashion designer, Versace, was actually Andrew Cunanan.

20. This is probably a reference to Teresa of Ávila. It is not that Angela doesn't get the name right or that she made a mistake; rather, that she says names as she has heard them, and often they are her own creation. The character applies her own unique imagination to names she has evidently heard, and brings them to life in her own manner.

CHAPTER 2

Latina Feminism Hits the Stage

Cherríe Moraga's *Waiting for Da God* (2003)

Cherríe Moraga, by permission of the playwright.

The Playwright/La Dramaturga

Cherríe Moraga was born in Whittier, California, on September 25, 1952, with Mexican origins via Sonora from her mother and French and Welsh origins from her father's Canadian- and Missouri-born parents.[1] She grew up "a stone's throw" from the San Gabriel Mission using theatre for social change in the heart of the valley where, as she writes "smog fell like an iron curtain between hope and us."[2]

In 1974, she received her Bachelor of Arts degree in English from Immaculate Heart College in Los Angeles, a small liberal arts nonsectarian and coed college, which in the early 1970s was the catalyst for much of Moraga's beginning politicization about feminism, race, and class. After college she taught high school for two years and then moved to the Bay Area with the intention of devoting herself full-time to her writing. While writing and supporting herself as a house cleaner, office painter, and waitress, Moraga enrolled in graduate school and in 1980 received a Master of Arts degree in feminist literature from California State University, San Francisco.

This Bridge Called My Back: Writings by Radical Women of Color, her acclaimed anthology of feminist writings, which she coedited with Gloria Anzaldúa in 1981, served as part of her master's thesis and became the single publication that would put Cherríe Moraga's writings on cultural, political, and literary maps. First published by Persephone Press in 1981 and rereleased in 1983 by Kitchen Table (Women of Color Press), *This Bridge Called My Back* has remained a text written, published, and distributed by feminists of color, culminating in its most recent edition by Third Woman Press of Berkeley in 2002.[3]

With the 1981 publication of *Bridge,* Moraga moved to New York City to work with Kitchen Table and complete her own collection of poetry and essays, *Loving in the War Years: Lo Que Nunca Pasó Por Sus Labios* (1983). In 2000, *Loving* was expanded in a twentieth-anniversary edition to include essays written in the late 1990s. Moraga is also the coeditor of *Cuentos: Stories by Latinas* (Kitchen Table, 1983) and *Third Woman: The Sexuality of Latinas* (Third Woman Press, 1989). After her return to California, Moraga published two works of nonfiction in the 1990s: *The Last Generation* (South End Press, 1993) and *Waiting in the Wings* (Firebrand Books, 1997), a memoir on motherhood.

Cherríe Moraga, an acclaimed poet, essayist, and playwright has brought a new and powerful voice to the theatre. Her work in theatre is extensive. Moraga's plays include *Giving Up the Ghost* (1986), a girl's coming-of-age story; *Shadow of a Man* (1990), directed by Maria Irene Fornes in the Latino Playwrights Lab at INTAR (International Arts Relations) Theatre; and *Heroes and Saints,* which premiered in 1992. Her more recent works are *The Hungry Woman: A Mexican Medea* and *Heart of the Earth: A Popul Vuh Story.* Originally commissioned by Berkeley Repertory Theatre, *The Hungry Woman* was produced as part of the Plays at the Border Festival at the Magic Theatre of San Francisco, under the direction of the playwright. *Heart of the Earth* first opened in 1994 as part of the Jim Henson Foundation's International Festival of Puppet Theatre, under the direction of Ralph Lee. Moraga's three published volumes of drama through West End Press (Albuquerque, N.M.) include *Heroes and Saints and Other Plays* (1994), *Watsonville/Circle in the Dirt* (2002), and *The Hungry Woman* (2001).

Moraga has been a significant voice for Chicana, feminist, and queer studies. In her introductory comments to *The Hungry Woman,* she writes: "I write to remember—*is there no other way to say it?*—because I fear (and hope, in my cowardice) that I will die before any revolution is born blood-red on the horizon. I write to imagine, which is a way of remembering, as are dreams, that 'we (women) were not always fallen from the mountain.'" As Jorge Huerta points out, "Moraga has dramatized some of the more complex issues of our time," and unlike Luis Valdez during his earlier work, she can now "take advantage of professional Latino theatre artists and companies to interpret those concerns: individuals and companies that were nonexistent in 1964" when Valdez first began.[4]

She studied with Maria Irene Fornes for one year, 1984–85, and comments on this work: "She allowed me to enter the art of playwriting through a poet's sensibility. Poetry, i.e. the expressive heart of character was always more important to Maria Irene than plot."[5] In *Conducting a Life: Reflections on the Theatre of Maria Irene Fornes,* edited by Maria M. Delgado and Caridad Svich as a tribute to Fornes's life and work in the theatre, Moraga reflects on how significant Fornes was to her own life in the theatre: "I remember I had never actually seen a live piece of theater (Ibsen or not) on a real stage until I began writing with Fornes in the mid-1980s. I say, 'Had I not begun writing plays with Maria Irene, I never would have become a playwright. Had I had to start somewhere other than my own voice, my own manner of telling story. . . . ' That's the point." Moraga recognizes that "it was not only play construction that Maria Irene had to teach me," rather, "she would also teach me how to appreciate my work (its poetry), defend my work, fight for my work, stand up to the master-teacher when I felt my vision was at risk of compromise." In essence, Moraga writes, "My work was illuminated by Fornes's touch," recalling the time that Fornes directed *Shadow of a Man,* "I remain ever-grateful for that experience, the only time in my life where another artist of Maria Irene's caliber and power, fell in love with my work enough to realize it so beautifully on stage."[6]

From 1991 to 1997, as playwright-in-residence at Brava Theater Center of San Francisco, Cherríe developed numerous works, including *Watsonville: Some Place Not Here,* which premiered in 1996, and the early versions of *The Hungry Woman: A Mexican Medea,* her most recently produced work. Both plays have been published in separate volumes by West End Press.

Moraga has received national acclaim, including a Theatre Communications Group (TCG) Theatre Artist Residency Grant (1996), the NEA's Theatre Playwrights' Fellowship in 1993, and two Fund for New American Plays Awards (for *Shadow of a Man* in 1990 and *Watsonville: Some Place Not Here* in 1995). As a San Francisco Bay Area writer, her work has premiered at Theatre Artaud, Theatre Rhinoceros, the Eureka Theatre, and Brava Theater Center. Brava's 1992 production of *Heroes and Saints* received numerous awards for best original script, including the Will Glickman Prize, the Drama-Logue Award, Critic Circles Award, and the Pen West Award.

Productions of her work have appeared throughout the Southwest and in Chicago, Seattle, and New York. *Heart of the Earth,* her adaptation of the *Popol Vuh,* the Maya creation myth, was commissioned by INTAR Theatre in New York City, and premiered at the Public Theater on September, 14, 1994, followed by its opening at INTAR on January 10, 1995, and subsequently premiering at the John F. Kennedy Center for the Performing Arts in Washington, D.C., in January 1997, all under the direction of Ralph Lee.

Since 1996, Moraga has continued as the artist-in-residence in the Department of Drama at Stanford University, where she works independently with student-playwrights and teaches courses in Chicano/Latino literature, performance and Xicana indigenous thought, intensive playwriting, and other creative writing courses. She is also a member of the core faculty of IDA, Stanford's Institute for Diversity in the Arts, where she mentors student artists of color in the areas of literary and performing arts, and she is proud to be a founding member of La Red Xicana Indígena, "a network of Xicanas organizing in the area of social change through international exchange, indigenous political education, spiritual practice, and grass roots organizing."[7]

Moraga completed a memoir on her mother's 2005 death after suffering from Alzheimer's disease, titled *Send Them Flying Home: A Geography of Remembrance.* She has also completed a new collection of writings, "A Xicana Codex of Changing Consciousness: A Decade of Discourse," forthcoming from Duke University Press. A volume of Moraga's children's plays tentatively titled "Warriors of the Spirit" is also forthcoming.

With her partner of over ten years, Moraga is the parent of two teenagers and the abuelita of two granddaughters. She is a founding member of La Red Xicana Indígena.

About the Play/Sobre la Obra

In *Waiting for Da God* we may glimpse this playwright's seminal concept of the struggles many of us face today. Moraga offers a poignant piece that resembles the short *acto* form developed by Valdez for weighty and heartfelt subject matter. The Valdezian use of humor is combined with the very difficult issues of aging, children caring and not caring for their elderly parents, and the tragedy of lost love. Jorge Huerta has compared Moraga's (especially in her work of the 1990s) with Valdez's approach to the topic of farmworker families in crisis; each has radically different means of exposing the problems and arrives at different solutions.[8] In this short dramatic piece, Moraga is exploring the changing nature of the family, religion, and the community in which the characters are trying to function.

The futile waiting for "God," the son, provides the background for the tantalizing hints of complex relationships that the playwright touches upon. In contrast to Angela's appeal to her entire spiritual community of celestial beings, her family, and her surroundings, enabling her to enact a miracle, here the daughter is on her own to bear the loss of family, loss of traditional religion, and loss of the larger community in which the characters have operated. As Moraga tells us in the next section, her intent for her audiences of this piece is a way to enact "politicized action" for compassion for her characters. Despite the son's wealth, it is the daughter who truly cares for her elderly parents. Besides dealing with her mother's dementia, she is also mourning the death of her partner. In the mother's view, the daughter's "wife" was "holding her down," but it is because of that lost love that the daughter now comprehends her mother's needs. Through an enchanting transformation, as though she enables the miracle within herself as the true source of spirituality, in contrast to the failed religion her brother represents, the daughter becomes a young male waiter who provides the solace her mother sought before slipping away forever.

The one-act *Waiting for Da God* is an earlier version of Moraga's *Mathematics of Love.*

Artistic Vision/Punto de Vista Artístico

ECR & CRC: Briefly describe your theatre experience.[9]

CM: After publishing my first titles as a poet and essayist in 1981 and 1983, I began writing plays. My first play, *Giving Up the Ghost,* emerged organically from my journals. It had not been my conscious intention to write for performance, but this writing distinguished itself from earlier autobiographical work in that for the first time, the "I" was no longer me. It was character. A character who spoke out loud with a body, and one who required a listener with a body; that is, a physically present audience. Thus, theatre. *Ghost* served as my application to work with Maria Irene Fornes in her playwriting lab at INTAR Theatre in NYC. There I fell in love with playwriting and upon returning to California, I began working in residency at Brava Theater Company (through grants such as the California Arts Council, NEA, TCG, and Fund for New American Plays, etc.) Several of my plays premiered during my tenure at Brava in the late '80s–early '90s. So, basically I have learned to write plays by writing plays and working with directors, designers, and actors in play development.

ECR & CRC: How did you decide to write and/or perform?

CM: All the genres I employ: playwriting, essays, poetry, fiction, are in conversation with one another in terms of my preoccupation as a politicized writer and thinker. I never "decided" to write. Making art did not feel like a real choice to me. As a young woman, when I was not actively engaged in writing, I felt my life to be meaningless. Choosing the genre of writing as opposed to other art forms grew out of economics mostly. Growing up, I did not have access to music or art training and little exposure to the arts. The pencils and paper used to write were cheap and easily accessible.

ECR & CRC: Why do you write what you do?

CM: I usually write to explore a question, a contradiction or silence I perceive in the world I inhabit, one which I believe whose censorship has caused us harm as a Chicano pueblo.

ECR & CRC: Who do you write for and what audience are you trying to reach?

CM: First and foremost, I write for myself because it is I who has the question that informs the writing. I write not to find an answer, but to express simply that the question, the contradiction, the invisibility or silence exists. As I have written professionally for over twenty-five years, I have come to believe that I am not alone in my questions. Still, oftentimes, in the act of writing, I feel that I am the first person, especially as a Chicana and lesbian, to bring up certain concerns in public. Therefore, my audience is anybody who is willing to share my considerations for a few hours one evening.

ECR & CRC: What message, if any, are you trying to convey to your audience with this work and/or with all of your work?

CM: My hope is that my reading or theatre audience will discover a compassionate identification with my characters and, in response, consider the politicized action required of such compassion. In *Waiting for Da God,* in particular, I would like my audience to reconsider questions of love and loyalty, their relationship to each other, and the prejudices we have attached to each. What does it mean to be loyal in love, as a spouse, partner, daughter, mother, sibling? Especially, as we age and begin to forget our short-term lives, what does the heart remember in the long run?

ECR & CRC: Who or what has been your major influence?

CM: As a playwright, my mother's and aunties' storytelling. In our home, there were no books on the shelves. A collection of *Encyclopædia Britannica,* I remember, and some abridged Reader's Digest collections. So my sense of story really came from the mouths of my female relations and the long hours I spent with them listening to their tales of romance and betrayal and economic hardship. Theirs was in the truest sense "spoken word," as the youth now call the performed poem. For me, those early testimonios completely informed the language of my first plays and impact how I write in every genre today. *Waiting for Da God* is close to an exact rendering of my mother's language as Peaches. I wrote the play in honor of her in that sense, as my true literary foremother.

ECR & CRC: What has been your biggest and/or most difficult struggle/challenge in life, in completing a play or getting it produced, etc.?

CM: The very subject matter of my writing queer, feminist, and indigenist in perspective and sensibility automatically removes my work from mainstream consideration in terms of production. The costs involved in staging a full-length large-scale work, as so many of my plays are, mean that larger theatres, which cater to white upper-middle-class audiences, will not even consider the work. The result is that few of my plays are realized, in terms of production values, as beautifully as I have imagined them in my writer's mind. Further, with cutbacks in the arts, alternative (including Chicano) theatres dedicated to producing multiply marginalized work are virtually nonexistent.

ECR & CRC: Can you offer any words of advice to aspiring playwrights/performers/directors/audiences?

CM: Self-discipline and rigorous devotion to your art form, regardless of monetary award or recognition, is what fundamentally distinguishes one's work. Through fearless commitment to removing self-censors and the daily discipline of writing and revisioning the work, the original voice will finally emerge.

Production History/Palabras Dramatúrgicas

This play was first conceived as part of a collaboration titled *Amor Eterno* with several Latino/a playwrights, under the direction of Diane Rodriguez. The project was initially commissioned by Latino Theatre Initiative of the Mark Taper Forum in Los Angeles in 2002.

The following is a developed version of the playtext performed as a workshop production at the Prosser Studio Theater in the Department of Drama at Stanford University, February 5–7, 2003. It was directed by Adelina Anthony; Alina Sánchez was the stage manager, with the following cast: Peaches—Micaela Días Sánchez; Poppa—Kem Ozbeck; and Daughter—Caroline Kuntz.

Contact Information

Direct all correspondence to www.cherriemoraga.com.

WAITING FOR DA GOD

Characters

PEACHES
POPPA
DAUGHTER (Daughter's changing appearance throughout the play reflects PEACHES's perception of her.)

Setting/Set

The lobby of a once grand hotel with a 21st century face-lift. Center stage sits a vintage-looking velveteen couch and a coffee table. A TV remote lies on top. Next to this are a stuffed reading chair and a small writing table with a laptop computer. A red velvet curtain hangs from the upstage wall.

Scene 1

(*POPPA, Anglo in his early 80s, sits before the hotel guest computer. He types out numbers very slowly and methodically with his two index fingers. The computer remains a kind of alien creature to him, yet he is forthright in his attempt to manage it. PEACHES, Mexican, slightly older, sits upright at the edge of the couch. She is the high energy her husband is not. She watches people in the lobby pass in front of her, trying to be well placed, clutching the purse in her lap. She wears heavy makeup, too much foundation, white against Indian skin.*)

PEACHES: What time is it? When are the kids coming?

POPPA: Real soon.

PEACHES: Where's your watch?

POPPA: It's busted.

PEACHES: We've been waiting too long.

POPPA: It hasn't been that long.

PEACHES: Not for you. You got something to pass the time. Numbers. That's all you know.

POPPA: I'm paying the bills (*like a foreign word*) e-lec-tronically.

PEACHES: How? Do you stamp out the money with your little soft fingertips? (*He looks at his soft fingertips.*)

PEACHES: Look at my hands. There is nothing soft about them. They're just tired hands. Sick and tired. Because I worked in my life and not in my head. Thinking is not working. Working is working. (*She stands up, straightens the pillows on the couch.*) Where are the kids? Shouldn't they be home from school by now?

POPPA: They don't go to school no more. They have jobs.

(*PEACHES is suddenly disoriented.*)

POPPA: They're all grown-up now, honey. We're at a hotel.

PEACHES: What hotel? (*She pulls out her compact; applies powder.*) What are you talking about?

POPPA: The kids. God said to meet him here. We've been waiting for him.

PEACHES: My son?

POPPA: Yes.

PEACHES: Don't try to make me crazy. My nerves can't take it.

POPPA: It's true. He reserved a room for us. The "honey moon suite" at the Biltmore!

PEACHES: He paid for it?

POPPA: You betcha.

PEACHES: The Biltmore?

POPPA: Just like you always wanted. Happy anniversary!

PEACHES: (*Looks around, for the first time noticing her surroundings*) The place looks so different.

POPPA: Oughta. They fixed it up pretty nice though, after all those years of letting it go all to pot. (*Beat.*) Hard to believe, fifty-five years together. Isn't it, honey, hard to believe?

PEACHES: (*Sighs*) That's a long time.

(*POPPA watches her for a moment, then returns to his work.*)

POPPA: First of the month comes like clockwork. Bills gotta be paid.

PEACHES: God is meeting me at the Biltmore. (*She rises.*) He took time off from work to fly in and see his mother.

POPPA: (*Not lifting his eyes from the keyboard*) That's right, honey. Should be here any minute now.

PEACHES: Will there be a party?

POPPA: Yep, tomorrow night. The whole family's gonna come. God's footing the bill.

PEACHES: I hope Cuca's kids aren't coming. They'll bring the grandchildren and the whole place will be like a zoo. I told Cuca that's what happens when you have kids too damn young, then the daughter goes and does the same thing, then her daughter, then the next thing you know you gotta big bola of brats on your hands and the grandma's the one that's gotta take care of them. Cuca's too damn old for that. She made fun of me for waiting, for only having two, but my kids turn out good.

POPPA: God told daughter to invite "only the closest relatives."

PEACHES: Bueno.

POPPA: Yep, he took care of everything. Put it on his credit card. He said he got one room for himself and one for us.

PEACHES: Is *she* coming?

POPPA: The wife? Tomorrow, I think. Tonight we have God all to ourselves.

PEACHES: It doesn't matter. My son is footing the bill.

POPPA: That's really something, isn't it, honey?

PEACHES: You better believe it. It's a miracle she let him open up the wallet for someone else besides her. (*She laughs at her own joke. Suddenly nervous.*) What I am going to wear? (*She rummages through her purse; takes out the compact again; more powder.*) Is this okay, what I got on?

POPPA: Daughter'll bring you a dress.

PEACHES: Where is she?

POPPA: She's coming.

PEACHES: I hope she doesn't bring the girlfriend.

POPPA: Virginia's dead, honey. Two months already.

PEACHES: Oh. (*Beat.*) Mejor. She's was holding her down. (*She crosses toward the upstage curtain, dreamlike.*) The Biltmore.

POPPA: Now, don't be goin' nowhere, sweetheart. The registration people told us to wait right here until God arrives.

(*PEACHES drapes the red velvet curtain around her like an evening gown. "Sunrise Serenade" by Glen Miller plays in her imagination. PEACHES dances in place for a few moments.*)

PEACHES: I remember all the beautiful hoteles, the elegant clubs, like in the Hollywood movies. When I was a girl in Tijuana, I worked only in the best places: The Agua Caliente, The Foreign Club where all the movie stars came . . . Gary Cooper, Jean Harlow. . . . even ese Mafioso, Al Capone. Puros americanos.

POPPA: Yep, that sure was something, honey.

PEACHES: (*Emerging from the curtain, she is all youth and "in charge." She mimes carrying a sales tray as a "cigarette girl."*) "Cigarettes, Candy, Chewing Gum!" (*Then "hat check" girl.*) "Check your hats and coats here please!" "Cigarettes, Candy, Chewing Gum!" "Check your hats and coats here, please!" They'd tip me good.

POPPA: They sure did.

(*DAUGHTER enters, a woman in her late 40s. She wears the Catholic school uniform of her childhood. Bobby socks, oxford shoes, plaid jumper skirt. Her arms are full of various items of clothing: an evening gown hung from a hanger and covered in dry cleaner plastic, a box of shoes, a tuxedo, etc. She crosses to PEACHES, kisses her on the cheek.*)

DAUGHTER: Hi, Mom.

PEACHES: Oh, mija. Eres tú. You look nice.

DAUGHTER: How could I, Mom? I'm still in my uniform. Just got outta work.

PEACHES: (*Confused*) Work?

DAUGHTER: (*Crosses to her father, kisses him on top of the head*) No God yet?

POPPA: He's late, I guess.

DAUGHTER: Figures.

PEACHES: Where's the baby?

DAUGHTER: Home.

PEACHES: Is your friend watching her tonight?

DAUGHTER: My . . . Rosa.

PEACHES: Sí, ésa.

POPPA: (*Softly*) She don't remember, Daughter.

DAUGHTER: Baby's big now, Mom. She can stay by herself.

PEACHES: Oh. (*Beat.*) And your brother?

DAUGHTER: (*To POPPA*) He didn't call?

POPPA: How could he call us here?

DAUGHTER: I gave you my cell. He's got the number.

POPPA: Oh, I forgot.

PEACHES: He forgets everything.

DAUGHTER: You got it on you?

POPPA: What?

PEACHES: He'd be an orphan on the street if it weren't for me.

DAUGHTER: The phone. Check your jacket pocket.

POPPA: (*Finds it, hands it to her*) I'm sorry, daughter.

DAUGHTER: (*Checking for messages*) Nada.

PEACHES: We haven't budged since we got here.

POPPA: We went to the bathroom a few times.

PEACHES: I told him I could go by myself. But no, he sticks to me like glue. I betchu God came and didn't see us, so he left.

DAUGHTER: Did you check on the reservation?

POPPA: No, I figured God'd show up any time now. She won't go to the room without him anyway.

DAUGHTER: I'm gonna go see.

PEACHES: Your brother took care of it.

DAUGHTER: Lemme just check, Mom. (*Beat, to POPPA.*) You guys eaten?

POPPA: Well, no. We wanted to wait for you, Daughter . . . so we could all eat together.

DAUGHTER: That's all right. I ordered sandwiches.

(She exits. PEACHES rewinds herself into the red drape. '30s music rises in her imagination.)

PEACHES: People don't believe it, but when I was a young girl in Tijuana, I used to dance with Rita Hayworth in the same clubs where she danced with her father. To see the two of them on stage, they were beautiful, like novios! When she walked off the stage, though, she was nothing. She could barely say two sentences, she was so shy. Then I found out why the father held her to him like she was on a leash.

POPPA: (*Half-listening*) Yep, she had a sad life, poor thing. Then the Alzheimer's . . .

PEACHES: She was rich and famous, but look how she suffered, five husbands, and I've lived twenty something years longer than her.

POPPA: Eighty-eight years old.

(POPPA begins to focus onto his work. The music has faded out.)

PEACHES: After my shift at the casino, I would walk home alone at two . . . three o'clock in the morning. The streets of Tijuana were not safe. If I turned the corner and found mi papa coming toward me, borracho, staggering, his belly full of tequila, I would real quick, before he had a chance to see me . . . before he looked up from the ditch his face had fallen into, I'd take a different way home. (*Pause.*) There was no one, really, ni papa, ni madre, to teach me about the ways of men. (*She looks over to see if POPPA is listening.*) There was a cousin, un primo hermano. My tía's son . . .

POPPA: (*Perfunctory*) He liked you.

PEACHES: Yes. He took his father's car, picked me up, as if by the trenzas and we went for a ride. He put his hand on my leg. I was thirteen.

(*POPPA looks over to her. DAUGHTER enters with the food.*)

DAUGHTER: You all hungry?

PEACHES: (*To Daughter*) At thirteen, you only want romance.

POPPA: Yep, we were getting a little bit hungry here.

(*Daughter looks back at her mother. POPPA, using a cane, moves laboriously from the computer to the stuffed chair. He waits for his sandwich.*)

PEACHES: (*Spying waiter offstage*) Joven, aquí, aquí.

DAUGHTER: Mom, the waiter isn't allowed to serve us in here. It's the lobby.

PEACHES: I just want to give him a tip. (*Conspiratorially.*) Es muy guapo.

(*PEACHES hurries over to her purse on the couch, starts rummaging inside it, pulling out several rumpled unused Kleenexes. She dumps the purse over, jiggles it, the compact, lipstick, and a holy card fall out*)

DAUGHTER: It's okay, Mom. I'll give him a tip when I bring back the dishes.

PEACHES: No. Espérate.

(*DAUGHTER prepares the sandwiches, PEACHES continues rummaging through her purse, opening and shutting zippers, digging her hands into its many empty pockets.*)

PEACHES: Yo sé que tenía dinero aquí.

DAUGHTER: Mom.

PEACHES: They stole all my money. It was the girls who clean the house. I tell him but he doesn't believe me.

DAUGHTER: Mom, I don't think . . .

PEACHES: It's all lost . . . I could make a list of all the things I lost every day. One two, three four five, but I am not the one with the numbers, he is. (*POPPA now sits at the chair waiting for his sandwich.*) He is always found, not lost, always fifty sixty seventy years, he is still here. I am perdida. I remember a lot of small things, important things that nobody gives a damn about no more. Sure, sometimes I forget if I've eaten breakfast or taken my pills, but that's natural, I'm no spring chicken. I don't even have to think about the bills no more, he says, I should feel lucky. It's not lucky to be useless.

DAUGHTER: You aren't useless, Mom.

(*PEACHES stuffs everything back into her purse, begins applying more white powder.*)

PEACHES: That's what you tell me, but you're trying to control me just like him. He took away my money, my credit cards, even the Penney's card, so I can't even buy a damn pair of calzones without asking permission from my husband. You think that makes me feel good?

DAUGHTER: No.

POPPA: Is there a sandwich there for me, daughter?

PEACHES: That's all he knows, when it's time to eat.

DAUGHTER: It's coming.

PEACHES: You might as well throw me into the garbage can, if I can't do nothing for myself no more, if I go around with my purse empty. But I got eyes. I can see what's going on.

DAUGHTER: (*Bringing a sandwich to POPPA*) Roast beef. Mayonnaise, no mustard. Pickles, no onions. Extra pepper.

POPPA: You got it! You sure are somethin,' daughter.

PEACHES: 'Cuz she pays attention. (*Beat.*) He doesn't believe me, but the mexicanos who clean the yard, they don't do a good job. And why should they? Is there a man around to tell them to pull up the weeds from the roots so they don't grow back in two days? No, there's no man around, just me, la vieja pendeja who's always complaining for nothing.

POPPA: Okay, okay, that's enough. Let's just enjoy our meal together.

PEACHES: Don't you try to shut me up.

POPPA: I'm not, honey, I just want us to enjoy this time with our daughter.

(*DAUGHTER serves PEACHES a sandwich.*)

DAUGHTER: Here, Mom. (*She opens a small jar of jalapeños.*) I brought you some chiles.

PEACHES: Do you think they respect him, those workers? They don't respect him because he's not a man.

DAUGHTER: Mom . . .

PEACHES: I only say it 'cuz it's true. They just steal his money. I try to treat them good. I know what it's like to come to this country new. I invite them in for a cup of coffee, a sweet bread or something. Then when my back is turn, they sneak inside the house. They steal my identification, my house keys . . .

DAUGHTER: Dad?

PEACHES: Why ask him? I could be hanging with my neck in a knot, he'd still be there with his face inside the computer.

POPPA: I love her, Daughter. She won't believe it. (*He starts to whimper.*)

PEACHES: I believe actions, not words. You think I wanted to marry you?

DAUGHTER: Stop it, Mom.

PEACHES: No, I don't give a damn no more what any body thinks.

POPPA: Fine, you didn't. Leave it at that.

PEACHES: It wasn't romantic. It was just need. I didn't love him.

POPPA: You barely knew me.

PEACHES: I know you now. Do you think I love you now?

DAUGHTER: Mom.

PEACHES: You bought a wife.

POPPA: Buy you! I barely had nothin' after the war. No family. Nothin.' I was free to—

PEACHES: Así son los gringos . . . free! What holds them to the dirt? They can buy it, but no feelings hold them to it. You couldn't have me, just cause of that piece of paper. You didn't buy me.

POPPA: Damnit! I didn't try to buy you!

DAUGHTER: C'mon, let's just forget it.

PEACHES: I don't forget nothing. I don't forget how I feel.

POPPA: I lost my appetite. I'm going back now. (*He doesn't move.*)

DAUGHTER: Where?

PEACHES: To the numbers. That's all he knows.

DAUGHTER: He's paying the bills, Mom.

PEACHES: Go 'head, take his side. Was he a father to you?

DAUGHTER: Mom.

PEACHES: Answer me the truth. What did he know about being a father? Nada!

POPPA: I admit it, I could've done better, but I had to work . . .

PEACHES: I taught your son how to be a man, not you!

DAUGHTER: You married him, Mom.

PEACHES: There's was nothing left for me in Tijuana. The casinos were closed already for a long time. We were poor. ¿No entiendes?

DAUGHTER: Sí, entiendo.

POPPA: (*A plea*) I just thought she was beautiful, Daughter. Is that a crime? You know your mother, a real lady.

DAUGHTER: I know.

PEACHES: Ya ves?

DAUGHTER: He said you were beautiful.

POPPA: Forget it. She don't wanna listen.

PEACHES: (*Softening*) Not to lies!

POPPA: (*Beat*) Yessiree, Beautiful. I asked her to marry me right there on the dance floor of the Paladium.

PEACHES: He did.

(*POPPA smiles.*)

PEACHES: I didn't let him touch me for whole month. It was in the Imperial Valley. We were staying with my tía Fita. They had put us in my primo's room. He was out picking walnuts near Sacramento. I drank two, three beers. Poppa looked good to me.

POPPA: She was drunk. (*They start laughing.*)

PEACHES: Afterwards, I was too tired to get up and clean myself. Pretty soon after, your brother was born.

POPPA: It was 1948. The war was long over. Truman was president. And I had a Mexican wife.

DAUGHTER: He was a love child then . . . God?

PEACHES: A what?

DAUGHTER: A child conceived in love.

POPPA: That's a good one, daughter.

(*They laugh and laugh and continue eating. Outside, the downtown cathedral bells begin to toll.*)

PEACHES: Mija, you know what I could use right now?

DAUGHTER: A beer.

PEACHES: Una nomás. Or you could share one with me . . . ?

DAUGHTER: (*Rising*) Nah, I'll get you your own. I'll tell the waiter. You want one too, Dad?

POPPA: No, no . . . coffee's fine.

PEACHES: It's nine o'clock.

DAUGHTER: What?

PEACHES: The church bells. It's nine o'clock, I counted them. In México, you tell the time that way. You don't have to look, you just listen.

(*DAUGHTER exits. PEACHES begins cleaning up, gathers together the paper plates and sandwich wrappings. SHE folds one of the unused napkins in half, then into quarters, then into eighths, then sixteenths. She repeats the folding several times. POPPA observes her.*)

POPPA: You don't have to do that, honey. Daughter'll take care of it.

PEACHES: I can't leave a mess.

POPPA: What time didya say it was?

PEACHES: What?

POPPA: The time.

PEACHES: I don't know . . . check your watch.

POPPA: I . . . doesn't matter. God oughta be here any minute now.

PEACHES: (*A bit martyred*) It doesn't matter.

(*POPPA studies her for a moment, then takes out the newspaper, which sits at his side and reads. PEACHES finally stuffs the napkin into her purse. She takes out her compact and reapplies more face powder. End of scene.*)

Scene 2

(*At rise, several empty bottles of beer stand in front of PEACHES, who stares out in an almost stupor, then lightly closes her eyes. POPPA has fallen asleep in the reading chair. DAUGHTER enters. She wears a waiter's formal attire. Her hair slicked back. She begins to clean up. She bends over the table, as PEACHES opens her eyes and sees the "WAITER." PEACHES reaches over and caresses "WAITER's" hair.*)

"WAITER": Mom?

PEACHES: I had a brother, Enrique. He was handsome like you. He used to work here in the Biltmore many years ago. A bus boy. (*She pulls "WAITER" to sit down by her side.*) One time, Rita Hayworth came in with a big group of people. Me and Enrique knew Rita when she was just Margarita Cansino and not famosa yet. Rita was the kind of person that she liked you, no matter who you were. The money didn't matter. So, when she saw my brother, she called, "Enrique! Enrique!" And there she was at a table with all of the rich people. But my brother felt ashame that he was only there to collect the dirty dishes. So, he pretended like he didn't hear her. It's sad, no? To be ashame of yourself like that.

"WAITER": Sí.

PEACHES: Work hard, mijo. Don't be ashame to work. Make something of yourself. Are you married?

"WAITER": I was.

PEACHES: Find a good woman. Not too pretty, but clean and neat and some body you can have confidence in.

"WAITER": I did.

PEACHES: When they betray you, leave them. Don't wait around. Take your children with you.

"WAITER": There was never another woman, Mom.

PEACHES: I'm not talking about that. I'm talking about a person who can only feel for themselves.

"WAITER": But you stayed.

PEACHES: You think it matters to me? All you really have is your children. (*Beat.*) Do you have a mother?

"WAITER": I. . . . Yes. She's you.

(*PEACHES laughs, lays her head against "WAITER's" shoulder, after a moment . . .*)

"WAITER": I miss her, Mom.

PEACHES: Who?

"WAITER": My wife.

PEACHES: Your wife.

"WAITER": Yeah.

PEACHES: You have a wife.

"WAITER": I did.

PEACHES: Ay! we're gonna make her so jealous.

(*Music can be heard coming from one of the ballrooms. A Mexican Ballad.*)

"Si Dios me quita la vida antes que a tí,
le voy a pedir consentir mi alma en la tuya."

"WAITER": Would you like to dance, Señora.

PEACHES: You want to dance with me?

"WAITER": Por favor.

(*PEACHES reaches for her compact. "WAITER" stops her, brings PEACHES to her feet, takes her into her arms. They dance.*)

PEACHES: (*Softly*) My whole life, lo único que quería yo fue casarme con un mexicano. To this day, when I feel a man with soft white hands, it gives me asco.

"WAITER": Why did you marry the gringo?

PEACHES: I had my God. (*Beat.*) Have you met my son, God?

"WAITER": Yes. I know him. (*Impassively. What follows as the closing dialogue of this scene occurs as dispassionately as possible. This is a true story told literally as a "matter of fact."*) When I was young, I had a brother by the same name. "Kneel down and call me God," he'd say.

PEACHES: ¿Cómo?

"WAITER": My brother. He'd play a game with me. He'd twist my arm behind my back and press it to the point of breaking.

PEACHES: Qué cruel.

"WAITER": Call me "God," he'd say. And I'd whisper, "God." And he'd go, "No, get down and say it louder." I resisted and felt the bone close to popping. Until I'd shout back "God! God!" and let my knees hit the floor.

PEACHES: I don't remember that.

"WAITER": I know.

(*They resume dancing. The music fades out.*)

Scene 3

(*PEACHES sits and folds towels at a hotel service laundry cart.*)

PEACHES: I wake up and got to think for a minute where I am. Sometimes a long time goes by before I remember. These are the things I think: I think I am going to stand up out of my bed and my teenaged children will be down the hallway asleep and my husband will smell of bad breath from his mouth open all night dreaming. I think I will get to the bathroom before all of them, wash my face and brush my hair before they start pounding on the door to get in. With me no one pounds on the door because I am always the first one up. Hours before the rest, I am already outside with the pajaritos, watering the earth beneath the rose bushes, before the wet morning air turns to smog with the heat.

But that isn't how it is now. That isn't the way I wake up. I wake up and sometimes I'm in the La-Z-Boy chair. Someone, I guess him, has put a blanket over me. I have piyamas on but I don't remember putting them on. I try to force my chair back down with my legs. But it's hard. He comes and helps me, and I start my day.

Siempre tengo mucho que hacer. The towels. I know how to fold them. First, I make the corners meet (*she demonstrates*) and then I press the fold along the line with my fingertips like this. And then I fold it again and press it again. My hands, como una plancha. Y así todo 'stá bien.

(*She observes her pile of folded towels with pride. POPPA enters.*)

POPPA: I was looking for you, honey.

(*She does not respond to him.*)

PEACHES: There he is.

POPPA: (*Nervous*) Honey, where'd you get the towels? You didn't take them, did ya?

(*PEACHES glares at him, threatened.*)

POPPA: You're doing a good job there, honey.

PEACHES: He doesn't know nothing.

POPPA: You fold them perfect.

PEACHES: He never fold a towel in his life.

POPPA: Yesirreee, honey . . .

PEACHES: "Yessiree Honey." "Yessiree." He sounds like a payaso.

POPPA: You finished folding?

PEACHES: A' course. Does anybody ever help me? (*She crosses with towels in her arms.*)

POPPA: I'll take them back for you. (*Taking the towels from PEACHES.*)

PEACHES: Okay, put them in the. . . . (*She is confused.*) Oh, you know where they go.

POPPA: Sure, I'll take care of it.

(*He starts to exit.*)

PEACHES: Poppa!

(*PEACHES crosses to him, and with sudden tenderness, tucks in a bit of his shirt tail.*)

POPPA: Thank you, honey. Don't know what I'd do without you.

(*He kisses her cheek as he heads for the service entrance. PEACHES opens her purse and takes out her compact; she applies face powder. Fade out. Sound of cell phone ringing in the darkness.*)

Scene 4

(*At rise, POPPA finishes a phone conversation. PEACHES paces, rearranging things here and there.*)

POPPA: Sure, son. You betcha. . . . Sure, we understand. . . . All right now. . . . Sure, God. . . . Love to the family. (*He disconnects the cell with some difficulty.*) He says he'll be here tomorrow by noon.

PEACHES: It's the wife.

POPPA: Let's get our things together, honey. As soon as Daughter comes back with the key, I'll take you to the room.

PEACHES: I got a bed at home. I don't need to stay in a stranger's house.

POPPA: It's the Biltmore, honey.

PEACHES: I don't care what the hell it is. I want to sleep in my own damn bed.

(*Stubborn, she sits on the couch.*)

PEACHES: Put on the TV, Poppa.

POPPA: Honey . . . ?

PEACHES: You heard what I said. It helps me sleep.

POPPA: But, Peaches . . .

PEACHES: And I don't want no party. You call my son back and tell him.

POPPA: It's for you, dear . . . for both of us.

PEACHES: Maybe for you, but it's not for me. You go by yourself if you want. (*POPPA hesitates.*) Put on the TV.

(*He gets the remote. They both sit down to watch TV. DAUGHTER enters wearing a nurse's uniform [her job].*)

DAUGHTER: I got the key, took your stuff up to the room. It's nice—

PEACHES: You go home, now, mija, it's late. You gottu work por la mañana.

DAUGHTER: No, I'll take you up.

PEACHES: Call me when you get there.

DAUGHTER: Dad?

POPPA: Your brother called. He won't make it tonight.

DAUGHTER: (*Beat*) Aren't you going to your room?

(*POPPA looks at DAUGHTER helplessly.*)

PEACHES: Don't forget to call the house the minute you get in the door. (*To TV.*) Ay! They don't leave nothing to the imagination. Change the station, Poppa. (*He does.*)

POPPA: Go on, Daughter. We'll be all right here.

DAUGHTER: Well here's the key. You'll go up later . . . ?

(*POPPA nods.*)

PEACHES: Ándale, hija.

DAUGHTER: . . . Okay. (*She kisses them both "goodnight."*)

PEACHES: Oh, and mija . . .

DAUGHTER: Sí.

PEACHES: You call the rest of the people. I don't want no party. I'm too old for that already.

POPPA: She don't know what she's saying, Daughter. It'll be all right tomorrow.

PEACHES: Como que I don't know! I don't want the party! He can have it, if he wants!

POPPA: I can't do that. (*Whining.*) Oh, I don't know what to do now. What're we gonna tell your brother?

DAUGHTER: Stop it, Dad.

PEACHES: (*Beat*) I'm so tired, hija.

DAUGHTER: I know, Mom. I'll tell God.

POPPA: No!

PEACHES: No, don't bother your brother. He's a busy man.

DAUGHTER: Okay, you just . . . rest tonight. G'night.

(*DAUGHTER kisses them both, whispering something to POPPA and exits. PEACHES and POPPA sit and watch TV in the hotel lobby. A late night show is on. Within minutes, PEACHES has fallen asleep, mouth open, head thrown back against the sofa. She snores lightly. POPPA observes her, and then returns to the TV program. He, too, dozes off. Gradually the hotel falls into a deep sleep. The lights fade on POPPA.*)

(*PEACHES remains in the sleeping light of the hotel, as a spot also rises on DAUGHTER driving home in a light rain. The neon of city lights, shimmering wet roadways and night traffic travel across her face.*)

DAUGHTER: My wife's name was Rosa, Mamá, Rosalinda. One night almost a year ago, I woke up and found her dragging herself across the floor to get to the bathroom. She felt eight-eight years old, she said. She was thirty-eight. It was leukemia, Mamá. You forgot.

(*The lights fade on DAUGHTER as they rise back on the hotel lobby. The TV has dropped out of signal, the snow of the screen reflecting off PEACHES's and POPPA's faces. POPPA awakens suddenly. A bit disoriented at first, his eyes scan the empty lobby. He rises to turn off the TV, observes his wife. She has not changed position.*)

POPPA: Honey? You coming to bed? (*No response.*) Honey . . . ? (*He crosses to her, lightly shakes her. Her head collapses onto her chest. POPPA looks up and around the hotel lobby nervously. He comes downstage. He does not know what to do.*) Daughter?

(*POPPA stands speechless in the center of the room. Moments pass. At last, he returns

to the sofa, takes off his jacket and lays it across PEACHES. He lifts her head gently back against the couch. He opens her purse, finds her compact, and awkwardly begins to apply face powder. She is a ghostly white. The bell tolls for the sixth time. He looks around again. It is morning. The sound of the ocean in the distance. Rose petals fall from above.)
End of play.

Notes

1. Biographical information courtesy of the playwright. Additional information from an unpublished memoir by the playwright: "Send Them Flying Home: A Geography of Remembrance." See www.cherríemoraga.com and Elizabeth C. Ramírez, *Chicanas/Latinas in American Theatre: A History of Performance* (Bloomington: Indiana University Press, 2000), 118–24, 156.
2. Playwright's responses to editors' biographical questionnaire, November 19, 2003, with additions in 2007 and correspondence on November 19, 2009, July 15, 2010, June 14, 2010, June 19, 2010, and October 25, 2010.
3. Since Gloria Anzaldúa's death in 2004, *This Bridge Called My Back* has been out of print, although hopes of reissue remain high.
4. Cherríe L. Moraga, *The Hungry Woman* (Albuquerque, N.M.: West End Press, 2001), x. Jorge A. Huerta, review, "Moraga's *Heroes and Saints:* Chicano Theatre for the 90s." *Theatre Forum* 1 (Spring 1992): 51.
5. Playwright's responses to editors' biographical questionnaire.
6. Cherríe Moraga, "The Zen Master," in *Conducting a Life: Reflections on the Theatre of Maria Irene Fornes,* ed. Maria M. Delgado and Caridad Svich (Lyme, N.H.: Smith and Kraus, 1999), 183, 184, 186.
7. Playwright's responses to editors' biographical questionnaire. The spelling of *Chicana* as *Xicana* is rooted in Third World feminism.
8. Jorge A. Huerta, *Theatre Forum* 1 (Spring 1992): 49–52; Ramírez, 118.
9. Playwright's responses to editors' biographical questionnaire.

PART II

Chicanas and Chicano Teatro

Staging Identity

Among all of the many Latina/Latino groups, Chicanas/Chicanos continue to be the largest.[1] The term *Chicana/Chicano* refers to the group of men and women of Mexican origin born and/or raised in the United States and those from Mexico who have lived in the United States for some time.[2] The term was used during the early stages of the Chicano Movement as activists arrived at defining a cultural and political identity unique to themselves as a group.[3] Besides the cultural and political aspects, as Emma Pérez and Devon Peña describe the climate, "the movement also spawned a literary and art explosion among Chicanos and Chicanas in the 1960s and 1970s." This political and social movement also spurred the Latina voice, calling for women's rights and equality within the Chicana/Chicano Movement and community. Significantly, given this larger group, the breadth of dramatic literature by Chicanas stands out since the inception of the Chicano Movement, and it should not be surprising that this collection includes more works by women of this group.[4]

Juan Gómez-Quiñones has pointed out that within the two decades of the beginning of the *movimiento,* "these years of sustained conflict and struggle had yielded some positive results" because they had led to "a cultural and artistic flowering," a distinct feature of the late 1960s, the 1970s, and the early 1980s. He adds: "as the 1980s unfolded, the Chicano community in the United States was at a historical juncture." Within that juncture, evidence shows that among all Latina/Latino groups, Chicanas' creative expression stands out in that renaissance. Vicki Ruiz also comments on how we "witnessed the emergence of distinct Chicana feminist identities: collectively and individually" in the decades following the beginning of the Chicana/Chicano Movement. The increased awareness of the sexism in the Chicana/Chicano community during the 1970s resulted in more and more interaction with other feminists and women who were experiencing change in ideology. Ruiz cites Teresa Córdova's point that we must bear in mind that

"Chicana feminists have struggled to find their voices—have struggled to be heard," and yet, while "our struggle continues," "our silence is forever broken."[5]

In *Chicano Narrative: The Dialectic of Difference,* Ramón Saldívar specifically comments on the particular significance of contemporary Chicana writers on the whole, noting how they "challenge not only the ideologies of oppression of the Anglo-American culture that their Chicano brothers confront, but they also challenge the ideologies of patriarchal oppression evinced by Chicano writers and present within Chicano culture itself." In *Postnationalism in Chicana/o Literature and Culture,* Ellie D. Hernández effectively articulates the climate of the period, in which "newfound language, political direction, and focus culminated with the publication of essay collections and political projects that ushered in the 'women of color paradigm' during the late 1970s and the 1980s. Chicanas were both instrumental and central to that development," as Hernández stresses.[6]

This emergent Chicana expression can be attributable to many factors. In writing about *la nueva chicana* during the period of Chicana/Chicano student activism, Vicki Ruiz, one of the most recognized Chicana historians, remarks on the actual physical act of "picking up the pen" becoming "a political act" for Chicanas.[7] Along with these new narratives, these women began to undertake primary roles in the entire development of the Chicana/Chicano Movement, and these emerging Chicana voices increased. With the greater number of Mexican-born people and/or Latinas/Latinos with Mexican ancestry, "Chicano" theatre groups quickly grew throughout the Southwest and the West.

Mainly reawakened in 1965 with the work of Luis Valdez and El Teatro Campesino, by the early 1970s, at least seventy-five Chicana/Chicano *teatros* had formed, with most acknowledging some influence stemming from Valdez and/or El Teatro Campesino, either from the published *actos* or from witnessing performances, while others had simply heard about Campesino's work.[8] The earliest account we have of a Chicana's *teatro* is of Teatro de las Chicanas, formed by students at San Diego State College in 1971. Felicitas Nuñez and Delia Ravelo were the principal members, with many young women participating through its long history. Starting with "the familiar *acto,*" as Ravelo recalls in *Teatro Chicano: A Collective Memoir and Selected Plays,* the stories soon grew to include a wide range of experiences developed by the group members.[9] Changing its name to Teatro Laboral, the group performed until 1977, then ceased production until reforming in 1979 as Teatro Raíces (Roots theater). The teatro performed mostly in Southern California near the Mexican border.

Perhaps the most critical event in the history of Chicana theatre occurred at the 1973 festival in San Jose, California, under the auspices of El Teatro Nacional de Aztlán (TENAZ), a coalition of *teatros* formed in 1971 for the purpose of coordinating regional and national events, publications, and exchange between theatre groups. A group of Chicanas performed at the festival, using the style of the *corrido* (ballad) that had been popularized by Los Marcarones, a *teatro* from Mexico, in a presentation that emphasized the Chicana as a vital and dominant figure within a chronicle of the Chicano Movement. The resulting volatile debate and criticism about the group and the performance led many participants to take sides on the issue of Chicana feminism. Either one was a proponent of women's voices or viewed the work as divisive to the movement.

As Alma M. Garcia explains, "a Chicana feminist movement originated from the nationalist Chicano struggle," and, "as the Chicano movement developed during the 1970s, Chicana feminists began to draw their own political agenda and raised a series of questions to assess their role within the Chicano movement. They entered into a dialogue with each other that explicitly reflected their struggles to secure a room of their own within the Chicano movement."[10] By the mid-1970s, Chicana alternative theatre groups had formed, and with these groups, the numbers of Chicanas working in *teatro* increased.

Yvonne Yarbro-Bejarano includes the work of Dorinda Moreno and Las Cucarachas in her dramatic piece titled *Chicana,* which was first performed in San Francisco's Mission District and subsequently presented in Mexico City at the fifth festival organized by TENAZ. Another group that must be mentioned here is Women in Teatro (WIT), a women's caucus established within TENAZ in 1978, in response to the growing call for attention to the contributions by Chicanas working in *teatro.* WIT's continued support of women has been instrumental in terms of networking and support.

Academic theatre programs also played an important part in this dramatic history. One of the most prominent of these was the collective work of El Teatro de la Esperanza (Theatre of Hope), formed by Jorge Huerta, along with six other students, in 1971, when he was completing his doctoral work at the University of California, Santa Barbara. Diane Rodriguez, whose playtext follows this introduction, was one of those students. It is important to get a glimpse of the kind of performance work Rodriguez participated in as a precursor to her subsequent work in theatre.

At first El Teatro de la Esperanza performed *actos* written by El Teatro Campesino, but it soon began to produce original works written by Huerta's students. In January 1974 it produced one of its most important works, *Guadalupe,* a docudrama derived from interviews, research, and improvisation, to document issues of civil rights. Huerta left the group in 1974, and the company began to create original works collectively. One of its most recognized works from this time is *La víctima* (1976), which traces a woman's crossings from Mexico to the United States, beginning with the 1910 Revolution and continuing to the present. Drawing from the tradition begun by El Teatro Campesino, musical narrative in the form of a *corrido* (ballad) informed the audience about the unfolding history.[11]

Yarbro-Bejarano discusses the significance of El Teatro de la Esperanza in the shift that began to occur in the 1980s from texts focused on the male subject, "through notions of class, 'racial,' and cultural identity that reinscribed tacit cultural definitions of masculinity and femininity within the heterosexual structure of the family," to texts that "while still concerned with class and cultural identity, attempt to focus on the female subject or address more directly questions of sexuality, including homosexuality." She adds that following their early experiments with the *acto* form, El Teatro de la Esperanza's distinct docudrama form "illustrated the difficulty of decentering the male subject of representation in narrative forms."[12]

As Yarbro-Bejarano points out, "These docudramas concentrated on the weakness and contradictions of the male protagonist, placed in dialectical relation to active female characters who possessed a clearer vision of the economic and social forces composing the dramatic conflict." This group's efforts "to distribute power within the group among both men and women involved not only decision-making, but also directing, collective creation, administration, and all aspects of production."[13] Thus, it is not difficult to comprehend how capably Rodriguez can assume so many types of leadership roles and continue her performance work as well.

The ability to assume participation in and often take leadership roles in all aspects of performance is a distinct feature of this period of renaissance for Chicanas in theatre. Chicanas have ushered in an entire movement of their own, "making an indelible mark in performance," and more and more representation by this group has surfaced.[14] Similar to Rodriguez's work, in Yareli Arizmendi's piece we witness how her Chicana perspective allows her to portray many Latinas, all emanating from her as center. Arizmendi begins her dramatic piece by first introducing us to her own speaking Mexican-born voice, one that has resided in the United States since 1982, and then walking into the shoes of a Chicana, in which she dramatizes the struggle of identity within this new character.[15] From there she broadens the scope so that we end up with the larger Latina voice identified through stepping into the many distinct character types she has created. In writing about themselves and their experience, we can observe the Chicana who has honed her acting craft through her experience in Chicana/Chicano *teatro* in Rodriguez, and the kind of actor who pursues actor training in one of the new academic programs offered to Latinas in Arizmendi. Both illustrate professional actors who have achieved success through very different methods of preparation.

In the following two chapters, we can examine how two Chicanas have undertaken positions "behind the footlights," so to speak, on stage, and further afield. Through their wide range of experience, both Diane Rodriguez and Yareli Arizmendi reveal how broad this involvement has become for Chicanas on the whole since the 1960s. While other women discussed throughout this collection can certainly fall into this category, these two women will serve as representatives for the topic under discussion.

Notes

1. U.S. Census Bureau, *The Hispanic Population: Census 2000 Brief* (Washington, D.C.: U.S. Department of Commerce, May 2001, C2KBR/01-3. See also data report, "Hispanic or Latino Origin by Specific Origin," in *U.S. Census Bureau 2006 Accuracy of the Data Report.* Both documents available at http://factfinder.census.gov.

2. Emma Pérez with Devon Peña, "Chicanos and Chicanas," in *The Oxford Encyclopedia of Latinos and Latinas in the United States,* ed. Suzanne Oboler and Deena J. González (New York: Oxford University Press, 2005), 1:323, 329.

3. See Marcelo M. Suárez-Orozco and Mariela M. Páez, eds. *Latinos: Remaking America* (Berkeley: University of California Press, 2002), 321–38; and Rodolfo Acuña, *Anything But Mexican: Chicanos in Contemporary Los Angeles* (London: Verso, 2000), 209–29.

4. Jorge Mariscal, "Chicano/a Movement," in *Oxford Encyclopedia of Latinos and Latinas,* 1:320; see also Emma Pérez with Devon Peña, "Chicanos and Chicanas," in ibid., 1:320–21, 329–31.

5. Juan Gómez-Quiñones, *Chicano Politics: Reality and Promise 1940–1990* (Albuquerque: University of New Mexico Press, 1994), 190–91; Vicki L. Ruiz, *From Out of the Shadows: Mexican Women in Twentieth-Century America* (Oxford: Oxford University Press, 1998), 124; Gómez-Quinoñes, 189–90; Ruiz, 124–25; see also Elizabeth C. Ramírez, *Chicanas/Latinas in American Theatre: A History of Performance* (Bloomington: Indiana University Press, 2000), 124.

6. Ramón Saldívar, *Chicano Narrative: The Dialectic of Difference* (Madison: University of Wisconsin Press, 1990), 173. Ellie D. Hernández, *Postnationalism in Chicana/o Literature and Culture* (Austin: University of Texas Press, 2009), 58.

7. Ruiz, 102.

8. Elizabeth C. Ramírez, "The Annals of Chicano Theater: 1965–1973," M.A. thesis, Department of Theatre, University of California, Los Angeles, 1974.

9. Laura E. Garcia, Sandra M. Gutierrez, and Felicitas Nuñez, eds., *Teatro Chicana: A Collective Memoir and Selected Plays* (Austin: University of Texas Press, 2008), xxiii–xxx, 11.

10. Alma M. Garcia, "The Development of Chicana Feminist Discourse," in *From Different Shores,* ed. Ronald Takaki, 2nd ed. (Oxford: Oxford University Press, 1994), 175–83.

11. Elizabeth C. Ramírez, "Playwrights," in *Oxford Encyclopedia of Latinos and Latinas,* 3:393.

12. Yvonne Yarbro-Bejarano, "The Female Subject in Chicano Theatre: Sexuality, 'Race,' and Class," in *Performing Feminisms: Feminist Critical Theory and Theatre,* ed. Sue Ellen Case (Baltimore, Md.: Johns Hopkins University Press, 1990), 133, 140.

13. Ibid., 140, 141.

14. Ramírez, *Chicanas/Latinas in American Theatre,* 93.

15. For further reading on the topic of Latina/Latinos and identity, see Jorge J. E. Gracia, "Latino/a Identities," part 1, *Latinos in America: Philosophy and Social Identity* (Malden, Mass.: Blackwell, 2008), 1–74.

CHAPTER 3

Chicanas Can Do It All

Diane Rodriguez's *The Path to Divadom, Or How to Make Fat-free Tamales in G Minor* (1985)

Diane Rodriguez, by permission of the playwright. Photographer unknown.

The Playwright/La Dramaturga

Diane Rodriguez was born in San Jose, California, in the 1950s.[1] Her mother was born in Blythe, California, and her maternal grandparents were from Mexico. Her father was born in San Angelo, Texas, and her paternal grandfather was from Texas and paternal grandmother from Mexico. She received her Bachelor of Arts degree in theatre arts at the University of California, Santa Barbara, where she studied with Jorge Huerta. Perhaps one of the most seasoned Chicana actors, she stands out for her experience with El Teatro de la Esperanza and El Teatro Campesino. She is one of the founding members of El Teatro de la Esperanza, founded at her alma mater, the University of California, Santa Barbara, and performed with the company. Following her departure, she was a leading female actor for the seminal theatre company, El Teatro Campesino, for ten seasons, where she toured internationally. She is also a founding member of the Los Angeles–based comedy troupe, Latins Anonymous, founded in 1988.

Rodriguez's experience in theatre is vast. She describes herself as "a multidisciplinary theatre artist," with her work as an accomplished actor, anthologized writer, regional theatre director, and now a producer at Center Theatre Group, Los Angeles. The Center Theatre Group is the new umbrella under which the Mark Taper Forum (Los Angeles) now falls, a theatre with which she has long been associated, now joined with both the Kirk Douglas Theatre (Culver City, Calif.) and the Ahmanson Theatre (Los Angeles).

Rodriguez's directing credits include numerous regional stage productions: *Bordertown*, by Culture Clash, Arizona Theatre Company (2004); *Spic-a-Rama* by John

Leguizamo, Actors Theatre of Phoenix (2002), featuring an actor from Phoenix in this one-man show; *Wait Until Dark,* by Frederick Knott, Mixed Blood Theatre, Minneapolis; *Inside Out,* with book by Doug Haverty and lyrics by Haverty and Adryan Russ; *Our Lady of the Tortilla,* by Luis Santiero, Phoenix Theatre, Arizona; *Heroes and Saints* by Cherríe Moraga, Borderlands Theatre, Tucson, Arizona. Her credits at Center Theatre Group are *Highest Heaven* by Jose Cruz Gonzalez, and *Drive My Coche* by Roy Conboy. Other credits include: *La Posada Majica* by Octavio Solis, for four seasons at South Coast Repertory; *Los Vecinos* by Luis Alfaro and Rodriguez, at Cornerstone Theatre; and Migdalia Cruz's *The Have Little,* which was produced at the Group at Strasberg in the Marilyn Monroe Theatre at the Lee Strasberg Creative Center in West Hollywood. Other directing projects include her work at the City Theatre in Pittsburgh, where she directed John Belluso's *Pyretown* (2006) and Lynn Nottage's *Intimate Apparel* (2007). She was among the group of actors in Heather Woodbury's recent *Tale of 2Cities,* jointly commissioned by P.S. 122 and UCLA Live, which garnered the 2007 Obie Award for ensemble.

Rodriguez has also directed workshops and readings at Hartford Stage and San Jose Repertory Theatre. She has worked with numerous playwrights on their new plays, including: Kirsten Greenidge, Octavio Solis, Cherríe Moraga, Polly Penn, Nilo Cruz, Jessica Goldberg, Oliver Mayer, Roy Conboy, Naomi Iisuka, Dan Guerrero, Julia Cho, and Lynn Nottage at Sundance Theatre Lab 2003. At the Mark Taper Forum, where she is currently associate producer/director of new play production, she commissioned, supported, and developed new works by Nilo Cruz, Jose Cruz Gonzalez, Octavio Solis, Oliver Mayer, Ricardo Bracho, Ann Garcia Romero, Alina Troyano, Marga Gomez, Rogelio Martinez, Michael John Garces, Evelina Fernández, and Cherríe Moraga, among others, while she was director of the Latino Theatre Initiative.

Rodriguez's acting credits are also extensive. She has appeared in over twenty premiere productions and on many of our leading regional stages, including La Jolla Playhouse, the Mark Taper Forum, Southcoast Repertory, San Diego Repertory, the Old Globe Theatre (San Diego), Cornerstone Theatre, and at the Los Angeles Theatre Center. She has also performed and toured with El Teatro Campesino. She has performed in such works as: Tony Kushner's adaptation of *Good Woman of Setzuan* and El Teatro Campesino's *Conference of the Birds,* under the direction of Peter Brook. Rodriguez has also worked in television and film for twenty years and has worked with film directors James Cameron, Sidney Poitier, the late Anthony Perkins, and Luis Valdez, among others. During the 2002–4 season at the Mark Taper Forum she originated the roles of Zoila in Lisa Loomer's *Living Out* and Minerva in Luis Alfaro's *Breakfast, Lunch and Dinner.*

Other recognitions include being the recipient of an NEA/Theatre Communications Group Directing Director's Early Career Development Fellowship (1998–2000), a New Generations Mentor Awardee from the TCG/Mellon Foundation (2003–5 and 2007–9), and she is an associate artist of Cornerstone Theatre Company. She published an anthology of her two plays with Latins Anonymous, titled *Latins Anonymous* (Arte Público Press, 1997), and she also released a comedy CD, *Laff Traxx* (1999). She is published in various anthologies, including in Alberto Sandoval-Sánchez and Nancy Saporta Sternbach's *Puro Teatro: A Latina Anthology* (2000).

It is evident from this brief description that Diane Rodriguez has been a valuable contributor to the U.S. stage. Her work with the Los Angeles Mark Taper Forum's Latino Theatre Initiative has been instrumental in assuring that Latinas' voices are heard on the stage, and her continuing work with the Center Theatre Group will insure greater success for Latinas and Latinos on both sides of the footlights.

About the Play/Sobre la Obra

The Path to Divadom, Or How to Make Fat-free Tamales in G Minor is an excellent example of a performance piece that both draws from Rodriguez's experience in Chicano *teatro* in its earlier form and also illustrates how she broadens her theatrical voice through her subsequent vast experience in theatre. As Rodriguez describes her work, her immersion in all aspects of Chicana/Chicano performance has resulted in her becoming a completely well-rounded artist of the theatre. This piece allows her to showcase her abilities in performing comedy, introduce new and different characters, and bring cultural traditions and experiences to her wide audience.

In *The Path to Divadom,* we find the style of an *acto* like those typically found in the early work of Valdez, filled with political and social satire. Skillfully using the monologue form, Rodriguez takes the stereotype of an overweight, "unhappy with herself" small-town California girl and shows her transformation into a "sexy bossy *nalgona mandona*" with "big ole hips and thunder thighs" who is transformed into a "Diva Royal." Within the context of a *tamalada,* Rachel, the narrator's fat-free-driven cousin, attempts to change the age-old tamal recipe in this traditional gathering of women in the family. As Rodriguez points out, "I think it's important to challenge tradition and question who imposed this tradition on whom." The playwright is "attempting to explore the notion of culture being alive and constantly changing." Amid feminist politics, social commentary, and bawdy humor, the result highlights the value of women upholding "la cultura" within a climate of change (see About the Play section).

Artistic Vision/Punto de Vista Artístico

ECR & CRC: Briefly describe your theatre experience.[2]

DR: In college, I was one of the founders of El Teatro de la Esperanza. After graduation I went immediately to San Juan Bautista to work with El Teatro Campesino. I was a core member of the ensemble for eleven years. In the mid-eighties, I moved with my husband, who was also an ensemble member, to Los Angeles where I started my own comedy group with three other actors. The group was called Latins Anonymous. In 1995, I was hired as the codirector of the Mark Taper Forum's Latino Theatre Initiative, which grew to be the largest Latino play development program in the country. I remain there today as associate producer/director of new play production.

ECR & CRC: How did you decide to write and/or perform?

DR: I come from a performing family. It was what the Esparza/Rodriguez' did. My father sang, my mother played the piano, my aunts and uncles sang in quartets, my cousins sang in bands and performed in school and church plays. By the time I was fourteen I had my sights set on performing and going to college to major in theatre. The passion for writing came much later out of a frustration over the lack of roles for me to play in television and films. Thus, tired of complaining I took my career into my own hands and began writing comedy sketches for Latins Anonymous that we self-produced.

ECR & CRC: Why do you write what you do?

DR: I have grown to have an amazing respect for writers. Their work, especially among writers of color, illuminates our communities with depth, humor, and understanding for each other. Writers do wonders for race relations. Had I had this epiphany earlier I might have concentrated more on writing as my primary discipline. Since I am a multidisciplinary artist, writing is only one component of my life as an artist. Lately, because I find so few young theatre writers coming out of the Chicano community, I feel the need to fill that gap and give voice to my community. The challenge is to do it in a smart, contemporary, and forward thinking way.

ECR & CRC: Who do you write for and what audience are you trying to reach?

DR: I write from a Chicana point of view in the First World. Chicanos generally relate to the nuances, references, and rhythms of my writing. But I am interested in a broader popular audience. I want to inspire and entertain. I want to reach a diverse audience in terms of race and age.

ECR & CRC: What message, if any, are you trying to convey to your audience with this work and/or with all of your work?

DR: With *Path to Divadom, Or How to Make Fat-free Tamales,* I'm trying to explore the notion of culture being alive and constantly changing. I think it's important to challenge tradition and question who imposed this tradition on to whom. Sometimes, tradition can be incredibly oppressive, especially between male and female. I constantly look forward and always referring back but never trying to re-create what has past. My writing helps me free myself from the past by looking forward.

ECR & CRC: Who or what has been your major influence?

DR: My years in the Teatro Campesino formed my notions of what it meant to be an artist and an activist. That time had a tremendous effect on my world view. The teatro was at its height in terms of aesthetic and respect internationally. We traveled constantly to Europe and, while on tour I was exposed to world-class theatre. The bar was always very high. Our commitment was so intent on representing our community in its best light that the company was heralded for its discipline and ground-breaking aesthetic. The second major influence has been my time at the Mark Taper Forum, where brilliant artists from diverse communities surround me on a daily basis. Their work has inspired me and expanded my vision of the kind of theatre I would like to produce and do.

ECR & CRC: What has been your biggest and/or most difficult struggle/challenge in life, in completing a play or getting it produced, etc.?

DR: If the Chicano/Latino community had had infrastructure: theatres that were respected, vital, and producing on a regular basis, with substantial budgets and staffing, I might have had more personal time to create and focus on my art at those theatres. But my generation, being the first Chicano generation to make a living as artists and writers and be taken seriously, had to create on the fringes or be arts activists because we did not have our own mainstream institutions to support us and produce our work. That has changed a bit, but we have much farther to go in terms of being represented on an ongoing basis. We still don't have anyone. That has been the biggest struggle. Much of my time is given over to other artists in order to create the support and structure that artists of my age did not have from mainstream institutions.

ECR & CRC: Can you offer any words of advice to aspiring playwrights/performers/directors/audiences?

DR: Be competitive. We should not be afraid of that word. It doesn't mean be cutthroat or backstab. It means be the best that you can be. Be great. Get training and listen. Never ever get so "big" you stop learning, stop being curious, stop listening. Never sit on past glories. Move forward constantly. Think of yourself as a spherical artist, able to do many things to survive.

Production History/Palabras Dramatúrgicas

The Path to Divadom premiered at Highways Performance Space, Santa Monica, California, in 1995. The following listing appeared in the September–November 1995 Highways calendar, in which this work appeared in a bill of three works by women, described as the *Trio Las Girlfriends*:

> Rodriguez! Gaitan! Sahaugun!
>
> Trio Las Girlfriends
>
> Thursday–Sunday, September 18–October 1
>
> A raucous theatrical ride with Trio Las Girlfriends. Untamed, uncensored, unleashed y que? Diane Rodriguez in The Path to Divadom, a playlet about femininity, power and fat-free tamales, Maria Elena Gaitan in Chola Del Mundo World Tour, a hilarious acto de resistance and cello playing too! Paulina Sahaugun in Nahuatl—Now What? A high tech Aztec in Gringolandia, self-help extravaganza."[3]

The play has also been performed at Diva LA (1995) at the Mark Taper Forum, Los Angeles; Sor Juana de la Cruz Festival (1996), Mexican Museum, Chicago; Trio Las Girlfriends Tour (1996), Guadalupe Cultural Arts Center, San Antonio; and La Mujer Latina Conference (1997), University of Wisconsin, Madison.

Contact Information

drodriguez@centertheatregroup.org

THE PATH TO DIVADOM, OR HOW TO MAKE FAT-FREE TAMALES IN G MINOR

The path to Divadom is a difficult one. The road is dark at times, dangerous. Filled with *bandidos* that steal your soul, making *your* ideas their own, slap you in the face with the thought that: you're too young, too fresh, too old, too weathered to know the ways of this *pinche* world. But somehow through this dangerous road, la *via loca,* you finally make it to the golden gates of "I don't give a damn what you think of me."

And yet, some of you women are completely unaware that you have entered the gates of the queendom. Like my cousin Rachel, a diva that didn't know it, and *needed* to be crowned.

And as I witnessed with mine own eyes, it took my "Aunt Liz," *la* know-it-all of the family and Diva Supreme, to show Rachel that she had entered the land of "I'm in charge."

I witnessed the crowning of Diva Rachel on a phantasmagoric December day.

Everybody was there at the chante of Rachel and Mac's 'cuz we were having a tamalada. It's a party. Everyone repeat after me. A tamalada. What does it mean? It means the Diva is making tamales, honey. Yes, making those delicious, delectable, delightful, sacred wrapped secrets.

Now Rachel is a sexy, bossy, *nalgona, mandona* big ole hips and thunder thighs. I hug her and I get lost in the softness of her 40 DDs. But in that embrace, I felt her go limp. Oblivious to her royal divaness. Shockingly, my sexy bossy *nalgona mandona* cousin was unhappy with herself and diligently watched her fat intake . . .

Ay, Diane. Look what I found for me and the kids at Ralph's: fat-free cookies, fat-free cakes, fat-free cokes, fat-free chips, fat-free cheese. Fat-free cookies, cakes, cokes, chips, cheese. Fat-free. And I'm just getting fatter.

Diva Rachel lives out in Gilroy, California, garlic capital of the world. Everything in Gilroy is about garlic. They're even opening GarlicLand. It's a theme park! Rides on big ole cloves of garlic. They entice you with garlic-smothered morsels of food. Then, as you escape their clutch they hand you a gift bottle of mouthwash. "Oh mouthwash. Thanks. Is this fat-free? 'Cuz I've got to stay thin and sexy for Mac, my honey."

Why? How can you even tell what oh-so-skinny Mac likes?

"How you doing, Mac?"

"Purty good."

"How's work?"

"Good."

"How are the kids?"

"Fine."

Mac, you are incredibly in-ter-es-ting.

Mac's a dentist. Homeboy Mac is a bona fide dentist with a practice and everything. Beautiful hands that worked the land are working your teeth, twisting and turning, irrigating, implanting, building root canals. Quiet or not the *nalgona mandona* married well . . .

(*Music underscores.*)

By the time I arrived at Rachel's on that fateful December day, she has the table all laid out, corn husks washed, the masa mixed.

La Tamalada, spreading of the masa on a corn husk. Masa, tamale dough premade and available at: (*Using television commercial voice as music segues into Mariachi music.*) *Panadería La Mejor, La Calle Glendale Blvd. y Escott en Los Angeles, California.* (*Throws grito.*)

Diva Rachel is brave. Real brave. She decides she's going to make her *masa* from scratch.

Masa from scratch? This is unheard of by any standards. Only the most experienced tamal maker attempts the difficult feat of creating the perfect blend of ground corn, lime and fat. Is this a foolish attempt or a brilliant one? I who have been around masters of *masa* making, have to admit, am impressed.

Finally, my "Aunt Liz" arrives, the authority on everything . . . IBM retiree, spiritual advisor, golfer, elder. She walks into the kitchen sniffing. Something doesn't smell right. She heads straight for the masa like a warrior after her prey. Like Patton looking over plans for the Battle of the Bulge. She plucks a piece of *masa* dough and examines it. Everyone holds their breath.

"Masa, as you know, is the secret ingredient of the tamal. In my day if the masa wasn't right the tamales were ruined, a disgrace, a humiliation. You could not show your face for a year or they would stone you at Von's."

"People talk about you. Whisper behind your back. Did you hear the Esparza's tamales were dry. Secos! Will they ever get it right?"

I plead. "Aunt Liz, taste the *pinche masa,* already."

She tastes it.

"Rachel, Rachel. How much lard did you use? It tastes a little corny, Rachel."

"Ay, Tía. I didn't use lard. I used shortening."

"What do you mean you used shortening?"

"I couldn't bear to use lard. No one cooks with lard anymore. Do you know what it is?"

"Of course I know what it is."

"It's the fat of hogs melted down and clarified. I looked it up in the dictionary. What is the big deal, anyway? Can't you see I'm getting fatter by the minute. I have to do something."

"You're damn right you have to do something. You are defying tradition, woman. This recipe has been in our family for hundreds of years. But you can save yourself. There's still the second batch. Mac, go to Los Amigos Bakery and buy a pound of lard! *Manteca!*"

(*Romantic Mexican music underscores.*)

Señoras at the Guadalupana Market on Sunset Boulevard . . . in Echo Park . . . wearing their aprons and two bobby pins holding their jet-black hair back . . . buying slabs of white lard wrapped in plastic. And they go to their home at the Echo Arms Apartments and put chunks of that lard in their frying pan, melt it down, throw beans in the mix, produce a huge flame, fire ÁY ya! Refried beans. Tradition. *Tradición.* Wait a minute. Stop. Cut.

Let's think about this. Did the Aztecs use lard?

(*Aztec music plays.*)

"Popolitzli, por favor. Pass me the lard for my corn cakes. Corn cakes with lard, food of the Gods. *Tradición.* Tradition. *Tradición.*

O.K. Let's take a vote.

Who thinks the Aztecs used lard?

(*The audience responds.*)

Who thinks they didn't use lard?

(*The audience responds.*)

You people need to take a Chicano studies course.

So the debate continues.

Any vegetarians out there, you might want to skip this next part.

The ritual on the yellow Formica table was mesmerizing. The melted lard literally smelled like pig. Aunt Liz poured the clear substance into the *masa.* Sizzling pools formed. Rachel handed her a spoon. Aunt Liz shunned her.

"I don't need that."

And with her bare hands she carefully mixed the corn dough . . . kneading it every so carefully.

"This is how you make tamales," said the high priestess, my Aunt Liz, as the priestesses, my aunts y la Rachel looked on. *La tamalada* is reserved for the female. But when she breaks with tradition the wise diva priestess breaks in and sets her back on the right path.

Rachel was humiliated.

"Can't you people see I'm fat! How long are we going to perpetuate this madness. I'm trying to make things better, improve the quality of my life, and I get shot down like some *ranchera* in a bad channel 22 movie."

(*Melodramatically.*) "Callate mujer." (*Fake slap*)

"Te odio y te voy a matar. Te voy a matar!" (*Slap*) . . .

I knew how she felt. I'm a big girl, too. I'm always on a diet. I try not to eat too many *chicharrones.*

Every year, on the day of my elementary class pictures, I willed myself to be petite, small, frilly, and every year the photographer made me wait until the end and then he'd put me in the middle of the back row of my class picture, 'cuz I was the biggest.

So, Diva, honey, sweetie, darling, doll, I know how you're feeling. All of us who've struggled on the path to Divadom, know how you're feeling.

So, just take a Tylenol and sit on anyone you don't like.

Finally, the tamales were done. And out of loyalty, I kept my mouth shut. Me and Rachel ate the not-even-close-to-fat-free tamales and everyone else, all 59 of my lard-eating relatives ate the loaded-with-fat ones. I have to admit when Rachel wasn't looking I sneaked into the kitchen and grabbed one of Aunt Liz's tamales. And they were so much better. Oh my god, grease is good.

My Aunts Lupe, Vickie and Sally chimed in: "Liz, you were so right. I don't know what got into Rachel. Too much Oprah. Too much Oprah! You know mother always made tamales with lard. They'd just roll off the husk and onto your plate. They were so good. Liz, you were so right."

Rachel was fuming at who she called "the wicked witches of San Jose." Aunt Liz looked quietly on.

"Excuse me. Excuse me. For your information, my chubby little tamales are artery friendly, ok? I thought you all might appreciate that. But I was sadly mistaken. And must I remind you this is my *tamalada*? Everyone repeat after me, *my tamalada.* It was my idea to bring this family together. Mine. No one else seems to care *when* or *if* we see each other. 'Cuz everyone's always too busy talking about each other's fat *nalgas* to notice who's lonely, who's sick, who needs some friendly advice or any advice at all. Uh, I give up. I'm gonna go into the kitchen and stuff my fat face. Low-fat tamales!"

Aunt Liz stopped her.

"Mija, mija don't be mad. I have to admit I sneaked into the kitchen and I tried one of your tamales and they were (*beats her chest*) good. A little secos, dry, but good. Congratulations. Congratulations. Now, I want you to eat one of mine. It will not kill you, but make you feel whole."

And at that moment the room stood still. No one moved. A pall of silence filled the air. We watched as the High Priestess, Aunt Liz, took la Rachel into the Temple of the Kitchen and handed her one lone sacrificial tamal.

Slowly, reluctantly, surprisingly, Rachel took a bite as Aunt Liz chanted.

"*Mija, mija.* Eat. Taste our hands, our love, our history and that which comes from the earth, from the pig. Feel it in your thighs, *tus piernas,* your *nalgas,* your *tetas.* Let our history live."

And as Rachel tasted of the holy food I saw with mine own eyes a crown descend from the grease-splattered ceiling and she became in front of all of us *la Diva Royal.*

"Say it, girl." I said. "Say it."

And Diva Rachel proclaimed.

"I'm a sexy, bossy, *nalgona, mandona,* big ole hips and thunder thighs.
Hug me and get lost in the softness of my 40 DDs . . ."

> Women, why do we shrink ourselves, make ourselves small,
> wrap ourselves, hide ourselves . . .
> Some women move it forward, others move it back.
> We are the priestesses of *la cultura.*

We are the keepers of the tradition.
La cultura. La Culture is an every-changing,
ever-growing big ole woman. La Culture is a woman.

Notes

1. The Playwright/La Dramaturga section is compiled from Diane Rodriguez, e-mail correspondence with the editors, November 4, 11, and 16, 2009, and from the playwright's responses to editors' biographical questionnaire, August 28, 2002. See also Elizabeth C. Ramírez, *Chicanas/Latinas in American Theatre: A History of Performance* (Bloomington: Indiana University Press, 2000), 94 and 144.
2. Diane Rodriguez, revised responses to editors' biographical questionnaire.
3. Diane Rodriguez, playwright's notebook, January 14, 2007.

CHAPTER 4

A Playwright's Many Voices

Yareli Arizmendi's *Who Buys Your Shoes?* (ca. 1989)

Yareli Arizmendi, by permission of the photographer, Joaquin Sedillo.

The Playwright/La Dramaturga

Yareli Arizmendi was born in the Ciudad de México (Mexico City) on April 24, 1964.[1] The story of her family origins is best told in her own words:

> My father was born from a Basque–Nueva España father and a 100% Mestiza mother. My paternal grandfather's family came from the Basque Country in the 1700s and settled in Guanajuato. Judging from the crypts that bear their names in the central cathedral, they became one of the powerfully rich families in one of the most important colonial cities. My grandmother, born in Celaya, Guanajuato, was the butcher's daughter. The soap opera ensued when they fell in love (class-racial struggle and all) and eloped. I think they then formalized their vows and led a very Catholic (bordering on Opus Dei-ish life). My father was raised in Guadalajara, Jalisco. He pulled himself up by his own bootstraps and moved to Mexico City, studied medicine, became a successful surgeon, and eventually a renowned psychoanalyst. He met my mother in the big city. But she didn't start out there.

She continues:

> My mother is Cuban—born in Galicia, Spain, and transplanted to Havana at the age of two. My grandmother was born in the Canary Islands, and my grandfather in La Coruña, Galicia. They met in Cuba after a first marriage that left both of them widowed. They married, had three daughters and at a time when the Spanish Republic appeared to be a possibility, my grandfather took the family back to Spain. That's when my mother was born. Two years later, Franco's men were looking for my grandfather, who quickly jumped on a ship back to Havana with the whole family. As a university student my mother was offered a scholarship to Paris or Mexico. In her words, she chose Mexico "because of the pyramids and Pedro Infante [famous actor of the golden age of Mexican cinema and singer]." That's when she met my father. Their firstborn, my brother, was born in 1960 and he is named Fidel. My name—Yareli—was my mother's creation. She combined her

name "Aralia" with "Yara"—the call for independence of Cuba known as "The call of Yara." It marked my life for good.

Yareli's education includes a Bachelor of Arts degree in political science with a minor in theatre and a Master of Fine Arts degree in theatre with a specialization in dramaturgy from the University of California, San Diego.

Yareli Arizmendi's extensive film and stage career goes hand-in-hand with her written work. Her work is at once entertaining and political. With both her Cuban and her Spanish lineages, this Mexican-born artist who has resided in the United States since 1983 provides a unique perspective with her "binational, bicultural reality," as she describes it. Perhaps best known for her performances on film, she had a starring role in the popular and critically acclaimed Mexican film, *Like Water for Chocolate,* and more recently, she collaborated with her director-musician husband, Sergio Arau, in writing, producing, and starring in the "mockumentary," *A Day Without a Mexican,* a much-talked-about documentary about a day in which all Latinos disappear from the State of California.

About the Play/Sobre la Obra

For this playtext the playwright provides a distinctive preface that describes the setting, the characters, and her intention with this piece before the play begins. The result is a sort of production promptbook, which illustrates the method this playwright uses in creating her work, namely, functioning as the playwright, director, and the actor in the piece. We have retained her playtext in its original form because of the value we have placed throughout on reading the playwright "in her own words."

Similar to the other playwrights in this book who strive to broaden their audience's view of the Latina/Latino experience in the United States through performance, Arizmendi has written numerous works that utilize an ironic tone reminiscent of what characterizes the *acto* technique, that is, short pieces filled with humorous satire that abruptly hit the spectator with stark political and social commentary while embedded within serious feminist issues.

In *Who Buys Your Shoes?* this dramatic-comedic "monologue for six" is conceived for one female actor who interacts with the audience through five different characters. The style is presentational and runs the gamut from comic to tragic, allowing the performer to display a wide range of emotions. This short work shows the skills that Arizmendi brings to the stage with her background in actor-training, using a kind of interior monologue that she has brought to life as she physically steps into the shoes of five different women, and thus, five distinct experiences.

This work would serve any female actor well because of the demands it places on the performer: one actor portraying an actor who becomes a chubby teenage Chicana girl, a pregnant teen who had thought of becoming a gynecologist but instead pursues fulfilling her dream of a family and marriage, a Chicana lesbian and rape survivor, a successful Puerto Rican thirtysomething professional who goes from a wealthy upbringing to dire poverty when she is thrown out of the house by her father, eventually succeeding on her own; and culminating with the narrator becoming politicized as she steps into the shoes of a "mature woman of eleven" who was born and perishes in the midst of the Nicaraguan Contra theatre of war.

Artistic Vision/Punto de Vista Artístico

ECR & CRC: Briefly describe your theatre experience. How did you decide to write and/or perform?[2]

YA: I started dancing at the age of four. As expected, my first theatrical experiences were in musical theatre. Soon I grew uneasy with the idea of prancing happily ever after on stage (as most musicals require) while the world was burning up. My declared double major in college was economics and nutrition—on my watch we would eradicate hunger and malnutrition. But I bumped into Dr. Jorge Huerta and enrolled in his Chicano Theatre Ensemble class playing Somoza's lover in *La Llamada,* a play by John Herschel-Dobles dealing with the downfall of the Nicaraguan dictator. During the semester, Teatro Campesino put out a call for a summer workshop. When I asked "Who is Luis Valdez?" Dr. Huerta jumped. "He's the creator of *Zoot Suit!* I'd pay to work with him, you should go." I confess, I still had no idea who Luis Valdez was, but one can not ignore Dr. Huerta's command! My experience with Teatro Campesino and Luis Valdez himself immediately led to a tour of Nicaragua with Teatro de la Esperanza during the first Sandanista elections (1984) and the Reagan reelections. It was clear that politics-economics and theatre could very well live together and work toward the same objectives. It was then I started to write original work and perform it myself or with ensembles created for that purpose. I haven't stopped since, although the genres and mediums have varied.

ECR & CRC: Why do you write what you do?

YA: My passion is acting. Interpreting reality in an attempt to expose an angle of the "same old story" the audience had not considered. Concerned with an individual's responsibility to the larger social reality and vice versa, I found that many of my concerns and perspectives were not being written about. I tried to create politically charged work with others (collective creation theater). It was not an easy task to get a group to commit and concentrate on creating work that would result in an actual play delivered before an audience, when the ideological fights erupted. It was exciting, but not very productive. That's what made me sit down at my kitchen table, take pen and paper in hand, and start writing. I would call on the group when I had something clear and ready for them to join. At times, I called on myself as the sole actress. The freedom that gave me was fantastic: performance art and one-woman shows became a very dynamic and immediate venue for me.

ECR & CRC: Who do you write for and what audience are you trying to reach?

YA: I think at first a writer sets out to reach everyone. It is hard to understand why others would not be interested and able to "get" what one wants to share. As an actor, armed only with the writer's words and one's interpretive quality, you feel yourself connecting or, what's worse, not connecting with the audience. In an attempt to make sense of the experience, you dissect it: Was the material over their heads, too long, too fast, too boring, confusing. To hold postperformance discussions is invaluable because it shows you that your intention and an audience's interpretation at times are completely different and sometimes right on. One either rejoices in that or becomes a control freak about it, giving the audience little room for interpretation. I want an audience to "get it," but yet be completely surprised by what they are feeling as they intellectually "get" the rational story. I seek an audience that has been disenfranchised, an audience whose story has not been told or has been misrepresented. I seek to provoke discussion; open the window into a room people knew existed, but had no idea where. My ideal audience does not run from intelligent discussion, facts or books, but above all it does not run away from emotions. My ideal audience has a tiny space in their brain forever tied to their heart; a little space that believes we can change the world.

ECR & CRC: What message, if any, are you trying to convey to your audience with this work and/or with all of your work?

YA: In the piece *Who Buys Your Shoes?* I call on the cornerstone of empathy "Put yourself in their shoes" to weave five different women's realities together, while reaching out to the audience and inviting them to walk in their shoes. In Latin America, Mexico specifically, the importance of shoes is paramount. An Indian goes barefoot or wears *guaraches,* but a civilized member of society wears shiny, clean, and well-mended shoes. Obviously, my own obsession with shoes prompted me to explore this silent, but loudly visual code of social placement. The device proved visually interesting for the audience to identify and follow the characters throughout. The monologues themselves explore how these characters wound up in their particular shoes; social, historical, and personal profiles if you will. My intent was to personalize historical circumstances and thus provide the audience with a glimpse into the minds of real people making choices within those conditions dealt to them.

ECR & CRC: Who or what has been your major influence?

YA: I can't point to one huge "Aha!" artist or moment. I can provide a list, though: *A Tale of Two Cities, Jesus Christ Superstar,* Antonio Gramsci, Cherríe Moraga, Les Luthiers, Jose Rivera, Luis Alfaro, García Lorca . . .

ECR & CRC: What has been your biggest and/or most difficult struggle/challenge in life, in completing a play or getting it produced, etc.?

YA: In life, I'd say my biggest challenge happened while I wasn't looking. Surviving a potentially paralyzing, damaging childhood, adolescence allowed me to find power through creating. At times I found myself in absolute isolation, with only my mind to keep sane. Forced to reach into the depths of my imagination to survive I found my creativity . . . my words, my views, my music. I didn't see it then, but that certainly charted my way into the arts and social activism.

ECR & CRC: Can you offer any words of advice to aspiring playwrights/performers/directors/audiences?

YA: Aside from honing one's craft, I think artists forget to actively search for their "band of thieves"; their tribe with whom the journey of idea to execution of your work will become a reality. While in training, keep your eyes wide open. Of your fellow students, whose words would you want to interpret? What performer "gets" your vision? Whose work sends you in a direction you had never thought of before? Make friends and nourish the friendship. It's a long road ahead . . .

ECR & CRC: If you studied with Maria Irene Fornes, please provide dates, place, and any commentary you wish to add about her impact on your work.

YA: I never formally studied with Maria Irene Fornes. The first time I heard of her work was in playwriting class when we read *Mud.* I was taken aback. At the time I was at a very politically militant stage of my writing and performing; very outward if you will. *Mud* was an intense, quiet peek into human behavior. And it was a woman writing this way. I would slowly come to understand her, since her images and words haunted me. Later, when I worked with her at South Coast Rep during a workshop of one of her plays, I watched this insightful woman open roads in my mind where I had not taken the time to go. "Layered" is how I would describe her; her writing as well as the woman she was.

Production History/Palabras Dramatúrgicas

The first performance of the English version of the play was at University of California, San Diego Cabaret, circa 1989, performed by Karen Sanchez and directed by Jim Peck. Yareli tells us: "Later that same year I performed it at the Festival de la Raza sponsored by the Mexican government in collaboration with San Diego City entities at the Tijuana Cultural Center. Funny trivia: I had recently met Laura Esquivel (writer of *Like Water for Chocolate*) and she was on her book tour in the United States. When she came to San Diego I invited her to the opening of my play, *Who Buys Your Shoes?* at UCSD! She liked it very much." Of course, Yareli ended up working with Esquivel for the film version of her work.

Contact Information

www.yareli.com

WHO BUYS YOUR SHOES?

The play is conceived for one female actor. Set and props are limited to five pairs of shoes scattered on the playing area, a chair and lighting when available. This dramatic/comedic monologue for five characters begins with the actor interacting with the audience and establishing the convention of the play: "You are your shoes." As the actor tells her story, she introduces friends and their tales, weaving one story into the next to paint a wide picture of women's experiences. There is Chela, the spunky teenager who "wished and wished she was Olivia Newton-John." Then comes Lizie, who's waiting to get her share of life "in love coins." Next is Luchi with a chilling story of rape that led her to drastic conclusions. After her comes Whitney with her explanation of why she joined the Corporate Ladder Hikers Club. Last is Norma, wishing she could have "risked more for the revolution." Intertwined with these five stories is the story of the actor, a story that is not finished: like the lives of the spectators, her story remains to be written.

Who Buys Your Shoes? establishes a dialogue recognizing both the validity and the limitations of personal experience as an absolute gauge by which to judge the world. It hopes to encourage individuals to try on other people's shoes, share their own, and join in the crafting of an entirely different line of footwear.

Characters

A monologue for six characters: One actor portraying five characters, namely, Chela, Lizie, Luchi, Whitney, and Norma, and herself.

Setting

Five pairs of shoes are strategically positioned throughout the stage. Along with a chair, they constitute the entire set and props for the piece. Designed lighting would greatly enhance the piece, but the absence of lighting equipment should not be an obstacle for the presentation of this play.

The female actor mingles with the audience prior to starting time. At a designated moment she takes the stage.

I have a little secret to share with you. (*Starts to take off her shoes, socks, etc.*) Something a little shocking and quite serious: I was born barefoot. Yes, really! (*Directing questions at specific audience members and waiting for their response.*) Were you? What about you? You too? So how come you all have shoes now? Excuse me, who bought your shoes? (*Ad lib responses to audience comments.*) And yours? Your Daddy? Well, isn't that nice. Actually most of us got our first pair of shoes from our parents, I mean you probably didn't get to pick them out. But what about the ones you are wearing tonight? Well, that's our story for today.

(*Deliberate pause; look around.*)

You see I have this theory: You are your shoes. *You are your shoes.* Makes sense? Of course it makes sense! Well, I'm going to tell you how I got into my shoes; actually out of them. But first let me expand on my theory. You see, as an actor I learned that the most distinguishing trait of any character was the way they walked (*demonstrates by reacting as an Old Lady, then a "lady of the night"*)—you get the point. So the sooner you figured out what kind of shoes your character wore, the faster you get into the character itself. I think that's also true for people in real life. So today, while I tell you my story, I'll introduce you to some of my friends and their shoes.

Ok. I promised to tell you how I got out of my shoes and into these actor's feet. When I was young I used to be really, I mean really scared of the dentist, so when I played with my dolls I'd pretend *I was* the dentist. "Let's see, I think you need to have all of your top teeth extracted. Nurse! Prepare 25 shots of anesthetic for this patient." Well now, any Freudian worth their couch could tell you I was "projecting" my fears. I guess I was . . . and it worked! I got through the orthodontist without too much permanent trauma—see (*smiles broadly*)—perfect teeth! Chela (*as she steps into the first pair of shoes*) used to play a similar game, only hers was a little bit more serious.

(*Transition into CHELA, a chubby teenage Chicana girl.*)

All my life I wished and wished I was Olivia Newton-John. You know, with her beautiful blonde hair, sparkling blue eyes. She is so skinny and looks great with those tight black satin pants. Oh and her voice, gorgeous high C's. (*Singing as high as she can and imitating Olivia's style.*) "I love you, I honestly love you. I'm not trying to make you feel uncomfortable, I'm not trying to make you anything at all, but these . . . (*Her voice cracks.*) Shit! I pray to God and to the Virgin and nothing. Every morning I rush to the mirror to check if my totally straight, jet-black hair has turned sunstroke blonde, and nothing. My eyes are still brown, "The color of shit," like stupid Stevie Baker said in fifth grade. And my hips, my stupid hippo hips. There is no way I'm ever going to be able to wear those kinds of pants with my hippo hips. I remember my mother trying to tell me that I'd grow up to have the kind of body that drives men crazy, "Shaped like a guitar," she said. That's all well and good, but they don't make black satin pants for guitars, now do they! And my voice, I sound like a boy! One day a friend of my parents asked me to sing along with him: (*"Te solté la rienda" a Mexican Ranchera song that requires a deep, melodic voice.*) "Se me acabó la fuerza de la mano izquierda, voy a dejarte el mundo para ti solito. Como al caballo blanco le solté la rienda, a ti también te suelto y te me vas ahorita." He tells my mom: "Oye Prieta, the next Lucha Villa's been born." Lucha Villa, Lucha Villa, oh great! They don't even know her in Hollywood! So I decided to take things into my own hands, you know, "take control of your life" like those positive-thinking books say. I set a routine for myself: Every night I soak in the bath tub and scrub hard with a loofah for at least 45 minutes. I'm sure the dirt will come out eventually. I can't buy hair dye, 'cause my mom would find out, but I heard beer is supposed to lighten up your hair, so twice a week I sneak one of my Dad's beers and soak my hair for about an hour. I'm still not sure what to do about my eyes: I can wear sunglasses forever, make it my gimmick, sort of like Elton John, remember him? Or maybe I'll just wait till I save enough money to buy those color contact lenses like they advertise in *Tiger Beat* and *Seventeen.* And the most important thing: Every night, while I soak in the tub, I vocalize. Efficient heh? (*Pause; taking herself in.*) Why didn't it work?

(*Transition back to "Actor."*)

Chela is doing Ok. She's still working through the trauma, but working. (*Taking off shoes.*) She dances folklórico and has her own dance company. (*Showing shoes to the audience.*) She certainly doesn't need these to dance the Jarabe Tapatio (*mocks a za-*

pateado). By the way, she got tickets to an Olivia Newton-John concert and met Olivia's hairdresser—"Clairol #9," he said.

There is another game I used to play right about the time I had two of my teeth pulled out: Mother. Not that one has anything to do with the other . . . well, come to think of it maybe there are some similarities. You see, my mother had just had my younger brother. We didn't have much room in the house, so his crib was in our room and I got to watch how you take care of babies. Well, I thought I knew what to do, all I needed was a baby! No, I didn't go out and get pregnant; come on I was ten or eleven . . . although you know it happens now a days, don't you. Anyway, I picked out my favorite doll and went all out. I mean all out: I gave birth—painful delivery I might add—I bought myself flowers, made a mini-crib and set the alarm clock for feeding—1:00, 3:00 and 5:00 am. Needless to say, the baby starved after the first two days. But you know I felt special. I started to really like being a girl. For once we could do something boys couldn't. I hadn't told anybody about my game. I wanted to tell my best friend Lizie, but she told me first. She told me about the birth, the feedings, the diapers, the thrill of knowing boys would never be able to do this. I think she liked it more than I, at least I hope she did. Five years later she met Salvador. I was at her wedding, you should have seen her dress, every girl's dream; and she was so skinny! She looked perfect. Then I saw her again. She'd put on a few pounds and traded her satin pumps for something more comfortable (*as she slips into the second pair of shoes*). She looked happy, yeah, she did.

(*Transition to Lizie, who is very pregnant. She looks happy and peaceful; the look of someone who's chosen and chosen well.*)

No, I didn't *have to* get married—it wasn't like that at all. At least not because of this (*touches her belly*). My parents had been hunting for a "suitable husband" for me. My grandmother married at 13, my mother at 14, so to them I was almost an old maid at 15. I was still in school. I was thinking of becoming a doctor, a gynecologist. But then I met Chava, (*smiles*) he was nice. You know what he did for my birthday—he sent me a red rose every day for 15 days and then, on the 16th, he sent me 15 red roses with one white rose in the middle: "Love and loyalty," he said. I could live with that. Sure, I'd miss school, but there I was only one more smart girl, not that that's bad, but it sort of seemed like anyone could be smart . . . it wasn't special. Not that I expected marriage would suddenly make me all that special, but it could help me get something that would. You see, ever since they showed us that film strip, you know, *Your Growing Body* in 6th grade, I wanted a baby real bad. Can you imagine, a person growing inside you. Think about it: a tiny person inside you and you are helping them get started. They're eating your food, breathing your air, they're sleeping inside you. And then comes the day of the birth, sort of like this new person is putting on their coat and hat and saying, "Thanks for the stay, nice bed, the food was great. See you soon." (*Lizie feels a slight labor pain.*) Real soon. And they're gone, on their own, but they don't forget the debt, they pay you back—in love coins. In love coins that just keep coming, in love coins that dent the earth reminding everyone you didn't just take, you gave, you mattered . . . in love coins, the strongest currency on the market.

(*Transition back to "Actor."*)

Next time I saw Lizie was the day Lizie Jr. was born. Lizie looked great, oh, let's use the cliché: She glowed! She asked me what I was up to and I told her about the college applications, the entrance exams. "So you are going to med school," she said. "Maybe I'll wait for the next one (*touching her belly*) till you can deliver her." (*Taking Lizie's shoes off.*) She was still wearing these old shoes, "They're comfortable," she said. I just laughed . . . she looked so . . . she glowed.

Lizie had her second child, and her third, but I never made it to med school. So what about my story? Let's see, I got over the orthodontist, and after being declared an unfit mother by the Council of Dolls, I fell right into my next traumatic experience—boys—and I've never recovered since. I didn't date too much throughout school, partly because of my parents, but mostly it was me. I didn't want to just be somebody's pretty prize and it seemed boys were into carrying trophies, so I stayed away from the tournaments. Except for Alex, but well, he was different. Anyway, it's all so complicated I thought of forgetting the whole "Men's scene." (*Slips into the third pair of shoes.*) My friend Luchi really did.

(*Transition to Luchi, an 18- to 20-year-old Chicana. She is uncomfortable in her body and fidgets a lot. She is rash in attitude and tone.*)

You know how they talk about it in the movies? Well, it's nothing like that, not even like the soaps, at least I didn't think so. Of course, I was a little young the first time, and the last time's been a while, but *no*body is going to convince me otherwise, *no* way. I bet you want to know how it happened, but I'm not going to tell you . . . maybe I should, not for me but for you. Maybe I can be a good Samaritan and save a soul. Well, I was eleven or twelve, what's that, 5th or 6th grade? I still don't call it by its rightful name, but like that theatre dude said, what's in a name, right?

So I get home from school one day and no one's there yet. And I make a mad dash for the freezer and sneak a whopping scoop of the ice cream I'm not supposed to have. Just as I'm licking the last of the bowl, this man, a friend of my dad's, knocks on the door and invites himself in. He says he's fixing some kitchen light my mom asked him to check out, which sounds weird to me, but what am I supposed to say, "Man, man go away, come again another day?" He had a screwdriver in his hand and he looked pretty ready to work. I want to leave, but the minute I move he says, "Me ayudas?" And well, I'm a good little Mexican girl who can't say no, right? He says he needs someone with small hands to pull the wires that are stuck inside this hole he is about to unscrew. So he wants me to stand on this chair and reach. And I get on the chair and I look into the hole, but I don't see no wires. He tells me to keep looking. Suddenly I feel his hands on my legs, "Para que no te caigas," me dice and I, toda nice "Thanks, I don't think I'll fall though." And I keep trying to find these wires, and I'm looking as hard as I can, and he keeps touching my legs . . . a little higher each time. I feel my head getting dizzy and my cheeks are burning, like with a fever. And I start wishing my mother would get home, but then I think about the ice cream bowl; I was going to wash it, but then this man came and . . . the screwdriver is right on my leg . . . (*Lets out a gasp.*) It's touching me there. He says, "No te muevas, ya casi terminamos." And all I can say is "Hurry, my mother's going to be home soon." I know he's going to push the thing up me. And I start trembling, and I want to cry, "Please God, I won't cheat on my homework or sneak on the ice cream ever again." He pulls my chones down, then I hear the screwdriver hit the floor. Please get this over with, just get it over with; I close my eyes and hope that when I open them someone will tell me it was all a dream. But then he does it, he shoves the damn thing up me and now I know for sure it's a nightmare. All I can see is the hole in the wall where the wires were supposed to be, while something is in me, digging inside me, sort of like my hands in that hole looking for the wires. But there is nothing there, just a hole . . . just a hole.

(*Transition back to "Actor."*)

Luchi is living with Silvia now. I mean not just living with Silvia, but living (*implying lesbianism*) with Silvia. We drifted apart, not just 'cause of Silvia, but . . . well, I tried to understand her, but you know, the whole thing was too weird! I don't think I was too helpful at the time. I wish I had been. Maybe I was a little scared. What if Luchi's answer was the right answer? (*Taking Luchi's shoes off.*) Talk about changing shoes! I mean, I had been through rough times with boys (*correcting herself*) excuse me, men—well, more boys than men—, and I had come to surprising conclusions of my own, but did it have to be that drastic?

About that time I met Whitney, Wit for short. She was intelligent, funny, beautiful and alone. She was the prototype dress-for-success woman of the 80s. While she was making serious, and I do mean *serious* money, I was starving double-time: mornings at the university and nights at the theatre. While she was ordering more bombs and missiles, I was joining the Committee Against Global Militarization. She was the first woman president of General Deathnamics nuclear parts division. That's why we met: I was at the picket line. (*Yells out the chants.*) "Bread not Bombs." "No Nukes," and she was the company spokesperson assigned to deal with the "unamerican ragtag rabble rousers." I'm not sure why she picked me, but she invited me to her office to (*putting on a Yuppie voice*) "interface, chat a little, network." We "compared notes" on the nuclear build-up, the meaning of socially responsible growth, what a "nice girl like me" was doing involved with those hippies—"Join the Yuppies!" she said. It was a little too much to take. (*Slips into the fourth pair of shoes.*) Just as I got up to leave, she stopped me cold (*stomps her pump on the floor*): She was going to talk to me straight.

(*Transition to Whitney, a Puerto Rican executive woman in her 30s. She's quick with language and hides behind it in a creative way.*)

You remind me so much of myself years ago, you know. I like you, I like what you do. (*Pause. She decides to open up.*) I guess there was one good reason for joining the Corporate Ladder Hikers Club: My father. Yes, of course there was the money, and the power, but it wasn't the money or the power. Well, actually yes, it was the money and the power, but not because of the money and the power, but because of what money and power can buy. (*Pauses; gauges the effect.*) Oh sorry, I was going to give it to you straight. In brief: Whitney Susana Thompson Buendia had a shitty childhood. Now we all know Cinderella. (*Mockingly, making light of what she is saying.*) Once upon a time, in a place . . . very close by, there lived a mean, mean tyrant: Whitney's father! Iron Hand was his name, but they called him Iron for short. Well, after killing Whitney's mother—actually after driving her to kill herself, he found himself another wife; one certified by the United States Import-Export Department: Snow Blonde. Blondie had two children of her own and guess what? You got it! They didn't like Whitney. Neither did Blondie for that matter, but Iron had decreed that his was a *happy* family, so everyone had to smile and smile and smile—of course they used "Colgate." Whitney didn't mind smiling as long as they left her alone to play with her toys. It was all well and good, but as Whitney grew older, Blondie, jealous and afraid that Whitney would remind Iron of his beautiful first wife, wished Whitney gone. Of course she couldn't say so out right, so . . . Blondie started plotting. She told Iron that Whitney was "acting up" and "giving her dirty looks." She said Whitney was being mean to her little brothers and that if he really cared for their family he should punish her. Iron reprimanded Whitney just to prove his love for Blondie, but this wasn't enough. So Blondie went and made up a big story: "I hate to be the one to tell you, but it's got to be said: Your Whitney is stealing money from the castle to pay for the 'slutty' makeup she wears with her 'sleazy' friends. And not only that, noooo: She's started smoking and (*thrusting her hips*) with the local druggies; for all we know she just might be pregnant." *Well,* Iron Hand was enraged: How dare anyone stain his honor; how dare anyone misbehave in the kingdom. Blinded by the rage and by Blondie's lies he summoned Whitney. (*A transformation slowly develops; we can tell Whitney is now really talking about herself.*) Of course he never asked Whitney if all these things were true. Well I mean, he did ask, but he had a whip in one hand and Blondie at his side. What could Whitney say? She did try to tell her story: No, she had not stolen any money; Yes, she tried her friend's mascara; no, she had not been dirty dancing with the boys; and No, she was definitely not pregnant.

(*Imitating Iron's voice in an attempt to return to storytelling.*)

"Oh, so I suppose your step-mother is lying?"

"No, well, yes, I mean.—"

"What!"

He cracked the whip and came closer, then raised his hand and let it drop on my back. He was out of control. It was one blow after the other—one, two, three, four, five. I was crying but he couldn't hear. He kept hitting me and hitting me and I yelled "Daddy stop, please listen, stop, stop, please Daddy!!" I stopped pleading. I couldn't tell when he finally stopped. All I could see was my body curled up like a little black and blue fuzz ball in the basement corner . . . paralyzed. (*Down on her knees, starts to take off one pump shoe.*) He told me to get out, "You disgust me, just get out!" Snow Blonde was watching, smiling.

"Can I stay here till tomorrow?"

"What's tomorrow?"

"Well, I could get my money from the bank tomorrow?"

"How much do you have?"

"Thirty dollars."

"Slut."

(*Rising to her feet and using the shoe in her hand.*) He slapped me across the face, but I didn't even feel it, he threw thirty dollars at me . . . and that hurt. Then he grabbed my hair and pushed me out the door and on to the street. I didn't know where to go, so I just stood there, spent the night there . . . like frozen. Next day he sent a man to take me to the bus station, that's the last I saw of home, of friends. Suddenly there I was, with an envelope of instructions pinned to a thick coat. I felt so dirty, so tricked, so *powerless*, so . . . so nothing. I didn't know where I was going, what was going to happen to me. Of course, I wasn't eighteen to decide that . . . and thirty dollars couldn't take me far. Just a black and blue fuzz ball being swept out of hell. I promised my aching body and my ripped out heart we would never, *ever* feel like that again, NEVER. What's the good of truth, honesty, principle, *reason*, when you have no way to make it count? So you see, between being right and being powerful, I (*appraises her surroundings*) . . . Now they call me Iron Wit.

(*Transition back to "Actor."*)

I didn't leave . . . well, not right away. The story sounded so . . . so familiar. No it was more than that, it was real; it was me eight years ago. I wondered if that meant I'd be like Whitney ten years from now. I wondered if I'd forget all the things I'd promised: To make the world a better place to live in; Power to the People; For the good of the majority. What if the majority turned their back on me. Would the majority feed me, would they take me in? The majority didn't even know who I was! No, I don't think Whitney was right, bombing the majority is not the best way to introduce yourself. I felt sorry for her, her shoes looked quite uncomfortable (*taking the remaining high-heeled pump off; drops it*) and they were, but she bought them herself, yep, all two hundred and fifty dollars' worth of alligator skin. You see, that's what I can't excuse: two hundred and fifty dollars for a pair of shoes when there are all these people . . . well I'm sure you know what kind of trouble our world is in. Maybe you don't, I didn't really know myself until an eleven-year-old girl told me. Yeah, an eleven-year-old woman. And I had to travel far to find her. It wasn't so much the distance in miles, but the distance in *minds*. There I was in my not-so-comfy—so I thought—college room, when I get a phone call. (*Mimes the phone with the pump.*) "Hello? Yes, this is she, aha, aha, aha. Would I be interested?! Sure! When, where? In two weeks, . . . Nicaragua. Nicaragua? There's a war going on down there! Oh, God, I'll have to think about that, I mean . . . Oh God. I'll get back to you, ok?" Nicaragua! A *theatre festival* in Nicaragua and they wanted me for the touring company?! Crazier things have happened, I couldn't think what, but I called back, said yes, and in two weeks I was landing at the airport of that burning piece of earth the size of Idaho. Smack in the middle of history and the daily news. But I'm not going to do the talking, (*she slips into the fifth pair of shoes*) I'll let Norma fill you in.

(*Transition to Norma, a playful, mature woman of eleven.*)

I was born in a war. I don't really remember all of them—my family was pretty big and I was pretty small. I know three of my brothers had already been killed by the time I was six. No one told me that, but I listened:

"What's wrong Mami?"

"Nothing."

I learned to tell when "nothing" meant no news and when "nothing" meant death. I didn't see Papi a lot, he was busy . . . real busy. "He's important," Mami used to say "He doesn't have time for little girls like you." But he made time. One night he snuck home real late. He was standing over me, just watching me. You know how you can feel when someone's watching you? Well I opened my eyes and there was Papi! I could see Mami through the little curtain that divided the room; she was crying, she always did when it was dark. Papi sat me on his lap and I told him about how me and my favorite friend Luli helped Mami fetch the water and grind the corn. "That's good m'hija. I want you to promise me you'll always take care of your mother." "I'll take care of you too!" I said. He hugged me real tight, almost squeezing me. I was going to say something, but he was crushing me. I hugged him back as hard as I could. That was the last time I saw Papi. Two weeks later I asked Mami, "What's wrong?" "*Nothing,*" she said. Luli heard her brother say Papi was a hero, that he held out to the end. Held out. He knew many names, they said. Names? Killed for holding out names? My mother didn't cry; she scared me, she was so serious. Almost like . . . dead. She told me we had to move to a neighboring town the next day.

"Can Luli come too?"

"No."

But the next day was too late. I remember the guards that night. They didn't knock, just came right in and started barking, really it sounded like dogs barking—they were so loud! Mami grabbed me and picked up Quique; their guns were looking straight into our heads. One of them yelled, "Give the baby to the girl." Mami just stood there. "I said, give the bastard to the girl, bitch." I took Quiquito from her and the minute I did, another one hit her on the back. I saw her fall and went to help, but the third guard pointed his rifle at me and Quique. I just stood there. They were beating Mami in the face . . . in the chest . . . in the stomach. Then the chief guard started talking.

"Look, I don't like beating women. I was born from a woman myself. The only thing we want is for you to tell us what you know."

"I don't know anything," she said.

"Well maybe this will remind you."

They started ripping off her dress and calling her names. The chief guard had his gun right on her throat. I was screaming for them to stop, but then one of them slapped me real hard and I thought I better keep quiet 'cause I might get them angrier and they'll hit Mami harder. Two of them were holding her arms and legs. She was all naked. And then the chief slid his gun from her throat to her belly, well not really her belly, but I don't know what you call that. He was hurting her—she was screaming so loud and they just kept on hurting her. Then they started saying Papi's name: (*painfully slow*) "Miguel Buendia . . . he was tough, but we broke him. We'll break you just as easy. You see, we start with your fingernails, then your fingers, then maybe your ears, then . . ." I must have fainted then, 'cause the next time I opened my eyes I was in Luli's house. Quiquito was there, but Mami wasn't. I was going to ask where she was, but then Luli hugged me real tight and I knew. I'm sorry, Papi, I know I promised, but there was nothing I could do.

I knew Luli's brother didn't like Tacho's guards, so I told him I didn't either and if there was something I could do.

"Are you sure?" he asked.

"Real sure."

"Alright, Compañerita."

My first assignment was to deliver a package to the bottom of the second hill. Someone would come get it when it was dark. They didn't say what was in the box, but I figured it was ammunition 'cause they told me not to shake it. Then I started delivering messages. We used to make a big ball of dough and stick the paper in the middle. It wasn't long till the word was out: Tachito and his guards had given up. I wished you could've been here! I wished I'd been able to do more for the revolution, but now we have a whole country to build and I'll have plenty of time.

(*Transition back to "Actor."*)

I never saw Norma again. I wrote, but I'm sure the letters never got there. I was living in a country that didn't like Norma's smile, her laughter. But a letter from Luli made it through the hatred curtain and I'm not sure I was glad to get it: Norma, my eleven year old woman, the builder of tomorrows was dead. Well no, not just dead: murdered, ambushed on the road to Matagalpa. Returned, (*she takes off shoes*) barefoot, to the earth, dust to dust . . .

Luli asked me to deliver this letter: (*takes out the letter from her pocket; read with Actor's voice*) I had a friend, Mr. President. My favorite friend. But you know what? Today I found out someone killed her—tore her eyes out and shot her. The bullet was marked U.S.A., they say. I wanted to know who did it. They say someone named "Contra" or something like that. I was very, very angry with him. When I asked where he was, they told me to talk to his boss—Ronnie. That's your first name, Mr. President. Why did you kill my friend, Mr. President? If you were mad at her you could have talked to her, but why did you make her dead? I can't forgive you ever, and I hope you don't forgive yourself because you did something very bad—you killed a friend of mine.
(*She looks to the audience.*)

I keep sending this letter to 1600 Pennsylvania Avenue, Washington, D.C., and I keep getting it back: NO SUCH ADDRESS. And I was thinking, well, I was thinking maybe *you* might have the right address.

Notes

1. Playwright's responses to editors' biographical questionnaire, January 23, 2007, and e-mail correspondence February 16, 2007 and November 1, 2010.
2. Biographical information provided by the playwright, January 23, 2007.

PART III

La Indígena/ The Indigenous

Staging Myth

Among numerous arenas, the collective expression of militancy and protest in the Chicana and Chicano movement at the close of the 1960s also manifested itself through language, culture, and traditions.[1] This stimulation caused Chicana/Chicano literary expression to flourish, and distinct ideology soon arose. The discovery and/or rediscovery of one's history and culture resulted in a desire for self-identity and self-determination, and attempts at rewriting history soon surfaced. Amid this cultural nationalism, as Arturo J. Aldama writes, "the cultural forces of the Chicano/a movement in its 1960–1970 renaissance included a revalorization of the indigenous aspects of one's identity and a desire to celebrate the accomplishments of the Aztec and Mayan past."[2] In Latina/Latino theatre, perhaps more than elsewhere, the collective body of work by El Teatro Campesino indicates how the company spearheaded the exploration of educating Chicanas and Chicanos about their culture and their historical past. By the 1980s, it was Chicanas who stood out in staging their own myth, using their own unique voices.[3]

In his overview of Mexican American literature, Raymund A. Paredes notes that "more than any other literary activity of the time, the Teatro Campesino demonstrated to Mexican Americans the power of art to provoke consideration of critical cultural and political issues." Various playtexts stemming from the annals of El Teatro Campesino during this period reveal this reconnection with history and myths drawn from an indigenous past that had not previously been examined. The group merged social and political ideology with an exploration of cultural identity, thus bringing new themes and forms to the stage. As Stan Steiner recounts or chronicles the company's earlier years, he recalls Luis Valdez remarking that "we know we have our own culture. . . . It's just that there has been nobody to express it—until now. We will change that. We are on the verge of it. The whole country will be amazed!"[4]

The cultural center that El Teatro Campesino began shows the depths that the group took to immerse itself in its culture and traditions, thus inspiring other *teatros* to focus on their indigenous past and to reconnect with their origins. In describing the new directions of the group, Valdez wrote that "our rejection of white western European (gavacho) proscenium theater makes the birth of new Chicano forms necessary—thus, los *actos* y los *mitos*; one through the eyes of man; the other through the eyes of God."[5]

In the case of Chicanas writing about the indigenous, Estela Portillo Trambley is one of the first playwrights to incorporate indigenous mythology in her writing. Among her published plays, both *Day of the Swallows* and *Blacklight* draw from indigenous concepts and symbols.[6] Cordelia Candelaria examines "the nature, and problematic, of Trambley's 'feminist legacy,' particularly in terms of her pioneering presence as a woman of the Chicano Renaissance." Candelaria writes about the significance of this playwright's receipt of the Premio Quinto Sol Award, given by "the germinally influential *El Grito* and (to my knowledge) as the first Chicana to dramatize lesbianism for the stage," remarking that "her intellectual impact was at least in part strongly sociological and historical." Candelaria stresses, however, that it was the literary impact that was "first." She adds:

> Certainly, in terms of her representations of gender, sexuality, and ethnicity/race and their intersection with the related material issues and nodes of social class and power, Trambley inscribed her point of view in unflinching and memorable tracings of one woman's Chicana imaginary. Characterized by a hybrid consciousness of Mexican-Texan biculturality, Spanish-English bilingualism, and resistance to the entrenched vestiges of conquest and colonialism, Trambley expresses the mestizaje of her imaginary through a pointed and unflinching concern with gender relations in the full compound meaning of the term, i.e., sex roles, sexuality, orientation, and identity; patriarchy, personhood, and power, etc.[7]

In both Valdez and Portillo Trambley, we find, as Jorge Huerta comments on the significance of these two playwrights, that they are the "most dedicated to creating a mythos employing indigenous belief systems," who are "also the first playwrights, a man and a woman, to publish plays about the Chicana/o reality." Recognizing the two dramatists as "the pioneers in the realm of Chicana/o playwriting," Huerta also notes that few others followed them in presenting the distinct ideology that these had invoked on the Chicana/Chicano stage. As Huerta adds: "Other teatros and playwrights invoke indigenous gods in their productions, but these examples are not as visible and accessible in print, especially as are Portillo-Trambley and Valdez." Yet, "the indigenous gods are not too far offstage in many other plays; proof that these two pioneers have left their indelible marks and will always be the starting point for any discussions of Chicana/o drama and a Chicana/o mythos."[8] In the next two chapters, we can examine the remarkable way in which Latinas stage the indigenous.

Celia Herrera Rodríguez and the Colorado sisters, Elvira and Hortencia, provide us with playtexts that display the kind of performative expression that results from the integration of indigenous ideology. Very much in a spiritual and religious vein, these three playwrights create the kind of "Latina subject" that Alicia Arrizón describes in her study on *Latina Performance*: "In challenging her assigned position, she begins to transform and transcend it. She is the radical intellectual, the taboo breaker, the feminist dramatist," representing "difference" and also "seek[ing] to uncover and confront the very space where her body converges or intersects in a performance that comprises her subjectivity and ethic cultural sense," adding that "Latinas today bring a rebellious sensibility to the task of dismantling the structures that have defined, silenced, and marginalized them."[9] As Sonia Saldívar-Hull writes in her introduction to the second edition of Gloria Anzaldúa's *Borderlands/La Frontera: The New Mestiza,* Anzaldúa's "claim of the Indian part of her *mestisaje* avoids simplistic appropriation," because

> the *indígena* in the New Mestiza is a new political stance as a fully racialized feminist Chicana. She appeals to a history of resistance by subaltern Indian women of the Americas and in that shared history narrates strong political affiliation: "My Chicana identity is grounded in the Indian woman's history of resistance" (43). This political alliance further strengthens her internal critique of Chicano cultural practices that deny the indigenous part of the *mestisaje.* Claiming all parts of her identity, even those that clash, she escapes essentialist categories and envisions one provisional home where she can "stand and claim my space, making a new culture—*una cultura mestiza*—with my own lumber, my own bricks and mortar and my own feminist architecture" (44).[10]

In Rodríguez and the Colorado sisters, we find a vision closely aligned to the insight that Anzaldúa shares with us, understanding that despite "the struggle of identities, the struggle of borders is our reality still," and that "one day the inner struggle will cease and a true integration take place." Finally, as Anzaldúa put it, "In the meantime, *tenemos que hacerla lucha. ¿Quién está protegiendo los ranchos de mi gente? ¿Quién está tratando de cerrar la fisura entre la india y el blanco en nuestra sangre? El Chicano, sí, el Chicano que anda como un ladrón en su propia casa.*" (We have to struggle to do something. Who is protecting the ranches of my people? Who is trying to close the fissures between the Indian and the White in our blood? The Chicano, yes, the Chicano who walks like a thief in his own home.)[11]

Rodríguez's work, as described by Cherríe Moraga, is "based in the language of the symbol," as a "directed gesture toward the recuperation of a history, a way of knowing," which had been "lost to Xicano/as." As such, through her work, the artist-performer is making history, as well as the "living practice of ceremony as understood through the elemental."[12] Rodríguez's memorial for Gloria Anzaldúa can attest to her reverence for the Chicana poet and philosopher. Dating back to her seminal work with the Royal Chicano Air Force in Sacramento, if not earlier, this artist has integrated various elements of performance, and it is captivating to examine how her present work shows this connection.[13] For Rodríguez, the performative act is ritual, profoundly capable of immersing her audiences into this experience.

The Colorado sisters have risen to prominence as playwrights whose work revolves around deeply rooted ties to our indigenous past, beginning with their inclusion in the highly acclaimed and widely distributed anthology edited by Kathy A. Perkins and Roberta Uno, *Contemporary Plays by Women of Color* (1996), followed by their photograph gracing the front cover of Elizabeth C. Ramírez's *Chicanas/Latinas in American*

Theatre (2000), as well as their extensive production experience over the years. In the case of the Colorados, theirs is much more an immersion of ideology through blood lineage and history as it informs present-day struggles for all Latinas and Latinos. They break traditional boundaries through their use of English and Native tongues.

Perkins and Uno describe Elvira and Hortencia Colorado's *1992 Blood Speaks* as a work that "identifies the moment of Columbus' mythical 'discovery' of the Americas as the turning point for Native people; their satiric deconstruction of history's lies is framed by spirituality and healing that celebrate the spirit of survival." Their method of interweaving the comic into the serious recalling of the past calls to mind the type of humor that Valdez and El Teatro Campesino first used in their serious messages about the Chicano condition. Alicia Arrizón has also written about their work, noting that "the staging of the native woman is especially remarkable" in their productions. In effect, "these dynamic performers draw on the narratives of the precolonial legacy, weaving stories of the indigenous goddesses along with their own personal and familial tales."[14]

Besides directly linking themselves to Coatlicue, the powerful earth goddess-virgin mother of the Aztec pantheon who gives birth to Huitzilopochtli, through their company name—Coatlicue Theatre Company—the Colorado sisters also interweave Nahuatl into their playtexts.[15] Arrizón insightfully observes that "this tactic helps affirm their survival as urban *mestizas* in contemporary New York City." Through their method of interweaving ancient mythology with contemporary social and political topics, "including racism and sexual oppression," as Arrizón points out, "the affirmation of pre-Hispanic symbols in their work counteracts a dramatic space embedded in interculturalism itself." As such, "the legacy of the native woman is implicated in discursive configurations of the neocolonial, precolonial, and postcolonial subjects." Thus, through the mixing of Spanish and Nahuatl with the dominant English in their work, the group "configures the intercultural location of the 'new' native woman."[16]

The playwrights in this section contribute to the discourse on language and its loss, cultural nationalism, and transculturalism, and especially the need to "recuperate the figures of cultural memory and the sites of political agency" through their artistic expression.[17] Through two distinct styles, creating visual and aural imagery, they stage sites for explorations of the sacred places of our forbearers in new and renewed mythologies. As Anna Marie Sandoval observes, "The re-visioning of myths, legends, and cultural symbols has always been a significant feature of the literature of Chicanas and Mexicanas."[18] As we turn to the next two playtexts, we can examine how these playwrights also draw from those resources as they reimagine their histories.

Notes

1. Jorge Mariscal, "Chicano/a Movement," in *The Oxford Encyclopedia of Latinos and Latinas in the United States,* ed. Suzanne Oboler and Deena J. González (New York: Oxford University Press, 2005), 1:320–21.

2. Arturo J. Aldama, "Native Americans/Mexicanos," in *Oxford Encyclopedia of Latinos and Latinas,* 3:251.

3. Sarah Ramirez, "Borders, Feminism, and Spirituality: Movements in Chicana Aesthetic Revisioning," in *Decolonial Voices: Chicana and Chicano Cultural Studies in the 21st Century,* ed. Arturo J. Aldama and Naomi H. Quiñonez (Bloomington: Indiana University Press, 2002), 232–37. See also Emma Pérez, *The Decolonial Imaginary: Writing Chicanas into History* (Bloomington: Indiana University Press, 1999), 23–27; and Sheila Marie Contreras, *Blood Lines: Myth, Indigenism, and Chicana/o Literature* (Austin: University of Texas Press, 2008), 71–78.

4. Raymund Paredes, "Mexican-American Literature: An Overview," in *Recovering the U.S. Hispanic Literary Heritage,* ed. Ramón Gutiérrez and Genaro Padilla (Houston: Arte Público Press, 1993), 42. Stan Steiner, *La Raza: The Mexican Americans* (New York: Harper and Row, 1970), 337.

5. Luis Valdez, *Actos* (San Juan Bautista, Calif.: Cucaracha, 1971), 5.

6. Jorge Huerta, *Chicano Drama: Performance, Society and Myth* (Cambridge: Cambridge University Press, 2000), 22.

7. Cordelia Candelaria, "Engendering Re/Solutions: The (Feminist) Legacy of Estela Portillo Trambley," in *Decolonial Voices: Chicana and Chicano Cultural Studies in the 21st Century,* ed. Arturo J. Aldama and Naomi H. Quñonez (Bloomington: Indiana University Press, 2002), 196.

8. Huerta, 55.

9. Alicia Arrizón, *Latina Performance: Traversing the State* (Bloomington: Indiana University Press, 1999), xvi.

10. Sonia Saldívar-Hull, "Introduction to the Second Edition," in Gloria Anzaldúa, *Borderlands/La Frontera: The New Mestiza,* 2nd ed. (San Francisco: Aunt Lute Books, 1999), 5.

11. Anzaldúa, 85. Translation by Elizabeth C. Ramírez.

12. Cherríe Moraga, *Sola, pero bien acompañada: Celia Herrera Rodríguez: January 5–March 31, 2006,* exhibition monograph, C. N. Gorman Museum, University of California, Davis, 2006. Available at http://gormanmuseum.ucdavis.edu/Exhibitions, accessed December 4, 2008.

13. Elizabeth C. Ramírez knew the artist-performer during the time she was teaching at California State University, Sacramento (1974–76), where Celia Herrera Rodríguez was an undergraduate student. The artist also appeared in one of the plays that Ramírez directed, *Regalos de Tristeza.*

14. Kathy A. Perkins and Roberta Uno, eds., *Contemporary Plays by Women of Color: An Anthology* (London: Routledge, 1996), 11. Alicia Arrizón, "Mythical Performativity: Relocating Aztlán in Chicana Feminist Cultural Productions," *Theatre Journal* 52 (2000): 34, 35.

15. See Arrizón, "Mythical Performativity," for further information on the topic of Coatlicue, the concept of redefining "Aztlán" within the context of Chicana/Chicano cultural studies and Chicana feminist discourse, and Anzaldúa, *Borderlands/La Frontera: The New Mestiza,* and Sonia Saldíva-Hull, *Feminism on the Border* (Los Angeles: University of California Press, 2000), among many other studies on these and related topics on the Chicana/Chicano revisioning of culture and history.

16. Arrizón, "Mythical Performativity," 35–36.

17. Ibid., 49.

18. Anna Marie Sandoval, *Toward a Latina Feminism of the Americas: Repression and Resistance in Chicana and Mexicana Literature* (Austin: University of Texas Press, 2008), 11, 18.

CHAPTER 5

Reconnecting with an Indigenous Past through an Artista's Canvas and the Stage

Celia Herrera Rodríguez's *Cositas Quebradas: Performance Codex* (1999)

Celia Herrera Rodríguez, by permission of the photographer, Cherríe Moraga.

The Playwright/La Dramaturga

Celia Herrera Rodríguez is a painter and a performance and installation artist born in Sacramento, California, on November 26, 1952.[1] The maternal side of her family migrated to the United States in the late 1930s and 1940s, from Sandias Tepehuanes, Durango, México, where they had been "desde que nació el sol," as her grandmother would say.[2] Her father, whom the artist never met, was from San Luis Potosí. Of her family history, the artist writes: "My mother came north in her teens. She worked in Tijuana with other young women from the rancho until my grandmother and uncle helped her cross over at Mexicali. According to Grandmother she was six months pregnant with me when she and my grandmother made that journey. My mother died very young at the age of twenty-five, due to an unknown (possibly lymphatic) cancer that took her life about two years after she gave birth to my brother. I was five years old. After her death, my grandmother raised me, and my brother was raised by his father in Stockton, Califas."[3]

Growing up with her grandmother, who had been born in 1907, proved to be fundamental to the artist's evolving identification as an indigenous Xicana and critical to the formation of the concepts that would guide her painting, installation and performance work.[4]

Celia Herrera Rodríguez received her B.A. from the California State University at Sacramento (CSUS) in 1979, almost a decade after she began her college studies in 1970. Although it had been her ambition since the age of nine to attend college and study art, the political fervor of the period found her leaving school after one semester and by 1971, working in the sugar cane fields of Cuba with the 4th contingent of the Venceremos Brigade.[5] Upon her return to the United States, she worked with Union Latina in Manhattan, N.Y., and then in 1972, moved with her two-year-old daughter to Los Angeles where she became a volunteer for CASA (Centro de Acción Social Autónomo-Hermandad General de Trabajadores) with Bert Corona at the helm. In 1975, after three years as a full-time advocate for undocumented workers' rights, she returned to Sacramento, where she continued to work with CASA while attending CSUS. The artist's integrated approach to art and cultural/political activism was in many ways born out of the time and place of her education (in and outside the classroom). She states:

> Although I was born and raised in Sacramento (Barrio Cinco) in a predominantly Mexican neighborhood, it was bordered by two rivers, canneries, packing plants, the Southern Pacific Railroad, and the downtown capitol. Integrated within the Mexican community were Blacks (from Texas and Louisiana), East Indians, Chinese, Filipinos, Romas (Gypsy), and California (and others) Indians. Also, the areas held what was left of the working-class white immigrant community—German, Portuguese, Italian, Greek and dust-bowl immigrants from Oklahoma. I grew up with a very diverse view of "community" and this has been an abiding influence. Plus I was raised in a woman-oriented household consisting of just me and my grandmother. This perspective gave me a very independent perspective on my life and education as an artist. Thus, as the Chicano Movement was gearing up, I was part of the *Chicana* movement that is not widely discussed: one influenced by Marxist philosophy, anti-imperialist struggles around the world, and the early feminist movement of color in the United States. As I see it, the best thing that happened for me as an art student was the Barrio Art classes, taught by Esteban Villa and Jose Montoya, which put me back in my own specifically Raza community, and provided me with an approach to viewing artists as cultural workers. Also deeply influential was what I observed as the role of artist in Native California culture. I especially credit my Native American professors for that—Frank La Pena and Brian Bibby.

Celia Herrera Rodríguez (CHR) was a member of the arts organization, the Royal Chicano Air Force (RCAF) between 1975 and 1977. Of her years with the RCAF, CHR states, "As a woman, it was a problematic association. I was criticized for being a 'feminist Third-Worldist.'" "In the end RCAF and I clashed. I was court-martialed," she adds, with a touch of cynicism. CHR attributes the origins of her ouster to having "commandeered" an RCAF wall in Chicano Park in San Diego, where she and a group of four other women artists from Sacramento painted the mural *Women Hold Up Half of Heaven*. This, "among other transgressions," she admits.

In 1987, Rodríguez received her M.F.A. in painting from the University of Illinois, Urbana-Champaign and went on to study art history, theory and criticism at the School of the Art Institute of Chicago. In her five-year tenure in Chicago, she exhibited extensively and became involved in installation and performance art. In the mid-1990s she returned to California, where she has made Oakland her home and has taught Chicano/Indigenous art and art history at the University of California, Berkeley since 2000. In addition to the UC Berkeley position, Rodríguez is currently teaching at the California College for the Arts, in Oakland. She has also taught Chicano art theory and practice and painting at colleges and universities across the country, including Stanford University, UC Santa Cruz, and the School of the Art Institute of Chicago.

Celia Herrera Rodríguez's work reflects a full generation of dialogue with Chicano, Native American, pre-Columbian, and Mexican thought. Hers is a conceptual art, inspired as much from the intricate embroidery work of her Mexican female elders of Sandias Tepehuanes in the state of Durango, México as the iconography of the pre-conquest Mexicas.[6] Her paintings, drawings and installation work have been exhibited nationally and internationally, including: Centro Cultural de Tijuana, Baja California; Centro Cultural Santo Domingo (Oaxaca, México); the Centro Colombo Americano (Medellín, Colombia); the Curtain Gallery, Columbia College of Chicago; the Institute of American Indian Art Museum (Santa Fe, N.M.); the Oakland Museum of California; the Mexican Fine Arts Center Museum (Chicago); Tufts University Gallery (Medford, Mass.); the Rike Gallery (University of Dayton, Ohio); the Mexican Museum (San Francisco); CAGE Gallery (Cincinnati Artists Group Effort, Cincinnati, Ohio); NAME Gallery (Chicago); the C. N. Gorman Museum (University of California, Davis); the De Saisset Museum (Santa Clara University, California); and the Wight Gallery (Los Angeles). Her work is permanently housed in a number of private and public collections, including the Mexican Fine Arts Center Museum in Chicago, the Institute of American Indian Art Museum of Santa Fe, and the C. N. Gorman Museum of the University of California at Davis.

Rodríguez has also performed in conjunction with her installations for more than a decade. In her installations, the cultural symbology of her paintings moves into the three dimensions of a materialized Mexican Indigenous history. When she enters the work, through performance, the result is a living (embodied) codex of contemporary Xicana Indigenous thought. Some of her most salient performances include

- *Woman Falling from the Night Sky* (2007) for the "Signatures of the Past—North American Drama" Conference, sponsored by the Université Libre de Bruxeles
- *A Prayer to the Mother Waters for Peace* (2006), performed at the Glass Curtain Gallery, Columbia College of Chicago
- *El Paso: Like a Rock Tossed on the Road* (2001) for "Fronteras y Migración, Espacios Reales y Imaginarios," Mexican/Chicana Conference, Centro Cultural Santo Domingo, Oaxaca, México

In recent years, Celia Herrera Rodríguez has also begun to apply the southwestern and mexicano indigenous elements of the staging of her performances into conceptual design for Xicana theatre, including Cherríe Moraga's *The Hungry Woman* at Stanford University in 2005.

About the Play/Sobre la Obra

In Celia Herrera Rodríguez's work we find a performance text created by a visual artist. This "Performance Codex," as the playwright describes it, is set within the context of an *altar* (pronounced in Spanish with the stress on the second syllable). Rodríguez tells us that the intent is "to relocate our attention and our bodies from contemporary assumptions about place, history, and experience to 'sacred' time and place." The "cositas quebradas" of the title refer to broken little things that encompass a huge mythological, indigenous and historical past. This painter creates a vast canvas filled with precious fragments of the mind and soul, tiny bits of the nation's memory that allow one to return to those images that have become lost in the present. Rodríguez's work is more sacred ceremony than spoken drama, in the vein of the experimental theatre forms of the 1960s, but is distinctly rooted in her native past.[7]

Artistic Vision/Punto de Vista Artístico

ECR & CRC: Briefly describe your theatre experience.[8]

CHR: I don't have a history of theatre. I am a visual artist, primarily a painter, who through my work as an installation artist and my own living understanding of ceremonial practice, gradually began to "perform." I first became aware of the possibilities of performance work while I was studying at the School of the Art Institute of Chicago (1988–89). I was taking classes in the Art History, Theory and Criticism Program, and took a class in ritual and ceremonial practice with Marilyn Houlberg, an artist-scholar of Haitian Vodoun. My fellow classmate Douglas Stapleton, an installation and performance artist, was performing "drag" and studying the enactment of gender in Queer performance. We struck up a conversation about sacred space and the enactment of the sacred, and he introduced me to some readings and artists which I never would have found my way to alone. I had been involved in Xicana/o and Northern Native ceremonial practice for about 16 years at this point. But spiritual practice always held a separate place in my mind from my art. It was "performance" that brought them together. Through the years of "sitting in ceremony" I had begun to understand the values that underlie the simple rituals, which remain intact in Mexican households and, on the surface, look completely mundane and functional. Things as simple as the manner in which my grandmother swept the kitchen before preparing a meal, or the way she insisted that a bed be made up. These mundane everyday *costumbres* were essentially the same used in the rituals I observed within the ceremonies.

- The act of preparation of the altar or sacred space
- The value given to the care of human-made and natural ceremonial objects
- The importance of order and sequence in the arrangement of proceedings within a ceremony
- The value given to consistency, to custom, and tradition in how things are done
- The attention given to detail
- The value placed on proper attitude

The way in which Doug and fellow performers began to self-consciously examine their "performance of queerness" also provided an entry way through which I could approach the performance of the "sacred" outside of the environment of commercial consumption promoted by typical museum and gallery spaces. In 1990, I was invited by Doug Stapleton to participate in a series called "Real Life Cabaret" at the NAME Gallery, an alternative performance space in Chicago. The whole point of the series was to (re)connect and to recognize the act of "art" within everyday contemporary culture. I agreed to do a performance because it allowed me the opportunity to bring in an aspect of Xicana/o Indigenous culture that is not only unrecognized within Mexican American culture, but also unknown within contemporary American culture.

This first performance was entitled "Sacred Hair Washing Ceremony," in which I set up a small "altar" consisting of a basin of water, a comb, generic shampoo, some towels, and a bundle of sage. First I explained what I was going to do to the audience, asking them to abstain from bringing any alcoholic beverages into the space, and then cleaning the space and the audience with sage smoke. After I set up the altar, the audience was invited to have their hair washed by me. A man and a woman volunteered. I asked the man to kneel over the basin in front of the altar, and began washing the man's hair. I did not speak or explain further to the audience. I just began talking quietly to the man, in the same manner that my family in México might wash each other's hair in the public baths of our pueblo or ranchito. In the ensuing quiet, the audience began quietly talking to each other about hair, exchanging their grandmothers' recipes for hair care, and the atmosphere of the space became almost reverent, relaxed, and very intimate. The mixture of herbs blended with the shampoo's fragrance, and both the sound of splashing, and the aroma of the steamy hot water in the galvanized steel basin (my grandmother's) changed the relationship of the audience from spectators to participants through a ritual that is practiced every day in our homes.

This "performance" led to other invitations to perform work in the Chicago area. I followed this up with another performance at NAME called *What Part Indian Am I, or How I Came to Be Mexican* (1990–91). Perhaps because I wanted the audience to be aware of the specificity of culture, I began to develop "altars" or sacred space that required something other than "stage" to contain the "performance." (I am still not convinced that what I do is actually "performance" in the theatrical sense of the word.) I think of the experience of performing within these "assembled spaces" as *dando palabra,* speaking from extraordinary place. I say "extraordinary" because, if the "performance" is going as it should, there is a way in which the "I" (that self-consciousness) disappears. The words are not mine alone. I guess what I am saying is that I am "performing ceremony," not "improvising" but creating sacred space within the context of contemporary American art space through which "vision" might enter. I am not looking for the exotic, the avant-garde. I am looking for ways to transmit or reignite what remains alive from that "old way of doing."

ECR & CRC: How did you decide to write and/or perform?

CHR: The act of performing happened pretty organically it seems, as I just explained. But the writing is something that I struggle to do. I am a visual artist, but I have always had a deep interest in history and what is referred to as mythology. I read voraciously as a child and absolutely loved fairytales and folktales. I grew up hearing my grandmother and her women friends exchange stories and life histories across the kitchen table. From then, I developed a high regard for storytelling. What interests me is what is held within the structure (form) of the story and how this shapes its intent (the inherent lessons and history) as given by the storyteller. I am drawn to the ways in which a story engages the imagination and transports the listener into the scenario. I remember that as a young artist people would often ask me to "tell the story" about the images or symbols that I painted. Although I loved explaining the symbolism or telling the story of the pieces, I did not really know what to make of the phenomena. I worried that I was not effective as a painter if the painting did not function to provide its own meaning. Yet I realized that I have always been attracted to drawing particular symbols, shapes, and imagery, more so than developing "scenes," which are more narrative. Since I began drawing I have felt compelled to trace these certain symbols that feel to me like barely remembered words at the tip of my tongue (or emerge almost close to the experience of déjà vu). Many years ago, a close friend, Regina García, who was studying with California Native healers, urged me to redraw the small "doodles" that I was always putting into the margins of books, on napkins, and onto scraps of paper. She felt that this was my "real work." It took awhile for me to recognize that what she had observed was true and even longer to accept the challenge of making the work with integrity. It gradually became evident to me that the symbols had much to offer my painting. In the process of studying and researching the symbols I began to understand the meaning of the symbols, and I realized that they were, in fact, "words"—doorways into a more expansive or profound understanding of what appeared to be a simple design or shape. Today my work—from painting to performance—reflects a recontextualization of the primordial and sacred symbols that are the legacy left to us as Indigenous people of this hemisphere.

I can only say that I feel the symbols, that the practice of painting is a prayer, a meditation that allows a conversation with the symbols that releases ideas, something close to words but visual in meaning. It is this form of "writing" in the "Old Way" that grew into the "text" for performance. The process of developing the installation/performance is similar to the manner in which I paint. I research and study the concepts, in conjunction with developing the materials and objects that I want to work with. Each performance is an organic response to the particular audience, place and time. The text is spoken and not scripted in advance. What is included in this particular version of *Cositas Quebradas* will never be spoken or performed again in the manner it has been written here. I don't write out the performance text ahead of time, because it seems that once the word is contained in the written (colonizer) language, the anima of the work could dissipate. I organize the performance in outline form, providing the framework of the material and its meaning, but I allow the content to emerge in real time in response to who is in the room, and what is happening in the historical moment we are sharing.

ECR & CRC: Why do you write what you do?

CHR: Again, for me it is not about writing: it is about the ideas or concepts that inform a work. In many ways I feel that my performance works are intended to counter romantic notions about American Indigenous identity. Romantic notions are the colonizers' implantation in our consciousness that all is lost and unrecoverable from indigenous histories. Romantic notions of identity and nation are seeded in a deep fear that there is no real possibility in recovering what was lost or in recognizing what is still alive and right in front of us waiting. To gain consciousness is to have deep and abiding faith in what we have been traumatized (tortured or taught) into no longer seeing, acknowledging, or believing. Romantic notions are basically pretensions that must be overcome in the only way I understand, which is to align ourselves with the most real and honest resistance to imperialism and colonization. This alignment requires that we listen, pay attention, learn to think, and dare to act. Political consciousness is required to make change that takes into account the complexities and contradictions of our historical times. Political consciousness is another way of saying that we have developed the skills of analysis and interpretation to be able to make connections, and have gained the ability to see, to en(vision) and to act definitively. The intention of my performances is to raise political consciousness in this sense.

ECR & CRC: Who do you write for and what audience are you trying to reach?

CHR: I am speaking to the Xicana/o Indigenous Peoples of our time. I'm using the current meaning of the word *Xicana/o,* which is inclusive of the Indigenous Peoples of Mexico, Central America, and South America, who are in diaspora across the United States. I am making this work for my mom-abuela, my mujer, our children and grandchildren because my nation resides within them. I am trying to reach us, nuestro pueblo, nuestro futuro—our youth—and I'm trying to reach us all as human beings.

ECR & CRC: What message, if any, are you trying to convey to your audience with this work and/or with all of your work?

CHR: *Cositas Quebradas* responds to tremendous loss that we suffered as the original peoples of the Americas. Sometimes the trauma seems so huge that it is a wonder to me that we survived at all. Yet the knowledge of that loss is something that we are told to negate. I am ever conscious that the Buddhist temples in Tibet and the early pre-mosques in Iraq that have been ransacked and destroyed are absolutely as necessary to our survival as every creature on that list of animals bound for extinction. The interruption of the continuity of our thinking as Indigenous peoples and the decimation of our creative efforts has impacted all of us on this continent and beyond. Thus *Cositas Quebradas* asks us to remember, to recall, what it means to lose the precious. What was (and continues to be) stolen from us the Indigenous Peoples has great value to the colonizers. To this day it is held captive in so-called "public" museums, art galleries, the private homes of wealthy collectors and in corporate headquarters. We have very little recourse to get it back. However, I also want us to realize that what was left behind—the everyday and mundane—that was considered of no value and remains undervalued by the colonizer, is still in our hands and has relationship intellectually and spiritually to what has been stolen from us. We are required to remember and give value to those remains that we have been taught are of no value.

Given the complexities of our historical time, I am simply asking, in all of my performance works, that we make the difficult journey toward home, that we continue to resist assimilation and cultural-political complacency in the face of the brutality, greed, and ignorance of neocolonization. I am praying that we decide to remain awake and responsive to every opportunity to regain control of our humanity, our spirit, and our relationship with our Madre Tierra and the rest of creation.

ECR & CRC: Who or what has been your major influence?

CHR: My influences are the People of Color writers and thinkers of the last 52 years that have shaped the foundations of our movement, and the everyday people—our ancestors—who have made sacrifices and lived their lives with us in mind. The list would include many people of which I name these few: the writers, Gloria Anzaldúa and Cherríe Moraga; the visual artist and poet, Frank La Pena; the activist, Victoria Mercado; the formidable Adaliza McHue of the Candy Story Gallery in Folsom, California; my Chicano/a professors at Sacramento State, including Olivia Castellanos; my grandmother, Domitila García, and the mujeres that sat at her table.

ECR & CRC: What has been your biggest and/or most difficult struggle/challenge in life, in completing a play or getting it produced, etc.?

CHR: As a Xicana visual artist who performs, I mainly have to deal with an art world that continues to be Eurocentric and exclusive. With a few exceptions, the Chicana/o work that receives the most attention from the mainstream art world (and I would even venture to say the Chicano Art establishment) is based largely on the tradition of social realism and less so on the kind of conceptual (spiritual) work that has been allowed within a Native American context. This bias is slowly changing in academic, artistic, and intellectual circles, but exhibition opportunities are developed by corporate-sponsored museum and private commercial galleries that have specific definitions of what is considered significant, representative, and worthy of discussion. So the biggest challenge is trying to find the appropriate venues that might be interested in the concepts and style of my work, securing representation, and just getting on with the business of making a living as an artist. I have always had children and a big life. Now I have (and have had) grandchildren who also need(ed) raising. I have made commitments to teaching and working with youth in terms of spiritual practice. I am involved politically in Indigenous women's international organizing efforts. I have always made work through difficult circumstances, but getting the work to the public—where it can be seen—remains the biggest struggle.

ECR & CRC: Can you offer any words of advice to aspiring playwrights/performers/directors/audiences?

CHR: Do it.

Production History/Palabras Dramatúrgicas

This published version of *Cositas Quebradas* was first performed by the artist in 1999 at Tufts University Art Gallery, Medford, Massachusetts, as part of the "Imágenes e Historias/Images and Histories: Chicana Altar-Inspired Art" exhibition curated by Dr. Constance Cortez. The performance accompanied Rodríguez's installation, "Red Roots/Black Roots/Earth Árbol de la Vida." Other performances of *Cositas Quebradas* include those at the de Saisset Museum, Santa Clara University, Santa Clara, California (2000); the National Association of Chicana and Chicano Scholars Conference, University of Arizona, Tucson (2001); the Department of Drama, Stanford University, Stanford, California (2001); "Encuentros: Perspectives on Latina/o History and Culture," Mills College, Oakland, California (2002); Casa Diocesana de Espiritualidad, Málaga, Spain, at the "III Congreso Internaciónal de Literatura Chicana," (2002); and the Humanities Center, De Paul University, Chicago (2003).

Contact Information

The playwright may be contacted through the editors.

COSITAS QUEBRADAS: PERFORMANCE CODEX

The following includes the artist's description of the concepts and personal history, which provide the basis for the performance, Cositas Quebradas. *Celia Herrera Rodríguez's spoken words, which occur in the actual performance, appear in quotation marks. ["Stage Directions" appear within brackets.]*

EL PROPÓSITO/LA PREPARACIÓN

Uno

Preparation begins with the determined purpose of the altar, the fireplace.[9] The altar is not made and then described. It is built with purpose, with the intention of its use determined for each and every time it is performed. In this case, *el propósito* (the purpose) is to relocate our attention and our bodies from contemporary assumptions about place, history, and experience to "sacred" time and place.

The return to this form is given by my grandmother. In her daily practice I locate my right to make this Old Way return. The sacred instruments left behind contain the method and the concept. Not that she said to me, "Pick them up after I die." What she did say was, *"Pon atención mijita. Cuando me muera vas a reconocer quien fui yo, y te va pesar no haber puesto atención en estas cosas que te estoy enseñando."*[10]

En/seña (sign).

> *This is how we speak of learning, literally learning to sign or read signs. Sign: image, picture, gesture, marking. Do it again and again and again, like the old time people make you do it. Again and again until you tire of doing it over and again. So you learn to do it right the first time. Take your time and think about it and do it right, so that you can walk away and*

> *know that it was done right. And this becomes habit and it slows you down. But the value of this way does not always function in this got-no-time society, where brightly scrubbed pots and pans that shine like new after twenty years of use mean nothing to anyone but you. There is configuration to the day's work in this Old Time way, where how you do a task is as important as the fact that it is done.*

Dos

I am very much of this time, a reader of books and a maker of marks. For as much as my abuela tried to deter me from "wasting" the precious materials (#2 pencils, ballpoint pens, and writing paper), as hard as she tried to dislodge the books from my hands for more immediate important tasks (the making of tortillas, ironing, and cleaning), she lost the battle, and with it a little bit of lo acostumbrado.

In her culture, in the quiet dusty ranchito of her girlhood, drawing and embroidery had an allocated time within the day. Like letter writing it was designated to the time between the required daily tasks.

> Rise before the sun, light the fire, then make desayuno. Get the men folk off to their labores. Start the morning chores of preparing the corn, sweeping, cleaning, washing, tending to the animales, and the care of the elderly and young.

Finally after the midday meal and preparations have been made for the cena, when the sun is high over head, we, mujeres and niñas, sit in the brightly lit doorways and visit and make the art (embroidery) that decorates the sparsely furnished adobes of my relatives. *Ramos y flores* and elaborately scripted names with poetic wishes for good sleep and the acknowledgement of love: "*Duerme Mi Amor,*" "*Querida Madre,*" "*Mi Hijo Precioso,*" "*Camerina,*" "*Florinda*"—imported mail order designs from some distant ciudad. Still, in the highly nuanced and intricate color schemes of intertwined rosales, I find the connections to older (native) forms, to relatives unnamed.

Born in the north, I was the first in my generation to shatter that fundamental connection to the order and use of a day. Lost in my dictionary and the "Blue . . .," "Yellow . . ." and "Purple Book of Fairytales," I was not present in the world of my abuela. Instead, I could be found wandering through the pages of some other lifetime and took no pleasure in the neatly organized laundry hanging from the line, or the way a stain could be lifted through careful application of detergent, bleach, and sunlight.

I think of a painting by Carmen Lomas Garza, of a mother making the bed for her children while they lay atop the rooftop gazing at the stars. This picture brings back to me the simple Sacra Victorian early summer mornings of the late 1950s and '60s, the sound of the ringer washing machine churning away, the swish of sweeping, water running out on the back porch, and my abuela's songs of loss and love, mixing with the smell of coffee and *frijoles* cooking on the stove. Me, lying under bleached, sun-dried and starched, embroidered linen, sneaking a last page of my book before rising to the chores ahead, already plotting ways to cut the corners of the workload in order to get back to the story.

Tres

Years later, as an adult, I dream. "There is an earthquake coming," the dreaming voice announces. I think, *I need to get those little things my Mom gave me.*[11] "Better hurry," the dream voice warns. I run up the stairs to the old Victorian house I grew up in. Rush through the door and through the trembling swaying kitchen into the dimly lit pantry. Grabbing a shoe box, I start tossing in the "*cositas*"—a salt shaker from one of the restaurants she cooked in, a little clay pre-Columbian style bird, a chile bowl shaped like a duck, a sugar bowl, and embroidered hand towels, their edges crocheted by her hand.

"Wait," I say to myself. "Where are the *precious* things?"

"Long gone, *como tu Mami,*" the voice responds. "Take what you can, the time is up." The shaking becomes more violent. The walls in the pantry crumble and the shelves begin dropping the familiar. I jump out and down the stairs in one leap. My "precious things" clutched to my heart. The house collapses behind me. I awaken.

THE PERFORMANCE

I come to this fireplace way over here in Boston through my mom's kitchen, bedroom, ironing board. I take the broom, like the broom she used, and I sweep. I prepare the "performance" space like she would do before any important event. "Primero se barre," she would tell me as we cleaned. "Chase out the lanas y malos espíritus, los pedos y malos pensamientos."[12]

Days maybe months before this day, I read in the effort to prepare. I follow the trail of an idea/image that leads to the place where this altar is to be. An elder tells me that the spirits know where to find me now, that they set up traps and lures within the books to catch my attention. "Como un coyote," my mother names my spirit. "*Esculcando, metida en donde no tienes negocio.*"[13] In spite of the warnings, I (re) search and assemble elements that fall into my hands.

> How is it that I came back, here, to this place so far from home? Can anybody name the thieves that took my home? Has anybody seen my relatives? Does anybody recognize my bones? What is that growling inside my chest, trying to get past the frozen vocal cords?

I sweep the space, then bring to the altar the elements rescued from the last world, the Quinto Sol, the fifth world of movimiento. I bring *las cositas* that did not fall into the crumbling ruin.

The Zapotec rug paid for out of the remains of the money my mom and I were given for our terreno, our land in Tepehuanes. We had no right to protest its sale. In the indigenous sense it was not even property to be sold. But sold it was and I take the rug, red/white/blue/black and lay it across the floor where I have swept. This rug is all that is left of my nation, my land, and my people, my connection to home.

I build the altar/fireplace with cut logs of oak and pine, two logs facing east/west, two more crossing at the edges facing north/south. Thirteen layers, sometimes 26 until the fireplace is as it should be. And I cover the logs with my *rebozo,* dress the fireplace with flowers and candles and lay down my ax, wrapped in red cloth, across the surface of this altar—Grandfather Fireplace, Sacred Fireplace.

All is prepared. All is performance.

[*The audience arrives.*]

I re-enter. I carry the stone, which will hold the fire and place it in front of the altar. I light the *copal*, *salvia* (sage), or the *cedro*. I bring in the Sacred and ask once again, in the correct manner for permission to be here in this way, like my mami used to, making sure both doors are open, so that what comes in and what has to leave have equal but separate doors. I ask in the right way, so that the dangers in the doing of this act are acknowledged.

Then on the blanket are placed the most important and elemental of all *cositas, lo que nos dió nuestra madre:* the water, corn, the carne, the fruit.

Así nomas. I speak.

"I invite you to sit in my nation, on what is left of my land, my nation. I invite those of you who remember how to sit on this blanket to join me. I invite those of you who are blocked of their memories to come and sit here in my nation. And those of you who have no connection, I invite you, too, but only if you promise to leave when asked to do so. Don't act like those white people who come for a visita and refuse to leave, confusing our hospitality for servitude. I ask you to sit where mine is not mine and yours is not mine."

"I say to you all, I have returned, I have come back.
I have come because you called me yesterday, a long time ago.
Here I find myself.
Llego como piedra que anda rodando
Como yerba desconocida
Aquí en este momento
En este tiempo
En este mundo.
Apache[14] *nuevamente.*
Soy el agua que reconoce su camino through man-constructed barriers.
Aunque no me esperan ya
Aunque muertos viven en el olvido contentos."[15]

"I invite you to re-member.
If you, any of you, remember how to sit up on this blanket,
I invite you, I do.
I invite you in real time to sit with me and remember."

[Members from the audience that remember (and some that do not but are trying) join me on blanket, where the sacreds (the elemental foods) have been laid out. I bless the food.]

"I give thanks for the food that has remained with us. I give thanks for us, all of us, memory impaired and the repaired. I'm grateful. I give thanks by passing the Water to you. I pass the corn. I pass the meat. I pass the fruit."

[The sacreds are passed among the audience. I say:]

"Drink this water, the corn, the meat, the sweet fruit of our grandmother."

[I ask:]

"Does anybody know what it means to have everything taken from you? To awaken and find what was true is no longer, what was home is shattered, what armed the day and moved the night is no longer. Does anybody remember what it is to witness one's loved ones disappear, pass into another time? Does anybody here know, remember what it is to lose the world familiar? What is that sound lurking in the heart frozen?

"Most of us don't remember, don't know. We are generations away from the witnessing, from the surviving of the burnings, the hangings, the chasing away from all that was familiar. We are generations removed from that initial invasion. Settled now into an acceptance of our dispersal. Having survived, we sleep, we wake, we move through our time, our world, certain that the world will not end, our god will not betray us, our shopping malls will always be there and our credit will always be good. We vote our certainty into government policy. Good citizens of this world, if we question, it is an inarticulate question, a vague discomfort with the present form."

[As the vessels holding the sacreds return, I too drink the water, take a mouthful of corn, meat, fruit. When they are emptied, I place the vessels back on the altar, and I ask again:]

"Do you remember, do you know what I mean? In the contemporary vernacular, I ask, 'do you feel me?' No? No? You, my oh-so-polite, softly-swaying-to-the-sound-of—my—voice audience. You, so cozy and warm, in the sacred light of my fireplace. Your loss safely distant and intellectualized."

[Nervous smiles on some faces, tears running down others; boredom on the sophisticated; already-know-this-why-can't-we-move-on-faces of the smug and self-certain. So I take the precious bone china cup made for the Boston elite via Manila so many generations ago . . . I take this precious fragile remnant of New England tradition, and I . . .

SMASH IT WITH MY AX.

I take the precious gold-gilded American-made serving tray with pictures of the Presidents, limited edition 1960-something, and I

SMASH IT WITH MY AX.

I take the precious cobalt Italian hand-blown glass, and I

SMASH IT WITH MY AX.

I SMASH. I SMASH. I MAKE FRAGMENTS OF IT,

And I ask:]

"Does it matter, in this time, that these things are gone?"

I place the ax covered in red cloth on the altar and I go back, careful not to step in the fragments of these *cositas quebradas,* careful not to pierce my feet on the fragments of the precious.

I return.

Notes

1. The biographical narrative and interview responses were developed by Celia Herrera Rodríguez in conversation with playwright Cherríe Moraga, who edited the work. Copyright © 2010 by Celia Herrera Rodríguez. The editors retain copyright for the questions on the biographical questionnaire, for the About the Play/Sobre la Obra section, and for the endnotes. Additional information for this chapter from e-mail correspondence with the playwright, October 24 and 31, 2010.

2. "Desde que nació el sol" translates as "since the birth of the sun."

3. Califas refers to the state of California. Most often heard at the height of the Chicano Movement, it is primarily used by Chicanas/Chicanos/Latinas/Latinos who live there.

4. The term *Xicana* is the term preferred by the playwright instead of *Chicana.*

5. At its homepage, the Venceremeos ("We Shall Overcome") Brigade describes its origins: "In 1969, a coalition of young people formed the Venceremeos ('We Shall Overcome") Brigade, as a means of showing solidarity with the Cuban Revolution" (http://www.venceremosbrigade.org, accessed August 1, 2010).

6. The term *Mexicas* refers to the Aztec people occupying the Valley of Mexico and builders of Tenochtitlan, the major site of urban civilization during the Classic period, situated in the Valley of Teotihuacán, 26 miles from México City. See Livie Isauro Duran and H. Russell Bernard, *Introduction to Chicano Studies* (New York: Macmillan, 1973), 583, 586; and Jorge A. Huerta, *Chicano Theater: Themes and Forms* (Ypsilanti, Mich.: Bilingual Press, 1982), 188.

7. See "The Living Theatre," "The Open Theatre," and "Happenings" along with the work of Artaud and Grotowski, which Peter Brook refers to as "Holy Theatre," and other examples in Oscar G. Brockett, "Toward Commitment: Theatre in the 1960s" (chapter 13) and "Reshaping the Theatre: 1968 and Its Aftermath" (chapter 14) in *Century of Innovation,* 2nd ed. (Boston: Allyn and Bacon, 1991), 343–428.

8. Responses to the editors' biographical questionnaire, August 24, 2007.

9. The word *altar* should be read with the Spanish pronunciation with the accent on the second syllable. Also, in this piece the altar and fireplace are one and the same.

10. Translation by Celia Herrera Rodriguéz: "Pay attention my daughter. When I die you are going to realize who I was, and you will regret not having paid attention to what I am teaching you."

11. The playwright explains that the terms "Mom," "Mami," "Grandma," and "Abuela" are used interchangeably throughout the text to refer to her grandmother, who raised her.

12. Translation by Celia Herrera Rodríguez: ". . . dust-balls, bad spirits, old farts, and bad thoughts."

13. Translation by Celia Herrera Rodríguez: "Searching, meddling in things that do not pertain to you."

14. In an old native language of the north, "apache" meant "strangers," according to the playwright.

15. Translation by Celia Herrera Rodríguez:

. . . "Here I find myself.
I arrive, a rolling dislodged stone
an unknown weed
Here in this moment
in this time

in this world.
A stranger once again.
I am the water who remembers her path
Through man-made barriers.
Although you no longer await my return
Although the dead live content in their oblivion
I invite you to re-member."
. . .

CHAPTER 6

Re-creating Myths

The Colorado Sisters' *Chicomoztoc: Mimixcoa—Cloud Serpent* (2000)

Elvira and Hortencia Colorado, by permission of the photographer, Rodolfo B. Ornelas.

The Playwrights/ Las Dramaturgas

Elvira and Hortencia Colorado, Chichimeca-Otomí, founded Coatlicue Theatre Company in 1987 and named it to honor the Mexica deity of the earth and creation.[1] The sisters tell us that "the Company was formed out of an urgency to address issues of identity, racism, appropriation, historical trauma, migration, and violence against women, which affects them and their communities."[2]

These two sisters come from "an oral tradition, listening to their mother and other family members tell stories, but also listening to secrets and silences—stories left untold." Their theatre work is "rooted in stories, memories, dreams, and their stories of creation." They "weave their stories much like the weaving of symbols on a woman's huipil (dress or blouse), in a rainbow of colors. Stories are a sacred, spiritual, powerful means filled with honor to educate, entertain, and begin a healing process with one's self, family and community."

Their plays include: *Caracol: Heart of the Earth—Flower of Hope; La Carpa de las Invisibles; Chicomoztoc: Mimixcoa—Cloud Serpents; A Traditional Kind of Woman: Too Much, Not 'Nuff, Open Wounds on Tlalteuctli; Huipil; Coyolxauhqui: Women Without Borders; Walks of Indian Women: From Aztlan to Anahuac; La Llorona; Tlaltilco: The Place Where Things Are Hidden*; and *1992: Blood Speaks*, which appears in *Contemporary Plays by Women of Color: An Anthology.*

These playwright-performers have received numerous grants. In 2004 they received a Ford Foundation Grant to develop *Caracol: Heart of the Earth—Flower of Hope* and premiere it in Belo Horizonte, Brazil, at the 5th Encuentro: Performing "Heritage": Contemporary Indigenous and Community-based Practices through the Hemispheric Institute of Performance and Politics of New York University. Other grants include those from the Jerome Foundation, Franklin Furnace, Dance Theatre Workshop, New York State Council on the Arts, Open Meadows, Rockefeller Foundation, Lila Wallace, New York Foundation for the Arts Fellowships, and the Ingrid Washinawatok Community Activism Award.

They are members of the Hemispheric Institute of Performance and Politics at New York University, the Network of Ensemble Theatres, and of the American Indian Community House, and founding members of Cetiliztli Nauhcampa Quetzalcoatl in Ixachitlan (the first Mexica dance group in New York City) and the New York Zapatistas. In New York City, they have performed at the National Museum of the American Indian, the American Museum of Natural History, the American Indian Community House, the Bronx Museum, and with the Thunderbird American Indian Dance Company. They have also appeared in museums, cultural centers, universities, and on reservations, including: Northwest Indian College, Bellingham, Washington; Southern California Indian Center, Long Beach; Tribal Health Services, Pendleton, Oregon; Mexican Fine Arts Center Museum, Chicago; Guadalupe Cultural Arts Center, San Antonio; and Rosario Castellano Women's Center, Oaxaca, México.

About the Play/Sobre la Obra

Chicomoztoc Mimixcoa—Cloud Serpents revolves around the two Colorado sisters' search for their ancestral roots. From their grandparents and parents, "who in spite of forced assimilation through religion and education, wove into their shame and denial threads of creation, language, stories, memory, food, traditions in their daily lives and in their dreams," these two sisters continue to "weave these threads for the generations to come."[3] The Colorado sisters explain the playtext as being "a journey through dreams, stories, time, and memory, across mountains and deserts, retracing the footsteps of the ancestors, traveling back to Chicomoztoc (the place of our origin), searching, digging up, and gathering stories that have been buried through centuries of shame and denial in our family, but which connect us to our past and identity. Some stories/secrets remain buried, and they are also part of who we are. We honor all those who struggled with their shame and denial. This is an offering to all of our relations."[4] Using rich imagery, song, and music, they reconnect with their family in Mexico as they explore their indigenous heritage, re-creating their past and bringing a sense of pride and renewal in their discovery.

Artistic Vision/Punto de Vista Artístico

The Colorado sisters' individual responses to the subject of artistic vision precede their responses to our biographical questions.

Elvira Colorado

I'm always being asked, what are you? Where are you from? How come you speak English so well? The Red people. You are the real Indians. You look just like my grandmother. I'm part Cherokee. It's terrible what they did to the Indians. Are there Indians living in New York City? You're Indian? I thought they were all dead. You're the first Indian I ever met, as he clasps both hands and bows to me.

Growing up on the south side of Chicago we were Mexican. We never identified as Chicana. When I would hear the word *Chicana* it was always said in a derogatory manner, but I don't know why. When mama would get angry at me she would call me India Meca, Meca. In Mexico, they would say, you're not Indian, you're gringa. In New York City, you're not Indian, you speak Spanish. At auditions for Mexican roles, you're too Indian looking. Ni de aquí—ni de allá. So much denial. But going back to recover that which was buried or lost has been an ongoing journey for me.

Why do I write? Rage at the injustices, exploitation, appropriation, loss of land, militarization, discrimination, violence and abuse of women, borders—those imposed and those we create between us and the continued colonization and genocide of Indigenous peoples. This is what motivates me to take action through the written word and turn it into performance.

Through theatre and our stories we transmit energy—a life force—that connects us with our audience and the response it generates is immediate—tears, laughter, anger that motivates action/transformation.

Whether working in the rainforest of Chiapas with the women's weaving cooperatives, health and education promoters, young girls transmitting Radio Insurgente, the street vendors in New York City defending their rights, HIV/AIDS patients, victims of domestic and sexual abuse, this is what inspires and feeds my spirit—the social, political, spiritual, and cultural struggles of Indigenous peoples and connecting the struggles of resistance to build a better world. Because it is we as artists who have the power to transform.

Hortencia Colorado

A las escondidas, hidden in a closet, my hiding place, I'd hear mama and Pera whispering about things I couldn't quite understand—bad things. Pepe and Fred did what? To whom? Oh, no! Images would pop up in my mind. Who could I tell? I wasn't supposed to be listening.

Secretos, stories, memorias, silences, shames—a tight-knit *familia,* not penetrated by outsiders. Punishments doled out with fierce love and humor. Shameful, hurtful memories of alcoholism, abuse, incest, loss of language and identity. Prayer, prayers, and more prayers to saints, virgenes, el Sagrado Corazón and little baby Jesus to make things right and heal our familia. These memories are a part of who I am. They evolved from the historical trauma of my ancestors. They continue to evolve in me and are transformed as I continue to heal. How to talk about this—to whom?

I had to leave my *familia*. I had to come to New York, almost lose my life, audition, audition, study and more study, Actors Studio, Grotowski with Manuel Martin, Theater of the Ridiculous, Off-Off, Off-Broadway, too Mexican to be a Latina, too Mexican to be Indian, finding myself at the American Indian Community House, finding a love, having a son.

But, I'm an actress. I'm not a writer. I can't write. Well, then stop complaining that you don't see yourself represented on the screen or on the stage—other than stereotypes. Well, then who is going to tell my story? I write. I direct. I perform. I fall down and get up again and again. And, because of the Otomí blood that runs through me, the love of my *familia,* my communities, meeting and working with Spiderwoman Theater, being gifted with stories from indigenous men, women, and children—from all of these come my inspiration.

I love the discussions with the audience after our shows. I remember after one of our first shows an African American woman remained to talk with us. She said, "You talk about your little grama, your grande chiquita, well, your little grama is my grandmother." Another time we performed at the Nez Percé Reservation. Before we started the performance we were blessed by one of the women elders and after the performance she told us: "You are truly Indian doctors."

This is what it's about for me.

ECR & CRC: Briefly describe your theatre experience.

EC: When I first arrived in New York I studied at the Gene Frankel Theatre for five years, doing street theatre, working in store front theatres, performing in experimental plays in Spanish with the Duo Theatre, working with a fantastic Cuban director, Manuel Martin, Viola Spolin Storytelling/Theatre Games workshop, and improvisational and storytelling workshops with the Talking Band. I was invited to participate in Theatre of the Oppressed workshops with Augusto Boal, whose technique has had a strong impact on my approach to conducting workshops in our communities. Also, working with another director, Ron Link, who cast me in *Women Behind Bars,* a play by Tom Eyen, which was a spoof on all the prison B movies.

HC: My fate was sealed when I registered at the Goodman Memorial Theater in Chicago, Illinois, where I studied for five years, going to night school four years and one year of day school. With all my studying I was ready for New York or regional theater. When I arrived in New York, not knowing a soul, I made rounds, auditioned, knocked on producers' doors and even Lee Strasburg of the Actors Studio. I was getting nothing, so I started taking classes with Gene Frankel and Andreas Voutsinas of the Actors Studio. Andreas coached me in auditioning for the studio. I was rejected because they felt the studio would ruin me!! I worked with Manuel Martin of the Duo Theater, working in the Studio and Grotowski techniques. The plays of Ron Tavel introduced me to Theatre of the Ridiculous. The playwright, Tom Eyen, and director, Ron Link, fed my love of theater. Theater for the New City was one of the first to produce Coatlicue's work and introduced me to Street Theatre. We found a home at the American

Indian Community House to present our first play and also formed another company, Off the Beaten Path, made up of Coatlicue Theater Company, Spiderwoman Theater, and Louis Mofsie of the Thunderbird American Indian Dancers. What an experience working on Broadway as understudy for Rita Moreno in the Ritz. It was a learning experience not wished on anyone. Or, how about, "you're too Indian to do Lorca." All part of the learning on my journey. Working with Spiderwoman Theater was a blessing. And, now learning from someone from a teacher whose work I have read, Augusto Boal. And I know there is more to come and all good.

ECR & CRC: How did you decide to write and/or perform?

EC: I began performing when I was six years old, dancing with a folkloric dance group, the Chicago Fiesta Guild. Mama would take us once a week to the Centro Social Mexicano to learn Mexican history and Mexican songs and dances from Sra. Celia Pedroza, a teacher from Mexico. But I also took tap dancing classes at the Masonic Temple in Blue Island, and I was the only Mexican all dressed in green who could dance the Irish jig. And I would put on shows in our backyard and would recruit my nieces and nephews. They were sometimes reluctant. But it was my sister who pushed me into taking acting classes when I came to New York. I was sick and tired of all the stereotyped roles I was being offered. One day we went to see Spiderwoman, another Native American theatre company, doing their version of *Lysistrata*. It was theatre like I had never seen before. I worked with them for several years, but we had our own stories that needed to be told, so we formed Coatlicue Theatre Company.

HC: In my mind I have always been thinking the words I needed to write, to speak, but for a long time they remained in silence. But, it was not until I saw my sister, Vira, writing her pieces and then working with Spiderwoman that the thoughts, silences, memories started to flow, tumble, and jump onto scraps of paper and then become living organisms on the stage.

I've been performing since I was in grade school—tap dancing, acrobat, ballet, *baile folklórico*, modern, Escuela Lazaro Cardenas with Sra. Pedroza teaching us the songs, dances, and poetry of Mexico, sitting in front of the radio with daddy listening to the operas, operettas, soap operas, country/western, and stories and music from Mexico. All of this was pushing me to Goodman Memorial Theater, where my fate was sealed.

ECR & CRC: Why do you write what you do?

EC: I used to read a lot when I was a kid. I'd spend a lot of time in the library, but I never saw myself, family, or community reflected, which was another form of making us invisible and silencing us. The silencing also came from my own family. We had to remain silent and speak when spoken to. Men were treated differently. They were more privileged. They could drink, beat their wives, and abuse their children.

Female sexuality was never addressed, so I was ashamed of my body. But later I discovered the power of female sexuality in all the deities, Coatlicue, Coyolxauhqui, and Chimalma. I feel a responsibility to members of my community and to the women I write about because I have been gifted with many stories on my journey and I am committed to telling the stories of women whose voices have been silenced, such as the murdered women of Juárez [Nuevo León, México], the victims of human trafficking, the Zapatista women who had to cover their faces in order to be seen and heard, the men and women in my family who were abused and were afraid to speak out. Stories were told to teach a lesson. They have a moral. Telling these stories and connecting them to what is happening now, the cultural, social, and political wars.

HC: It is that something knocking at my heart wanting to be released, to be expressed—one word among many. *Ya no más silencio, ya no más secretos,* say the grandfathers and grandmothers. I hear how their voices were silenced to their spirituality, traditions, and language. It can be a headline, a snatch of words overheard that scream out to be written and heard. Our generations to come need to read and see these words of how we existed.

ECR & CRC: Who do you write for and what audience are you trying to reach?

EC: I write for whoever will listen. I write for my community because sometimes they can't always come to see us perform because they work. We go to them and translate some of our plays into Spanish or perform excerpts. And when we perform, people identify with the stories and they see themselves reflected, whether it's the native community or the Latino community.

HC: I write and perform for all peoples of all ages and genders as I have done and will continue to do. I do it for my family, and maybe someday they will see their reflection.

ECR & CRC: What message, if any, are you trying to convey to your audience with this work and/or with all of your work?

EC: Our identity—who we are—where we come from. That is what connects us to the past, present, and the future generations. That is the thread that runs through our work. It is my ancestors who guide my spirit and motivate me to write the words that come to me. They are always present.

HC: Open your minds and hearts to hear, see and feel my words expressed through my writing and performance.

ECR & CRC: Who or what has been your major influence?

EC: *My* inspiration comes from many sources. Sometimes the radio, a conversation on the subway, a newspaper article, my family, my friends and my sister who has taught me so much and Shan, my nephew—who are always there when I need them.

HC: All the elders, men, women, youth, children, all the indigenous communities I have spent time in, all the books I have ever read, my family, my son, my sister, and Gloria Anzaldúa.

ECR & CRC: What has been your biggest and/or most difficult struggle/challenge in life, in completing a play or getting it produced, etc.?

EC: Oftentimes our work is not touched because it is too political. We address issues that make some people feel uncomfortable. Also, our plays are nonlinear. It is a continuous circle. In the past we have not had the luxury of devoting all our time to writing and performing. We do all of the administrative work, writing grants, securing venues because we don't have a booking agent. Once a play is written, we perform it a few times and go on to the next project. Rewrites are done when we perform it the next time. Sometimes we are asked to do 15- to 20-minute performances on a particular theme. So, we have a lot of short pieces that later develop into full-length plays. Most of our work comes from those who have seen our work. Roberta Uno has been instrumental in producing our work at New World Theater and so many other ways that I am so grateful to her, and Diana Taylor has also been so nurturing.[5]

HC: For the longest time it was completing a play before the first performance. Working all day, raising a son, writing, and rehearsing were a challenge. Now I have a little more time to go back to our earlier plays and do revisions, because sometimes they were only performed one weekend or two at the American Indian Community House or Theater for the New City. No one really knew about us. When I started attending conferences I was aware that the same groups or individuals were always working even though we kept submitting our material. I thought, how will they ever get to know us if they don't take a chance? Then along came Roberta Uno, who has supported our work, encouraging us in every way possible. And then along came Diana Taylor, who has been super-supportive. It's all blessings.

ECR & CRC: Can you offer any words of advice to aspiring playwrights/performers/directors/audiences?

EC: Take risks, don't play it safe, keep a journal, and have a sense of humor.

HC: Keep writing and don't stop. Don't censor yourself. Start a writers group in your community. Study. Read a lot—everything. Listen. See as many plays as you can. Perform whenever and wherever you can. Create your own work. Don't ever lose your vision.

ECR & CRC: Elvira, you are among the playwrights who studied with Maria Irene Fornes. Can you provide any commentary about her impact on your work?

EC: I first met Maria Irene Fornes in 1975 when I was invited to participate in a workshop at INTAR [International Arts Relations] Theatre in New York City to develop an original play. The play was a bilingual theatre piece with music, titled *Cap-a-Pie* (Head to Foot), comprised of personal childhood memories and fantasies of eight actors. It was performed at INTAR (May–June 1975), Lincoln Center Outdoor Festival (August 1975), and Theater for the New City (January 1976). The play had an overwhelming response and it was subsequently revived at INTAR. My memories of Maria Irene were her delicious sense of humor and the simplicity, delicacy, and beauty with which she encouraged us to bring our stories to life. We taped them, wrote them, performed them, and sang. What an incredible experience that was for me. One of my stories was a personal reminiscence of going to see my idol, Lola Beltrán, in the Mexican movies. There was always a nightclub/bar scene with people smoking, drinking, and laughing, and La Lola would make her grand entrance. As I describe Lola's entrance I transform myself and become Lola singing "Por un amor." Maria Irene would always bring her mom to the rehearsals, and one day she was watching a rehearsal and I wasn't doing it fully and her mom got worried. She said to Maria Irene, "Que le pasa a la Mexicana?" That's what she called me. And Maria

Irene said: "Nada mama, she's just marking it." The other vignette was the crush I had when I was ten years old on one of the boarders in our house. My mom took in boarders who came from Mexico to work. And one day I came home from school and he was gone. A neighbor had reported him, the *migra* deported him, and I never saw him again.

Production History/Palabras Dramatúrgicas

This play was performed as a work-in-progress at New World Theater (NWT) in July 1996 and commissioned in 1997 by NWT and the New England Foundation for the Arts in Partnership with Inquilinos Boricuas en Acción of Boston, Massachusetts; the University of Massachusetts Department of Theatre in Amherst, Massachusetts; and Brown University's Rite and Reason in Providence, Rhode Island, for the New Works for a New World Series. Subsequently, the play was rewritten and presented at the American Indian Community House in New York City as part of Indian Summer Festival 2000. In 2001 it traveled to Xicanindio, Mesa, Arizona, and to Multicultural Education (MECA) in Houston, Texas; Stanford University, California; and University of California, Riverside.

Contact Information

coatlicuetheater@gmail.com

CHICOMOZTOC: MIMIXCOA—CLOUD SERPENT

Dedication: We honor our antepasados, our mother, Maria, and our father, Regino, and our abuelitos and abuelitas, who in spite of forced assimilation through religion and education, wove into their shame and denial threads of creation, language, stories, memory, food, traditions in their daily lives and in their dreams, and we continue to weave these threads for the generations to come.

E enters SL with drum. H enters SR with rattle. Both walk to C, face each other and honor the four directions. E sets down drum SL and H sets down rattle SR. E picks up basket of flowers SL and H picks up basket of flowers SR and both walk to C. Both begin the invocation while walking and scattering flowers, making a full circle.

E: I call upon you mis abuelitas.
H: My grandmothers.
BOTH: Help us to remember
E: To dream your stories
H: And make them live.
E: I call upon you my grandmother Toci.
BOTH: Tonantzin, Coatlicue, Cipactli, Tlaltecutli, our mother the earth.
E: Yaocihuatl, Warrior Woman.

H: Llamateuctli, with your tears you bring the rain.

BOTH: Givers of life and death.

H: Grandmother Huixtocihuatl, Salt Woman, wipe away my tears.

E: Grandmother Chalchiutlicue, Jade Skirt, wash away my pain,

H: my shame,

E: my denial

BOTH: with your cleansing waters.

H: Grandmother Tlazoteotl heal my body and my spirit and make it whole again.

E: Grandmother Mayahuel let me suckle your maguey juice for strength, sustenance and joy.

BOTH: Grandmother Cihuateteo who died giving us life help us to follow the path of the sun.

E: Grande chiquita, little grandma, Grandma Rafaelita, protect and guide me.

H: Grandma Amada, I never knew you but your blood runs through my veins and sustains me.

BOTH: Coatlicue, Tonanztin, Cipactli, Tlaltecutli, our mother the earth.

H: Coyolxauhqui, sister moon, bathe me in your light.

E: Cihuacoatl, Snake Woman, Fertility Woman.

H: Ixpapalotl, Obsidian Butterfly, Warrior Woman.

E: Maria Sabina, mama.

BOTH: Our grandmothers, our mothers who gave birth to us, all of our ancestors,

H: Clear the path and sweep away the lies,

E: my shame, abuse and denial.

BOTH: Help us to remember, to dream your stories and make them live.

(*E goes SL, leaves basket and returns. H goes SR, leaves basket, and both return to C and H goes to SR.*)

E: When did my journey begin?

H: When did my journey begin?

E: It began the day I was born under the sign Macuilli Acatl Xihuitl, in the year 5 Reed.

H: It began the day I was born under the sign Ome Tecpatl Xihuitl, in the year 2 Flint.

BOTH: I was baptized with the sign of the cross and given the name, Elvira Elizabeth.

H: Maria Hortencia.

E: Don't look at those dirty books. Don't say that dirty word. Don't see those movies, they're condemned. Don't touch yourself here or there. Don't do this. Don't do that. Don't! Don't! Don't!

(*Music cue: "Chain of Fools." Both dance to music and music slowly fades and both transform words to:*)

BOTH: Shame, shame, shame.

(*Both bring 2 chairs with make-up bags and fake braids to C and H rolls in table. Both, as children, are getting dressed and putting on lipstick and fake braids as they prepare to perform.*)

E: Are you almost ready? You don't have your braids on yet.

H: Hey, those are mine.

E: No, mine had red ribbons.

H: Well, these aren't mine. They're all messed up.

E: That's 'cause you don't take care of them. Hurry up they're going to take our pictures.

(*Both go to C and pose 3 times. They return to makeup table.*)

H: Are you chewing gum? You better swallow it.

E: Go peek and see who's out there. (*H gets up to look.*) Are there lots of people? Do you see anybody we know?

H: I can't see without my glasses.

E: Well I'll go look then.

H: Hey, they just turned off the lights.

E: Are those your chones falling down?

H: Mensa, that's my slip. Hurry give me a safety pin.

(*Music cue: "Las Chiapanecas."*)

E: Come on the music's started.

(*Both dance to "Las Chiapanecas." Dance ends and both take bows and take off braids. E goes SL. H goes U behind scrim.*)

E: (*As museum tour guide.*) We are entering the hall of the Gran Chichimeca, the Dog People, a fierce nomadic tribe. They hunted with bows and arrows, eating wild weeds. They were primitive. They wore skins of animals. The women were bare breasted. And, they lived in thorn huts. (*Goes behind scrim.*)

H: Chicomoztoc is our birthplace. We live here with our mama.

E: I am Citlantlicue, Star Skirt, mother of the Mimixcoa, the stars and all the deities. Quetzalcoatl and Tezcatlipoca are my sons. In the beginning I gave birth to the Tecpatl, the sacred flint stone knife. (*E squats and lifts up skirt pulling Tecpatl [knife] from between legs, as if giving birth.*) It fell from the sky onto Chicomoztoc and from the Tecpatl were born the Mimixcoa (*the stars*). (*She lets Tecpatl fall and sprinkles confetti.*)

(*Both come out from behind scrim and shoot arrows.*)

H: Our papa, el sol, taught us how to hunt with bows and arrows.

E: I'm tired of hunting for our brothers and sisters.

H: Me too. How come they don't get their own food?

E: Yeah. Let's go drink some more of that delicious maguey.

BOTH: Orale! (*They move to DC and drink. They fall over and look up.*)

E: Five more brothers and sisters!

H: Five more Mimixcoa!

E: Papa gave them sharper weapons and taught them how to use them against us. Let's play a trick on them. (*Whispers in H's ear.*)

H: Orale! Where are they?

E: They must be hiding. (*Both signal to go behind scrim to look.*)

(*Both with knives sneak up on their brothers and kill them. Both slump over each other.*)

BOTH: Our hearts and blood nourishing our mother the earth and our father the sun.

E: We are the Mimixcoa.

H: The cloud serpents.

BOTH: The souls of our Chichimeca ancestors.

E: We were present at the beginning of all things.

H: From Chicomoztoc. . . .

E: we emerged, (*Both begin crawling from beneath scrim.*)

H: seven clans. . . . .

E: from seven caves.

H: Birds.

E: Butterflies.

H: Pumas.

E: Monkeys.

H: Tigers.

E: Dogs.

H: Serpents.

(*E moves chair from SL to U off center and sits. H sits SR facing front.*)

E: Sister Mary Dennis drilled us over and over.

H: Don't have anything to eat or drink the night before Our Lord comes into your hearts.

E: I was so excited and nervous. I forgot and drank some water. Oh, my God! If I tell anyone I won't be able to make my First Holy Communion. I had my white dress, my white shoes, my veil, prayer book, my rosary, everything! What if I don't tell anybody? It would be a secret between God and me. No one will ever know.

H: Except God.

E: I can't imagine that God who suffered and died on the cross for all my sins will send me to hell. You won't send me to hell will you God? He didn't answer, so I took it as a good sign.

(*Both bring table and chairs SR and sit.*)

H: Daddy would sit at the kitchen table drinking his Miller's six-pack and I would sit there with him. We both sat there in silence. I liked sitting there with him 'cause it was like we were talking to each other even though we didn't speak. Sometimes he would throw his head back and laugh.

E: Like when he would take us to El Piojo, the old Mexican movie house. It was so old it smelled viejo. He'd fall asleep and wake up laughing when everyone laughed. Sometimes I close my eyes and I try real hard to remember the sound of his voice. Mama would say, "Go tell your papa to come and eat." He slept in the basement right next to the furnace. Why? I would go down to the basement and he would be staring out the window. Like he was somewhere else. Remembering.

H: Mama told daddy to leave. Stop! Stop! Daddy's got a gun and he said he's gonna kill himself! No daddy! No daddy! Everybody was trying to take the gun away from daddy. Oh, no, he said he's gonna lay down on the railroad tracks and let the train kill him. No daddy! No daddy!

E: Su padre se va ir al infierno because he doesn't go to church.

H: Oh, please baby Jesus, don't let daddy go to hell. He loves us. I always thought that we'd all go to heaven together holding hands. (*Begins to sing.*) Ay, miniño, mikiko, miko, miko, miko.

E: Why are you singing that song? That's daddy's song.

H: Daddy used to sing that song to me.

E: No! Daddy would lift me up and sit me on his knee. And, he would sing: ay, miniño, mikiko, miko, miko, miko.

H: Ay, miniño, mikiko, miko, miko, miko. (*Both fight.*)

E: With an address I pulled from my memory, P.O. Box 265, the following day we took the bus to Cuero, Texas.

BOTH: The "Turkey Capital of the World," the bus driver told us as he dropped us off wishing us luck.

H: At city hall a woman searched for family records. No Colorados!

E: No Colorados? Then, as we were leaving she called to us, "Wait, I found the address to the P.O. Box. There are no Colorados living there. Someone named Matilde Mendez lives there."

BOTH: Matilde Mendez?

E: Maybe she's related. (*Looking at each other.*)

H: Do you think we should go anyway?

E: Let's call first.

H: No! Let's just go, 'cause maybe she won't want to see us.

(*Both begin walking in place.*)

E: So many beautiful old houses. I had a dream about my grandma, daddy's mama. That's what we always called her. A dream about the house she lived in. These houses and this road are not like the ones in my dream.

(*Both stop and look down*).

BOTH: Railroad tracks! (*Look at each other.*)

H: Daddy worked for the Rock Island Railroad.

E: We rode the train back and forth to school and work.

H: We had a garden by the railroad tracks.

E: We used to pick strawberries by the railroad tracks. (*Both cross tracks.*) Look! It's a dirt road, just like in my dream and the houses are built on top of cement blocks.

(*Both look for the house. They find it.*)

E: That's it. That's the house.

H: I just saw somebody looking out the window.

E: Let's go knock.

BOTH: (*Knock. The women open the door.*) Somos las hijas de Regino Colorado.

H: We hugged her and she said, "Pasen, pasen, come in." Finally a connection to daddy's side of the family, but we didn't really know each other.

E: And then she told us to sit on the sofa. I searched her face. The movement of her hands. The way she talked and walked. Her smile. To see if there was something of her in me.

H: We only have one picture of Grandma Amada. Do you have any more?

E: Matilde brought out a large cardboard box filled with family pictures.

H: We got down on the floor as she pulled out picture after picture of our uncles, aunts, cousins, and grandma. Indian faces.

E: Pictures like the ones buried in the trunk in our basement.

BOTH: They all look like us.

H: There's Minnie. And she said, ya murió, no tuvo suerte con los hombres.

E: Uncle Leandro.

H: Uncle Apolonio.

E: Grandpa Lorenzo.

H: Grandma Amada.

E: Santos.

BOTH: They all died.

E: We never got to know them. Why?

H: Every summer we would drive through Texas on our way to Mexico, but we never stopped to visit them. We would only visit mama's side of the family. Why?

(*As they enter they look around.*)

E: Worn-out linoleum.

H: Life-size statute of the Immaculate Conception.

E: Piles of quilts everywhere that she makes.

H: And lots of plants.

E: Look, there's your picture on the wall. How come mine isn't there?

H: She said, "Your mama sent it to me."

E: Then Matilde took us into the kitchen and through a large kitchen window she pointed to a house, "That's the house your grandma lived in."

(*Both look at the house and each other and feel a sense of loss and recovery expressed through organic gestures.*)

H: Matilde we want you to come and have lunch with us.

E: Ay no, gracias, it's almost time for my telenovela and I don't want to miss it.

(*Both look at each other.*)

H: Can you believe it she'd rather watch a telenovela than be with us?

E: Well, we were strangers. We never kept in touch. And after so many years we show up at her home. What did we expect?

H: We told her we were going to Mexico and she said, "You have familia in San Luis Potosí. Go to Ciudad de Maíz and you'll find them. I can't travel anymore."

E: We hugged her tight one more time, not wanting to leave.

(*Music cue: "Paso Doble"*)

H: I would sweep across the dance floor with Manuel, Mary's husband. He was my dancing partner at celebrations like weddings, birthdays, fiestas patrias.

E: Bautizos, First Holy Communion, confirmations, bodas, crismas. Mama, Grande Chiquita, Tía Petra, Joan, Trini, preparing the masa to make tamales.

H: Mama would always call us on our birthdays.

BOTH: Que linda está la mañana en que vengo a saludarte . . .

H: Making piñatas for birthdays.

E: Hot dogs, cheese macaroni, White Castle hamburgers, Italian sausage, Polish sausage, drive-in movies with all of our nieces and nephews and cousins piled up in the old Ford.

H: Cornflakes, pancakes, pozole, chorizo, sweet rolls, pan dulce, grapefruit with lots of sugar.

E: Prince Castle banana splits, lime rickys, sloppy joes, chocolate phosphates, Creamsicles, popsicles, Fudgesicles from the Good Humor man.

H: Fresh-made flour tortillas with butter, enchiladas, tostadas, mole made on the metate, gorditas 2 inches thick with melted lard.

BOTH: A la rorro, niño a la rorro, duermete niñito y duermete ya.

E: Kiss the little baby Jesus and take a candy. Then mama would put baby Jesus in the manger.

H: And we would all sit down to eat buñuelos, tamales and strawberry atole.

E: Picking nopales in the sand dunes at Miller's Beach, then dumping them in the washing machine to get rid of the needles.

H: Pepe and Fred getting drunker and drunker and drunker and drunker. "Don't let them touch you." But, you didn't say anything, mama . . .

E: Swallow a raw egg. Mama would wash me by the stove in the winter. "Don't let anyone touch you here or here or here." Corridos, mambos, paso dobles, cha-cha-chas.

H: "Don't speak half English, half Spanish, a la trocha y mocha."

E: "You're not like the girls from Mexico. You're so frescas."

H: I bleached my skin so I could get whiter and whiter.

(*Music builds.*)

BOTH: Dirty Mexican! Dirty Mexican! Dirty Mexican! Dirty Mexican!

(*Music ends.*)

E: Are you Indian?

H: No, I'm Mexican.

E: Dirty Mexican! Dirty Mexican!

(*E goes around chair SL and H goes around chair SR*)

BOTH: We took the plane, we took the train, we took the bus.

H: We missed the bus.

E: There was no bus. Don't you remember? (*E and H sit.*)

H: It's a long ride from New York City to Temoaya.

E: Women on the bus speaking Nahuatl, Hñäñhu.

BOTH: Look! Look! The Ceremonial Center!

(*Both get up and walk around.*)

E: Huge stone columns for the days of the week.

H: Serpents carved and painted all around.

BOTH: Temezcales.

E: In the center on the ground was the sacred fire painted on stones.

BOTH: Let's burn some copal and sage.

(*Both C.*)

H: Music was playing, everybody was dancing, getting ready to leave Guadalupe Tepeyac in Chiapas and these guys come over and one of them asks, "Where are you from?"

BOTH: We're from New York City.

E: He says, "You look like us. You are one of us. You are Chichimeca-Otomís living and walking your path in New York City."

(*Both look at each other.*)

BOTH: Daddy's coming home! Daddy's coming home!

E: I'll race you. (*E from SR and H from SL run and meet DC.*)

BOTH: I won! I won! Daddy! Daddy! Papa, papa, papacito! (*Both fight with each other trying to get to Daddy.*)

E: (*H takes E and sits her SL.*) One day he picked me up from school and stopped at George's Tavern to drink with his buddies. "Here's some potato chips. Sit here and wait for me."

H: (*H pulls E from chair to C.*) How many times have I told you not to go into the tavern with your father? Now, kneel down and put your hands up over your head and don't get up until I tell you.

(*E kneels DC and H sits SR*)

E: No, mama I'll be a good girl. I won't do it anymore.

H: Ahora veras, me la vas a pagar, muchacha visionuda. I'm going to die.

E: No mama, don't die.

H: Yes, I'm going to die, and then I'm going to come back from the dead and eat you up. Ha, ha, ha.

E: No mama, no mama! (*E crawls over to H and grabs her around legs.*)

E: San Luis Potosí. Hills of gold. Mountains of red earth. (*E touches earth and smells it.*) Desert, cactus all around. Daddy's birthplace. (*E gets up.*) Guachichiles, red sparrows. They painted their hair red. First people of San Luis Potosí. (*Both walk and climb on chairs. Chairs are used as mountains.*)

BOTH: We're walking on the same ground daddy walked on.

E: This is where he walked when he was a little boy.

H: Was that lake always there?

E: He left and never returned.

H: What if we went all the way back, as far back as we could?

E: What would we find?

H: Who we are—our ancestors.

E: Grande Chiquita would be there.

H: Mama, daddy, all of our relatives.

E: And they would welcome us.

H: Speak to us in Nahuatl, Hñähñu.

E: And they would tell us, "this is who you are."

H: "This is how you came to be on this earth."

E: And there would be no more shame.

H: No more denial.

E: (*Jumps off chair C as Chimalma.*) I want all you beautiful, big-breasted women, todas las gorditas, to form a squadron and give the men time to regroup.

H: Chimalma led us women into battle.

(*H stands on chair SL and E stands on chair SR.*)

E: Orale, come on women let's show those men how brave we are.

(*H goes SL and E goes SR and both wind up C.*)

H: We charged, slapping our bellies and showing our beautiful breasts. Mixcoatl shot arrows at Chimalma and all of us, but they passed right through us and when we women came face to face with the enemy, Chimalma gave the order.

E: Attack women!

H: We squeezed our breasts, squirting milk into the faces of the enemy blinding them.

BOTH: Cowards! Cowards! We won! We won! The cowards are running away!

BOTH: Primitive, salvaje, evil, sneaky, pagan, india pata rajada.

(*H goes UR and gets table with book—E gets two chairs and both sit C.*)

E: I can't do this anymore! Hundreds of handwritten names. Victoriana, Teofila, Getrudis, Josefina, Agustina, . . . It's hard reading these names. They're all blurred. 1842 . . . 1843 . . . 1844 . . . 1845 . . . My eyes are burning. I can't see straight anymore. Aaaaaaayyy! I found her. I found grandma. Amada Loredo born 1845. (*E and H look at each other and continue looking.*)

E: But it doesn't say she's Indian.

H: I wanted the birth certificate, the baptismal certificate to say, Chichimeca-Otomí, Pame, Hñähñu, Indio, something written, some proof of who we are. Tell me que somos Chichimeca-Otomís I want to hear it.

E: Tell me que somos Chichimeca-Otomís. I want to hear it. I want to hear it.

(*H takes book and chair to UR and E takes chair SL and both put on First Communion veils.*)

(*Music cue: Gregorian chants.*)

E: I walked up the aisle with all the other girls in my class. I knelt down and stuck out my tongue. (*H pokes E and giggles.*) I waited for something terrible to happen, but nothing happened. I went back to my pew. (*E rises and walks around to SL and returns and kneels.*) Think holy thoughts, think holy thoughts. I tried to swallow the host, but it got stuck. (*E tries to push it down with her tongue or finger and chews it.*) It's all crumbled up. I chewed what was left of the body and blood of Christ. Oh my God, I killed Jesus! I killed Jesus! The devil's gonna come to get me with his pitchfork and I'm gonna burn in the fires of hell! I killed Jesus! I killed Jesus! (*Music ends.*) (*H moves cart to UR and E goes to C and kneels.*)

(*E goes to C and kneels as mama grinding ingredients on metate and H SR.*)

E: (*Sings as mama.*) "Si a tu ventana llega una paloma, trátala con cariño que es mi persona. Un poquito de jonjoli, unas semillas de calabaza, chocolate, a little bit of this and a little bit of that. Un señor me preguntó si yo era italiana."

H: "A man asked you if you were Italian?" What did you say mama?

E: "Pues yo le dije que sí."

H: You said yes, Mama?

E: Zas, zas, zas con el molcajete. Same circular motion. Hand to stone, stone to hand. Making fresh tortillas de harina every morning and rolling them up with mantequilla. "Ay, ay, ay, ay, Diosito de mi vida! Mi pajarito Jantzi se lo tragó el gato. (The cat swallowed my little bird, Jantzi.) Dónde estás condenado gato? (Where are you stupid cat?) Ay pobrecito de mi Jantzi. (My poor little Jantzi.) (*Sings.*) Si a tu ventana llega una paloma, trátala con cariño que es mi persona." (*E rises and goes to SL.*) Mama getting all dressed up to go out and putting on her corset, rolling her medias down below her knees, making a little nudito so they won't fall down. Pond's cold cream, Coty dusting powder.

E: She kept all her jewelry in special little boxes in her tocador. Cedar box filled with important papers, estampitas of all the saints, San Juditas, San Antonio, la Virgen del Carmen, la Imaculada Concepción, San Martín de Porres, el Sagrado Corazón de Jesús, la Virgen de San Juan de los Lagos and of course, la Virgen de Guadalupe. She would light candles and pray for miracles. Mama, la curandera who healed us with yerbitas, manzanilla, ruda, estafiate, and rubbing manteca on our bellies. Mama was a great storyteller. She scared us with stories about brujas, little lights in the night, and the woman who swallowed balls of hair. She loved telling bawdy stories.

One of her favorite stories was the "Talking Rooster." Once there was this viejo who was a real penny-pincher. He never gave his wife enough money to buy food and he always wanted to have carnitas for dinner. And if she didn't have carnitas for him to eat, he would beat her. One day she couldn't take it anymore. "Ahora veras, viejo stingy, me la vas a pagar." (Just you wait, you stingy old fool, you're going to pay for this.) She had no meat and she didn't want him to beat her. So she went into the kitchen and grabbed the butcher knife, lifted her skirt and sliced a nice fat juicy tender piece of meat from her buttocks. She threw it into the frying pan with tomatillos, onions, and chiles making a very tasty guisado.

H: Cucurucú, nalgas de vieja comemos aquí. (Cock-a-doodle-do, old lady's buttocks we're eating today.)

H: (*As husband*) Ay vieja these carnitas are so tasty. Where did you get such tender meat? Give me some more.

E: (*As wife*) Ay viejo, I'm so glad you like them.

H: Cucurucú, nalgas de vieja comemos aquí.

H: (*As husband*) Vieja, what's the rooster saying?

E: (*As wife*) Nothing viejo, he's just singing because he's happy.

H: (*As husband*) No, vieja, listen he's saying something.

H: Cucurucú, nalgas de vieja comemos aquí.

E: (*As wife*) "Don't pay any attention to that old rooster. I'll be right back with some more carnitas." But the viejo got suspicious and he followed his wife into the kitchen and just as she was lifting her skirt to cut him another slice of meat from her nalgas (buttocks) . . .

H: (As husband) Ay, vieja cochina, you've been giving me your dirty nalgas to eat.

E: (*As wife*) "What did you expect me to give you, viejo pendejo, penny-pincher. You ought to be glad I gave you my nalgas to eat. Ya basta! I've had enough. I'm leaving you and you can starve to death viejo penny-pincher." And the husband se petateo. He died because he had no more nalgas to eat.

H: Cucurucú, no más nalgas de vieja comemos aquí. (No more old lady's buttocks to eat.)

(*E sits SL and H sits SR.*)

H: Mama que somos? What are we?

E: Mexicanas.

H: No, que indias somos? You know, like Aztec.

E: Como van a ser Indias, son Mexicanas.

H: Pero, what kind of Indians are we?

E: Ay que mis niñas, you're not Indian. Why do you want to be Indian?

H: But, look at Grandma Chiquita, she looks Indian.

E: She's Spanish.

E: I was Indian without knowing I was Indian. I was Mexican.

H: India Meca, Meca.

E: No, no, I'm Mexican. I don't want to be India, Meca, Meca. Indian pictures in books, on calendars, statues. Relatives we visited who spoke Nahuatl. They were Indian. I was Mexican. I could tap dance, do the Irish jig, baile folklórico, the stroll, the Mambo and the Cha-Cha-Cha. I'm not an India Meca, Meca. No soy India Meca, Meca.

H: Shame, Shame, Shame. Have you looked in the mirror? What do you see?

(*H as nun, goes to E who is sitting SL.*)

H: (*As a nun*) No, no, no! Put out your hand. (*H hits E with ruler.*) How many times have I told you that's not the way to write a 9? (*H takes E by the hand and locks her in broom closet, behind scrim.*)

E: No, I don't want to be locked up in the broom closet. It's dark in here. I'm scared. And it smells funny. I have to go pee-pee. I have to go pee-pee real bad. I can't hold it anymore. Oh no, it's running down my legs. I'm all wet and it's going out the door. (*E starts to clean it up as H walks to open door behind scrim. H grabs E and takes her to SL chair and E sits and H goes to SR to sit.*)

H: She did pee-pee. She did pee-pee.

H: Maybe we're Apache! I mean because of our name—Colorado.

E: Maybe we're related to Mangas Colorado.

H: Or Joe Colorado. "My people are Apache—not Mexican. Mexicans killed the Apaches."

E: We gotta do something about it. They're casting for this big Indian film. Them Mexicans are taking all the Indian parts. (*Both freeze.*)

(*Music cue: "La Tierra Es Mi Madre."*)

E: The only good Indian is a Wall Street Indian.

H: The only good Indian wears Gucci moccasins.

E: The only good Indian is a card-carrying Indian.

H: The only good Indian is an urban Indian.

E: The only good Indian lives in a tepee.

H: The only good Indian runs the other way.

E: The only good Indian is a BIA Indian.

H: The only good Indian hears no evil and sees no evil.

E: The only good Indian is a commodity Indian.

H: The only good Indian is a Republican Indian.

E: The only good Indian makes love the Indian way, which is any which way.

(*H goes D.*)

H: I walked into the American Indian Community House—JTPA office. I was sweating. I filled out my application and I wrote "Apache." Someone passed me in the hall.

E: You Apache? (*H looks to R and L and shakes head yes.*)

H: He gave me the Apache handshake. (*E and H do mock handshake.*) I had passed the test. I wore my turquoise jewelry, my Southwest skirt, my cowboy boots and tried very hard not to look Mexican, hoping no one would speak to me in Spanish.

E: Mescalero or White Mountain?

H: No, I'm Apache.

E: From where?

H: From New Mexico. I was lying. I didn't know what kind of Indian I was. My face was getting red and I was sweating. Why did they have to ask all those questions. Why didn't they just give me my card.

E: Shame. Shame. Shame.

E: The only good Indian is a Hollywood Indian.

H: The only good Indian is an Apache Indian.

E: The only good Indian is a bad dog Indian.

H: The only good Indian is a Mystic Warrior.

E: The only good Indian wears buckskin and dances with wolves.

H: The only good Indian is a Sioux Indian.

E: The only good Indian is a Mexican Indian.

H: The only good Indian is a full-blood Indian.

E: The only good Indian doesn't talk Indian.

H: The only good Indian is an Arthur Murray dancing Indian.

E: Are they saying they're Indian? They speak Spanish. They can't be Indian.

H: Tell them you're Indian from here because they don't want Indians from the other side.

(*Music cue: "La Tierra Es Mi Madre."*)

(*Both freeze. End music.*)

E: The only good Indian is a Wannabe Indian.

H: The only good Indian doesn't believe in sharing.

E: The only good Indian shares everything.

H: The only good Indian is a politically correct Indian.

E: The only good Indian is a cigar-store Indian.

H: The only good Indian buys on credit.

E: The only good Indian has no credit.

H: The only good Indian is white on the outside and red on the inside.

E: The only good Indian shops at Walmart's and eats at McDonald's.

H: The only good Indian is a dead Indian.

BOTH: Ha. Ha. Ha. fooled you. We're still here.

(*E sits SL and H sits SR.*)

E: Grande Chiquita. She spoke Otomí but nobody knew it. She was tiny like a bird, a hummingbird. Nobody really knew how old she was. Her nose was like a beak, long and elegant. Her hair was pulled back in a neat little bun like a nest on her head. When she walked her long skirts rustled like the wings of a bird. She didn't speak English and very little Spanish. She spoke Otomí, but nobody knew it. Her hands were always in motion, making gorditas, tamales, healing herself with her yerbitas, telling me cuentos. When they rested she would place them one over the other on her lap. She spoke Otomí but nobody knew it. When was she silenced? She kept her songs locked in her heart where only she could hear them.

H: Grande Chiquita was a maid in grandpa's house and then when grandpa's wife died Grande Chiquita stayed on with Grandpa Flores and they got married. They say that grandpa's family came from Spain. And, when grandpa's family came to visit grandpa would take our little grandma to a back room and lock her up so his family wouldn't have to look at our little grandma's Indian face.

(*H takes E behind scrim.*)

BOTH: (*E goes around chair SL and H goes around chair SR.*) We took the plane, we took the train, we took the bus. (*Both go C.*) It was pouring rain.

E: We wound up in a hotel by the railroad tracks.

H: The clerk asked 15 minutes or an hour.

BOTH: No, we're staying overnight.

H: After we had checked in we noticed people coming in and out without any luggage.

E: It was then that we realized it was a hotel for hookers.

H: We checked out early the next morning.

H: When we arrived in San Luis Potosí we didn't know anyone. A stranger asked us, "What are you doing here?"

E: We're looking for familia. Do you know any Colorados?

H: "Yes, my sister has a good friend whose name is Colorado. The family owns a cab company and grocery store."

E: They were all waiting for us. Consuelo and Rosalio. Genoveva and Trinquilina.

H: The room was filled with cousins, grandchildren, nieces, and nephews.

E: Even a taxi with the name Colorado.

H: Genoveva looks like you.

E: Trinquilina looks like you.

(*E goes C and sits.*)

E: How old am I? I'm not gonna tell you. I am as old as the earth. I am Cipactli, the earth before it was shaped and formed. I am Red Woman. I am the womb, the earth, the sacred fire. I come from the belly button of the moon.

H: Trinquilina, come visit us in New York.

E: I will never leave this land. My belly button is buried here in this earth.

(*E goes SL and puts on veil and H goes SR and puts on veil. E walks S and stops.*)

E: I saw myself walking down the aisle. All dressed in white. I was going to be the bride of Christ. (H kneels.)

Music cue: "I Will Follow Him"—omit second stanza.)

(*Both dance.*) I will follow him. Follow him wherever he may go. I love him. I love him. I love him. And where he goes I'll follow, I'll follow. He'll always be my true love, my true love, from now until forever, forever, forever, forever. (*Music ends.*)

(*Music cue: Gregorian chant.*)

I read all the lives of the saints. How they fasted and did penance. Some were stoned to death. Some were burned at the stake. Some were shot with arrows. I could be a martyr, maybe even a saint! (*H passes out holy cards and relics.*) There will be holy cards with my picture on it and statutes and relics with pieces of my hair or clothing. People will pray to me and they'll kiss my feet and leave flowers and money. (*E goes out into audience.*) I could perform miracles, make the deaf hear, the crippled walk again, the blind see and bring the dead back to life! (*Music cue ends. Both take off veil.*)

And, I could punish Sister Mary Ethel for locking me in the broom closet by sending her to hell!

BOTH: (*Singing*) Ay miniño mikiko, Ay miniño mikiko.

H: Why is it so deserted?

E: Where are all the people?

H: Only 25 families living here.

E: Where did they go? Why did they leave?

H: After they shut down the mines there was no more work, so the people left.

E: Is that when you left daddy?

H: There he comes, daddy, daddy, daddy, (*both start running*) arms full of potato chips and cookies.

BOTH: Daddy, daddy, I love you so much daddy. (*E falls down.*)

E: Oh no, my elbow's bleeding. And, there's a hole in my blue chaqueta mexicana, the one you bought me daddy. It hurts. Blood runs. It hurts as I remember. Why doesn't the hurt go away? So much to say. All those times you were staring out the basement window. What were you thinking about? I never asked. What were grandma and grandpa like? I never asked. Why didn't we ever visit them? There's a hurt that won't go away. (*E gets up wiping blood and running SL and U to D.*)

E: Wake up daddy! Wake up! Don't leave me now. There's so much that hasn't been said.

H: Ay miniño mikiko, miko, miko, miko. (*Repeat several times.*)

(*E joins singing and goes to sit SL.*)

H: (*As priest*) You must be the Indian relatives from New York City. I've been to New Mexico.

E: Oh, that's nice.

H: Our niece, Jennie said, "Tío Pete looks so good. I guess it must be his Indian blood."

E: Oh, no! My daddy is not Indian! My daddy is not Indian. Shame, shame, shame.

H: (*As priest*) What does the feather signify?

E: Protection so he will have a safe journey. When you see an eagle.

BOTH: When you see an eagle and a serpent perched on a nopal you will know you have arrived. Petey was going home.

H: Nobody in our family says they're Indian.

E: Pera spoke Otomí.

BOTH: Liar.

H: In Mexico, people ask me, "Where are you from?"

E: I'm Chichimeca-Otomí from New York City.

BOTH: Ha, ha, ha. You're not Indian. You're a gringa.

E: Nobody in my family wants to be Indian. Pera spoke Otomí. Grande Chiquita spoke Otomí. Why was the truth denied? Why? Why? Why?

BOTH: (*Song and dance.*) Shame, shame, shame.

(*Both go to UC.*)

(*Sound cue: wind.*)

E: I am standing here in Buenavista.

H: I am standing on the Cerro de San Pedro.

BOTH: And, we're here searching for Las Peñitas, your birthplace, daddy.

H: What were the original names before the Spaniards changed them?

E: Railroad tracks.

H: A train passes.

E: I see the mountains. I think about all the stories mama told me. I look at the oldest tree, laurel de la India. I wrap my arms around it. I feel its strength.

H: What were the stories that daddy never told.

E: And we never asked.

H: How many stories have been seen and heard? How many secrets lie buried here?

E: The spirits stop to rest. I listen.

H: I hear their voices.

E: The old ones, the warriors, the children. I hear their cries, their songs, their stories.

H: I keep walking.

E: I listen again.

H: They're calling me.

E: I stop.

BOTH: Do not forget us. Do not forget us. (*Repeat.*)

E: I see the bark banner fluttering in the wind and I know they are present. Mis abuelitas—los ancianos—mama—daddy. I see their faces.

H: The Mimixcoa.

E: Our ancestors.

BOTH: The Cloud Serpents.

E: They are whispering: "No nos olviden. Do not forget us. Do not forget us."

BOTH: We travel to Mictlan.

H: The Place of the Dead.

E: We gather up the bones.

BOTH: And breathe life into them.

H: They are calling us.

BOTH: Back to the beginning. Back to the beginning. To Chicomoztoc.

Notes

1. Correspondence from Elvira and Hortencia Colorado, including materials received February 20 and April 10, 2003; press kit materials, received April 10, 2003; and responses to editors' biographical questionnaire, July 20 and August 1, 2007. See also Elizabeth C. Ramírez, *Chicanas/Latinas in American Theatre: A History of Performance* (Bloomington: Indiana University Press, 2000), 136–39. A photograph of the sisters appears on the cover of the paperback edition of *Chicanas/Latinas in American Theatre.*

2. Responses to the editors' biographical questionnaire, July 20, 2007.

3. See the dedication to the play.

4. Elvira and Hortencia Colorado, video performance description, American Indian Community House, May 2000, New York City. See http://hidvl.nyu.edu/video/NYUb13557251.html, accessed November 30, 2008.

5. Roberta Uno is the program officer for arts and culture at the Ford Foundation in

New York City. She is the founder and former artistic director of the New World Theater in Amherst, Massachusetts, and with Kathy A. Perkins she is coeditor of *Contemporary Plays by Women of Color* (Routledge, 1996), in which the Colorados' play, *1992: Blood Speaks,* appears. Diana Taylor is currently a professor of performance studies and Spanish at the Tisch School of the Arts at New York University, as well as the founding director of the Hemispheric Institute of Performance and Politics. She has published extensively on the subject of Latin American theatre and performance, politics and performance, and feminist theatre, among other topics.

PART IV

"Race Matters"

In a climate of heated debates over immigration, the ever-present threat of English-only measures, and the 2010 "open season" on anything Mexican in Arizona with Governor Jan Brewer's proclamation to pursue anyone who is in the state illegally, among other political domination in the United States affecting Latinas/Latinos, race certainly does matter. In this section we can explore the impact of race through performance. Among other reasons, staging race valuable in trying to understand the differences among Latinas. Tessie Liu addresses the useful nature of the study of race for comprehending the distinctions between women. She writes that "by focusing on race as an analytical category in accounting for the differences among women, we are in fact studying race as a principle of social organization and racial metaphors as part of the process of defining hierarchies and constituting boundaries of privilege." Thus, "understanding this process allows us to see how much the identities of different groups of women in the same society are implicated in one another. Although their experiences of oppression differ dramatically, these differences are nonetheless relationally constituted in identifiable social processes."[1]

The common factors in the study of race are ancestry, that is, the bloodline, and commonality. When we use performance as a means of this investigation, we can examine the racial metaphors that playwrights provide for us in order to understand the communities they create.[2] In that sense, race functions as a unifying force, binding characters through those ideas we have investigated previously, including family, religion, and community. Understanding the multifaceted nature of race, including "ancestry, color and appearance, class status, gender, and behavior, all of these perceptions and assessments intertwined" in the lives of the groups we can investigate with regard to performing race, is very difficult, as Martha A. Hodes insightfully observes: "Making sense of racial categorization is an elusive historical endeavor, doubly so when historical actors and their ancestors crossed racial boundaries and lived their lives across geographical borders, from Africa and Europe to North America and the Caribbean. Transnational journeys expose the malleability of racial classification and thus add an important dimension to our understanding of the constructed nature of race."[3]

In effect, racial classification has the power to "circumscribe lives, to categorize, distinguish, and separate people, to subjugate some and elevate others," as Hodes explains. She further adds, "transnational journeys illuminate, with equal certainty, the potency of racial malleability in local, daily lives," commenting on the fact that "the abiding power of race lies precisely within" its "mercurial nature."[4]

The following two chapters allow for an investigation of the performativity of race. In the playtexts of Josefina Báez and Evelina Fernández, we find two distinct views on matters of race, with very different styles of writing in their approach. Báez's work can best be described as "dando palabra" or "spoken word," which is also known as "performance art." Several Latinas have made their reputations in performance art, or what some playwrights call "spoken word."[5] Among the playwrights we have already discussed, Celia Herrera Rodríguez, Yareli Arizmendi, the Colorado Sisters, and Diane Rodriguez can all fall into this category. These women all use the dramatic form to tell us about their life experiences, using the first person to relate their memories as well as incorporating a variety of staging of their experiences.

Going back to the 1970s, this form is characterized by drawing from a wide range of forms, such as visual arts, dance, music, and various visuals and elements of the theatre. The playtexts may be written or improvised, and we may see a solo performer or more than one performer. As Oscar Brockett and Robert Ball describe it, "perhaps the essence of performance art is that there are no rules about what is allowed." Performance pieces by Latinas may be distinguished from others in the manner through which they draw from their culture as the subject of their autobiography. In *Voices Made Flesh,* a collection of performing women's autobiography, editors Lynn C. Miller and Jacqueline Taylor discuss the theory and practice of women's autobiographical performance: "Creating an autobiographical narrative reconstitutes the self, the audience, and surrounding cultural contexts. It makes sense of the self, gives each part a voice and a body. We can safely say that until a life is shared through writing or performance, it does not exist at all, or at least it does not resonate in the broader realm of public consequence." Within the story of their autobiography, they add, "is the story of resistance to the disembodied, traditionally masculine 'universal subject,' whose implicit denial of skin color, gender, sexual orientation (other than the heterosexual), and economic disparity constrained many women as 'others' with no voices or physicality." But, as Miller and Taylor point out, through women's autobiographical performance work, we can analyze "how the body is reclaimed, celebrated, and complicated."[6]

For us, the rich field of Latina performance artists well illustrates how they have negotiated their experiences and arrived at this kind of recovery. As Heather Carver observes in her chapter in *Voices Made Flesh,* "For women to even begin to write the autobiographical 'I' acknowledges that we can be the subjects of our own stories, and thus expands traditional notions of whose voices may take center stage," and hence, the "many challenges in creating autobiographical works are multiplied as women begin to speak the unspoken and to embody the selves previously unperformed for audiences."[7]

With regard to race, as Alicia Arrizón mentions, "for Latina lesbians the performing (or narrative) aspects of coming-out acts balance their sexualized bodies with other important categories, such as race and ethnicity, providing the opportunity to democratically mark the evolution of the gendered subject."[8]

Other Latinas, such as Denise Chavez, Amparo García, and Ruby Nelda Perez, also "use performance art to communicate the entire spectrum of Latina life and experience in their respective communities," as Alberto Sandoval-Sánchez and Nancy Saporta Sternbach mention in their entry on the genre in their anthology of Latina performance pieces, concluding that, "by staging their own life experiences, Latina performers have transformed Latino theater. In their irreverent and provocative way of doing theater, and by telling and staging their own autobiographies, Latinas have created a space for a self-defined Latina protagonist."[9]

Thus, "while intent on seeing themselves and their families realistically represented on the stage, they simultaneously continue to tackle issues that are of vital importance to them and their communities." As Sandoval-Sánchez and Sternbach further add: "Their work centers on their relationships with men, with other women, and with their families, a revisioning of history, political consciousness, open sexuality, and a cross section of representation of Latina life in its myriad forms. In this sense, these performers stage the multiplicity of roles that they have been performing both on and offstage for the last three decades." Unquestionably, Latina solo performance was a hallmark in the 1990s, both highly visible and resulting in a large number of works. As Sandoval-Sánchez and Sternback note in their companion study, *Stages of Life: Transcultural Performance and Identity in U.S. Latina Theater*: "Latina solo performance constitutes a genre in its own right. A concrete derivation of Latina playwriting, solo performance in its many manifestations—dare we say it?—has become the most highly original, irreverent, and innovative theatrical art form Latinas are producing today."[10]

Josefina Báez offers a vast canvas that encompasses transnational, transcultural, and transglobal views from a Dominican American perspective. The very dynamics of transculturation are at the core of Josefina Báez's *Dominicanish,* a work where "multiple cultures coexist and collide in a compelling collage of text, music, and movement," where the artist explores "migration—marginality—language—identity."[11] Given, as we shall see, the population of Dominicans in the United States, her voice is important to include.

According to the 2008 Pew Hispanic Center report on Hispanic women in the United States, nearly all of the 13 percent of immigrant Hispanic women from the Caribbean were born in Cuba or the Dominican Republic (Puerto Ricans are not included in this group). With regard to Dominicans, in *Harvest of Empire: A History of Latinos in America,* Juan Gonzalez tells us that between 1961 and 1986 there were more than 400,000 people who legally migrated to the United States from the Dominican Republic. In addition, he writes, another 44,000 moved to Puerto Rico, "while thousands more entered both places illegally." By 1990, Gonzalez documents that there were more than 300,000 Dominicans living in New York City, with the total "expected to reach 700,000 early in the millennium, making Dominican migration one of the largest to this country of the past forty years." Given the U.S. Census 2000 Brief and the projections released in August 2008, there is little reason to doubt that these numbers will continue to grow.[12]

With the growing number of Dominican Americans in the United States, we are fortunate to be able to include in this anthology a contemporary playwright, Josefina Báez, who stands out for her achievements in advancing the Dominican American experience through her work. Under the leadership of Josefina Báez, the artistic director of Latinarte Inc., as Lara W. Walker describes it, the group's goal is to "tackle the challenges and possibilities of Dominicans in the United States through an experimental theatrical expression that avoids linearity both of text and dramaturgy." She adds: "A black woman whose ancestral line links her directly to the African-descended sugarcane workers of the *bateyes* (migrant camps) in La Romana, Dominican Republic, Báez draws on the mental transformations set in motion by migration to peruse many of the social, political, and cultural myths of the Dominican Republic."[13]

In contrast to the "spoken word" form used by Báez, Fernández uses a traditional play structure in her work. Because she develops her characters fully, we can better study the challenges they face. Fernández's *Luminarias,* which originated with the Latino Theater Company in Los Angeles under the direction of her husband, the acclaimed director José Luis Valenzuela, is a serious drama with comedy that revolves around professional Latinas in a growing middle-class Chicana/Latina setting.[14] In *Luminarias* we encounter how racism is a part of their daily lives. As Jorge Huerta observes, this work is "an important play for many reasons, but perhaps mostly because it deals with the Chicana/os internalized and externalized racism, challenging notions of culture and stability." Most importantly, just as Báez is able to accomplish, Fernández presents a universe that reflects "the totality of the Mechicana, Mechicano and Latina/o experiences in the United States."[15]

For both Josefina Báez and Evelina Fernández, their approach to performance exemplifies a means of constructing and deconstructing identity, and through performance we can investigate how they negotiate operating in a universe in which "race matters."

Notes

In the title of this part introduction, the words "Race Matters" appear within quotation marks in acknowledgment that Cornel West has used them in the title of his book, *Race Matters* (Boston: Beacon Press, 1993, rpt. 2001). That book was one of the primary resources and assigned reading for coursework that Elizabeth C. Ramírez developed for the Ethnic Studies Program at the University of Oregon during the time that she was director of the program.

1. Tessie Liu, "Teaching the Differences among Women from a Historical Perspective," in *Unequal Sisters: A Multicultural Reader in U.S. Women's History,* ed. Vicki L. Ruiz and Ellen Carol DuBois (New York: Routledge, 1994), 571, 576, 581.

2. See Brandi Wilkins Catanese, "'How Do I Rent a Negro?': Racialized Subjectivity and Digital Performance Art," *Theatre Journal* 57 (2005): 699–714; and Dorinne Kondo, "(Re) Visions of Race: Contemporary Race Theory and the Cultural Politics of Racial Crossover in Documentary Theatre," *Theatre Journal* 52 (2000): 81–107.

3. Martha A. Hodes, "The Mercurial Nature and Abiding Power of Race," in *American Dreaming, Global Realities: Rethinking U.S. Immigration History,* ed. Donna R. Gabaccia and Vicki L. Ruiz (Urbana: University of Illinois Press, 2006), 38, 58.

4. Ibid., 58. See also José A. Cobas, Jorge Duany, and Joe R. Feagin, *How the United States Racializes Latinos: White Hegemony and Its Consequences* (Boulder, Colo.: Paradigm, 2009); and Jorge J. E. Gracia, *Race or Ethnicity? On Black and Latino Identity* (Ithaca, N.Y.: Cornell University Press, 2007).

5. Elizabeth C. Ramírez, "Playwrights," in *The Oxford Encyclopedia of Latinos and Latinas in the United States* (New York: Oxford University Press, 2005), 3:395.

6. Oscar G. Brockett and Robert J. Ball, *The Essential Theatre,* 9th ed. (Boston: Thomson Wadsworth, 2008), 226. Lynn C. Miller and Jacqueline Taylor, introduction, *Voices Made Flesh: Performing Women's Autobiography,* ed. Lynn C. Miller, Jacqueline Taylor, and M. Heather Carver (Madison: University of Wisconsin Press, 2003), 3, 4.

7. M. Heather Carver, "Risky Business: Exploring Women's Autobiography and Performance," in *Voices Made Flesh,* 15.

8. Alicia Arrizón, *Latina Performance: Traversing the Stage* (Bloomington: Indiana University Press, 1999), 139.

9. Alberto Sandoval-Sánchez and Nancy Saporta Sternbach, *Puro Teatro: A Latina Anthology* (Tucson: University of Arizona Press, 2000), 227–28.

10. Ibid. 227, 228, 95.

11. From the collection of reviews and other documents provided by the playwright, Josefina Báez.

12. Pew Hispanic Center, *Hispanic Women in the United States, 2007,* update, May 14, 2008. Juan Gonzalez, *Harvest of Empire: A History of Latinos in America* (New York: Penguin, 2000), 117. On the 2000 census data: Jeorge Zarazua, "U.S. Hispanic Population May Become More Like Texas," *San Antonio Express-News,* August 14, 2008, 8B. See also "An Older and More Diverse Nation by Midcentury," August 14, 2008, available at http://www.census.gov/newsroom/releases/archives/population/cb08-123.html, accessed September 1, 2010; and *The Hispanic Population: Census 2000 Brief,* May 2001, available at http://www.census.gov/prod/2001pubs/c2kbr01-3.pdf, accessed September 1, 2010.

13. Lara A. Walker, "Playwrights, Caribbean," in *Oxford Encyclopedia of Latinos and Latinas,* 3:399–400.

14. Jorge Huerta, "An Overview of Chicana/o Theatre in the 1990s," *Latin American Theatre Review* (fall 2000): 224.

15. Jorge A. Huerta, *Chicano Drama: Performance, Society and Myth* (Cambridge: Cambridge University Press, 2000), 84.

CHAPTER 7

Dando Palabra/Spoken Word

The Dominican Experience in Josefina Báez's *Dominicanish*

Josefina Báez, by permission of the photographer, Jorge Vismara.

The Playwright/La Dramaturga

Josefina Báez was born in La Romana, the Dominican Republic, in January 1960, and she has lived in New York since 1972. Her family origins are Dominican. She is an actor, writer, educator, and director. She is also the founder and director of Latinarte/AyOmbe Theatre, which has been in operation since April 1986. Under her guidance, the group has an institute structured as international annual retreats, and the themes studied include from performance techniques to physical and mental health for the artists. Her work is multidisciplinary in context and intercultural in scope. Her work is highly subjective. She has participated in many international theatre festivals and workshops in Europe, Asia, Latin America, and the Caribbean. Her written work has been published in *Forward Motion Magazine* (New York City), *Brujula/Compass* (Latin American Writers Institute, New York City), *Ventana Abierta* (University of California), *Tertuliando/Hanging Out* (Anthology of Dominican women writers in New York), *Vetas* (Dominican Republic), *Caribbean Connections: Moving North* (NECA/Washington, Ojo Paralelo, New York City), *Dominicanish* (New York City), and *Beacon Press 2001 Anthology*, among others. From 1981 to 2004, Báez taught creative writing and theatre in public schools and cultural centers in New York City, in collaboration with Teachers & Writers and the Arts Connections and Creative Art Laboratory (CAL) at Teachers College, Columbia University.

Josefina Báez's *Apartarte/Casarte* performance-dialogue project, in houses and apartments, is in its twelfth year. She is also performing in public spaces—locally, nationally, and internationally—as part of her Wandering Soul series (Aparecer Al Parecer A

Perecer/Apariciones y Acciones); and performing this piece, *Dominicanish,* directed by Claudio Mir.

Josefina has been working independently since 1986, using various techniques and creative sources as her main references (biomechanics, Chinese calligraphy, meditation, yoga, World music and dance). In her own words, the playwright describes her theatre experience: "I am a theatre writer, actor, director. I create, sponsor and promote my work. The most rewarding (or the instance when I learn the most) aspect of my work is teaching/directing. There, the levels of alertness are transparent, detached, protective of the other, unending process, true and of the highest caliber to my whole system of life."[1]

About the Play/Sobre la Obra

As the playwright tells us in her prefatory words to the playtext that *Dominicanish* changes every time it is published, not every time it is performed, "since the work is set out to explore non-linearity." Rather, what has changed every two years in the performance is what she presents in the videos, which the playwright uses as part of the set. Báez's performance texts focus on the life of her people as a "cultural, political, and linguistic minority in the United States," according to Lara A. Walker. Walker adds that, as "a black woman whose ancestral line links her directly to the African-descended sugarcane workers of the bateyes (migrant camps)" of her homeland, La Romana, in the Dominican Republic, she "draws on the mental transformation set in motion by migration."[2] Her style is extraordinary, displaying a wish to both experiment in her writing technique and in her performance of it. This particular emphasis on the written playtext is evident in this playwright's printing specifications for the play, including special vertical spacing, line breaks, font size, capitalization, and bolding, including the special typography of the playtext title itself, and varying play with the written text. Every effort has been made to accommodate her request in this edition.

Reviewing her performance of May 22, 2001, at the Bats Theatre in New Zealand, Timothy O'Brian writes: "A *trumpeter* precedes Josefina Báez on to the stage. His music immediately places us somewhere Hispanic yet, as Báez enters behind him, her hands over her head in an Indian dance gesture, we're dislocated." He adds: "And that sets the mood of this piece which is about the flow of movement and language across cultures—not just language as spoken but the language of the body itself as migrants adapt and remake themselves from one social reality into another." For O'Brian, the performance "awakens the emotions at a deep level reminding the audience of sensations of loss, belonging, identification and change." He adds: "that emotional power is summed up perfectly in the final image. Báez is almost motionless on one side of the stage while the video on the other shows a boy rolling a hoop down the main street of a Dominican country town as the trumpet similarly fades away from us. It's an image of memory and exile, the past and the present mingling to express what it is to be Dominican but not quite—an identity you might describe as 'Dominicanish.'"[3]

Báez refers to *Dominicanish* as

> Language acquisition with soul
> Beyond ESL (English as a second language)
> Where worlds collide
> A nonlinear expression of our nonlinear life
> Poetic and nonsensical texts tapping into unofficial stories and undocumented history.

The imagery is profound, drawing from the realities of everyday life juxtaposed against "social, political, and cultural myths" along with the ancient texts of Adi Shankara and the Panchatantra stories. But the piece is heroic in tone and entertaining in its lilting poetic fashion. In the playwright's words, *Dominicanish* is:

> An eclectic use of symbols, times and places
> Dominicanish, a language created by the awareness of the ordinary in the here, today, now.
> Dominicanish, just an exercise.
> A non-linearity exercise organized in a distinct way every time that is published; containing stories within stories (bold and non-bold letters; the text in its entirety are some of the possibilities).[4]

In Walker's words: "The linguistic, racial, religious, and ethnic diversity of New York fuels the discourse of her performance texts, which ingeniously indict the negrophobia, conservatism, misogyny, homophobia, Eurocentrism, and upper-class bias characterizing official Dominican discourse. At the same time she celebrates the cultural hybridity that diaspora Dominicans normally develop while poking fun at the xenophobic prejudice that often causes others in the larger American society to raise a disapproving brow in the face of Dominican difference."[5]

For Juleyka Lantigua, editor of *Urban Latino Magazine*, in writing about the published playtext, "Báez truly has a gift of language—Spanish, English and Dominicanish," referring to "poetic crevices" where "we find Báez at her best and where the true drama of the immigrant experience in her work lies." Lantigua adds: "Taking on another language is equivalent to taking on another identity. There's no escaping it and the only hope is that you—the reader, the immigrant, the woman, the man—will find yourself somewhere between transformation and alienation."[6]

Ramón H. Rivera-Servera has written about Báez's production at Dance Theater Workshop during its premiere in November 1999 in New York City. In "A Dominican York in Andhra," he describes the performance piece in which Báez "utilizes kuchipudi movement, a classical Indian narrative dance form, as a strategy for exploring and critiquing the experiences of the Dominican diaspora in New York City." Rivera-Servera's analysis of the use of the body in movement provides valuable descriptions of the performance he witnessed: "the body in movement performs an act of decolonization by reinscribing the vernacular, the language with which the marginal community historically identifies. The body of Báez's performance confronts its marginality, recovering a history that is at times painful, to travel assertively through the uncertain geographies of the global, while moving pleasurably to perform identity."[7]

Through this piece, Báez takes us through a whirlwind journey that highlights her bilingual, bicultural experience in the United States, facing the harsh reality of racism, a desire for higher education despite insurmountable obstacles, among other ventures, and culminating in a world truth, namely, "home is where theatre is."

Artistic Vision/Punto de Vista Artístico

ECR & CRC: Why do you write what you do?

JB: What I write is just part of my path-life-phases-commentaries in this present filled and full of past and future; but today, now, here; how I make sense of this world; how I laugh or cry; how I see myself (me the actor/audience/performer and observer ever-present-me the other of the others); how I learn; how I elucidate this or that; how I relate/live/make community in the many communities that I am able to experience.

ECR & CRC: Who do you write for and what audience are you trying to reach?

JB: I write for whoever decides to be my audience.

ECR & CRC: What message, if any, are you trying to convey to your audience with this work and/or with all of your work?

JB: No message to convey. My prophetic abilities are personal, limited, contradictive and too simplistic to be shared. My work is just a very subjective commentary that might start (or continue) a dialogue. It might resonate with some people. The audience 's personal histories (the potential entanglement between the two) are an integral part in these conversations.

ECR & CRC: Who or what has been your major influence?

JB: My major and constant influences have been the people closest to me (myself-family-friends), home (where I was born, where I live, where I work–where I have been–where there is . . .); people in general; possibilities; fallacies; close or open doors; dreams, day and nightmares; words and gestures heard and seen. Definitively, my major influence is my present packed with its recipe that includes heavy doses of childhood memories and possible future; ingredients that are sweet, sour, pungent, bitter, a combination of these flavors or its sharper duality feature, even if we want them or not in our menu.

ECR & CRC: What has been your biggest and/or most difficult struggle/challenge in life, in completing a play or getting it produced, etc.?

JB: I do not belong to any theatre circuit where my work is produced. Thus, I do just few things that are seen (at a pace that I can afford); I do more creative things that are not shared with a larger audience. All this is done with no regrets and so much sanity and wholeness.

Production History/Palabras Dramatúrgicas

This play premiered in November 1999, at the Dance Theatre Workshop in New York City, under the direction of Claudio Mir. Performances of this work are numerous, including: the 3rd International Theatre Festival, Santo Domingo, the Dominican Republic, October 2001; New Zealand (tour produced by Magdalena Aotearoa and Fuel Festival, Hamilton, New Zealand) in May and June 2002; a festival in Magdalena, Australia, in April 2003, the European Women's Festival (Finland and Sweden) in June 2005; the 22nd Festival International de Teatro Hispano–Teatro Avante in Miami, July 2007, and the LATC (Los Angeles Theatre Center) Opening Festival in Los Angeles, December 2007.

Contact Information

The playwright may be contacted at ayombetheatre@yahoo.com

DOMINICANISH

Every time the text is published, it will be organized in a different way.[8] *Its nature, its non-linearity, frees even the original written structure. And the piece within the piece, the highlighted text, will also be different. Other readings are created, maintaining a freshness, other possible layers and relationships.*

D**OM**inican**IS**h

Gu nai
Di Ar   di tu   iu
IU
You OM IS
Celebrando Abril
march to take back our streets
march against police brutality
hoy no fio
mañana sí
brujo Haitiano brujo   Colombiano   brujo de las Matas
rooms for rent
a muchacha seria que trabaje
a pareja **sin** hijos
a hombre que no fume
sin cocina
con derecho al buzon
sin **telefono**
sin derecho a nevera

cerca del tren
cerca del hospital
cerca de bodegas
cerca del beauty parlor
cerca del laundry

paga aquí tus biles
lavamos, secamos y doblamos a tu deseo
GED ESL free classes
GED ESL citizenship classes
smokeshop 24 hours calls 19 cents a minute
2 dollars 3 dollars 5 dollars 10 dollars calling cards
uñas korea
uñas Hanoi
uñas La China
Unisex Tropical
Envios Tuyos
pupusas y tamales de elote D' Ellos
Paquetes El **primo**
frituras delivery
Da' heights art.

como es arriba es abajo
bilingual bicultural bacá
Here there **everywhere**
mala vaina y yo poquita
se vende se alquila se arrienda
por motivos de viajes vendo
se vende esta mejora
se vende esta **gallera** for sale
pais paisaje paraje pasaje
gone sold
Con los tuyos en navidad
I ain't no Juanita shit
como es arriba es abajo **miñinguiando el alma**
como soy aquí soy allá sold vendido sol y mar
como es arriba es abajo como **soy de allá** **estoy aquí**
S O L D

repeat after me repeat after them
repeat after them repeat after me

1 2 3 4 5 6 7 8 9 1 **187** 781 718 1 0 2 201 212
Ar
Er
Ir
as A is in **love**
M as in apple
You pero iu **you**
repeat after me iu you
me da verguenza poner la boca **así**

suerte que la 107 se arrulla con Pacheco
Pacheco tumbao añejo
Pacheco flauta
Pacheco su nuevo tumbao
el Maestro el artista
tremendo cache compartido en Cruz
juntos de nuevo como al detalle
tres de **café y** dos de **azucar**

Aquí los discos traen un cancionero
discos del alma con afro

la lista crece la lista creció
presente
pasado
simple
futuro compuesto
crece creció creciendo
creciendo
con el swing del tumbao y reculando
como ciguapa
me chulié en el hall
metí mano en el rufo
craqueo chicle como Shameka Brown
hablo como boricua
y me peino como **morena**
la viejita de abajo no e' viejita na'
el super se esta tirando la **culona** del 5to piso
jangueo con el pájaro del barrio
me junto con la muchacha que salio preñá
salgo con mi ex

hablo con el muchacho que estaba preso
garabatie paredes y trenes

Arrrr
Err
Ir

I thought that I will never learn English
no way I will not put my mouth like that
no way jamás ni never no way
Gosh, to pronounce one little phrase one must
become another person with the mouth all twisted
yo no voy a poner la boca **así como un guante**
don't get me wrong yo sé **un chin**
yo me sé girl loves you
me Tarzan you Jane
you me mine love you do does and doesn't
been very very very good to me mine myself
an' da' si'

past perfect **si** perfect past **si**
regular **si** irregular
an' da' si'

I went back there on vacation
There is La Romana
here is 107th Street Ok.
¿Tú sabes inglés?
Ay habla un chin para nosotros ver si tú sabes.
I was **changed** they were **changed**
he she it were **changed** too
pretérito pluscuamperfecto indicativo imperativo.
back home home is 107th Ok
full fridge **full of morisoñando con minute maid**
as a maid in a minute

a mor and more add more
add more signs
special signs
signs of specials donde Roy
Foodurama o el 10 cent
Gimbels o Korbette

10 for 1.99 and free with purchase
pay for it   **it is free**
Alexander the grape   wach you ma' call it
repeat after me   wach' you ma' call it

Once in a while   every sin'
son sin'   something sin
every sin is vegetable
ve   get able   veg e table
refri girator   refrigirator   fridge
com   fort   able   comfort   able
comfortable
Wednesday   sursdei   zersdeis
ando cantando
ing **singing**
very very **very good**

you you
you in a secret   iu   in a whisper
in a cloud of smoke I found my teachers
in an LP jacket I found my teachers
stitched suedes   **bell bottoms** on
openly displaying their horoscope signs
gemini Capricorn piscis leo lio
in that cover I found my teachers
Los hermanos   Bomba-Tonga   Isley
Los hermanos Isley
The Isley Brothers

Last saturday my teachers sang in **Soul** train
Now, I don't care how my **mouth** look
I like what I'm saying
Boy girl loves you   she does   she doesn't
Herself   **myself**   themselves   Denzel   himself girl loves you

a e o   i u   you
Ar   Er   Ir
as A **is** in love
M as in apple
Adam and new year's eve
one Juan   one Juan   one Juan   one Juan   one Juan
five Juanes uanes

S **es** double the consonant
el orden del factor no altera el valor
antes de P y B?
all of the above
Naigu

Aquí los discos traen un cancionero
discos del alma con afro
con afro black is beautiful
black is a color
black is my color
my cat is black
but first of all
baseball has been very very very good to me

pero iu
repeat after me
me da verguenza poner la boca así
you see si crooked
crooked cupid
a women named city
hips swing male or female
we swing creating our tale
male or female we swing
no one to **blame** or **complain**
but **go**
just **go**
let go
go slow
go fast
but **go**

Crooked city
a women named cupid
city glorifying the **finest brutality in blue**
city nuestro **canto con viva emoción**
city a la **guerra morir** se lanzo
Suerte que la 107 se **arrulla** con Pacheco
Pacheco tumbao añejo
Pacheco flauta
Pacheco su nuevo tumbao

el **Maestro** el **artista**
compartido en Cruz
de nuevo
tres de café y dos de azucar

con el swing si
city
I pulled the emergency cord

Repeat after me
pull **the emergency cord**
again and again
De nuevo
y la lista crece
y la lista creció
De nuevo
presente
pasado simple
futuro compuesto
crece creció creciendo
Más de lo mismo
De nuevo

One way to Santo Domingo
exchange today
sell 43.50
buy 52.50
euro better
yen best
yembe
bembe
libras esterlinas radio bemba
dollar canadiense
rupias no incluidas
no ñapas
no gracias
hoy **no** fio
mañana si
trips to the airport
Que viva el jefe pa' matalo otra vez
Balaguer leave us the fuck alone leave us alone man leave me alone

Dominican cake any occasion
Seguimos
march to take back our streets
march against police brutality
cerca del laundry
again and again

Mar travel
Sol travel
STD ISD PCO STD ISD PCO
Fax to let
best of both worlds
for hire please sound horn veg. non veg. hotel
India moves with Modi xerox
Ashoka Birla Supreme
Maha cement
I want my thunder
Ajjanta weds Ellora
Nuclear weds **Namaste**
Mira weds khrisna
traffic police
for you with you always
Saraswati travels Durga travels **Surya travels**
government approved officer's mess

frequent flying to the dictionary
grooving it diggin' it
fight the power **fight the power** fight it
past is not present you know better than anybody else
how I used to die to sing like FaustoRey
but past is not present
el present is a gift
cool as a cucumber like peter thru his house
leather leather leather **lederísima**
tell me with who are you hanging out
and I will tell you who you are
por H o por R that **doesn't ring a bell**
out of the woods just out of the boat
with two left feet

Let's go to the house of the Lord
brujo haitiano brujo colombiano brujo de las matas

let's be real let's do the impossible
recordando al Che
let's remember Ernesto
tour of idiomatic expression
class consciousness
fight it fight it fight it regular fight it irregular
ING the sweetest of actions
boy girl loves you she did she does she will
chi tu chi sa chi be chi mu
chi cho que bien
ain't no place I'd rather be than with you yeah
loving you well three times
well well well

Repeat after them
my teachers the Isley brothers
repeated a **whisper**
whispered a little louder
sing a song sang a song
sang a whisper
the list grows the list grew
grows grew growing
growing smooth soft hard
growing hard sweet memory
growing soft sweet passion
horizon promise **everlasting**
each and everyday you are the **heaven** I need to see

you are **real** you are **constant**
you are the top in **my priority**
in my priority you are the top
in the top you are my priority
in my priority you are the top
are you the top in my priority?
top top top priority
top top top priority

Although zip coded batey
water Con Edison **galore**
aquí también los pantis se tienden en el baño

"But then again kings and servants depend on each other*
there can be no king without a servant and no servant without a king
for silk comes out of a worm gold out of rocks
fire from a piece of wood
but have you heard of a friendship of a king?
as you have heard a gambler that is honest
a snake that forgives a passionate woman who is calm
an impotent man who is brave a drunk with discrimination
but then again how can servants be well?
it is said that the poor the sick the dreamers and the fools always go into exile
poor sick dreamers and fools exile"

Yesterday in homeroom **and today** in the cafeteria the bilingual students me cortaron los ojos they looked at me with the who-you-think-you-are-bitch attitude and the north-americans laughed at my corny vocabulary
I ain't no bilingual nerd I'm just immersed in the poetry of the senses **poetry that leads to acts of love** like a prayer like foreplaying poetry taught by my teachers
The Isley brothers
a turn before the guitar solo side side side
point turn stop point turn stop point turn stop

Now I am part of my teachers' tour
smoke and all **the garden**
smoke and all the Apollo
smoke and all the Great Hall in San Francisco

No no no Samantha Ronald is the cutest and then Marvin

repeat after **me** repeat after **them**
repeat after **them** repeat after **me**

Mister Juarez my ESL teacher and later Mrs. Kisinsky my monolingual teacher
were amazed 'caused I had the vocabulary found in **wet tongues** and hookie party goers
And I believe it or not was none of the above
Me the Dominican miracle in 84th street in Brandeis **representin'**
writing phrases and sentences in perfect syntax
filled and full of sensual images
SAT scores doubled but in no university catalog I found my teachers: The Isley Brothers
I did not see no class department major minor sororities
fraternities grooving' with **soul**

---

*Panchatantra[9]

repeat after **them**   repeat after **me**

take   take   take off every safety pin in your way
unleash this starched sari
let its prints and colors play wild ragas
foreplaying to the juiciest kalankhan
foreplaying in the juiciest **dulce de leche**
But you see   there's no guarantee
now   I'm another person   mouth twisted
güiri güiri on dreams
güiri güiri business
even laughing
laughing in dOMinicanish
there's no guarantee
ni **aquí**   ni **allá**
there's no guarantee
here   there   anywhere
there's no guarantee
without accent   PhD or CEO

Higher education took me to places of pain and pleasure
history in black and white
distinguished teachers: Pearl Bailey
Earth fantasy
Wind September
Reasons and Fire
Ella Fitzgerald   Louis Armstrong
and the dearest of all   **my favorite**
Ms. Billie Holiday
Lady Day **teaching** me the ups and downs of the heart
Lady Day in the other side of love
Where love resides
Love is like a faucet   it turns on and off
love is like a faucet   it turns on and off
in off   baseball has been very very very very good to me
in off   very very good to me
in off   enough to me
in off   enough   in off
I have been very good to baseball too

God bless the child travelin' light

"For example you see a rope   and think it is a snake**
as soon as you realize that the rope is a rope
your false perception of the snake stops
and you are no longer distracted by the fear which it inspired
Therefore   one who wants to liberate herself
must know the nature of the real self and the unreal
When appearances cannot distract you any more
then comes knowledge
then comes complete discrimination of the real and the unreal
When the vision of reality comes
the veil of ignorance is completely removed
When our false perception is corrected   our misery ends"

SA RI GA MA PA DA MI SA
loud colors
on silent faces
rude dances
on angels faces
sounds dancing   angels facing **loud silence**
silence   on color faces

Do-did-will
nuclear   do weds namaste.
Did-do-will-will-did-do
And yet   thanks to the Ganga   gracias al Ganjes
los tigre de bengala no enchinchan la sed
el salto del tigres hace rato que no es tántrico
thanks to the Ganga   bengal tigers don't move me
long gone tantrick attacks
Did do

But
if you want to be **prompted** in English   press one
if you want to be prompted in Spanish   press two
enter your card number
to place a domestic but not a national call dial   8 0 9
todos los circuitos están cerrados   trate su llamada luego
1 KK   no progreso
su llamada   no progreso   1 KK   no progreso
Please leave your message at the sound of the beep

** Shr Adi Shankara[10]

Although zip coded batey
water   Con Edison   galore
aquí también los pantis se tienden en el baño

SA   RI   GA   MA   PA   DA   NI   SA

Forgotten deities looked at me   recognized me
in the process they became tumeric yellow
I   jet black
home is where theatre is

Notes

1. Josefina Báez, notes e-mailed to the editors, February 24, 2007, July 8, 2009, and November 4, 2010.

2. Josefina Báez, notes e-mailed to the editors, July 31, 2008. Lara A. Walker, "Playwrights, Caribbean," in *The Oxford Encyclopedia of Latinos and Latinas in the United States,* ed. Suzanne Oboler and Deena J. González (New York: Oxford University Press, 2005), 3:400–401.

3. Timothy O'Brian, *Dominion* (Wellington, New Zealand), May 22, 2002, from notes from the playwright, December 7, 2006.

4. Josefina Báez, notes, July 31, 2008, and February 24, 2007.

5. Walker, 3:401.

6. Juleyka Lantigua, "Domincanish: A Performance Text" (book review), *Caribbean Studies Newsletter* 28:2 (winter 2002): 6.

7. Ramón H. Rivera-Servera, "A Dominican York in Andhra," in *Caribbean Dance From Abakuá to Zouk: How Movement Shapes Identity,* ed. Susanna Sloat (Gainesville: University Press of Florida, 2002), 153, 161.

8. Playtext copyright © 2000 by Josefina Báez. Alex Guerrero created the graphic art in the 2000 printing.

9. Vishnu Sharma, *Panchatantra: The Complete Version,* trans. G. L. Chandiramani (Calcutta: Rupa and Co., 1991), 9, 43, 44; the texts were edited by the playwright to suit the structure of the playtext.

10. The words of Adi Shankara's work are from Viveka Chidamani/Crest Jewel from three translations: Swami Prabhavananda and Christopher Isherwood (Hollywood, Calif.: Vedanta Press, 1978); and La joya suprema del Discernimiento, trans. Roberto Pla (Mexico, D.F.: Costa-Amic Editores S.A., 1980); and by Swami Chinmayananda (Mumbai: Centra Chinmaya Mission Trust, 1989). The texts were edited by the playwright to suit the structure of the playtext.

CHAPTER 8

Race, Gender, and the Professional Woman
Evelina Fernández's *Luminarias* (1996)

Evelina Fernández, by permission of the photographer, Jose Luis Valenzuela.

The Playwright/La Dramaturga

Evelina Fernández was born in East Los Angeles, California, on April 28, 1954.[1] Her father was born in Mexicali, Mexico, and he was raised in Rey, Arizona. Her mother was born in Jerome, Arizona. Her maternal grandparents were from Jalisco, Mexico, and the origins of her paternal grandparents are unknown. Evelina attended East Los Angeles College and California State University, Los Angeles, before dropping out to perform in *Zoot Suit.* She has been involved in theatre ever since.

Her writing credits include numerous plays. *How Else Am I Supposed to Know I'm Still Alive?* has been produced throughout the United States and adapted into an award-winning film for the Universal Hispanic Film Project, winning the CineFestival Special Jury Award; it was published in Kathy Perkins's and Roberta Uno's noted collection, *Contemporary Plays by Women of Color*. Other works are *Premeditation, Dementia,* and *Luminarias.* She has been recognized internationally for her writing and her performances, winning an award for Best Actress at the Festival de Cine Iberoamericano de Huelva (Spain) for her performance in *Luminarias.* She received a Golden Eagle Award for her performance in *American Me* and for Outstanding Writer for *Luminarias.* She also received the Alma Award for her performance in *Hollywood Confidential.* She was honored with the prestigious GLAAD Award for Outstanding Theater Production in Los Angeles with *Dementia,* which also garnered four Ovation Award nominations, including the categories of New World Premiere and Best Ensemble. In 2007 she was a finalist for the 2007 Humanitas Prize for her writing for the PBS animation series *Maya and Miguel.*

Her stage acting credits include roles in *Dementia* and *Luminarias,* with the Latino Theater Company (LTC). She was in *August 29* and *La Victima,* both with LTC and the Los Angeles Theatre Center (LATC). She was also in *Roosters, Stone Wedding, King Lear,* and *Etta Jenks* at the LATC, and she was Della, the female lead in the original stage production of *Zoot Suit* at the Mark Taper Forum. After *Zoot Suit* she toured nationally and internationally with El Teatro de la Esperanza. Among her many appearances, she has performed at the New York Shakespeare Festival and the Denver Center for the Performing Arts. A founding member of the Latino Theater Company, she also has film credits in acting in both *American Me* and in *Luminarias,* and she also adapted the latter for the screen from her stage play.

Evelina is also a poet and a motivational speaker, performing for and speaking to youth and adults in schools and community centers throughout California and the Southwest. She and her husband, Jose Luis Valenzuela, artistic director of the Latino Theater Company and professor of theater at the University of California, Los Angeles, have two children.

About the Play/Sobre la Obra

Like *Roosters,* this play went from stage to screen. Jorge Huerta writes that "*Luminarias* is an important play for many reasons, but perhaps mostly because it deals with the Chicana/os internalized and externalized racism, challenging notions of culture and stability." Its distinction lies in its attention to middle-class issues confronting professional Chicanas, rather than, as Huerta points out, "the usual working-class themes that predominate in most Chicana and Chicano plays." While Fernández was seeking performance roles for herself and other Latinas with this work, the attention to the "feminist themes it addresses even as it critiques both male and female chauvinism within and without the Mechicano communities" is also noteworthy.[2]

The story follows four Latina friends who meet regularly at Luminarias Restaurant. According to journalist Don Shirley, "*Luminarias* takes an approving view of romances between Latinas and non-Latino men." Valenzuela, the play's director, pointed out to Shirley that "this is a tough proposition for our audience, because in most of our plays we're victims." Shirley reports that Valenzuela "believes 'the Latino population is transforming every day' and that his company's plays should take note." In the world of this play, as Joseph O'Connell puts it, "one [woman] is a lawyer involved with a Jew, another a therapist attracted to a recent Mexican immigrant. An artist dates a Korean, while a trendy clothing store owner comes to grips with her gay brother and gives up sex for Lent." O'Connell quotes Fernández as saying: "It's inevitable that we're all going to fall in love with each other—all races."[3]

Reviewing the stage play, Diana Rico writes about the serious nature of the work: "Although Fernández's tone is light, the subjects she dredges up are heavy indeed: Latina/o self-hatred (the result of internalizing the racist values of the dominant culture), hatred of Anglos (the outcome of centuries of oppression of Latina/os and our ancestors), the painful issues brought up by mixed ethnic dating, deep mistrust of people not of one's own race—I could go on." Rico found *Luminarias* "a deeply illuminating treatment of the serious damage done to everybody when one segment of society holds dominion over other segments."[4]

In this play as in all of her work, Fernández creates positive roles for Latinas and Latinos, aiming to "build community self-esteem and encourage visibility for those who are otherwise invisible in today's media market." At least two film reviewers called attention to the film version's distinctive qualities. The *New York Times* notes that "*Luminarias* is enjoyable for Ms. Fernández's feisty performance [playing the leading role], its high comic spirits and its messages of sisterhood, brotherhood and hope," and the *Los Angeles Times* observes that "*Luminarias* takes us into a world all too rarely seen on the big screen: that of upwardly mobile Los Angeles Latinas."[5]

Artistic Vision/Punto de Vista Artístico

ECR & CRC: How did you decide to write and/or perform?

EF: I began writing prize-winning short stories at Rowan Avenue Elementary School in East Los Angeles, California, and began acting at Robert Louis Stevenson Jr. High School in East Los Angeles. I dropped out of high school and eventually made my way to Cal State, L.A., where I became involved in the Chicano Movement and Chicano Theater. I began writing again after many years while working with El Teatro de la Esperanza in Santa Barbara, California, using the Collective Creation method and I wrote my first original play, *How Else Am I Supposed to Know I'm Still Alive?* in 1989.

ECR & CRC: Why do you write what you do?

EF: I write about the contemporary Chicana/o reality. My plays and the stories and characters within them are based on what I know and have experienced, nothing more.

ECR & CRC: Who do you write for and what audience are you trying to reach?

EF: I don't think much about who I write for. I believe that specific makes the work universal.

ECR & CRC: What message, if any, are you trying to convey to your audience with this work and/or with all of your work?

EF: I don't think about a message when I write. However, I know that there are messages in my plays. I guess ongoing themes are tolerance, understanding, equality, justice, but not in a didactic sense. Many of my plays explore male-female relationships and sexuality. I try to place Chicanas in present-day situations dealing with current issues in order to break the stereotype of the domesticated, submissive, and uneducated. I find these images to be unrealistic, but still prevalent in many Latino and Chicano pieces.

ECR & CRC: Who or what has been your major influence?

EF: I've been inspired and influenced by very independent, passionate women: my grandmother, mother, aunts, sisters, and now my daughter. I continue to be influenced by and am in awe of the unique diversity of the Chicana/o culture. The dichotomy and contradictions of who we are offer me infinite possibilities for the stage.

ECR & CRC: What has been your biggest and/or most difficult struggle/challenge in life, in completing a play or getting it produced, etc.?

EF: Writing for the stage is my passion, but I also write for film and TV. The challenge is to make a living writing for the stage. I am very fortunate to belong to a theater company, the Latino Theater Company, where my plays are usually produced. Getting my plays produced in other regional theaters has been difficult but it isn't something I have actively pursued. However, they have been produced by many Chicano theater companies throughout the United States.

ECR & CRC: Can you offer any words of advice to aspiring playwrights/performers/directors/audiences?

EF: Live and observe life and then write about it.

ECR & CRC: If you studied with Maria Irene Fornes, please provide dates, place, and any commentary you wish to add about her impact on your work.

EF: I took a three-day writing workshop with Irene at the Mark Taper Forum hosted by the Latino Theatre Initiative's Luis Alfaro. I found the exercises interesting and I continue to find them useful.

Production History/Palabras Dramatúrgicas

Luminarias premiered in May of 1996 at the Los Angeles Theatre Center. It was directed by Jose Luis Valenzuela, with the following cast: Andrea (A Divorce Lawyer)—Evelina Fernández; Sofia (A Therapist)—Marta DuBois; Irene (A Chicano Studies Professor)—Dyana Ortelli; Lilly (An Artist)—Angela Moya; Joseph (A Divorce Lawyer)—Dean Schofield; Joey (Andrea's Son)—Danny Garcia; Concha (Andrea's Aunt)—Angela Moya; Tonia (Andrea's Aunt)—Dyana Ortelli; Pablo (A Waiter)—Rick (Andrea's Cousin); and Jesus (Andrea's Brother)—Geoffrey Rivas.

Contact Information

The playwright may be contacted at Los Angeles Theatre Center, 514 S. Spring St., Los Angeles, CA 90012, 213-489-0944, and at hoop@THENEWLATC.com.

LUMINARIAS

PROLOGUE

The County Courthouse

ANDREA VALENZUELA, wearing a business suit and with a briefcase at her feet, sits on a bench with her client, CINDY RODRIGUEZ, a pretty homegirl, 19, with bleached hair and red lips.

CINDY: (*Heavy Chicana accent*) I never thought it would come to this.

ANDREA: We never do.

CINDY: When I met him, he was so sweet.

ANDREA: They always are.

CINDY: I thought I was gonna spend the rest of my life with him.

ANDREA: Yeah.

CINDY: Who would've thought he would turn out to be such an asshole . . .

ANDREA: Amazing, isn't it?

CINDY: Why do you think it is? I mean, that there are so many divorces nowadays?

ANDREA: I think women are more independent now. They won't tolerate the things they used to.

CINDY: You mean, women don't wanna put up with anymore shit?

ANDREA: Yeah.

ACT ONE

Scene 1

Lights up on LUMINARIAS, an East-side nightclub. Three women, SOFIA, wearing a trendy outfit, IRENE, wearing a tight skirt and a revealing blouse and LILLY, a little plump, wearing a plain flowered dress, sit at the bar.

LILLY: I know, I shouldn't feel this way, but I do.

SOFIA: Well, you gotta be honest about your feelings.

IRENE: Even if he is an asshole.

LILLY: Okay, so I'm in love with an asshole . . .

IRENE: Who doesn't have a job or money . . .

SOFIA: . . . and who's married with five kids.

LILLY: I know, I'm stupid.

(*A waiter arrives.*)

WAITER: Anything else ladies?

SOFIA: Another round. Brandy. Courvoisier.

IRENE: Long Island Ice Tea.

LILLY: Give me a Zombie.

WAITER: A Zombie?

LILLY: (*Defensive*) Yeah!

(*ANDREA, wearing a silk blouse and a tight skirt, arrives.*)

ANDREA: (*To waiter*) I'll have a shot of tequila.

(*The women give her a look. The waiter leaves.*)

IRENE: (*To Andrea*) Mario dumped her.

ANDREA: Again?

(*Lilly nods.*)

SOFIA: (*To Lilly*) You need to work on your self-esteem. People respond to the signals you put out. You don't think you deserve to be treated well, so you attract these jerks . . .

LILLY: Don't start analyzing me, Sofia. I'm not one of your patients. I don't go around looking for a man who's gonna hurt me.

IRENE: You don't?

LILLY: No. I'm just attracted to . . .

SOFIA: Wetbacks.

(*Lilly glares at Sofia.*)

SOFIA: Sorry—undocumented workers.

IRENE: Who don't work.

ANDREA: Wait a minute. What's his name . . . uh . . . Pedro—he worked.

LILLY: Yeah. I met him while he was working.

IRENE: King Taco.

SOFIA: Right. Dos tacos de pollo and it was love.

(*They laugh.*)

LILLY: Hey, enough already. If you can't be supportive . . .

SOFIA: I'm trying, but it's hard. I don't understand how you go from relationship to relationship . . .

LILLY: I want a husband, okay? It's all I've ever wanted. I wanna have babies, Sofia, and the alarm on my biological clock is about to go off.

SOFIA: Well, you're going about it all wrong . . .

LILLY: Oh, really? What should I do?

IRENE: Go out with white guys, like you?

ANDREA: You mean, white, rich guys.

IRENE: With little dicks.

SOFIA: It's not the size of the vessel . . .

ANDREA: It's the size of the bank account.

LILLY: I judge people by what's in their heart, not by the color of their skin.

SOFIA: Me too!

IRENE: Oh, come on, Sofia. Don't tell me all those rich guys have good hearts.

SOFIA: Don't criticize it until you've tried it.

ANDREA: No thanks.

ANDREA: What'd they do, get transplants? White guys can't get it up.

SOFIA: How would you know?

ANDREA: Irene told me.

(*Sofia looks at Irene.*)

IRENE: Hey, I've been with two white guys and neither of them could get it up.

SOFIA: So, what are you saying? That all white men are impotent? How do they reproduce?

(*Andrea and Irene shrug.*)

SOFIA: Look, I've had them all; brown, black, yellow, red and white. There are good and bad lovers in every color.

(*They look at her.*)

ANDREA: You've had yellow?

SOFIA: Well, not exactly . . .

IRENE: You've had red?

SOFIA: Latinos are red . . .

ANDREA: Sofia, you've had brown . . . back in the '70s and you've had white and that's it.

SOFIA: I've been with a Cubano and that counts as black.

IRENE: Whatever. But, now you stick to white. Why's that?

SOFIA: Because all men are assholes. So, if I'm gonna be with an asshole, he might as well have money.

IRENE: There are Latinos with money.

SOFIA: Name one?

(*They can't.*)

IRENE: Well, give me a fine-looking Latino anyday.

SOFIA: Anyday? You've been celibate for a year.

IRENE: Ten months and five days to be exact; and it has nothing to do with Latinos, Sofia, it has to do with a promise I made to La Virgen de Guadalupe, okay?

ANDREA: Yeah, La Virgen didn't get any so why should we?

IRENE: Andrea!

ANDREA: I'm kidding. (*She looks upward.*) I'm kidding.

SOFIA: Why would you promise not to have sex for a year?

IRENE: It's called sacrifice, Sofia. Something you know nothing about.

SOFIA: Catholicism can be such a crock. What are you punishing yourself for?

ANDREA: What are we, our grandmothers? Making mandas to the Virgin, making sacrifices thinking that she's gonna come through for us?

LILLY: She comes through.

IRENE: Yeah. Remember that time I promised not to drink for a year and I lost all that weight?

SOFIA: (*To Andrea*) She's serious, isn't she?

IRENE: Yeah. And when my year is up, in exactly two months and twenty-six days, I'm gonna give it up to a fine-looking Chicano. You know, one of those dark brown, black-haired, Emiliano Zapata–looking ones.

SOFIA: Who's gonna find him for you? La Virgen?

ANDREA: Look, we all make choices in our life. We're all screwed up and we shouldn't judge one another. You like white guys, you make promises to virgins, Lilly, you go for losers and me . . . I'm getting a divorce after 15 years.

LILLY: What?

ANDREA: He asked me for a divorce.

SOFIA: You're kidding.

ANDREA: He's in love with somebody else.

LILLY: Oh, Andrea, I'm sorry.

IRENE: Do you know who she is?

ANDREA: No.

LILLY: I can't believe it. Not you and Joe. You guys were always so . . . perfect together.

IRENE: Yeah, you were the ones that held out. You were the one that married your high school sweetheart, had a child . . .

LILLY: What we always wanted, but somehow never had . . .

SOFIA: I never wanted that . . .

LILLY: I was referring to Irene and me.

SOFIA: He's going through a midlife crisis . . .

ANDREA: Again? Look, I know how much you guys like Joe, but he's been cheating on me for years.

SOFIA: You never told us.

ANDREA: I know. I guess I didn't want to disappoint you.

SOFIA: Why'd you stick it out for so long?

ANDREA: I don't know. For Joey. And I guess I thought he'd change.

WOMEN: Hmmm . . .

ANDREA: I know . . .

LILLY: I bet it hurts.

(*Andrea tries to shrug it off.*)

ANDREA: I just feel kind of numb. Maybe, it hasn't hit me yet. I'm gonna focus on my son, my work . . .

SOFIA: I sense a bit of denial, Andrea.

IRENE: Must you always analyze us?

SOFIA: I can't help it!

LILLY: Don't worry, Andie. There's a lot of fish in the ocean.

IRENE: Not like Joe. He's the ultimate Latino. And boy is he fine, hmmm, hmmm, hmmm. (*She catches herself.*) I'm sorry.

ANDREA: It's okay. It's true.

(*The waiter enters and begins to clear off the table.*)

SOFIA: Men are men. What's so special about Latinos?

WAITER: When you find out girlfriend, let me know.

(*They think.*)

ANDREA: I don't know . . .

LILLY: The way they sweet-talk you.

IRENE: The way they call you "reina."

SOFIA: And even though you know it's bull . . .

LILLY: It feels so good to hear it.

IRENE: The way they call you "Mami." "Ay, Mami, que rica estás."

ANDREA: The way they move.

IRENE: The way they dance.

LILLY: The way they hold you.

ANDREA: The way they look into your eyes and make you feel like you're the only one.

LILLY: And you wanna believe it . . .

SOFIA: But, you know you can't . . .

IRENE: The way they make you open up your heart.

ANDREA: And then they break it.

SOFIA: Yeah . . .

(*They stop. They look at each other.*)

WOMEN: Latinos suck.

ANDREA: But, you know what, Sofia?

SOFIA: What?

ANDREA: The thought of being poked by a little pink penis really grosses me out.

(*The waiter re-enters.*)

WAITER: Ladies, can I get you anything else?

WOMEN: Tequila.

(*A pager goes off. All four women pull out their pagers.*)

LILLY: It's for me. My therapist.

(*Lilly scoots out of her seat.*)

LILLY: Excuse me.

(*Sofia rolls her eyes as Lilly walks away.*)

SOFIA: Why would she pay someone when she can talk to me?

(*Andrea and Irene give Sofia a look.*)

(*The waiter arrives with shot glasses.*)

ANDREA: Leave the bottle.

(*They do the tequila ritual. Andrea raises her shot glass.*)

ANDREA: Here's to . . . lost love, lost hope . . . Here's to Joe. I hope his dick falls off.

SOFIA: I hope it shrivels up and dies.

IRENE: I hope he can't get it up.

ANDREA: I hope it turns little and pink.

WOMEN: Salud.

(*Irene notices something offstage.*)

IRENE: Hey, is that Lilly . . . dancing?

SOFIA: Yeah.

ANDREA: Wasn't she crying just a minute ago?

SOFIA: What is he, Asian? I hope he has a green card.

ANDREA: Why? That would only turn her off.

(*The song ends. They see Lilly heading back.*)

IRENE: Here she comes.

(*Lilly returns for her purse. The women pretend not to be talking about her. And before they ask—*)

LILLY: His name is Lu and we're going to eat. Anybody wanna join us?

SOFIA: What did your therapist say?

LILLY: To stay away from you.

SOFIA: Where you going?

LILLY: Don't know yet.

(*As Lilly walks away they hear her ask Lu—*)

LILLY: Do you like Mexican food?

(*She's gone.*)

IRENE: (*Mocking Lilly*) "Do you like Mexican food?" Eat me!

(*The women laugh.*)

Scene 2

The County Courthouse
CINDY waits on the bench, putting on her makeup. She outlines her lips in a mirror like only a homegirl can—slow and deliberate. She puts on her lipstick, dark red. Andrea, a little hung over, enters.

ANDREA: Hi. How you doing?

CINDY: Okay, just nervous. Are you okay? You look sick.

ANDREA: (*Running her fingers through her hair*) Yeah, I think I uh . . . got the flu . . .

CINDY: Oh, I had it. It's that Chino flu that's going around. Drink a lot of manzanilla.

(*Andrea's cell phone rings.*)

ANDREA: Excuse me. (*She answers it.*) Hello? Hi, Carmen. She called in sick again? She's got morning, noon, and night sickness. It must be a boy. Only a man can make you that sick. Did you call the temp office? Okay, talk to you later. Bye.

(*She hangs up.*)

CINDY: Andrea, I know I promised you I'd pay you when I got some money from Tony, but I had to pay my rent because I was behind or else the landlord said he would evict me. Can he do that?

ANDREA: Yeah.

CINDY: Shit. If I don't pay you are you gonna drop my case?

ANDREA: I thought you were gonna look for a job.

CINDY: I can't find one.

ANDREA: Where did you look?

CINDY: In the *L.A. Times*. All the ones that pay good, you have to have a degree and shit. And I'm not gonna work in no sewing factory. I went to one and those fucking Chinos don't pay shit. They take advantage of people 'cuz they're desperate for work, you know, and those poor mojados can't say shit 'cuz they'll fire their asses . . .

(*Andrea's cell phone rings. She answers.*)

ANDREA: Hello? What do you mean she quit? Okay. Oh, Carmen? I need that brief by this afternoon. (*Carmen yells on the other end.*) Okay, calm down. (*She hangs up.*) Shit.

(*She sits on the bench, next to Cindy, opens her briefcase and downs some aspirins.*)

CINDY: Andrea, do you think I'm doing the right thing? The other day he called to ask about the baby. He was so sweet . . . And I thought about it . . . I guess, in a way, I still care for him. I mean, he's my baby's father . . .

ANDREA: Cindy, he broke your jaw. He broke your heart. He won't be happy until he breaks your spirit. Don't let anybody do that. Nobody.

CINDY: Yeah . . . you're right.

ANDREA: Whatever you do, don't look into his eyes.

(*Cindy's husband, TONY RODRIGUEZ, 20, good-looking, enters with his lawyer, JOSEPH LEVINSON, good-looking, early forties.*)

CINDY: There he is. He always looks so smug. Nobody would ever believe he can be as mean as he is.

ANDREA: Relax, we'll bring it all up in court. It's a female judge.

CINDY: Hmmm . . .

JOSEPH: Ms. Venezuela?

ANDREA: (*Correcting him*) Valenzuela.

JOSEPH: Sorry . . .

ANDREA: Just think of Fernando.

JOSEPH: I beg your pardon?

ANDREA: Fernando . . . Valenzuela?

(*Joseph doesn't get it.*)

ANDREA: Never mind. What can I do for you Mr. Levinson?

JOSEPH: Mr. Rodriguez would like to try to reach an agreement regarding visitation out of court, if possible.

CINDY: We already tried that, remember?

JOSEPH: Yes, but I don't think it was under the best of circumstances.

(*Tony approaches them.*)

CINDY: (*To Andrea*) Tell him I don't want to talk to him. I don't wanna look into his eyes . . .

TONY: Come on, Cindy. I was angry, you were angry. We can work this out.

CINDY: (*Not looking at him*) You're always angry. That's why I left you. 'Cuz, I'm tired of getting my ass kicked.

TONY: Please, Cindy. I'm gonna change, baby . . . Cindy, look at me . . .

CINDY: Fuck you.

JOSEPH: Listen . . .

CINDY: Fuck you, too!

ANDREA: Cindy . . .

JOSEPH: You know, Ms. Venezuela, I can inform the judge of your client's behavior . . .

ANDREA: Look, Mr. Levinson, don't try to intimidate my client or me. When your client's behavior is revealed in court, you've got a problem and you know it.

JOSEPH: How is she planning to support her child? She doesn't even have a job.

ANDREA: Yes she does.

(*Cindy looks at Andrea. Subtext: "I do?"*)

ANDREA: She works for me. She's my receptionist.

(*Cindy looks at Andrea. Subtext: "I am?" Andrea picks up her briefcase.*)

JOSEPH: I wasn't expecting this . . . hostile behavior.

ANDREA: I don't know what you're talking about.

JOSEPH: (*To Tony*) Hey, we tried.

(*Joseph and Tony begin to walk away.*)

ANDREA: Hey!

(*Joseph turns.*)

ANDREA: It's Ms. Valenzuela, not Miss Venezuela. Do you have beauty pageant on the brain? Or is it that learning disorder that doesn't allow you people to remember a Latino name correctly?

JOSEPH: Sorry. (*To Tony.*) Come on, let's go.

CINDY: Go girl!

ANDREA: Shhh . . .

CINDY: How much are you gonna pay me?

ANDREA: Minimum wage.

CINDY: Man, you're worse than the Chinos.

Scene 3

Luminarias

The women are in their usual spot.

IRENE: Jan Hoffmeyer.

LILLY: The immigration lawyer?

IRENE: Yeah.

LILLY: Isn't she her friend?

IRENE: Not anymore.

SOFIA: Who?

IRENE: You wouldn't know her. She does those Spanish-language commercials. (*Mocking a gringo accent.*) "Yo le puedo ayudar con sus problemas de inmigracion. Yo soy su amiga." I never did like that bitch.

(*Andrea arrives. She sits. The women look at her.*)

IRENE: Andrea, I never did like that bitch.

LILLY: Me either.

IRENE: Yeah, you know how gabachas are. They see a good-looking Latino and their legs flop open.

SOFIA: Okay, before we get into a "white women are loose bitches" frenzy let's think about whether we dislike her because she's white or because she's screwing Joe?

ANDREA: Both.

SOFIA: You can't blame it all on her. Joe played a part in this.

ANDREA: Oh, I'm not defending him.

IRENE: If there's one thing that pisses me off, it's seeing a Chicano with a gringa. Strutting around with her hanging on his arm like she's a status symbol of some kind. Why do Latinos do that shit?

SOFIA: Because they can get away with their Macho bullshit by saying "It's a cultural thing, baby." Latinos can't handle a strong woman and that's the truth.

IRENE: That's bullshit. Not every Latino is a Macho.

SOFIA: And not every white woman is a loose bitch.

ANDREA: Every one I've met is.

SOFIA: You are so racist!

ANDREA: I am not! Sofia, my husband is divorcing me for Jan Hoffmeyer. Can I process this without being politically correct?

SOFIA: I'm just saying . . .

LILLY: Sofia, shut up! Go on, Andrea . . .

(*A profound sadness comes over Andrea.*)

ANDREA: He's gonna marry her. And the worse thing is . . . I still want him back. He's my husband, he belongs to me. Joe is mine. And I miss him. I still reach over for him at night. When he told me he was gonna marry her, he looked into my eyes and if he would've asked me back I would've said "yes" . . . I know I shouldn't feel this way, but I do . . .

SOFIA: Well, you gotta be honest about your feelings.

IRENE: Even if he is an asshole . . .

Scene 4

Andrea's House

Andrea's son, JOEY, 17, is channel surfing. Andrea enters and puts her things down.

ANDREA: Hi, mijo.

(*She kisses him.*)

JOEY: Hi, Mom.

ANDREA: Have you been here long?

JOEY: No.

(*Andrea notices that something's wrong.*)

ANDREA: Are you okay?

JOEY: No. (*Pause.*) I saw Dad today. He told me about . . .

ANDREA: Jan?

JOEY: Yeah.

(*She goes to him.*)

ANDREA: I'm sorry . . .

JOEY: I thought Dad would come home just like he always does.

ANDREA: I know.

(*Silence.*)

JOEY: I guess I'm just feeling . . . dysfunctional. I miss Dad. I miss waking up and finding him cooking in the kitchen, making his huevos rancheros . . . And seeing you and him dance together. It always made me feel, I don't know . . . good. And seeing you hugging and kissing and laughing? You know how Dad makes us laugh.

ANDREA: Yeah.

JOEY: I was always so proud that I had my Mom and my Dad. Now, I'm just gonna be like everybody else. Can't you fix it, Mom? Can't you guys try?

ANDREA: He doesn't love me anymore. He's in love with somebody else.

JOEY: An ugly white chick.

ANDREA: Hey, watch your language.

JOEY: Sorry. An ugly white woman. What's up with that?

ANDREA: I don't know.

JOEY: And he always used to say, "Mijo, when you get married make sure you marry a Mexican girl who can afford to hire a maid who knows how to make tortillas." I mean, what can they have in common? He likes Mexican food, Mexican music, he shops at the Montebello Mall. She's probably never been east of La Cienega.

ANDREA: Maybe that's the attraction. I don't know. I'm sorry this is so hard on you.

JOEY: Don't worry. I'm not gonna go ballistic or anything.

ANDREA: Are you gonna go do drugs?

JOEY: Nah. Maybe a little pot.

ANDREA: Yeah, I'll pot you.

(*They laugh.*)

JOEY: (*Pause*) He wants me to go to the Dodger game on Saturday . . . with him and what's-her-name.

ANDREA: Jan.

JOEY: Yeah.

ANDREA: And?

JOEY: I don't know if I want to.

ANDREA: Why not?

JOEY: 'Cuz, the Dodgers suck.

ANDREA: Yeah, but that shouldn't stop you from going to a game.

JOEY: I know. I just don't want you to feel bad . . .

ANDREA: Hey, if you want to go, go. It's fine, really.

JOEY: But, will you feel bad?

ANDREA: No. You're gonna have to get to know her sooner or later. She's gonna be your stepmother.

JOEY: Ugh! That's a gross thought.

ANDREA: I know it is, mijo. But, you're gonna have to face it like a man.

(*Joey laughs.*)

JOEY: Mom, does this mean you're gonna have to learn how to cook?

ANDREA: No, it means you do.

(*They laugh. Joey hugs Andrea.*)

JOEY: Don't worry, Mom. I'll take care of you.

ANDREA: We'll take care of each other. How's that?

JOEY: Okay.

ANDREA: Mom . . .

ANDREA: What?

JOEY: I just wanna say . . . That you're my Mom and no one will ever take your place, ever . . .

ANDREA: I know that, mijo . . .

Scene 5

Luminarias

Lights up on LUMINARIAS. Sofia, Irene, and Lilly are sitting in their usual spot.

SOFIA: She feels like shit, she looks like shit. It's depression. I've seen it a thousand times.

LILLY: Sofia, isn't it unethical for you to discuss your patient's cases with us?

SOFIA: She's not my patient. She's my friend.

IRENE: Who goes to you for therapy.

SOFIA: She doesn't pay me.

IRENE: I hope not.

SOFIA: Look, I think we need to help her.

LILLY: How?

SOFIA: We need to give her advice.

IRENE: I'm in no position to give anyone advice.

LILLY: Neither am I.

SOFIA: Well, neither am I. I mean, just 'cause I'm a therapist doesn't mean I know anything.

IRENE: Gee, don't tell your patients that.

SOFIA: I think she needs to start dating.

LILLY: Why?

SOFIA: Because if she doesn't accept male companionship now, she may never learn to trust a man again.

IRENE: Do we really want her to?

(*A new, very handsome, waiter, PABLO, appears.*)

PABLO: Buenas noches, Senoritas. What can I get you this evening?

SOFIA: Brandy. Courvoisier.

IRENE: Long Island Ice Tea.

LILLY: Sex on the Beach.

PABLO: Gracias.

(*Sofia glances at the waiter as he leaves.*)

SOFIA: Is that a new waiter?

IRENE: Yeah . . .

SOFIA: Anyway, I invited a friend . . .

LILLY: Here?

IRENE: Tonight?

LILLY: Is he . . .

SOFIA: Jewish.

IRENE: Pinche Sofia!

LILLY: You should have asked her first.

SOFIA: He's a great guy. A lawyer. I would've gone for him myself, but I'm (*to Irene*) "making the sacrifice."

(*Andrea enters.*)

ANDREA: Hi.

WOMEN: (*Pretending not to be talking about her*) Hieee . . .

ANDREA: Were you guys talking about me?

SOFIA: Of course not. Lilly was filling us in on her new boyfriend. What's his name?

LILLY: Lu.

SOFIA: Yeah, Lu. Go on.

LILLY: He owns a 7-Eleven.

SOFIA: That didn't get burned down during the riots . . .

LILLY: Rebellion, Sofia, rebellion.

SOFIA: I'm sorry, honey. But, a rebellion is organized. That was a riot.

IRENE: Uprising.

SOFIA: Whatever.

IRENE: It turned into a black and white issue anyway.

ANDREA: Hey, there're Latinos in South-central.

LILLY: Yeah. Most of the looters arrested were Latino.

IRENE: Those were Salvadoreans and Nicaraguans, not Mexicans!

LILLY: Would you stop! Now, you're pointing your finger at other nationalities.

IRENE: Hey, Mexican's aren't thieves.

ANDREA: Neither are Salvadoreans or Nicaraguans or African Americans. The only thieves around are . . .

SOFIA: Don't tell me. White? Right? Here we go with the white-bashing.

IRENE: Hey, they stole our land and they haven't stopped since.

SOFIA: Is that what you teach in your Chicano studies classes?

IRENE: Exactly!

SOFIA: And then we wonder why we can't get along.

ANDREA: Not all those people in the street were thugs or looters either. They were poor people who wanted a piece of the pie, that's all.

IRENE: All I know is when I saw Latinos looting on television, I felt ashamed. It's not our way.

ANDREA: It's not anybody's way, Irene! Damn you're hard headed!

LILLY: Can I go on with my story?

WOMEN: Go on . . .

LILLY: His cousin lives in Monterey Park. He's the one that brought him here that night.

SOFIA: How old's his cousin?

LILLY: Married.

SOFIA: Shit.

ANDREA: What is he, Chinese?

LILLY: Korean.

IRENE: Oh, shit . . .

LILLY: What?

IRENE: You know how Korean's feel about Latinos.

LILLY: Well, Lu doesn't!

ANDREA: Okay, go on . . .

LILLY: Anyway, so far we've gone out to eat a couple times . . . We've gone to the movies, dancing . . .

IRENE: Have you gone to bed?

LILLY: Just a couple of times. I don't want him to think I'm loose or anything.

ANDREA: He's gonna find out sooner or later.

LILLY: No, really, you guys. I think I really like him. I've never been attracted to anyone like him.

SOFIA: You mean Asian?

ANDREA: Or single?

IRENE: Or with a job?

LILLY: All of the above.

(*Pablo returns with their drinks.*)

SOFIA: (*Smiles*) Gracias.

PABLO: (*To Andrea*) What can I get you, Señorita?

ANDREA: Mineral water.

PABLO: Con gas o sin gas?

ANDREA: Con gas.

(*Pablo begins to leave.*)

ANDREA: Make it a shot of tequila—El Patrón.

(*Sofia checks Pablo as he walks away.*)

SOFIA: God, he's gorgeous.

(*Looks at Sofia.*)

ANDREA: Hello?

(*Joseph Levinson approaches. Andrea frowns. Irene and Lilly smile politely.*)

SOFIA: Joseph, hi!

JOSEPH: Hi.

SOFIA: This is Irene . . .

IRENE: (*Dryly*) Hi.

SOFIA: Lilly . . .

LILLY: (*Flirting*) Nice to meet you.

SOFIA: And Andrea . . .

JOSEPH: Hello.

ANDREA: We've met.

SOFIA: You have?

JOSEPH: Ms. Fernando, right?

(*Andrea begins to correct him—*)

JOSEPH: Just kidding.

(*Andrea forces a smile.*)

SOFIA: Do you know each other?

ANDREA: Our clients are divorcing each other.

LILLY: What a small world.

ANDREA: Yeah.

SOFIA: Sit down.

JOSEPH: Thanks. (*To Andrea.*) Actually, I was going to call you . . . regarding the case.

ANDREA: Uh huh. Do you come here often?

JOSEPH: No, it's my first time. Sofia invited me . . .

SOFIA: (*Cutting him off*) I can't believe you know each other.

(*Irene and Lilly get up from their stools.*)

IRENE: Excuse us.

SOFIA: I'll go with you.

(*Andrea fumes. Pablo approaches as the women leave. Sofia bumps into him.*)

SOFIA: (*Breathless*) Perdón.

PABLO: Pase.

(*The women continue on their way.*)

PABLO: What can I get you tonight, sir?

JOSEPH: I'll have a beer. What kind do you have?

PABLO: Bohemia, Dos XX, Tecate, Corona . . .

JOSEPH: (*To Andrea*) Which do you recommend?

ANDREA: Just don't order Coors.

JOSEPH: Okay, I'll have a Bud.

(*Pablo leaves.*)

(*Silence.*)

Scene 6

Luminarias

Special lights on Joseph and Andrea. Joseph pulls chair closer to Andrea once the others leave.

JOSEPH: I guess this is the chance you take when you agree to a blind date.

ANDREA: Is that what this is?

JOSEPH: Sofia didn't tell you?

ANDREA: I guess she knew better.

JOSEPH: I really think you got the wrong impression of me the other day.

ANDREA: It doesn't matter, really.

JOSEPH: It does to me.

ANDREA: Why's that?

JOSEPH: I don't like being accused of being a . . . what were you accusing me of?

ANDREA: I wasn't accusing you of anything. I just wanted you to stop playing that male dominating, racist bullshit game you were playing. Your testosterone level was way up. You should really have it checked.

JOSEPH: (*Laughs*) I'm not a sexist and I'm certainly not a racist. In fact I used go out with a Mexican girl.

ANDREA: (*Not impressed*) Oh, really?

JOSEPH: Yeah, her family had a great spread in Puerto Vallarta.

ANDREA: Oh? And I bet she took you to all the best Mexican restaurants in L.A.

JOSEPH: (*Detecting her sarcasm*) What part of Mexico are you from?

ANDREA: East L.A.

JOSEPH: Oh, that explains it.

ANDREA: Explains what?

JOSEPH: That . . . edge.

ANDREA: (*With an edge*) What edge?

(*Pablo returns with Joseph's beer and notices they're at odds. The women return from the bathroom.*)

JOSEPH: (*Gringo accent*) Gracias.

IRENE: (*Nonchalantly*) We're gonna go.

(*They gather their things.*)

ANDREA: I'm leaving, too.

SOFIA: Do you have to?

ANDREA: Yeah. I have an early appointment.

JOSEPH: Listen, I'll call you regarding the joint custody proposal.

(*Andrea stops.*)

ANDREA: The what?

JOSEPH: Joint custody . . .

SOFIA: Listen, I can see you guys need to talk.

IRENE: We're out of here.

WOMEN: Byeee . . .

(*The women leave.*)

(*Silence.*)

ANDREA: You'll be lucky if you get unsupervised visitation.

JOSEPH: I don't know. I think the judge likes my client, actually. You never know which way she'll go. He's gone through some intense rehabilitation. I think part of his rehabilitation is being able to care for his son. I have letters from his doctors, his parole officers, close friends. And they're all willing to testify. Look, it's not personal. I'm representing my client's . . .

ANDREA: You represent a man who abuses women, Mr. Levinson.

JOSEPH: Doesn't he deserve a chance? Isn't that what you want for your client? He's a young kid who wants a crack at being part of his son's upbringing. Is that so bad? I mean, look at your client. She's rowdy, foul-mouthed . . .

ANDREA: But, she's honest, a good mother and a hell of a worker!

JOSEPH: I can say the same for Tony.

ANDREA: Can you really?

JOSEPH: (*Honestly*) Yes, I can.

(*Silence.*)

ANDREA: Okay. I'll convey the message. But, I'm not convinced he's changed.

(*She begins to gather her things.*)

ANDREA: (*To Waiter*) Check please.

JOSEPH: I've got it.

ANDREA: Thanks. Goodnight.

(*She gets up to leave, then notices somebody offstage. She goes back to the table.*)

ANDREA: I think I'll have another shot after all.

JOSEPH: (*Surprised*) Great.

(*She sits back down, then turns her attention to Joseph.*)

ANDREA: (*Flirtatiously*) So, where did you say you were from?

JOSEPH: (*Not sure what to think*) I didn't.

ANDREA: (*Giggles coquettishly*) That's right you didn't . . .

JOSEPH: I'm from here . . . L.A.

(*Andrea looks offstage, then back at Joseph.*)

ANDREA: (*Pretending to be very interested*) Are you really?

JOSEPH: Yes, I am.

(*She takes his hands in hers. Joseph doesn't understand, but goes along.*)

JOSEPH: (*Laughs*) What's going on? Why so friendly all of a sudden?

ANDREA: See that man over there?

JOSEPH: The really good-looking one?

ANDREA: Yeah. He's my husband.

(*Joseph begins to pull his hands away, but she doesn't let him.*)

ANDREA: Relax, we're getting a divorce. That's his girlfriend. They're engaged. Please, go along with this . . . please.

JOSEPH: Okay.

(*He touches her face. He kisses her hand. He bends over the table and kisses her lips. Andrea gets a tingle.*)

ANDREA: Okay . . . I think we've made our point . . .

(*He kisses her again. Pablo returns, shocked to see them kissing.*)

ANDREA: They're gone.

(*Trying to compose herself.*)

ANDREA: Thank you.

JOSEPH: My pleasure.

ANDREA: (*To Pablo*) I'll have another shot please.

PABLO: A shot for you, sir?

JOSEPH: Uh . . . sure.

(*Pablo leaves . . . confused.*)

JOSEPH: So, are you gonna fill me in?

ANDREA: He's in love with being in love.

JOSEPH: And you're in love with him.

ANDREA: I . . . I guess so. I'm sorry. I shouldn't have done that to you.

JOSEPH: Hey, I know how to role-play. I'm a lawyer, remember?

(*She cracks a smile.*)

JOSEPH: Actually . . . (*He takes back her hand.*) It felt kind of good.

(*Andrea pulls her hand back. Pablo arrives with tequila, lemon, and salt.*)

ANDREA: Salud.

(*They drink the tequila.*)

JOSEPH: You know, my father was the same way. Affair after affair and my mother always took him back.

ANDREA: Are they still together?

JOSEPH: They were until he died a few years ago. But, she became so bitter from all the pain he caused her, she made his last years miserable. They stayed together for us kids. Now, we're all scared to death of marriage.

ANDREA: See, I don't want that to happen to my son. I'm afraid he's getting a distorted view of what marriage is supposed to be.

JOSEPH: Who's to say what it's supposed to be? Is it about possession and fidelity? Is it about trust and freedom? Is it about habit and complacency? What do you think it's about?

ANDREA: (*Thinks*) I think it's about time for another shot of Patrón. How about you? (*To Pablo.*) Dos más, por favor.

(*She's got a buzz.*)

ANDREA: So, have you ever been married?

JOSEPH: No. I've always wanted to, though. But, it hasn't happened. Somehow I scare women away before we walk down the aisle.

ANDREA: Have you been in love?

JOSEPH: Once.

ANDREA: With the rich, Mexican girl, right?

JOSEPH: No, with a rich, Jewish girl.

ANDREA: So, what happened to the Mexican?

JOSEPH: She dumped me.

ANDREA: For who?

JOSEPH: For her best friend.

ANDREA: Did you know him?

JOSEPH: Her.

(*Andrea laughs.*)

ANDREA: I'm sorry.

JOSEPH: It's okay. I wound up in therapy. That's where I met Tess.

ANDREA: Was she in therapy, too?

JOSEPH: No, she was my therapist.

(*Andrea laughs again.*)

ANDREA: So, you date your therapist?

JOSEPH: Not anymore.

ANDREA: Why not?

JOSEPH: She's nuts!

(*They laugh. Pablo brings their shots. They slam them.*)

ANDREA: Can you handle one more?

JOSEPH: Sure.

PABLO: Two more? Ju got it.

JOSEPH: Did he say "Jew"?

(*Andrea laughs.*)

ANDREA: You're really funny, you know that? I haven't laughed this much since . . .

JOSEPH: Since the last time you were out with a Jew?

(*Pause.*)

ANDREA: No. Since the last time I was out with Joe.

(*Silence.*)

ANDREA: I've never been out with a Jew.

JOSEPH: Ju're out with one right now.

ANDREA: Weren't we meeting about the case?

JOSEPH: Something like that.

ANDREA: (*Moves close*) What was your proposal?

(*Joseph whispers something in her ear. She smiles. A slow oldie plays.*)

ANDREA: You wanna dance?

JOSEPH: Sure.

(*They get up and hold on to each other. Her knees buckle. They kiss . . . long and juicy.*)

Scene 7

Andrea's Office

The phone rings and Cindy, dressed in her version of office attire, answers the phone.

CINDY: Good morning, law offices. Oh, hi Mary. No, she's not in yet. Did you try her house? So did I. No answer. I know Joey stayed at Joe's last night. She has a client waiting.

ANDREA: Hi. Are you my nine o'clock? I'm sorry I'm late. I'll be right with you.

CINDY: (*On the phone*) Hold on.

(*Andrea enters, wearing sunglasses.*)

CINDY: Are you okay? You're an hour late. Your Mom's on the phone.

ANDREA: I'm fine. Tell her I'll call her back.

(*Andrea opens up her briefcase and takes out some aspirins.*)

CINDY: Mary, she'll call you back. Okay, hold on.

(*Cindy hands her the phone.*)

CINDY: She said "No."

(*Andrea takes the phone.*)

ANDREA: Hi, Mom. Yeah, I overslept.

(*Cindy hands Andrea her messages.*)

CINDY: Sofia . . .

ANDREA: No, I haven't been drinking. No, I haven't met anyone.

CINDY: Irene . . .

ANDREA: I gotta go. I have a client waiting. I'll see you this weekend.

CINDY: and Lilly . . .

ANDREA: I promise. Bye.

(*She hangs up.*)

CINDY: They all wanna know where you are. You really should call in when you're gonna be late, you know. That's really unprofessional of you. So, where were you?

ANDREA: I can't talk now. I have a client . . .

CINDY: It's okay. She's my friend. She wants a divorce. I told her she could pay you in payments.

ANDREA: What?

CINDY: She's married to an asshole, Andrea.

(*Andrea looks pissed.*)

ANDREA: Cindy, sit down.

(*Cindy sits.*)

CINDY: I'm sorry. I know I shouldn't have told Isabel that she could pay you in payments. But, I just felt so sorry for her, you know. Her husband's in jail for murder and he's never getting out. She has three kids and she wants to start a new life. Nobody would do this for girls like us. You know that?

ANDREA: Yeah, I know. (*Pause.*) Cindy, Tony wants joint custody.

(*It sinks in.*)

CINDY: Doesn't that mean that the baby will live with me sometimes, then with him sometimes?

(*Andrea nods.*)

CINDY: (*She shakes her head "No"*) Uh uh, Andrea, I don't want my baby living with him. He's crazy.

ANDREA: I . . . I'm gonna have to refer you to another lawyer. My colleague, Frank Gutierrez . . .

CINDY: How come?

ANDREA: Because uh . . . ummm. . . .

CINDY: I want you to be my lawyer. Don't you do custody cases?

ANDREA: Yes, but . . .

CINDY: Yeah?

(*Andrea can't bring herself to tell her.*)

ANDREA: I . . . Ummm . . . We could lose, you know.

CINDY: How in the fuck can we lose, Andrea? He's a fucking maniac!

ANDREA: First of all, you're gonna have to watch your language! If you go into court talking the way you do you're gonna get kicked out of the courtroom, you understand me? Now, he has a very good lawyer . . .

CINDY: Better than you?

ANDREA: No.

CINDY: Shit, I hope not. I'm busting my ass out there. I expect some good representation.

ANDREA: But, he has a good case because Tony has gone through therapy, counseling. You know, all the things I asked you to do when we began this case and you didn't.

CINDY: You just suggested it, you didn't say I had to!

ANDREA: Okay, forget it. There's nothing we can do about it now.

CINDY: Should I go to counseling now?

ANDREA: It couldn't hurt. And there're parenting classes you can attend . . .

(*The phone rings. Cindy answers.*)

CINDY: Good morning, law offices. (*She covers the phone.*) It's that fucking . . . I mean fricking . . . It's Tony's lawyer.

(*Andrea takes the phone.*)

CINDY: Tell him we're going to court. And tell him I'm going to counseling and to those mothering classes. Go on, tell him.

ANDREA: I will. Can you leave my office please?

CINDY: How come? I wanna know what he says.

ANDREA: Cindy, I take my calls in private . . .

CINDY: But, this is about me . . .

ANDREA: Cindy, get the fuck out of my office, now!

(*Cindy gets up to leave.*)

CINDY: (*To herself*) What's her problem?

(*She exits.*)

ANDREA: (*Into the phone*) This is Andrea.

(*Lights up on Joseph on the phone . . . wearing sunglasses.*)

JOSEPH: Hi. How you doing?

ANDREA: Fine. Just busy.

JOSEPH: I just have one question.

ANDREA: Yeah?

JOSEPH: Who hit me over the head?

(*She laughs.*)

JOSEPH: I had a great time last night. Can we get together sometime this weekend?

ANDREA: Uh . . . I . . . have so much work. I . . . I'm really sorry about last night.

JOSEPH: Sorry?

ANDREA: I don't know what got into me. I mean, I guess I was feeling vulnerable and I was really drunk.

JOSEPH: We were both drunk . . .

ANDREA: I don't think it's a good idea for us to see each other again.

(*Silence.*)

ANDREA: It's unethical and I'd have to drop Cindy's case and that wouldn't be fair to her. I hope we can keep this . . . incident confidential.

JOSEPH: Sure.

ANDREA: I'm sorry if I made you think that there could be anything between us. I mean, I shouldn't have let it go as far as it did. I don't normally do that kind of thing.

JOSEPH: I know you don't. And I'm sorry you feel this way. But, I understand. And don't worry, I'll keep it to myself and I won't call anymore . . . I mean, personally. It'll be strictly business. Okay?

ANDREA: (*Pause*) Okay. My client refused the offer. She wants to take it to court.

JOSEPH: (*Strictly business*) Alright, see you in court.

(*Lights down on Joseph. Andrea slowly hangs up the phone. Silence.*)

Scene 8

Andrea's Office
There's a knock on the door.

ANDREA: Yeah?
(*Lilly pokes in her head.*)
LILLY: Hieee . . .
ANDREA: Hi. What are you doing here?
LILLY: I was just in the neighborhood and I thought maybe you wanted to talk.
ANDREA: About what?
LILLY: Oh, I don't know . . . I was worried about you. It was all Sofia's idea . . .
ANDREA: I know.
(*Pause.*)
LILLY: Did you screw him?
(*Andrea nods.*)
ANDREA: I saw Joe with Jan and I got drunk . . .
LILLY: Did Joe talk to you?
ANDREA: He was so into her, I don't think he even knew I was there . . .
LILLY: And so this guy . . .
ANDREA: Joseph . . .
LILLY: Comforted you?
ANDREA: Yes. We had tequila and one thing led to another.
LILLY: He seemed like a very nice man. I got very good vibes from him.
ANDREA: He's nice, but . . . he's white.
LILLY: Nobody's perfect. Is he a good person? Does he have a good heart? Did you feel comfortable in his arms?
ANDREA: Yes, I did. Isn't that funny?
LILLY: What did you feel?
ANDREA: When he kissed me, Lilly. I felt . . . a tingle.
LILLY: That's great . . .
(*Irene enters.*)
IRENE: Hi. Lilly, I didn't know you were here . . .
IRENE: (*To Andrea*) So, what happened?
ANDREA: Nothing.
IRENE: Lilly, tell me what happened.
(*Lilly nods.*)
IRENE: You screwed him?
ANDREA: Shhh . . . I really don't think this is the time or the place . . .
IRENE: You mean he got it up?
ANDREA: Would you please be quiet . . .
IRENE: (*To Irene*) Did he?
(*Lilly nods.*)

IRENE: You did it with someone who doesn't believe in Jesus or La Virgen de Guadalupe?

LILLY: (*Worried*) Neither does Lu . . .

IRENE: Don't you know those gringos just want to be with Latinas because it makes them feel superior?

ANDREA: I know. I was drunk . . .

(*Sofia enters.*)

SOFIA: Hi . . .

ANDREA: Oh God. What is this?

SOFIA: What happened?

IRENE: She did it with your friend.

SOFIA: You did? I just wanted you to meet, not . . .

IRENE: She got drunk.

LILLY: She saw Joe with Jan and she needed companionship and Joseph gave it to her and she felt a tingle.

ANDREA: Lilly . . .

LILLY: Isn't that all that matters, Andrea? When it comes down to it. Two human beings, two bodies, two spirits intermingling in the universe. Entering one another's energy. We're like all these little particles in space and sometimes we collide with one another and create an explosion. Both lights coming together and creating that warm glow, that bathes you and consumes you.

IRENE: Lilly, you did a lot of drugs when we were in school, didn't you?

SOFIA: (*To Andrea*) That good, huh?

ANDREA: It had been so long anything would've felt good.

SOFIA: When are you gonna see him again?

ANDREA: I'm not.

LILLY: Is he married?

ANDREA: No.

SOFIA: So, what's the problem?

LILLY: His color.

SOFIA: He's Jewish . . .

ANDREA: He's white. He looks white, he acts white. The only thing not white about him is the size of his thing, okay?

IRENE: Really?

SOFIA: You know, Andie, you're letting your racism get in the way of the possibility of developing a relationship with a decent human being.

ANDREA: I am not a racist. I'm a victim of racism.

SOFIA: Come on, Andie. This isn't the '70s. You're a professional, you've made it. Get rid of that chip on your shoulder. It's getting ugly.

ANDREA: It's not a chip, it's a boulder. And I wear it proudly.

SOFIA: What for?

ANDREA: For a lot of things, Sofia. But, how far back do you wanna go? Let's see . . .

How about for when my first-grade teacher changed my name from (*Spanish pronunciation*) Andrea to (*English pronunciation*) Andrea.

IRENE: That's nothing. My high school counselor laughed when I said I wanted to be a teacher.

LILLY: Mine told me to take homemaking because I'd probably have five kids by the time I was 25. I wish . . .

ANDREA: I wear it for the immigrants that were beat up in El Monte and for every Latino that has gotten his or her ass kicked by the cops when there were no video cameras around.

IRENE: That's right! And what about proposition 187!

LILLY: And affirmative action?

ANDREA: But, the main reason I wear it, Sofia, is for every time a white person mispronounces Valenzuela!

SOFIA: Boy, do we have a problem . . .

ANDREA: Yeah, with white people and I'll be damned if you'll catch me screwing one!

SOFIA: Too late, Andie, you already did . . . And you liked it!

ANDREA: Fuck you!

SOFIA: Oh, please. Must we resort to this kind of language? What are we, cholas?

ANDREA: Sofia, why don't you go back to the West Side, where you belong.

LILLY: Hey . . .

SOFIA: You know what, Andrea? I'm tired of you playing this "Holier than thou" bullshit with me. You think I'm a sell-out! A vendida because I don't live in Montebello or Fontana or Diamond Bar! Well, I don't have to prove anything to you, Andrea! I am who I am! And if you don't like it you can kiss my brown ass!

ANDREA: You are who you are? Oh, please. When was the last time you visited that old lady who still lives in that worn-down house in East L.A.? Huh? Remember? Your mother? When was the last time you drove your Mercedes into that driveway? Or are you afraid someone might break your windows?

SOFIA: You leave my mother out of this!

IRENE: Yeah. Heaven forbid we go there!

LILLY: Irene!

IRENE: It's true!

SOFIA: You've got a lot of nerve. Miss "My brother isn't gay, he's confused!" Talk about denial!

IRENE: He is confused!

SOFIA: He's a drag queen Irene. He dresses like a woman and calls himself Carmela for Christ's Sake!

IRENE: He's a performance artist!

(*Lilly loses it.*)

LILLY: Stop it! And don't any of you start on me! I'm all fucked up and I know it! My sister drinks too much, my nephew's a gang member, my mother takes Prozac and goes from man to man. But, please, don't tell me about it! It hurts too much . . . Why are we hurting each other so much?!?

(*Cindy enters.*)

CINDY: What the hell is going on in here? Do I have to remind you ladies that this is a place of business? We have a client out there! Fuck!

Scene 9

The County Courthouse

Joseph is sitting on the bench looking through documents. He talks into his tape recorder.

JOSEPH: Monday. Meeting with Ms. Vene . . . Valenzuela to exchange documents. Need to schedule Ms. Rodriguez' deposition. Pick up clothes at cleaners and call your mother. Joseph, call your mother.

(*Andrea arrives.*)

ANDREA: (*No smile*) I have the documents you requested.

JOSEPH: Thanks. I need to schedule your client's deposition.

ANDREA: Fine.

(*She hands him an envelope and takes out her electronic organizer.*)

ANDREA: When is good for you?

JOSEPH: The 19th?

ANDREA: Fine. I'll let her know.

JOSEPH: Thanks.

(*He looks into her eyes.*)

ANDREA: What?

JOSEPH: I loved kissing your breasts.

ANDREA: Don't.

(*She picks up her briefcase and begins to walk away. Joseph does the same. Andrea stops and turns.*)

ANDREA: Hey!

(*He stops, turns and walks back.*)

ANDREA: I'm on to your game. You said we could keep this a secret, but you don't intend to, do you? You guys . . .

JOSEPH: What guys?

ANDREA: You! I mean you! You'll do anything to get the upper hand, won't you? What happened the other night . . . makes you feel superior, doesn't it?

JOSEPH: What are you talking about?

ANDREA: I'm talking about that superiority game you white guys play . . .

JOSEPH: Superiority?

(*He laughs.*)

ANDREA: Why am I wasting my time?

(*She turns and walks away.*)

JOSEPH: Hey.

(*She stops. She doesn't turn.*)

JOSEPH: Why are you wasting your time?

ANDREA: (*Still not turning*) I don't know . . .

JOSEPH: I don't want you to go.

ANDREA: Why not?

JOSEPH: Because I like you.

ANDREA: Well, I don't like you . . .

JOSEPH: Oh, baby, who are you kidding? When I held you the other night . . . The way you made love to me from head to toe . . . I know you like me and I like you.

ANDREA: No, I don't!

JOSEPH: Then why won't you look at me?

(*Andrea turns to look at him.*)

JOSEPH: This isn't about me being white and you being Hispanic . . .

ANDREA: Latina . . .

JOSEPH: Latina . . .

ANDREA: Chicana . . .

JOSEPH: Chicana . . . Whatever. This is about a man and a woman who are a little lonely and who enjoyed each other's company. It happens all the time, baby, and there's nothing wrong with it. There's nothing wrong with feeling good. There's nothing wrong with wanting to be happy.

(*Silence.*)

JOSEPH: Come here.

(*They go to each other, drop their briefcases and kiss passionately.*)

END OF ACT ONE

ACT TWO

Scene 1

Andrea's Parents' Back Yard

Lights up on a typical Chicano family party. People speaking Spanish, English, and Spanglish. Andrea is with her aunts TONIA and CONCHA, both in their sixties. She looks as if she's expecting someone.

TONIA: Relax, Mija. He'll show up.

CONCHA: Who, Mija?

TONIA: She has a new boyfriend she's invited.

CONCHA: You do, Mija? Oh, I'm so glad.

ANDREA: He's just a friend . . .

TONIA: Then why are you so nervous?

CONCHA: Your mother was getting worried about you. She thinks you need a man.

ANDREA: My mother thinks everybody needs a man.

TONIA: Everybody does.

(*Andrea spots Joseph offstage.*)

ANDREA: There he is.

CONCHA: Is that him?

ANDREA: Yes . . .

TONIA: (*Impressed*) Ohhhh. . . . Oh, he's kind of cute. Is he . . .

(*Concha elbows her.*)

CONCHA: Mija, your boyfriend is . . .

ANDREA: Jewish . . .

TONIA: A gringo!

CONCHA: Ay, que bueno! What does he do?

ANDREA: He's a lawyer . . .

TONIA: Like Joe?

CONCHA: Callate! Not like Joe. Verdad, Mija?

ANDREA: Let's hope not.

TONIA: Does he have money?

CONCHA: Tonia!

TONIA: Well, it doesn't hurt!

(*Joseph arrives.*)

ANDREA: Hi!

JOSEPH: Hi!

ANDREA: I guess you met my mother, inside.

JOSEPH: Yes, I did. Sorry, I'm late. I'm not familiar with this part of L.A.

CONCHA: I'm Andrea's Aunt Concha.

JOSEPH: How do you do.

TONIA: (*Flirtatiously*) And I'm her Aunt Tonia. But, you can call me Tonie.

JOSEPH: How do you do.

TONIA: How do I do what?

JOSEPH: I beg your pardon?

(*Andrea quickly adds—*)

ANDREA: Oh, and I want you to meet my son, Joey. (*She calls out.*) Joey!

(*Joey enters.*)

ANDREA: Joey, this is Joseph. This is my son, Joey.

(*Shaking Joey's hand.*)

JOSEPH: Hi, Joey. They used to call me Joey when I was a kid.

JOEY: My name is José. José Valenzuela.

JOSEPH: Like Fernando, right?

JOEY: No, like my father, José Valenzuela.

JOSEPH: Well, it's nice to meet you, José.

JOEY: Thanks.

(*He exits.*)

ANDREA: (*Trying to break the tension*) Can I get you something to drink? A beer?

JOSEPH: What, no tequila?

ANDREA: Uh uh—family rule.

JOSEPH: Why so?

ANDREA: A deep, dark family secret . . . My aunts start taking off your clothes.

JOSEPH: (*Remembering*) Oh, yeah . . . Okay, a beer.

(*Andrea leaves Joseph standing alone with her aunts. They look at him and smile. He smiles back. They don't know what to talk to him about. After a long moment.*)

TONIA: Do you like Mexican food?

JOSEPH: Yes, I do.

CONCHA: Good. We'll be serving in a minute.

JOSEPH: Okay.

(*Silence.*)

TONIA: You know, Concha used to have a grin . . . a . . . an American boyfriend when she was young.

CONCHA: (*Proudly*) Yes, I did. He's was a very nice boy. His father was the owner of the town store.

TONIA: Yeah, she'd get all dressed up just to go buy a loaf of bread. (*To Concha.*) Te acuerdas?

CONCHA: Yeah.

ANDREA: But, then she met Frank and she dumped him like a hot potato.

JOSEPH: Frank?

CONCHA: My husband.

TONIA: Yeah, Frank came home on leave one day. He looked so handsome in his uniform. (*To Concha.*) Te acuerdas?

CONCHA: (She sighs) Yeah. It took my breath away . . .

TONIA: And boy could he jitterbug. (*To Concha.*) Te acuerdas? That little gringo didn't stand a chance.

CONCHA: We got married before he went back. That's the way it happened back then. The boys would come home, get married, then go to war. A lot of them never came back.

JOSEPH: Where's Frank now?

CONCHA: (*Snapping out of the memory*) Huh? No me acuerdo. Oh . . . (*She looks around.*) He's over there.

TONIA: Yeah, the big fat one with the can of beer in his hand. And you see the ugly skinny one next to him? That's my husband. Old father time can be a mean son of a bitch, que no?

CONCHA: Ay, Tonia!

(*They crack up. Andrea's cousin, RICK, 30ish, dressed in an expensive suit approaches.*)

RICK: Hey, how you doing? I'm Andie's cousin, Rick.

(*They shake hands.*)

JOSEPH: Joseph. Pleased to meet you.

RICK: Pleasure. Is that your BMW out there?

JOSEPH: Yes, it is.

RICK: Nice. Divorce lawyer?

JOSEPH: Yes.

RICK: Play much tennis?

JOSEPH: Yes, I do as a matter of fact.

RICK: Great. We should get together and play sometime.

JOSEPH: Sounds great.

RICK: Nice meeting you, Joseph.

JOSEPH: Same here.

(*Rick leaves. Andrea returns with Joseph's beer.*)

ANDREA: How are you doing?

JOSEPH: Okay, I think.

JOSEPH: I keep hearing people whisper "gringo," "gabacho."

ANDREA: Terms of endearment.

(*They laugh.*)

ANDREA: First time in East L.A., huh? What do you think?

JOSEPH: Well, it isn't what I expected.

ANDREA: No?

JOSEPH: Well, I turned off the freeway and pulled over to take a look at my Thomas Guide and I see these two guys . . . you know . . . gang-banger types walking toward me . . . They're looking at me suspiciously, you know. So, without thinking, I lock my doors and roll up the windows. They pass me by and I watch them through the rear-view mirror. They look back at me then head back toward my car.

ANDREA: Yeah?

JOSEPH: One of them comes up to my window and motions for me to roll it down.

JOSEPH: So, I crack it . . . around an inch. He says "Hey, are you lost man?" I say "Yeah." "What street you looking for?" I tell him. I'm thinking these guys wanna shoot me and they turn out to be really nice guys. They tell me how to get here and then they ask "You got an alarm on this car? I say "Yeah." They say "You better put it on." And they leave. That's when I took a breath and said, "Joseph, you're gonna be okay."

(*Andrea smiles.*)

ANDREA: See, most of us are good. We just got a bad rap.

JOSEPH: It's a shame isn't it? That we haven't gotten past all that? Is it naive to think that we're all just people?

ANDREA: Yeah, it is.

JOSEPH: I mean, now I'm here and I look around and I think this isn't much different than my family.

ANDREA: Oh, come on.

JOSEPH: No, really.

JOSEPH: (*He looks offstage*) You see those two old people there?

ANDREA: My Nana and Tata?

JOSEPH: Their wrinkled skin. It's no different from my grandparents . . . just darker. The silver hair . . . the crooked fingers, the look of wisdom in their eyes. That look that says (*Jewish accent*) "If you knew what I know . . ." They're no different.

(*Andrea smiles and looks into his eyes.*)

JOSEPH: Did you talk to Cindy about the case?

ANDREA: Yeah. I referred her to my associate. I told her the conflict of interest was the fact that she's my employee and my friend.

JOSEPH: Was she okay with that?

ANDREA: Yeah.

JOSEPH: Are you?

ANDREA: Yeah. It was getting way too personal with her working for me and all.

(*He tries to hold her hand. She pulls away.*)

ANDREA: You want some food?

JOSEPH: Sure.

ANDREA: Salsa?

JOSEPH: Poquito.

(*Andrea leaves. Joseph feels a tap on the shoulder. He turns to face JESUS, 30ish, a hard-core-looking cholo type with his hair slicked back, a goatee, shirt buttoned up, pants worn high.*)

JESUS: (*Stonefaced*) Hey, what's happening?

JOSEPH: Not much. I'm uh . . . Joseph Levinson.

JESUS: My sister's friend, right?

JOSEPH: Your sister?

JESUS: Andrea.

JOSEPH: Oh, yeah.

JESUS: Jewish, right?

JOSEPH: Right. And you're . . . ?

JESUS: Catholic.

JOSEPH: I meant your name.

JESUS: Jesus. I'm named after Jesus.

JOSEPH: Nice to meet you.

(*They shake. Jesus tries to shake Chicano style, but Joseph doesn't know how.*)

JESUS: Who are you named after?

JOSEPH: My grandfather.

JESUS: No, I mean, where does the name Joseph originate? From the father of Christ?

JOSEPH: I guess . . .

JESUS: But, you don't believe in Christ, right?

JOSEPH: (*Uncomfortable*) Yes. I mean, we believe he was a good Jew. We just don't believe the Messiah has arrived.

(*Jesus nods and strokes his goatee.*)

JESUS: Interesting. Well, nice meeting you, Joseph.

JOSEPH: Same here, Jesus.

JESUS: By the way, did you meet my mother . . . (He smiles) Mary.

JOSEPH: Yes, I did.

(*He leaves as Andrea arrives.*)

ANDREA: The food's not ready yet. I see you met my brother.

JOSEPH: Yeah.

JOSEPH: I met your cousin Rick, too. Nice guy.

ANDREA: Good. You met the Ph.D. and the drug dealer in the family.

JOSEPH: Is your brother really a drug dealer?

ANDREA: No, my cousin Rick is. My brother's a professor at Berkeley.

(*Joseph's car alarm goes off. Everybody runs to see what happened. Andrea notices Joey off by himself, sulking. She goes to him.*)

ANDREA: What's wrong?

JOEY: Nothing.

ANDREA: He's just a friend.

JOEY: Yeah, right! I saw the way he was looking at you.

ANDREA: What is this? It's alright for your Dad to have someone . . .

JOEY: I never said I liked it . . .

ANDREA: . . . but, it's not alright for me to go out with someone?

JOEY: It's different, Mom!

ANDREA: Why?

JOEY: Because, the thought of you with another man (*obviously referring to Joseph*) . . .

ANDREA: Joey . . .

JOEY: You said we'd take care of each other. Remember?

ANDREA: Me having a friend doesn't change that . . .

JOEY: Well, I don't like him!

ANDREA: You don't even know him!

JOEY: And I don't want to know him. I don't wanna see him around the house either!

ANDREA: Don't you talk to me that way!

JOEY: Hey, I'm the man of the house now . . .

ANDREA: What?

(*Jesus comes up from behind.*)

JESUS: Hey!

(*Joey stops.*)

JESUS: I don't wanna hear you talking to your mother like that.

ANDREA: It's okay, Chuy. I can deal with this.

JESUS: You better go tend to your friend.

ANDREA: He's my son . . .

JESUS: And he's my Godson. Remember?

(*Andrea hesitates. Jesus motions her to leave.*)

JESUS: Go on.

(*She does. Jesus goes to Joey.*)

JESUS: What's wrong, mijo?

JOEY: Nothing.

JESUS: Don't like your Mom's friend?

(*Joey shrugs.*)

JESUS: Hey, I understand how you feel.

JOEY: You don't understand, tío. You've never been through this.

JESUS: No, I've never been through it. But, I watch you, my man. I'm your Nino, remember?

JOEY: Yeah.

JESUS: You don't wanna share your Mom? Hey, I can understand that. Look, your Mom loved your Dad. Man, she loved him more than you'll ever know. You're Mom's a beautiful woman. But, she wasn't enough for your Dad. And let me tell you something. We men . . . (*He looks around to make sure nobody's listening.*) Sometimes we can be real pendejos you know that? Don't get me wrong. I like your Dad. He's my homey from way back. My compadre. But, if he loses your Mom, he'll lose a good thing. Your Mom's still young, full of life and full of love and as hard as it is, mijo. You have to know that we all need to be loved. Your Mom needs to be loved. It's what dios put us on this earth for. Entiendes?

JOEY: But, she has me.

JESUS: (*Chuckles*) Mijo, there're some things that just can't be explained. But, believe me, in a couple of years you're gonna understand. You're gonna see a fine-looking young lady and sas! It's gonna hit you. You're gonna know the difference between loving a woman and loving your Mom. Mark my words.

(*Joey nods.*)

JESUS: And as far as your Mom's friend is concerned. Well, I'm not telling you to love the guy. Just give him a chance. Don't make up your mind about him in such a hurry. I want you to be a man, mijo. For your Mom, okay?

(*Joey nods.*)

JOEY: Okay, tío.

(*They embrace.*)

JESUS: Now, let's check out the damage to homeboy's BMW.

JOEY: Nothing happened. I just kicked it.

(*They exit.*)

Scene 2

Luminarias

The women are sitting in their usual spot.

ANDREA: Why do I need a man?

IRENE: Well, for one thing . . .

ANDREA: Besides sex?

(*Silence.*)

ANDREA: I mean, how do I explain to my son that I need a man? Why do I need a man?

LILLY: Well, I don't know why you need one. But, I need one . . . I don't know. To feel good about myself. To feel attractive . . .

SOFIA: That's sad. You need a man to validate yourself?

LILLY: That's not what I mean . . .

IRENE: It's human nature. We're women, we like men . . .

SOFIA: Not all women like men.

LILLY: That's true.

ANDREA: I can't hate men. I'm raising one! We're pretty messed up, you know that! It's all about men! We fall in love with them, we marry them, we have them, we raise them, and it goes on and on . . .

SOFIA: The vicious cycle.

WOMEN: Yeah . . .

LILLY: They gotta get to know each other . . . it'll work itself out.

(*The waiter arrives.*)

WOMEN: Tequila.

PABLO: Sí, Señoritas.

SOFIA: Gracias . . . Pablo.

(*The women notice a certain "something" between Sofia and the waiter.*)

IRENE: Pablo?

SOFIA: That's his name.

LILLY: Since when?

SOFIA: Since he was born, I guess.

ANDREA: Since when do we call him by his name?

SOFIA: Since . . . I've been seeing him, alright?

ANDREA: Say what?

IRENE: You're seeing a waiter?

SOFIA: He's a bartender.

ANDREA: A bartender?

SOFIA: Alright, a waiter.

LILLY: Who probably has a wife and kids in Mexico.

SOFIA: No, he doesn't!

ANDREA: How do you know?

SOFIA: Because he's from El Salvador.

WOMEN: Oh, no!

SOFIA: Just kidding. He's from Jalisco.

WOMEN: Ay, no . . .

ANDREA: Sofia, I know I got on your case about not being around your people, but isn't this a little extreme?

(*Pablo returns with the drinks.*)

SOFIA: Gracias, Pablo.

(*As he leaves.*)

IRENE: (*Mocking Sofia*) Gracias, Pablo.

(*They laugh.*)

SOFIA: Cabronas!

LILLY: Guess what. Lu's parents are coming in from Korea. He wants me to meet them.

ANDREA: Oh, how sweet.

IRENE: Do they know you're Mexican?

LILLY: I don't know. Do you think it matters?

(*Silence.*)

LILLY: Gee . . . I hope it doesn't matter.

(*Silence.*)

IRENE: (*Changing the subject*) I ran into Joe the other day.

ANDREA: Oh, really?

IRENE: He was asking about you. Says he worries.

ANDREA: Uh huh.

IRENE: Are you really over him, Andie?

(*Pause.*)

ANDREA: The other night I woke up in the middle of the night and I saw Joe sitting on my bed. At first I just watched him. His silhouette in the moonlight. That beautiful indio profile of his . . . It seemed so normal, him sitting on my bed. Then it hit me like a real bad flashback. How we're not together anymore, that he left me for somebody else. I said "Joe, what are you doing here?" He said he needed someone to talk to . . .

WOMEN: Uh huh . . .

ANDREA: I could tell he'd been drinking. I told him that he couldn't just come into my house whenever he wanted to. Then he came close and said, "I just need to know that you still love me."

WOMEN: Ummm . . .

ANDREA: I asked him about Jan and he said, "Oh, come on, Andie. You know that wasn't for real." He went on about how much he misses me and Joey and our home. Then he said all the stuff they say when they wanna come back, you know . . .

WOMEN: Uh huh . . .

ANDREA: About how he's an asshole . . .

LILLY: "I don't know a good thing when I have it . . ."

IRENE: "I don't know what's wrong with me . . ."

ANDREA: Yeah, all that. Then he started to cry and he said he wanted to come home. He kissed me and I started to cry . . .

WOMEN: Hmmm . . .

LILLY: You still love him, don't you?

ANDREA: No. I cried because I don't. After all these years . . . After all we've been through together I said the words I never thought I'd say to him . . . I said, "Joe, I don't love you anymore." I never thought I could love another man. But I do . . .

Scene 3

Andrea's House

Joey and Joseph are sitting on the couch watching a Dodger game. The tension is thick. Joseph tries to break the ice.

JOSEPH: So, what do you think of Hideo Nomo?

JOEY: He's alright.

JOSEPH: Do you think this is Tommy Lasorda's last season?

JOEY: I hope so.

JOSEPH: Yeah.

(*Silence.*)

JOEY: (*Calling out*) Mom!

ANDREA: I'll be right out.

JOEY: She'll be right out.

(*He continues to watch the game.*)

JOSEPH: You don't like me, do you?

JOEY: Not really.

JOSEPH: (*Laughs*) Come on, you don't even know me.

JOEY: I don't have to.

JOSEPH: Don't you think you're being a little hard on me?

JOEY: I know what you're up to. You like my Mom so you're trying to make points with me, right?

JOSEPH: Right. I mean, that's part of the reason. But, I'd like for us to get to know each other. I mean, I don't know if I'm gonna like you either. So, why don't we give it a try, huh?

(*Joey shrugs.*)

JOSEPH: Go ahead. Ask me anything you want.

JOEY: Anything?

JOSEPH: Sure.

JOEY: What are your intentions?

JOSEPH: I beg your pardon?

JOEY: Yeah. What are your intentions with my Mom?

JOSEPH: Well . . . I like her and I'd like to continue dating her . . . But, I can't say I have any . . . intentions at this point.

JOEY: That's what I thought.

JOSEPH: What?

JOEY: You just want one thing. It figures.

JOSEPH: Joey, your Mom and I enjoy each other's company.

(*Joey rolls his eyes.*)

JOSEPH: Okay, yes, it is . . . that, but it's not only that. Honest.

JOEY: She can't cook, you know.

JOSEPH: I can.

JOEY: Do you know how to make huevos rancheros?

JOSEPH: No. But, I make a mean salsa.

JOEY: Where'd you learn how to make that?

JOSEPH: In Puerto Vallarta.

JOEY: I'm number one in her life, you know.

JOSEPH: Yes, she's already made that clear to me.

JOEY: She has?

JOSEPH: Yeah, and she told me how close you are to your Dad.

JOEY: We're like this. (*Putting up two fingers.*)

JOSEPH: I have no problem with that.

(*Joey looks at Joseph.*)

JOEY: Hey, if you don't mind being number two . . .

JOSEPH: (*Points to Joey*) Numero uno. (*Then to himself.*) Numero dos.

(*Joey laughs.*)

JOSEPH: Anything else?

JOEY: Yes. When they circumcise you guys do they really cut it in front of your whole family and shit?

JOSEPH: Sometimes. Not too often anymore.

JOEY: Shit, that must hurt.

JOSEPH: I don't remember.

JOEY: They say sex feels better if you're not.

JOSEPH: I've heard that. I also heard it hurts a hell of a lot the first time if you're not.

JOEY: Shit . . . Do you practice safe sex?

JOSEPH: Yes, I do.

JOEY: Good.

Scene 4

The Courtroom

A Latino attorney, FRANK GUTIERREZ, is questioning Cindy on the stand while Joseph and Tony are seated at a table facing the audience. A female judge, JUDGE ADAMS, is heard, but not seen.

CINDY: That day me and Tony were over my Mom's house and little Tony was playing and he accidentally knocked over a little ceramic figure my Mom had on a coffee table. Tony grabbed him by the arm and slapped him, hard. I got mad and told him not to hit him like that. Well, he got very angry and said "Let's go." I didn't want to go home with him because I knew what was gonna happen, but he insisted and I left 'cuz I didn't want him to make a scene at my Mom's.

ATTORNEY: What happened when you got home?

CINDY: He put little Tony in his room and he took me in the bathroom and beat me up. (*Cindy tries not to cry.*) Then, he grabbed me and the baby and threw us out of the house. I called my Mom and Dad and when they saw my face they took me to the hospital and they called the police.

ATTORNEY: I have no further questions, your honor.

JUDGE ADAMS (OS): Mr. Levinson.

JOSEPH: Thank you, your honor.

(*Joseph goes to the podium.*)

JOSEPH: Mrs. Rodriguez, Mr. Gutierrez asked you why you divorced Mr. Rodriguez. Can you tell us why you married him?

CINDY: Because . . . I love . . . d him.

JOSEPH: Why did you love him?

CINDY: Because he was cute . . . and nice.

JOSEPH: Nice?

CINDY: When I first met him.

JOSEPH: And when you were living with him, was he nice, then?

CINDY: Sometimes.

JOSEPH: What would you say the percentage of the time was that he was nice and what was the percentage of the time that he was not?

CINDY: Most of the time he was nice.

JOSEPH: Say, 90 percent of the time?

CINDY: (*Thinks*) No, 80 percent of the time he was nice and 20 percent of the time he was mean.

JOSEPH: Mean, meaning abusive, right?

CINDY: Yes.

JOSEPH: Why do you think he was mean?

CINDY: I don't know. He would just go off.

JOSEPH: Just go off?

CINDY: Yes.

JOSEPH: When he would go off. Did you ever think maybe he had a problem?

CINDY: You mean like that he was nuts? Yeah.

JOSEPH: You thought maybe he had a psychological problem?

CINDY: Definitely.

JOSEPH: So, you thought he was sick?

CINDY: Uh huh.

JOSEPH: Did you know that people with violent tempers can be treated medically?

CINDY: I guess.

JOSEPH: What would you say if I told you that Mr. Rodriguez has undergone aggressive treatment for his violent temper?

CINDY: I would say . . . he's up to something.

JOSEPH: What would you say to his doctors who agree that his violent temper is under control?

CINDY: I would say they don't really know him.

JOSEPH: What would you say to his doctors who agree that Mr. Rodriguez is capable of caring for little Tony?

CINDY: I would say . . . they're wrong!

JOSEPH: Mrs. Rodriguez, these are professionals who've evaluated Mr. Rodriguez . . .

CINDY: I don't care who they are! I would say they're full of shit!

JOSEPH: Your honor . . .

CINDY: And that they fell for his bullshit!

JUDGE ADAMS (OS): Mrs. Rodriguez!

CINDY: I would say that that motherfucker should win a fucking academy award!

JUDGE ADAMS (OS): Order!

CINDY: He fooled all of you! (*She looks at Tony.*) But, you can't fool me, you motherfucker!

JUDGE ADAMS (OS): That's enough!

CINDY: I've seen you when you get ugly and I know who you really are!

JUDGE ADAMS (OS): Mrs. Rodriguez, you are in contempt!

CINDY: Fuck you!

Scene 5

Andrea's Office

Andrea is lying on a couch and Sofia is sitting on a chair.

SOFIA: Are you feeling guilty because you dropped the case?

ANDREA: I guess. (*Pause.*) When Frank called her in here and he told her they lost, she just stood there, Sofia. No, tears. No, emotion. But, I knew her heart was breaking.

SOFIA: What the hell happened?

ANDREA: She fell apart. Joseph pushed the right buttons and she just went off! The worst part is they say she looked so bad and Sofia, she's so good, you know.

SOFIA: Hey, the judicial system sucks, you know that.

ANDREA: Thanks for the "words of wisdom." Do people really pay you for this?

SOFIA: Yeah.

ANDREA: Damn, I'm in the wrong field.

SOFIA: (*Laughs*) I could never do what you do.

ANDREA: I know you couldn't.

SOFIA: What is it with you and this girl?

ANDREA: I don't know. She's a fighter, a guerrillera.

SOFIA: Like you?

(*Andrea looks at Sofia.*)

ANDREA: Yeah.

SOFIA: Then, she's a tough cookie, believe me. She had a session with me, remember? She's been through more in her life than we ever will.

ANDREA: I know.

SOFIA: By the end of the session, I was asking her for advice . . . and girlfriend was giving it, too!

(*Andrea laughs.*)

ANDREA: Really? What did she say?

SOFIA: That I'm crazy for falling in love with a mojado. (*Pause.*) He wants to marry me, Andrea. It was going so great and now he wants to marry me.

ANDREA: What are you gonna do?

SOFIA: One part of me says, "Are you crazy? You're gonna marry a Mexican bartender . . .

ANDREA: Waiter.

SOFIA: " . . . waiter." And another part says "Forget about what you wanted before. Go for the love." You know, I've been trying to fit in with white people all these years. I even began to resent who I am, because no matter what, no matter how hard I tried to fit in, I was always different. But, I'm tired. It's always a fight out there. I have to be ten times better because I'm Latina. I have to prove that I fit in. But, you know what? The only time I'm really myself . . . is when I'm with my own people. Isn't that sad? (*She chokes up.*) And I don't know if I'm in love with Pablo because of who he is or because he reminds me of who I am. It's like I'm falling in love with who I am for the first time. And now every time I'm around white people, I feel this . . .

ANDREA: Be careful, Sofia. That shit can wear you down, too.

SOFIA: You oughtta know.

ANDREA: Yeah. I'm tired, too. Tired of being angry. I just want some love, some peace of mind. Is that wrong? Is it wrong to want to be happy?

SOFIA: No, it's not wrong.

Silence. Lilly and Irene arrive. Lilly is distraught.

ANDREA: Hi.

(*Lilly sits down.*)

IRENE: It's Lu . . .

SOFIA: What happened?

LILLY: He invited me to dinner at his house. He said his Mom had cooked a traditional Korean dinner in my honor. He picked me up and he held my hand in the car, I felt it. I felt his love . . . When we got there we walked in and he introduced me to them and they looked . . . confused. They said something to him and he explained that he had told them that I was an American and he guessed they were surprised that I wasn't a blonde. He smiled and winked at me. But, I felt something was wrong. We sat down to eat and I began to speak, to explain why I'm not blonde and blue eyed and Lu gave me a look, like he wanted me to be quiet. And I said "Lu, I want them to know what I am . . . Tell them that I'm a Mexican." I could tell he didn't want to, but he did. And his mother looked at me and said something to Lu in Korean. His father left the table without saying a word. And as we sat there in silence I could feel his mother's disdain for me. I excused myself from the table because I had to throw up. Lu took me home. He didn't hold my hand. I asked him what his mother said and he said she said that Mexicans are garment workers and that she refused to sit and eat with one. He said he was sorry and left. He didn't kiss me good-bye.

ANDREA: So, what's gonna happen?

LILLY: He says he has to think. He loves his parents.

IRENE: Those damn Koreans . . .

ANDREA: Oh, man, Chicanos are the same way.

IRENE: (*Gives Andrea a suspicious look*) Since when?

SOFIA: My Dad never wanted me to marry anyone but a Mexican. Not even another Latino.

IRENE: But, there's something about holding on to the culture. You know, preserving it. It's like it takes so long to figure out who you are. Then when you finally do, you wanna savor it for a while. You don't wanna mix it up with anything.

ANDREA: But, when you really think about it. We are who we are because we're a mix.

IRENE: So, what are you saying, Andrea?

ANDREA: I don't know what I'm saying anymore. You know, I always wanted Joey to marry a Chicana. I don't know why. I guess I thought it would be easier. But, guess what? He has a girlfriend named Laura Johnson.

IRENE: A white girl?

SOFIA: You're kidding.

LILLY: What'd you tell him?

ANDREA: What could I tell him. I'm in love with a gabacho . . .

(*Pause.*)

LILLY: I'm in love with a Chino . . .

SOFIA: I'm in love with a mojado . . .

IRENE: Give me a Chicano anyday . . .

(*The women look at Irene.*)

Scene 6

Andrea's Living Room

Lights up. There is a pounding on the door. Andrea enters pulling on a robe and opens the door. Cindy enters in a panic.

ANDREA: Cindy, what's wrong?

CINDY: He hurt my baby, Andrea. That motherfucker hurt my baby!

ANDREA: What? What happened?

CINDY: He says it was an accident . . . that he fell, but I know he did it. I know it! They called me from the hospital . . . I went over there . . . (*She sobs.*) He broke his arms.

ANDREA: Oh, Cindy, I'm so sorry . . .

CINDY: I wanna press charges! I wanna get him, Andrea! I wanna put him away!

(*Andrea holds Cindy. Joseph enters from the bedroom with no shoes and no shirt. Cindy looks at him in shock. Then, she looks at Andrea, confused.*)

CINDY: What is he . . . (*She looks at Andrea in disbelief.*) You . . . Oh fuck!

ANDREA: Cindy . . .

CINDY: You've been fucking him all along?

ANDREA: No . . .

CINDY: That's why you dropped my case?

ANDREA: Cindy, listen!

CINDY: That's why my baby is lying in the hospital with broken arms? You sold me out! You fucking bitch!

JOSEPH: Hey!

CINDY: (*To Joseph*) Fuck you! Motherfucker!

ANDREA: Stay out of this, Joseph!

CINDY: You're nothing but a fucking whore!

(*Cindy slaps Andrea and runs out. Joseph goes to Andrea and tries to hold her.*)

JOSEPH: Baby . . .

(*Andrea turns away.*)

ANDREA: Don't . . .

ANDREA: That baby has two broken arms because I didn't defend him . . .

JOSEPH: Oh, come on, Andrea. You don't believe that, do you?

ANDREA: Yeah, I do. And you know what else I believe? I believe you defended the wrong person, Joseph. Now get out.

JOSEPH: I can't believe you're gonna let this come between us . . . You're gonna let that little . . . street kid. That stupid little . . . (*He stops himself.*)

ANDREA: That stupid little what? That stupid little Mexican? Go on, say it!

JOSEPH: I would never say that!

ANDREA: You know, that thing you called "an edge." It's not an edge. It's a hurt. And I've still got it. You see that girl out there. She's got it, too. I'm just like her. No different.

JOSEPH: No, you're not like her.

ANDREA: Yes I am!

(*She cries.*)

I've been fooling myself. I've got this rage inside of me, Joseph, that you'll never understand.

JOSEPH: I love you, Andrea.

ANDREA: I'm sorry . . .

Scene 7

Andrea's Living Room
Joey is combing his hair.

ANDREA: Nervous?

JOEY: A little.

ANDREA: Why? Because I'm gonna meet her?

JOEY: Yeah . . . Mom, are you disappointed because Laura isn't Latina?

(*Andrea embraces Joey.*)

ANDREA: Mijo, please, don't let my hang-ups get in the way of your happiness, okay?

JOEY: What do you mean?

(*Andrea strokes his hair.*)

ANDREA: You know, mijo. We have a lot of stuff going on inside of us, we . . . Latinos. We've got these great feelings of love. We love who we are. We love being who we are. And . . . we have this rage inside of us. This rage that comes from all the hurt, all the stuff we've been through and our ancestors have been through. And it comes from way back. It's like it's part of our genetic memory. And that's good, too. Because it keeps us strong, it keeps us fighting. Because we know things aren't fair. But, mijo . . . don't ever let that rage take over. Don't let the rage get in the way of love.

JOEY: I love you, Mom.

ANDREA: I love you, too.

(*The doorbell rings.*)

ANDREA: (*Playfully*) And don't worry. Your Mom can hang with a white girl.

JOEY: Mom . . . Laura's not white.

Scene 8

Luminarias

Sofia and Lilly are at their usual spot. There's a gift on the table. Lilly is writing in a card.

LILLY: Has she seen him?

SOFIA: No.

LILLY: I thought she was in love.

SOFIA: I thought so, too. Have you heard from Lu?

LILLY: No. I don't think he's back yet.

(*Andrea arrives.*)

ANDREA: Hi.

LILLY: Hi.

ANDREA: Where's Irene?

LILLY: She's gonna be a little late. Listen, how's this? "Dear Irene, Now that your year of sacrifice is over we hope you find yourself a beautiful, brown man, with muscles and hair and a great big . . . heart."

SOFIA: Did you think that up all by yourself?

LILLY: Yeah.

ANDREA: It's a gem.

SOFIA: Unpolished, but a gem nonetheless.

LILLY: Thanks.

SOFIA: So, did you get Joey off to the prom?

ANDREA: Uh huh.

LILLY: With the white girl?

ANDREA: She's black.

SOFIA: Black? How do you feel about that?

(*Pause.*)

ANDREA: I think I'm okay. But, we better schedule a session.

(*Irene arrives.*)

WOMEN: Hieee . . .

IRENE: Hi.

(*She looks at the gift.*)

IRENE: Thanks, you guys.

LILLY: Open it.

(*Irene opens the gift. It is a sexy camisole.*)

IRENE: It's beautiful. Thanks.

(*Pablo arrives with a bottle of tequila and shot glasses.*)

SOFIA: (*In love*) Gracias . . .

(*Pablo bends over and kisses her.*)

PABLO: De nada, mi reina . . .

(*He leaves.*)

SOFIA: I took him home to meet my Mom.

ANDREA: How is she?

SOFIA: Old and fat and so soft I couldn't stop hugging her. She smelled delicious. Like Masa Harina.

(*The women smile a knowing smile.*)

SOFIA: I just sat and watched her and Pablo talk for hours. It was heaven. I'm gonna marry him. I'm gonna marry a Mexican waiter.

ANDREA: Congratulations.

(*Lilly pours the tequila.*)

LILLY: Let's drink to you getting married and to Irene going a year without it.

(*They hold up their shot glasses.*)

ANDREA: To two very courageous women.

(*They drink their shots. Irene takes a breath.*)

IRENE: You guys . . . I have a confession to make.

SOFIA: A confession?

IRENE: All these months I've gone without being intimate with a man and it's been tough. And all these months I've been fantasizing about who I would want to give myself to when my year was up. And there's always been one person in my mind. It's someone we all know and I just want to put it out there . . . because completing this year has been a great accomplishment for me. So, I want to come clean here. (*Pause.*) I've been fantasizing about . . . Joe.

ANDREA: My Joe?

IRENE: Uh huh.

SOFIA: That's understandable . . .

LILLY: You're gonna give yourself to Joe?

IRENE: My intent has always been to come here tonight and ask Andrea if she'd mind . . .

ANDREA: Irene . . .

IRENE: Hold on. I've decided against it.

WOMEN: Good.

IRENE: Because I met the most beautiful, brown creature you can imagine . . .

LILLY: Oh . . .

IRENE: He's kind of young . . . he's 20.

ANDREA: Wow . . .

IRENE: And he's a virgin.

WOMEN: Oh . . .

IRENE: Well, I'm a born-again virgin! And we're gonna give ourselves to each other tonight. Isn't it perfect?

ANDREA: Yeah.

IRENE: So, I gotta go. Wish me luck.

WOMEN: Good luck.

IRENE: (*To Andrea*) Do you forgive me for my . . . impure thoughts?

ANDREA: Sure.

(*Andrea and Irene embrace.*)

IRENE: I love you guys . . .

(*She leaves.*)

SOFIA: She's such a . . . Catholic.

(*A pager goes off. The women check their pagers.*)

SOFIA: One of my patients. Excuse me.

(*She leaves as another pager goes off.*)

LILLY: It's for me. My curandera.

(*Lilly leaves. Andrea sits alone.*)

(*Crossfade to Joseph as he enters. He sees Andrea and walks over to her.*)

JOSEPH: Hi.

ANDREA: Hi.

JOSEPH: How've you been?

ANDREA: Good. I've been good.

JOSEPH: That's great.

(*A slow oldie plays.*)

JOSEPH: Would you like to dance?

(*Pause.*)

ANDREA: No . . . Thanks. . . .

JOSEPH: Okay. It was nice seeing you again . . .

(*He begins to walk away.*)

ANDREA: Hey.

(*He turns. She looks into his eyes. Silence.*)

ANDREA: Maybe later.

(*He leaves.*)

EPILOGUE

The County Courthouse

Andrea is sitting on the bench looking through documents. She looks at her watch as if she's expecting someone. Cindy enters carrying a box.

CINDY: Damn, that parking lot is far. Where's Isabel?

ANDREA: She hasn't shown.

CINDY: Hmmm . . .

ANDREA: I know. She was having second thoughts.

CINDY: Hmmm . . .

ANDREA: I know . . .

CINDY: The guy's in jail for life. What's she gonna do? Save it for the afterlife? Has she given you a payment yet?

ANDREA: No.

CINDY: Hmmm . . .

(*Andrea gives Cindy a look.*)

CINDY: (Defensive) What?

ANDREA: Forget it.

(*Andrea looks away.*)

CINDY: You know what, Andrea?

ANDREA: What?

CINDY: Ever since we had that fight . . .

ANDREA: What?

CINDY: You seem so sad . . . Like there's no light in your eyes.

ANDREA: (*Smiles*) It's still there. It's just burning low right now, that's all. That's the way it is with us women. We have this little flame in our heart. Like a little luminaria that burns with the hope that one day we'll find love, happiness, peace of mind. Sometimes it burns so low you think it's out. Next thing you know it's burning so bright that you can barely stand it. Mine is burning low right now . . . That's all.

CINDY: Did you love Joseph?

ANDREA: I don't know. But, I know I wanted to.

(*Silence.*)

CINDY: I ran into Tony the other day.

ANDREA: Yeah?

CINDY: He smirked at me. He thinks he's tough shit 'cuz he got away with it. But, that's okay, he'll get his some day, huh?

ANDREA: Who knows.

CINDY: It was funny, though. When I saw him. Even though I hate his ass so much. There was still something there, you know. Like my heart felt sad . . . because it was so full of love for him before. I would've done anything for him. All I wanted was for him to love me back. I felt kind of empty, you know. But, like you say. I guess I won't feel this way forever. My flames just burning low like yours. It'll come back, huh?

ANDREA: Yeah.
CINDY: It's all about love, isn't it?
ANDREA: Yeah, it's all about love.
(*THE END*)

Notes

1. Evelina Fernández, notes and responses to editors' biographical questionnaire, February 24 and 27, 2004, October 24 and 30, 2010, and November 1, 2010.

2. Jorge Huerta, *Chicano Drama: Performance, Society and Myth* (Cambridge: Cambridge University Press, 2000), 84.

3. Don Shirley, "Setting the Latino Theatre Company Stage," *Los Angeles Times* (home edition), Entertainment Desk, Calendar, May 4, 1996, F2. Joseph O'Connell, "Pair of Latino Films Shine at SXSW Film Fest," *San Antonio Express-News,* March 23, 1999, 3E. See also Elizabeth C. Ramírez, *Chicanas/Latinas in American Theatre: A History of Performance* (Bloomington: Indiana University Press, 2000), 139.

4. Diana Rico, "'Luminarias' Sheds a Bright Light," Entertainment Desk, *Los Angeles Times,* May 27, 1996, calendar, F:3.

5. Ramírez, 139. Lawrence Van Gelder, "Film in Review: 'Luminarias,'" *New York Times,* October 6, 2000. Kevin Thomas, *Los Angeles Times,* Entertainment Desk, May 5, 2000, calendar, F.

PART V

Where Is Home and How Do We Get There?

In these last three chapters, we emphasize the role that home plays in the work by Latinas. As Donna R. Gabaccia and Vicki L. Ruiz comment, "for immigrants, images of 'home' conjure up a myriad of meanings—from a birthplace far away to the *casita* [little house] down the street," for "women and men engage in making home both literally and figuratively." As in the case of one of our playwrights, it can be imagined despite never having put foot on the land of her parents. Gabaccia and Ruiz cite Yen Le Espiritu on her remarks on the definition of "home," telling us that Espiritu "offers the most incisive definition of 'home making,' which she describes as 'the processes by which diverse subjects imagine and make themselves at home in various geographic locations.'"[1] Making home also ties into a great many other pertinent concepts that our playwrights remind us of through the worlds they create, including colonialism, past, and present.

Although other works have also revolved around the subject, we have selected these playtexts to address the groups that these particular playwrights represent. Carmen Peláez's Cuban American view is an intimate, personal reconnection with her parents' homeland. We first heard about her when she was highlighted in a *New York Times* feature article, "For Those Who Fled, a Retort to Cuba," about Cuba and its exiles in the United States. In her work, we can experience her yearning for the Cuba she has never known along with her joy at reconnecting with her ancestral homeland.[2] As Gerald E. Poyo points out, "Cubans have resided in the United States for almost two centuries." and their experience "is characterized by a great deal of diversity but also by common elements that provide the basis for a cohesive approach to the Cuban American story." Given their long history in the United States, Poyo adds, "Cuban integration into North American society cannot be understood as a linear trajectory of assimilation, but rather as a complex, multidimensional process influenced by nationalism, an exile dimension, ethnic consciousness, and solidarity with other Latina and Latino and Hispanic groups. This guaranteed an ongoing and distinct Cuban presence in the United States for almost two centuries."[3]

The two final playtexts are by Puerto Rican playwrights. With regard to Puerto Rican theatre in the United States, as John V. Antush reminds us in his collection, *Nuestro New York: An Anthology of Puerto Rican Plays,* "a popular misconception among non-Hispanics has been to view the Puerto Rican Traveling Theater (PRTT)" and "other Hispanic touring companies as unique entities that sprang spontaneously from the political upheaval and agit-prop theatre of the times." In the large migration of Puerto Ricans to the mainland, they also "brought with them the seeds of a theatre that would blossom in the 1960s and dominate Hispanic theatre in New York City." Forward-looking toward the new century, Antush assessed the state of Puerto Rican theatre on the U.S. stage, noting that this group would continue to dominate Latina/Latino theatre in New York City: "Hispanic theatre's *gran floricanto* in New York City in the 1960s and 1970s continued unabated through the 1980s, and now Hispanic theatre moves forward into the twenty-first century stronger than ever with a firm sense of purpose to forge a new understanding of what it means to be a Latino/Latina in the United States. With dozens of Hispanic plays produced each year throughout the city, and with several festivals, Hispanic theatre has become a major force in New York Theatre."[4]

Carmen Rivera's *La Gringa* is one of her growing number of successes on the U.S. stage as well as in her parents' native Puerto Rico, providing an excellent example of the transnational audiences that Latinas have garnered for the stage. In our final entry, Migdalia Cruz, one of the most prolific Latina dramatists in our day, shows us one of the many types of plays she has written with *Another Part of the House,* her adaptation of Federico García-Lorca's classic play, *The House of Bernarda Alba.*

For all three of these playwrights, their work exemplifies a means of constructing and deconstructing identity, and we are fortunate to be able to present the varying ways they each negotiate arriving at the place they call home.

Notes

1. Donna R. Gabaccia and Vicki L. Ruiz, *American Dreaming, Global Realities: Rethinking U.S. Immigration History* (Bloomington: University of Illinois Press, 2006), 6.

2. David Gonzalez, "For Those Who Fled, a Retort to Cuba," *New York Times,* March 10, 2008.

3. Gerald E. Poyo, "Cuban Americans," *The Oxford Encyclopedia of Latinos and Latinas in the United States,* ed. Suzanne Oboler and Deena J. González (New York: Oxford University Press, 2005), 1:438, 448.

4. John V. Antush, ed., *Nuestro New York: An Anthology of Puerto Rican Plays* (New York: Mentor, 1994), ix, xv.

CHAPTER 9

A Cuban American's Search for Home

Carmen Peláez's *El Postre de Estrada Palma* (1998) and *My Cuba* (1998)

Carmen Peláez, by permission of photographer, Abigail Collins.

The Playwright/ La Dramaturga

In her own words, the playwright tells us about her family origins:[1]

My parents were born and raised in Cuba and both escaped Havana in the 1960s. My mother was thirteen when she was sent to the United States through the Catholic Church on the Pedro Pan flights. My father had to be smuggled out of Havana at 17 after a public confrontation with the rebel leader Camilo Cienfuegos.[2] Their parents stayed in Cuba believing Castro would eventually collapse on his own cynical farce and democracy would be restored. Nevertheless, civil liberties systematically disappearing, each set of grandparents decided to join their children in Miami, leaving behind the only life they'd ever known. In exile, all they had left was each other, and their way of keeping Cuba alive was to pass it down to us.

My little sister and I were raised between the two Abuelos' houses—our grandparents were our babysitters. Between the Spanish lessons, the sardonic nurturing, and the meriendas—my sister and I had a very Cuban upbringing. And even though we lived in the States, we were always made very aware of the fact that there was another life that we belonged to and would inevitably return to. Our upbringing ensured a seamless homecoming . . . one day.

On my father's side, my grandfather's sister was the great Cuban painter, Amelia Peláez.[3] Every time I colored anything, it was looked over for traces of her genetic influence. I was told wonderful stories about her years in Paris and how she painted every day of her life. They weren't able to bring any of her work, but they'd tell me about it in great detail. Three of my grandfather's sisters still lived in the family's house in Havana,

> and we would write them letters telling them about our life, and when they wrote back they would sometimes send snapshots of her work—which would only inspire me to color more. I loved the comparison—it made Cuba real for me.
>
> On my mother's side, my great-uncle was a political prisoner, so my great-aunt and great-grandmother stayed in Cuba so as to not leave him alone in his courageous stand against dictatorship, without ever thinking that they were taking their own *stand by staying with him.* I remember writing them letters that we couldn't send because I criticized the revolution and it infuriated me. If I felt something and wanted to say it in a private letter to my great-aunts, why couldn't I? Instead I had to write them small-talk letters that betrayed my frustration, and their letters to us were filled with the same chatty silence.
>
> There was no way for me to grasp the entirety of what my family was surviving, intellectually, but emotionally, I knew something great had been lost. And my only way of comforting my amazing family, was to honor their sacrifice and embrace the traditions that helped them transcend what they would've thought impossible to become—a family with no origin to return to.

Born in Miami, Peláez obtained an Associate of Arts degree in liberal arts, an Associate of Occupational Studies degree from the American Academy of Dramatic Arts, and, as she describes it, from "every museum I have ever gone to." In his *New York Times* feature article about several individuals who lived under Castro that "clash with popular views," David Gonzalez described Peláez as a "liberal with a deep laugh and a great sense of the absurd," adding that "all of those qualities are tested when she encounters fellow New Yorkers who still admire Fidel Castro."[4]

Using Peláez's one-woman show, *Rum & Coke,* as the basis for her views on Cuba, Gonzalez points out that Peláez "channels relatives on both sides of the Florida Straits and wary Habaneros stuck on an island forgotten by the outside world." Gonzalez ascertains her reasons for writing this acclaimed work: "The play was her retort to the fascination with Che T-shirts, solidarity tours to Cuba and the endless praise of the revolution's twin pillars of health and education." He cites her views about the play after the show closed its monthlong New York run: "When I started writing the play, I thought people just didn't know what was happening in Cuba. . . . But the longer I live here, the more I realized, they don't care." She added: "I had somebody come to me after a show and say, 'Don't ruin Cuba for me!' Well, why not? They're holding on to a fantasy."[5]

Peláez began writing *Rum & Coke* soon after graduating from the American Academy for the Dramatic Arts in New York. She received a 1997 New York Foundation of the Arts Fellowship, which led to its eventual production in New York City. The piece has been honed through various performances. It was optioned by Fox Theatricals in 1999–2001, and she performed it at Chicago's Pegasus Theatre, the HBO Workspace in Los Angeles, PS NBC in New York, and Wellesley College in Massachusetts, where the work is now part of the curriculum. In the Coconut Grove Playhouse's 2003–4 season, the run was extended because of its popularity. She performed at the 10th annual New York International Fringe Festival in New York City in 2006, and following other performances, *Rum & Coke* opened Off-Broadway in February 2008 at Abington Theatre in New York City, where it won the 2008 Outstanding Solo Performance Award from the Hispanic Organization of Latino Actors (HOLA) in New York. It was also optioned for publication.

In Caryn James's review of *Rum & Coke,* appropriately titled "A Cuban-American's Wish to Find Her Ancestral Home," James describes the effective use of two forms as Peláez uses her famous Aunt Amelia, the artist, and her Aunt Ninita, and other Cuban and Cuban American women: "the actress Ms. Peláez enlivens two overused forms: the one-person show and the personal memoir." James was particularly struck by her acting: "Ms. Peláez (who might have stepped out of one of the Dove soap ads featuring real-life women) acts these characters beautifully, from the slumped body language of her grandmother to the defiant stance of a prostitute who was sent out to work by her own mother when she was 12." For James, Peláez "obviously honed each piece to its essence," adding that through the artist's travel to Havana to visit her aging great-aunt, "her sketches become poignant as she discovers an identity—the courage of survivors and a heritage of artistic, strong-willed women—that she could not have understood from a distance."[6]

Reviewer Lee Hernández was equally struck by the performance: "Peláez gives a fearless, invigorating performance as each of the quirky characters she created: An eccentric *santera* who owns a chicken, a Cuban prostitute, a man in a night club looking for some 'action,' and an elderly aunt," finding the play "entertaining and moving." Noting that the play appeared shortly after Fidel Castro resigned from his position in the Cuban government, he gives us an insight into Peláez's sentiments: "'I hope Cubans come together and establish a free and Democratic Cuba,' says Peláez, 'Fidel's stepping down is the first step. He's very much Cuba's abusive father, and his resignation is going to have a big impact.'"[7]

About the Plays/Sobre las Obras

The playwright tells us that *El Postre* "has an incredibly special place in my heart."[8] It is easy to comprehend why. Once her visa to Cuba is approved, Cami, the narrator, is filled with thoughts about her grandmother and the stories she would relate to the young woman about life in Cuba. Through a poignant story of colorful memories about her grandparents' life in Cuba, we glimpse the effects of exile on Cubans who were driven from their country. With the descriptions of a special dessert, "el postre de Estada Palma," as it was called by her grandparents, the playwright reveals unforgettable memories about how she came to know "a combination of all the best Cuba had to offer." In a story akin to that told by Cherríe Moraga and her mother, we meet Abuela, the narrator's grandmother, who is stricken by Alzheimer's disease. Yet, despite the memory loss, she is incredibly lucid as she relates a poignant and memorable story to her granddaughter that influences whom she will visit once on the island.

The dessert was something she learned to make from Cachita, a neighbor who was also a *santera.* The grandmother believes Cachita is practicing witchcraft until Cachita helps save her young son, Cami's father, at which point the grandmother realizes she is indeed a healer. Through the story about a traditional dessert, the playwright captures the poignant story that informs us about other traditions in her grandparents' native land. Cami arrives at this reconnection to Cuba through her family's past, and her visit allows her to continue a long lineage of traditional views.

Both *El Postre* and the next short playtext, *My Cuba,* introduce characters that have impacted greatly on this playwright. About *My Cuba,* Peláez tells us that it is "the old monologue that I pulled sections from for *Rum & Coke.*"[9] In *My Cuba,* Cami, the narrator, is actually on her way to Cuba. Her description of the flight is comic in tone, introducing us to the difficulties relatives have in reconnecting with family who have remained in Cuba. Her Great-aunt Ninita, living in the same house as her Great-aunt Amelia, the famous artist, greets her with mistrust, knowing that everyone who visits the house is after something of Amelia's artistry. Yet, Ninita soon comes around to wanting Cami to return.

In the end, Cami finds "my Cuba" as a place that "isn't a tropical paradise or a communist example." It also "isn't captured in a foreigner's dollar or a government's yard sale." Rather, "it seeks freedom and isn't limited to its island's borders." We discover that for this young girl, she sees that "it exists in the stretch of a teenage girl's back and the gaze of an exile trying to figure out what happened." As Cami says at the end of the play: "My Cuba blows away like ashes, while those that need it try and keep it safe in their longing. And when all is said and done my Cuba will forgive those that have ravaged it and welcome me home." Through both playtexts, Peláez's personal biography entices us to want to know her homeland, too, and these are ideal doorways into that world.

Artistic Vision/Punto de Vista Artístico

ECR & CRC: Briefly describe your theatre experience.[10]

CP: All my training has been as an actor. From high school to college to the wonderfully well-rounded education I received at American Academy of Dramatic Arts—my focus has always been acting. But once I was out of the shelter of school, out of necessity I have written and produced as well.

ECR & CRC: How did you decide to write and/or perform?

CP: When I was fifteen I saw Whoopi Goldberg's one woman play *Whoopi on Broadway* and I knew I wanted to one day do the same kind of work. So I auditioned for the Players class in my high school. I had no experience and when they told me that I had to present two monologues, I greenly wrote them. Afterwards I learned that I should've chosen monologues from published work, but I still got in and I was as hooked. Years later, when I graduated from the American Academy of Dramatic Arts I was annoyed by the parts available to me as a Cuban actress. They were clichéd, ridiculous, and boorish. I didn't want to act if that was all I would be asked to act in. I had told a friend of mine my Whoopi Goldberg story, and when she heard of a variety night at a theatre—she signed me up. I used a monologue I had written for movement class, and the audience response was amazing. The ability to write the roles that I wanted to play is what brought me into the world of playwriting . . . but being able to create worlds that I wanted to be in kept me there.

ECR & CRC: Why do you write what you do?

CP: The things that catch my eye are usually things that I feel are misunderstood. Be it a person or a moment in time. There's something about stories that have been unjustly diminished or ignored that make me crazy and inspire me to put them in a context through which they can have their say. I feel compelled to give their voice a space. It's often where laughter and devastation live in the same breath. And it's not a particularly noble instinct . . . it's a compulsion.

ECR & CRC: Who do you write for and what audience are you trying to reach?

CP: I can't really say that I write for any one audience. I pride my work on being universal. But I would say that my work is really emotionally sincere. I like writing about the most tender and most painful of moments the way that we live them . . . quietly and without much flash. Of course, being Cuban—whatever I write will naturally be filtered through my cultural perspective, usually only perceptible to Cubans. But even if I'm writing about a specifically Cuban story—I focus on what is universal about it so that it translates. If it doesn't translate—it's pointless to even bother with it.

ECR & CRC: What message, if any, are you trying to convey to your audience with this work and/or with all of your work?

CP: I want nothing more than for people to see themselves reflected in my work and feel understood. There's something that happens when a person feels "seen" that is truly amazing . . . there's a shift and a lightness that comes with it. Whether art reflects something painful or joyful is irrelevant—it's the recognition that counts. It's our only proof that we are part of something greater. I love when I am sitting in an audience and feel it and being in the position to give that experience to somebody in an audience is a gift.

ECR & CRC: Who or what has been your major influence?

CP: Two things: art and family.

My family, without question. My grandparents and their generation, the way they lived their lives with dignity, grace and tender irreverence in the face of incredible sadness and struggle in exile and under dictatorship, has had an incredible influence on me. My father, who always insisted on me believing I could do anything I wanted. And my mother, who taught me the value of hard work. My sister, who is actually working on becoming a pastry chef specializing in Cuban desserts thanks to my Abuelo's influence, constantly challenges me to be fearless in my writing. My family always influences me with their examples and their faith in my work.

I am also greatly influenced by art. Since I began writing monologues I started looking at paintings like monologues. The artists had one opportunity to make me see what he/she wanted seen. I began to study how they did it—what colors, composition, and layers did they use? How did they transport, convey emotion, or move me? My appreciation of art started when I saw my first *Amelia* in person.[11] I was profoundly moved and felt instantly transformed. It has evolved in such a way that going to a museum has the same effect on me as going to a sporting event—my reactions as immediate. Regardless of when something was created or by who—if it has "it," something clicks in me and my own instincts are sharpened.

ECR & CRC: What has been your biggest and/or most difficult struggle/challenge in life, in completing a play, or getting it produced, etc.?

DR: I don't think life is easy or fair for anybody. Struggle, for better or worse, is subjective. I've had more than my fair share of it, but I still consider myself incredibly fortunate. I don't know—I think when you know how ugly your world can get—it makes you fight for a better one. And ultimately—I'm thankful for that impulse because it's what makes me write.

In completing a play—rewrites—I loathe them. They itch until I get them done, but I truly struggle with rewrites.

Professionally, getting produced is always difficult for everybody—it's the nature of the beast. But I try and compartmentalize my struggles—otherwise one bleeds into the other and both suffer the consequences unnecessarily.

ECR & CRC: Can you offer any words of advice to aspiring playwrights/performers/directors/audiences?

CP: Nothing I could possibly say could prepare anybody for what a dysfunctional business this is. Until they live it—they won't believe it. But if you're signing up for the fight—go for it! Write without thinking of your limitations. Don't waste time on complaining—attack the page and the stage. The time that you spend working will be the only time you will derive true happiness from this career, *así que goza* every minute you can. Be bigger than the business.

Production History/Palabras Dramatúrgicas

El Postre de Estrada Palma was performed at Aaron Davis Hall, New York, in the Playwrights in Performance series, May 1999.

My Cuba was performed at a one-night event in New York City called Moth Bar, June 1998.

Contact Information

The playwright may be contacted through the editors.

EL POSTRE DE ESTRADA PALMA

Cami stands center stage and talks directly to the audience.
(Lights come up on Cami.)

When my visa was approved to go to Cuba I thought a lot about Abuela Carmita. Living in Miami, my grandmother had raised me on afternoons in Cuba and the thing that always brought on the stories was dessert.

My grandparents were incredible cooks. Both of them. They worked in the kitchen for hours, carefully making sure that every dish was perfect. I was surprised that my grandfather was such a good cook because in Cuba he was a businessman. When I asked him who taught him to cook he answered, "Exile, Cami, the exile."

But I don't think you can "learn" how to cook the way they cooked. They made meals that made you happy for days. And their desserts. . . ."It's twenty-three egg yolks per spoon? Fantastic! You guarantee that I will gain a pound if I eat that *tocino del cielo*? Well, they don't call it *tocino del cielo* for nothing—get me a spoon!" So you grow an inch here and there, or two, it didn't matter because my grandparents made it. And when they cooked it was special because they did it together and they did it together because it was all that they could do to hold on to their life in Cuba.

Every *postre* had a memory attached to it. A cousin that balanced in the lace of the *merengue*. A family dinner, protected, in the caramel moat of a *flan*. I loved desserts more than anything because they were just over the top. A combination of all the best Cuba had to offer, the amalgamation of everything that is good and too much.

We weren't allowed in the kitchen, which only made me insanely curious about my grandparents' ceremonial cooking. And there was this one dessert that they took very seriously. "El postre de Estrada Palma."

I first tasted it when I was ten. After our lunch my grandfather winks at my grandmother and says "*Anda, trae el postre.*" My grandmother obediently goes to the kitchen and quietly appeared with it, gently setting it on the table.

My sister and I gasp. My grandmother slices it. What is this? Could it be the best possible combinations of our favorites? I glance over at my father and he understands something. I get the first piece. I wait quietly for everybody to be served and stare at the delicacy in front of me. Then I take my bite.

Aahhhhh . . . *panetela* infused with *natilla* and covered with this thick not-too-sweet, not-too-light, *merengue*. This bite dances in my mouth and I am loving my life. Immediately I ask my grandparents why they'd never made it before. Apparently it's very difficult to get right. It was years before they were able to make it in the United States, something about the eggs not being any good here.

Later on that afternoon, I ask my grandmother to teach me how to make this gem of a cake. And she promises that when I'm old enough she will, but I had to wait because it was more than a postre. It was a very special memory. Her friend Cachita taught her how to make it. They were neighbors and when I got older she would tell me the story behind el postre de Estrada Palma.

And now here I am years later. In Cuba, sitting at the eighty-year-old dining room table that a lot of those recipes made their first appearance. And I can't remember the sound of Abuela's voice but I remember her desserts.

(*The pre-recorded voice of Ninita, her great-aunt, is heard.*)

"Cami, *vamos que se nos va el dia.*"

"O.k. Ninita." My great aunt, Ninita has taken me all over Cuba. She's an eighty-six-year-old firecracker. In Havana, I see a lot of things Abuela had told me about, but I can't remember her stories about them. I was too young when I first heard them. I start to wonder if her neighbor Cachita still lives next to the old house. That's one story I could never forget. It was the last one Abuela Carmita ever told me.

Abuela started getting Alzheimer's after my father died. I spent a lot of time with her and really didn't want to believe it was happening. But one day she came over to me and asked me to please write down the names of her four grandchildren and their birthdays.

"Ay Abuela, you know us! You would never forget our birthdays." But she begged.

(*As her grandmother*) "Please Cami, *por favor.*"

(*Surprised by the moment*) "O.k. Abuela, don't worry about it. I'll do it."

My grandmother had always been a very dignified woman. Always neatly dressed with her hands perfectly manicured. I was definitely her *niña* and pretty much got away with everything. (*As an aside.*) Except I never saw her bottom teeth. I can't remember why I was so obsessed with seeing them. But I always tried to trick her into letting me see them and she would never let me. Once she got sick, I was able to sneak a peek; but by that time she had dentures. Whatever. It was one of those things that when you're little you fixate on.

Anyways, I had to start helping my grandfather bathe her and dress her, which was shocking. She was the one that took care of me. But my grandfather needed my help. We'd comb her hair and put her makeup on. And together we'd try and help her look the way she would have wanted.

The only thing my grandfather wouldn't let me do was help him cook. I hated seeing him in the kitchen alone, but he absolutely refused my help. Always, (*as her grandfather*) "No, no, no! Set the table. I'll cook." It had become his way of holding on to her.

When I was sixteen my grandfather had to have an emergency operation and I had to sleep at their house and take care of my grandmother. I was freaking out because my grandmother was getting up in the middle of the night and walking around the apartment and I'm a very heavy sleeper so I thought. "Great, I'm going to fall asleep and she's going to get up and fall." But I was the only one that could stay over, so I had to do it.

I didn't change into my pajamas. I watched TV until around two. Then I went to her bed. I was lying there with one foot on the floor, terrified. I knew that I had to be strong but all I could do was cry. Not even cry, I could only manage a whimper. How was I going to take care of my grandmother? My weakness woke her up, and she didn't get up or turn around to me. She just started talking, "Did I ever tell you about *el postre de Estrada Palma?*"

"Abuela, you can tell me tomorrow." I thought she was just babbling. But she sits up in bed and she continues.

(*Light change. Cami becomes her grandmother.*)

When Cachita and her family moved in next door I was afraid of them. Cachita was a Santera. I thought that *Santería* was witchcraft and I was afraid that if I made her mad, she would put a spell on me. Santería belonged to *los Africanos,* and I was Catholic. A few days after they moved in she brought over *el postre* as a welcome gesture and I thanked her and told her that if there was anything she needed to please call us. I didn't even invite her in.

She smiled and walked back to her house. I took the cake, cut it in half to see what was in it. I don't know what I expected, but all I saw was the *panatela, natilla,* and *meringue.* It looked beautiful, but I didn't dare taste it. I threw it in the garbage. Your grandfather couldn't believe that I'd done that. He was furious, *pero* once it was done, I couldn't undo it.

Bueno, months passed and we were cordial to each other but kept our distance. Your grandfather went to Santiago on business, and your father got a very high fever. After being up all night, I took him to the doctor and the doctor gave him medicine but didn't really know what was wrong.

And your father couldn't stop crying. He cried all night. When I finally got him to fall asleep, I went into the kitchen. Your grandfather wasn't due back for another couple of days and your father was not getting any better. I didn't know what to do.

Cachita's kitchen and my kitchen faced each other. Our shutters were closed, but I could see that the light in her kitchen was on. She must have heard me crying and she called out whispering, "Carmen. Carmita."

I was embarrassed but too tired to care so I opened the shutters and I saw her cutting the pieces of *panetela* for the *postre.* I think she was more surprised than me that I responded. She asked me what was wrong and I told her. She said that she was going to ask her saint, Elegua, what needed to be done.[12]

"No, no, no, Cachita. I don't get involved with those things. I'm sorry I bothered you." And I closed the window. A few hours later your father woke up screaming, *pobrecito,* he was only four years old. *Desesperada,* I didn't know what to do. So I went next door and asked Cachita for help. Without saying a word she motioned me in and I followed.

She took me to her special room and lit all the candles, prayed an Our Father and continued. She took shells out of a bag and started rattling them and asking questions in Yoruba. Then she looked up at me and told me that your father was going to be alright. But we had to perform a *despojo.* Imagine how I felt, because you know how I am, but I knew I needed to listen to her.

Bueno, Cachita prepared everything. We cleansed your father with the holy water and flowers and we put him to bed. Cachita promised me that in the morning he would wake up fine. I thanked her and she went home. I fell asleep in a rocking chair in your father's room and I dreamt that San Lázaro, Babalú Ayé, came and told me that he would take care of your father from then on.[13]

The next thing I hear is your father laughing. I open my eyes and he's playing in his bed with the dog. I look at my watch and it was 11:30 in the morning. I take his temperature and he is completely normal. I run next door to Cachita. As soon as she opens the door I throw my arms around her and tell her Juliancito is fine and what can I possibly do to repay her. She tells me to wait in the living room. She goes to the kitchen and brings out *el postre de Estrada Palma* and tells me to eat it this time. I look at her without knowing what to say and she just smiles. "I'm sorry Cachita." She forgave me. And I took *el postre* home. She was the best friend I ever had.

(*Light change. Cami back to herself.*)

Then Abuela laid back down, turned, and turned away from me. It had been years since my grandmother had spoken to me with that kind of clarity.

(*As her grandmother*) "Come here, don't cry. I'm here to take care of you *mi niña.*" Then still with her back to me she put her hand out to take mine and she makes me cuddle up to her. I asked her, "Will you teach me how to make el *postre de Estrada Palma* tomorrow?"

She answers yes and I fell asleep and we both slept through the night.

I was hoping that it was some sort of remission or change in her Alzheimer's, but the doctor told me that those kind of things happen pretty randomly. The next morning, she didn't remember what had happened.

A few days later Abuela asked me if she had taught me how to make el *postre,* and I told her yes. And she smiled and laughed a little, then fell asleep in her chair.

(*Ninita's voice-over*) "We are almost there, Cami."

Abuela Carmita died when I was eighteen. She didn't know my name anymore, but she always knew it was me when I came to see her. I was able to convince my grandfather a few years ago to teach me how to make *el postre.* But the *merengue* didn't turn out right and he refused to continue.

(*Ninita's voice-over*) "Let's see if Cachita still lives next door. You know she was your grandmother's best friend. She's a *santera.* Nobody ever knew how your grandmother and her became such good friends."

Ninita rings the doorbell and knocks on the door.

(Ninita's voice-over) "Cachita?"

This older, beautiful woman comes to the door.

(*Cachita voice-over*) "Ninita! I haven't seen you in years! *Entra! Entra!*"

Ninita introduces me and Cachita's face lights up. Her black eyes turn into pools and she tells me that I look like my grandmother. When I see Cachita's face I feel my grandmother's hand reach out to me. When Cachita calls out my name, she does it with Abuela's soft voice. I can hardly speak, but I ask her for one thing.

"Cachita, can you teach me how to make *el postre de Estrada Palma*?" She smiles, understanding that I know the story, and lowers her head a little bit and says,

(*Cachita voice-over*) "But I can't buy any eggs."

"Don't worry, I'll go and get everything we need. I just need you to teach me how to make it."

(*Cachita voice-over*) "Me encantaría, Cami, I would love to."

In one Cuban afternoon, Cachita taught me how to make *el postre de Estrada Palma.* And for a few hours I was able to remember all that was good and too much.

(*Lights fade down on Cami.*)

THE END

MY CUBA

I've been raised on countless stories of what Cuba was and what it could've been. I was born in Miami, but I've always had an eighty-year-old Cuban patriot running through my psyche. At the age of six, I was a sight, but at twenty-six, I needed to make Cuba mine.

Growing up, Cuba was like smoke. Even when it filled me, it disappeared as quickly as it came. I could never completely catch it. And now I was going and even though I had a very strong idea of what my Cuba was—I was on my way to discover what it actually is. Images of everything from Ricky Ricardo to my grandparents were racing through my head, and I still had no idea what to expect.

When I get to the Miami airport I realize that I'm the only person on the Havana flight with only one suitcase. Everybody else in the customs line has these huge stuffed duffle bags filled with things to give to their families. And, because you are charged for extra checked weight, people are literally wearing decorated pots. On their heads, Osterizers covered in fabric and bows so that they can get them through without being charged extra for them.

The woman in front of me, Daisy, confesses that she has cut two perfectly equal pieces of cured beef into squares so that she can put them in the special shorts she's wearing under her pants. She also has five heads of garlic, in her bra. Her family lives on the interior of the island and they haven't had meat in a year and garlic costs a dollar a head. The average working Cuban only makes seven dollars a month so Daisy brings her family everything she can stuff into a duffle bag or wear on the plane.

A few minutes later I complain that my hands feel a little dry and she pulls out a bottle of lotion, also from her bra, readjusts the heads of garlic, and asks me if I will help her get all her carry-ons on the flight. I tell her I will as long as she promises to stuff the cured meat in one of the bags and not in her contraband special shorts, 'cause we got seated together. She agrees and I help her out.

On the plane, I keep smelling bacon cheeseburger but I tell Daisy that under no circumstances do I want to know where it is coming from. There is a man, Juan, sitting next to us. He left Cuba on a raft three years ago and it's the first time he's going to see his wife and daughter, who just turned five, since.

Cubans aren't allowed in the Cuban airport and as we land, I see hundreds of people waiting outside in huge fenced-in areas. Still, though, being as Cuban as I am, I think I'm going to touch down and instantly feel at home. But these Cubans are different than the ones I grew up with. Their names—Vladimir gives me my visa and Yaskiaveli looks through my bags. Meanwhile, Daisy has been bribing everybody for no reason. At every checkpoint she winks at the person and slips them a five. I don't really have any trouble getting in except that they take away my copy of the *New York Times* because it's considered subversive.

I see Juan's reunion. His wife is carrying his daughter and telling her that she shouldn't be scared because that's her father, and Juan and his wife are hugging and crying. Then

I hear my great-aunt Ninita calling out, "Cami!" She stands out in the crowd like a little merengue with her white hair and shiny black eyes.

She takes me straight to the house and on the way there I see hundreds of people on the streets and everybody is kind of . . . hanging out. There's a lot of movement but everybody is kind of standing still. We get to the house, Villa Carmela, and it is a big wedding cake sitting in a garbage can of a block.

My great-aunt Ninita has stayed there all these years to protect her sister's work. Her sister, my great-aunt, Amelia was a painter and the house is home to some of her most amazing paintings. It's already considered a museum by the government. National patrimony. The government is just waiting for her to die out of it.

The rest of the family left all sorts of belongings in Ninita's care. There are wardrobes that hold doll collections, and porcelains. Fifty-year-old pictures, old antique medicine jars and books. And everywhere I sit, there's a rocking chair.

But I can tell Ninita doesn't completely trust me. She senses I want something, everybody that comes to the house usually does. And I'm not going to lie. I want something too, but I don't know what it is. So I ask her different things about everything I see in the house. She decides to keep me at a comfortable distance by offering me a tour of Old Havana.

When we get there I can hardly breathe. It's just beautiful. I get to meet a lot of people and I start to recognize some of the more enduring Cuban qualities. Cuban vanity is ever present. This woman tells me, (*as the woman*) "Imagine that I have to wear shoe polish as mascara sometimes!"

(*As self*) "What about maybe not wearing mascara?" I ask innocently. And all the women of the group crack up and look at me like "Poor thing." And Ninita adds that I was born "over there." To which they all reply, "Ahh . . ." and this makes me crazy 'cause in the U.S., when people ask me where I'm from, I always say "Cuba!" But here I say the same thing and it means something completely different.

"But you are a Cuban-Americanita, right?" And I don't want to answer yes, but I have to. Even still, everybody is great. A generosity of spirit that could only come from people that don't have anything.

Government taxis, all of them brand-new Mercedes Benzes, whiz by a line of people waiting for the bus that won't come for another couple of hours. There is a huge flea-market type thing behind the Havana Cathedral where tourists are buying books on the Cuban Revolution and Che Guevara berets. They are eating up Castro's pop revolution marketing. This one guy hears me say something in English and is thrilled that I'm a Cuban he can actually talk to.

(*As the guy*) "Oh your Cuba is a wonderful place. The music! So sexual. I'm being consumed by this old-world charm. Thank God Castro has saved it from us."

(*Shocked*) "If Castro has saved it from us, how come you get to go and eat in restaurants that my family can't even walk in to?"

(*As the guy*) "Oh honey, don't tell me you are one of *those* exiles. If I could only live here."

"Why don't you?" I am genuinely curious.

He answers that he can't leave his business, as he buys his Che Guevara T-shirt in American dollars. A capitalist communist. Typical. This is something that I deal with all the time in New York. "One of *those* exiles." Why are people so angry at the Cuban exiles? For seeking freedom? *The Sound of Music.* People didn't think the Von Trapps were a mafia. But my grandparents, who crossed an ocean instead of climbing a mountain, are responsible for any problem Cuba has today. Not "el Comandante," the great Communist leader. A bunch of wounded people in Miami are the reason Cuba has been devastated.

I am so frustrated I tell Ninita I want to go home. Walking towards the taxi, we pass this tourist, an old man with a putrid stench, holding the hand of a thirteen-year-old Cuban girl. The driver opens the door and tells me as I get in, (*as the driver*) "When somebody finally realizes what's going on here. things will change." And I don't have the heart to tell him that people do know what's going on here, that's why they come.

I start to think about the way cigars have made Cubans a brand and not a people. That Old World charm that guy was talking about is intoxicating, but it's crumbling into the streets with the exception of a few hot spots that have been restored.

The house has become my sanctuary, Amelia's paintings put me in the Cuba that my grandparents protect in their nostalgia and after seeing as much as I have, I'd rather be there. I stay home for the next couple of days and I start to feel guilty. Guilty as if I had been responsible because I was born in Miami, and I've benefited from the Cuba I was given, while the people that live the Cuba they have, are slowly disappearing. I was afraid that I would discover that I was too American and was saddened to find out that I was more Cuban than I wanted to be, because I can't wait to leave. Not because I don't love it, but because it hurts too much to be in Havana knowing that I CAN leave.

My week has come to an end and as I'm packing I look over at the brushes sitting on the dresser. I stayed in Amelia's room and there are these two huge jars full of paintbrushes. And I really want a paintbrush. But I don't know if Ninita will give me one.

I'm so tempted to just take one. Instead I call out for Ninita and I say, "I'm going to ask you for something but don't freak out. And it's too late to go anywhere so don't even think about calling the taxi driver."

She looks me straight in the eyes and says, (*as Ninita*) "WHAT?"

I take a deep breathe and state, "I want a paintbrush."

She stares at me but I don't back down. She looks up at me and shrugs her shoulders, (*as Ninita*) "They're dry. You can't paint with them." She answers.

"I don't want to paint with them. I just want a piece of the family. Just one."

(*As Ninita*) "Fine, take however many you want." And she walks away. I run after her and hug her. She blows me off pretending not to understand my request.

She takes me to the airport and I see Juan and his family. His little girl is now locked in his arms and doesn't want to let go. It looks like his eyes are going to fly out of his head from the pressure of trying to hold back the tears, and his wife is the same.

I can't hold back—I've cried in the taxi all the way to the airport. When I go to say good-bye to Ninita, she says, "Mama used to say that good-bye is written in tears. Don't say good-bye, you'll be back. You've got to convince me to give you a painting." And she laughs. I know she'll never give it to me, and she knows that it's not why I'll come back.

"You know what Ninita, you're not a merengue. You are a little pearl."

"Leave! Before you run out of tears!" And she pushes me towards the door she's not allowed to walk through.

My Cuba isn't a tropical paradise or a communist example. It isn't captured in a foreigner's dollar or a government's yard sale. My Cuba seeks freedom and isn't limited to its island's borders. It exists in the stretch of a teenage girl's back and the gaze of an exile trying to figure out what happened. My Cuba lives in the argument of a Conga drum, not because it turns me on, but because its sets my rhythm, no matter where it may find me. My Cuba blows away like ashes, while those that need it try and keep it safe in their longing. And when all is said and done, my Cuba will forgive those that have ravaged it and welcome me home.

Notes

1. Biographical information is from the playwright's responses to the editors' biographical questionnaire, dated through December 14, 2008, and October 29 and October 31, 2010.

2. Camilo Cienfuegos (1932–1959), a Cuban revolutionary born in Lawton, Havana City, became one of the key figures of the Cuban Revolution, along with Fidel Castro, Che Guevara, Raúl Castro, and Huber Matos.

3. Amelia Peláez del Casal (1896–1968), an important Cuban painter of the Avant-garde generation. This internationally recognized artist was born in Yaguajay, in the former Cuban province of Las Villas. In 1915 she moved with her family to Havana, where she studied art and subsequently established herself in Paris. In 1934 she returned to Cuba. Known as a painter and ceramist and also made murals. She died in Havana in 1968.

4. David Gonzalez, "In New York, with Beliefs That Still Challenge Cuba," *New York Times,* March 10, 2008.

5. Ibid.

6. Caryn James, "A Cuban-American's Wish to Find Her Ancestral Home," *New York Times,* theatre review, February 15, 2008.

7. Lee Hernández, *New York Daily News,* February 26, 2008.

8. Carmen Peláez, e-mail to the editors, May 9, 2008.

9. Ibid.

10. Carmen Peláez, biographical questionnaire.

11. According to the playwright, the works of Amelia Peláez are known as *Amelia*s.

12. Carmen Peláez, e-mail to the editors, July 20, 2008: "I found this definition for Elegua. He is the saint that Santeros talk to when your cards or shells are read—also all

those things below: Elegua: Trickster God of Crossroads, Beginnings and Opportunity. See www.mythicjourneys.org.

"He's the Guardian of the Crossroads of Life. Whenever there are decisions to be made, he provides opportunities and second chances. If you're lucky. As a Trickster God, the childlike Elegua can sometimes make things even more complicated. At a whim he can turn a simple choice into a vast conundrum of paradox. He's also messenger to the higher Gods, and he does like to be noticed. He's partial to cigars and rum, but he is very good with children. See www.godchecker.com."

13. In Cuban Santeria, Babalú Ayé has been syncretized with Saint Lazarus, who is commonly referred to as the father of the world. Lázaro is one of the most important saints in the Cuban society because of his connection with health and disease. Babalú Ayé is also the saint of diseases.

CHAPTER 10

An Off-Broadway Success
Carmen Rivera's *La Gringa* (1996)

Carmen Rivera, by permission of the photographer, Candido Tirado.

The Playwright/La Dramaturga

Carmen Rivera was born in New York City on 1 October 1964.[1] Both of her parents were born in Puerto Rico and came to live in the United States when they were eight years old. They quickly adapted to the American way of life and learned English quickly; consequently, she was raised in a household that did not speak Spanish. Her parents felt that if Carmen's first language was English, she would have more success in U.S. society. Her only exposure to the Spanish language was through her two grandmothers and her family in Puerto Rico. Carmen has a Bachelor of Arts from New York University in economics and Latin American literature. It was at NYU that Carmen really learned to speak Spanish, albeit with a U.S. accent. Learning Spanish opened up a whole new world for her, where she was really able to communicate with her Spanish-speaking family. Carmen discovered she had wonderful storytellers in her family, who fed her blossoming writer's voice. Carmen returned to New York University to earn a Master of Arts, where she created her own course of study that combined playwriting, Latin American theatre, and educational theatre. For nearly twenty years she's been working in the theatre as a playwright, producer, and teaching artist in the New York City public schools.

Rivera is a prolific writer. Following the success of *La Gringa* in 1996, *La Lupe: My Life, My Destiny* opened Off-Broadway at the Puerto Rican Traveling Theatre (PRTT) in 2001, receiving an ACE Award from the Association of Journalists and Writers for Best Production, and was produced in Dallas, Texas, in 2004 by Martice Enterprises. *Julia de Burgos: Child of Water* was produced in spring 1999 at the PRTT and was videotaped for the archives at the Lincoln Center Library for the Performing Arts in New York. *To Catch the Lightning* was produced at the PRTT in spring 1997 and was nominated for an ACE Award for Best Production. *The Next Stop* has been workshopped at New York Theatre Workshop and at INTAR (International Arts Relations) Theatre and was also produced by Repertorio Español as *La Próxima Parada.*

Other plays by Carmen Rivera are *Ghosts in Brooklyn, Betty's Garage, Caravan of Death, The Next Cycle, The Power of Words, Plastic Flowers, La Pesadilla (The Nightmare), ameRICAN, The Nurse, Julia, A State of Bliss,* and *Delia's Race;* she cowrote *The XY Stories.* Her work has appeared at INTAR, La MaMa Experimental Theatre Club (E.T.C.), and the Theater for the New City, and other venues in New York City, Philadelphia, and other cities in the United States. Internationally, her plays have been produced at theatre festivals in Moscow, Chile, Puerto Rico, Colombia, and Bolivia.

Among other accomplishments, Rivera's *Betty's Garage* is included in *The Women's Project and Productions: "Rowing to America" and Sixteen Other Short Plays,* and she is also included in *Women Who Make Theatre. Delia's Race* is included in the anthology *Positive/Negative—Women of Color and HIV/AIDS. Julia* has toured the New York City Public Schools and is included in *Nuestro New York,* an anthology of Puerto Rican Theatre. Her work can also be found on the online archive, Alexander Street Press. Carmen has been the recipient of grants from the National Endowment for the Arts (NEA) and New York State Council of the Arts (NYSCA).

The playwright's most recent success was a special project she undertook with her husband, the playwright Candido Tirado, titled: *Celia: The Life and Music of Celia Cruz.* This musical on Celia Cruz, the queen of salsa, made its Off-Broadway premiere on September 26, 2007, at New World Stages, New York, where it was performed in both Spanish and English. In an announcement about this production in the *New York Times,* Stephanie Goodman mentioned that, without a background in musicals, the playwrights turned to the show's musical director, Isidro Infante, who had served the same role in Cruz's last tour and who appeared in this production. The playwrights also turned to the producers of *Celia,* a team that had been behind a 1999 theatrical work about Héctor Lavoe, another salsa star who was the subject of a 2006 feature film starring Jennifer Lopez and Marc Anthony. According to Goodman, the producers had been "looking to develop more stage shows for Hispanic audiences, but their focus had long been concerts by Latin artists."[2]

Celia seems to have quickly found a ready audience. The success of this production is evident by its nine-month run, closing on May 25, 2008. *Celia* has toured in Miami, Puerto Rico, the Canary Islands, and Chicago. Other recent projects that Rivera has undertaken are beginning a new play about the Dominican dictator, Trujillo.

About the Play/Sobre la Obra

La Gringa is a longer work than most already presented in *La Voz Latina.* While it is not quite a full-length play, the characters in this work are more fleshed out than those in many of the previous works examined. In this Off-Broadway production, Carmen Rivera brings us a delightful insight into a Puerto Rican family as a young woman from New York goes to Puerto Rico in search of her extended family. Through this Obie Award–winning play, we find a fascinating twist in glimpsing from the outside in, with characters who, as D. J. R. Bruckner wrote in his review, "have a strong streak of the ridiculous in them, and it is precisely that quality that makes them familiar and lovable."[3] Bruckner added: "The play was a crosscultural experience for Ms. Rivera as well; she wrote it in English and it was translated" for the performances he observed.

In *La Gringa,* María, a second-generation Nuyorican just out of college, decides to take a trip to her mother's homeland, Puerto Rico, instead of going to Europe for Christmas. This recent college graduate is in search for her roots, and she is thrilled to discover foods, people, and places that she has only heard about and now can experience. She quickly bonds with her mother's brother, Tío Manolo, who is revived from his deathbed with the enthusiasm and interest that María takes in wishing to reconnect with Puerto Rico and her family. Despite a sour aunt and cousin, she is able to find connections to her past and desires to continue her lineage as part of this homeland. Her journey to El Yunque, the rainforest where the goddess Atabey resides, leads to a magical discovery of reconnection, and in doing so, the entire family is able to understand that despite some of the family having departed for the United States out of economic necessity, they are all joined by the cultural ties that Puerto Rico offers.

Artistic Vision/Punto de Vista Artístico

ECR & CRC: Briefly describe your theatre experience.

CR: I had another life until 1989 . . . I worked in corporate America; the brokerage and insurance businesses, until I decided I had to give my love for theatre a try. In 1990 I returned to NYU to pursue a Master's degree in playwriting, Latin American theatre, and educational theatre. Ever since, I have been extremely blessed to have a life in the theatre. I met my husband, playwright Candido Tirado, at an Off-Broadway production of one of his plays, *First Class,* and we started a theatre company, Shaman Repertory Theatre, in 1989 with some other friends/theatre artists. It was there that I wrote a one-act play, *The Universe,* that eventually evolved into *La Gringa.* After eleven years, Candido and I decided to leave Shaman and start another company, Education Play Productions (EPP), which creates one-acts plays about social issues, such as violence prevention and teenage pregnancy, for the public schools. I also have been actively producing and writing plays, which have appeared in such theatres as Repertorio Español, INTAR, La Mama, E.T.C., the Women's Project, and in theatre festivals throughout the United States, Bolivia, Colombia, Puerto Rico, and Russia.

ECR & CRC: How did you decide to write and/or perform?

CR: For as long as I can remember I've always wanted to tell stories and I've always loved the theatre. I can't remember a time when that love did not exist in me. My mother was very influential in my life. She used to take me to the library every week for two books, and in the summers there were puppet shows and readings that I loved attending. I started reading at four years old and started keeping a diary when I was eight. When I was ten, my mother started college; she was an English literature major. She had to see plays for her classes and I always went with her. I started to see many different types of plays, including Shakespeare, at eleven years old and I was completely fascinated by the theatre. There was also this television show that I loved, *Lost in Space.* I wrote a part for myself in the show; the assistant to the captain married the captain's daughter and they had a baby girl—me. I actually wrote out scenarios and designed clothing for myself in my journal. Writing always seemed to be a part of my life. As an actual profession, it all began in 1989, when I quit corporate America.

ECR & CRC: Why do you write what you do?

CR: That's such a difficult question to answer. I guess I write because that's what I do. Twice in my career I decided to stop writing; I packed away all of my work, determined to have a normal life. But sure enough, within 24 hours of my decision, the papers and notebooks were back out and my love of writing just picked up where it had left off.

ECR & CRC: Who do you write for and what audience are you trying to reach?

CR: I write for myself, knowing full well that if I don't have an audience it's not theatre. I guess all writers want the largest audience possible, regardless of background. While I am writing I do not target an audience per se, but I know that my audience does begin with Latinos and like concentric circles expands outward to anyone else who wants to join in . . . I always hope.

ECR & CRC: Who or what has been your major influence?

CR: Definitely Absurd Theatre: especially Arthur Adamov and Eugène Ionesco. Latin American writers: fiction—Horacio Quiroga, Julio Cortázar, Gabriel García Márquez; theatre—Griselda Gambaro; all of Albert Camus's work—novels, plays and essays; and the work of playwright Candido Tirado—he is my husband and I really admire and respect his work. Several of his plays do inspire me: *Momma's Boyz, Fish Men,* and *King without a Castle,* which was written in a style from Argentina called fantastic realism (it is not magical realism). Fantastic realism has two basic principles: (1) limited characters and limited situations (usually characters who have been marginalized by society), and (2) a fantasy serves as the inciting incident for the action of the play. Candido had briefly studied with an Argentine playwright, Guillermo Gentile, who was one of the proponents of fantastic realism. My graduate thesis was based on Guillermo's and Candido's work. I also wrote a play in that style, *To Catch the Lightning,* which was produced Off-Broadway in 1997.

ECR & CRC: What has been your biggest and/or most difficult struggle/challenge in life, in completing a play or getting it produced, etc.?

CR: I recently wrote a play about my grandmother and she is very ill. I couldn't finish it for three years. I can't give you a concrete reason why. I'm still trying to figure it out—but I hated the play. I couldn't do the rewrites; it made me cry all the time. Somehow I made it through—it's had several readings and a workshop production and now I'm very proud of the piece.

ECR & CRC: Can you offer any words of advice to *aspiring* playwrights/performers/directors/audiences?

CR: For writers—just write and write and do not let negative forces in your circles. For other theatre practitioners—find ways of practicing your art, especially when you are in between gigs . . . for example, produce showcases with your friends. Keep busy. Study and be prepared. For lovers of the theatre—support theatre any which way you can; buy a ticket, bring a friend, volunteer, produce a play . . . and on and on. . . .

Production History/Palabras Dramatúrgicas

La Gringa, in which Rivera has played the title role, has been in repertory at Repertorio Español for nine years (February 1996–present). It is part of the New Voices Series that received an Obie Award in 1996 and was presented at the Brooklyn Academy of Music (BAM) as a part of their Spanish Voices Series. The Repertorio Español provides a Study Guide for *La Gringa* at its website, which includes the playwright's biography, a synopsis of the play, commentary from Rivera about the origin of the play, and study guide questions for discussion.[4]

La Gringa was also featured at the 3rd International Theatre Festival of La Paz (FITAZ) in Bolivia (2002) and the 8th Iberoamericano Theatre Festival of Bogotá in Colombia (2002). In 2001 the screen adaptation of *La Gringa* was a finalist in the International Latino Film Festival/MTV Screenplay Competition. The play was produced in 2009 at El Ateneo de Puerto Rico in San Juan and published that same year by Ateneo in Spanish, in *Anthology of Nuyorican Plays.* Also in 2009, Samuel French published the play in both English and Spanish.

Contact Information

The playwright may be contacted through the editors.

LA GRINGA

Para Manuel—Thank you for that night at the ranch, where you recited poetry with the Gods.

To my grandmother Elisa—thank you for your gift of story and song.

> Our World is a Contradiction . . .
> . . . la tierra prometida eres tú
> . . . you are the promised land
> —Clemente Soto Vélez
>
> To the generation of Puerto Ricans who are absent from their native soil, lest they become a lost generation.
> —Loida Figueroa Mercado PhD
>
> There's a lot of Puerto Ricans out there that don't speak Spanish and aren't into the Spanish music, a lot of them, and they're still proud to be Puerto Rican. But if you don't know nothing about it, if you don't try to learn about it, then you're gonna be lost in the sauce.
> —K.T., the Emcee for Latin Empire

Characters

María Elena García: 22-year-old Puerto Rican woman born and raised in New York City.
Manolo Cofresí: Early 60s. Her uncle.
Iris Burgos: Maria's cousin. 24 years old.
Norma Burgos: Maria's aunt; Iris's mother; Manolo's sister. Late 50s.
Victor Burgos: Norma's husband. Early 60s.
Ramon "Monchi" Reyes: A neighbor. 24 years old.

Place

Las Piedras, Puerto Rico (El Campo—The countryside).

Time

The present.

Definitions

ATABEY: (also—Atabex, Atabei, Atabeira) One of the four names given to the highest Taíno Goddess. Referred to as Mother of the Waters and/or Mother Earth.
BENDICIÓN: A request for a blessing.
COQUIES: A small frog-like animal, indigenous only to Puerto Rico. Makes the sound *co-qui!*
COQUÍ SONG: This is a magical song that is a spiritual connection. Ideally the song is lyrical and played on a string instrument.
GÜIRO: A percussive instrument, which is commonly made out of a gourd. A pick is used to scrape the side of the gourd to yield its sound.
JÍBARO: Farmer, peasant who works the land.
MARQUESINA: Many houses in the hills of Puerto Rico are built on cement stilts. The cars are parked underneath the house. This area is the marquesina. Manolo has an apartment right next to the cars.
QUEBRADILLA: A deep brook in which swimming is possible.
YÜISA: One of the known female Taíno caciques (chiefs) of the area known now as Loíza Aldea. It is also believed her control reached to El Yunque, the National Rain Forest, which lies to the south of Loíza Aldea.

Food

ACAPURRÍAS: Fritters made from plátanos, stuffed with meat or crabs.
ARROZ CON DULCE: Rice pudding, with coconut, milk, sugar, raisins and cinnamon.
ARROZ CON GANDULES: Rice with pigeon peas.
BACALAO: Codfish fritters.
MAVÍ: Birch beer.
ÑAME: Edible tuberose root of the yam family.

PANAPÉN: Bread fruit.

PASTELES: Rectangular-shaped patties stuffed with meat, olives, beans, raisins, and other assorted foods. They are usually wrapped in plátano leaves or wax paper.

PERNIL: Roast pork.

PLÁTANO: Plantain.

YAUTÍA: an indigenous root.

YUCCA: an indigenous root.

ACT ONE

Scene 1

It is very close to Midnight on December 27th. Norma enters.

MANOLO: You didn't knock. (*He's lying in a bed. He does not get up.*)

NORMA: I don't have to, it's my house.

MANOLO: Did she arrive?

NORMA: Iris and Victor went to pick her up.

MANOLO: I can't wait to see *la nena.*

NORMA: I don't know why she's coming here for. (*Norma holds up tea to Manolo's lips.*)

MANOLO: Ah again! (*Manolo will not open his mouth.*)

NORMA: You will keep drinking this orange tea until you're cured.

MANOLO: I'm dying Norma, nothing is good for me. (*Norma forces the tea into Manolo's hands.*)

NORMA: You just decided to give up and die . . .

MANOLO: Everyone dies. (*Norma stares at Manolo hard. She reaches under the bed.*)

NORMA: This is what is killing you! (*She takes out a bottle of beer.*) Who's bringing it to you? If you die, it's not my fault . . . (*The sound of a car arriving is heard.*) They're here . . . God protect the person who brings you beer. (*Norma exits with the bottle of beer. Lights shift. The slam of a car door is heard, and a very irate Iris storms in.*)

IRIS: Your niece, Miss Puerto Rico, is here. Today was the most embarrassing day of my life! Let Miss Puerto Rico help him . . . I got my boyfriend's car to bring her here, that's enough . . . Mami, she's taking pictures of everything. She took a picture of the guy who picked up her bags. And then she made me take a picture of her kissing the ground, oh no, the sacred Puerto Rican ground!

NORMA: Iris she's never been to Puerto Rico before. She grew up as an American.

(*Through the door bursts Maria Elena Garcia. She has on a hat and a jacket with a Puerto Rican flag on them. She is carrying a suitcase.*)

MARIA: Hold it! (*She puts her suitcase down and begins taking pictures. Speaking in incorrect Spanish.*) No tía, don't look at me. No mira me.

IRIS: (*Correcting her Spanish.*) No me mires. Don't look at me!

MARIA: I want a spontaneous, I mean a natural picture! . . . How are you? . . .

NORMA: (*Norma is very cold to Maria. Maria kisses her, but Norma doesn't reciprocate the kiss.*) Fine.

MARIA: Wow, I'm so psyched! (*In bad Spanish.*) ¡Qué maravillo! Smell the air, it's so pure. OH Listen to the CO-QUIS. (*She stands still to listen and take it all in.*)

MARIA: That's excellent!

IRIS: Virgen Maria.

MARIA: It's like listening to a symphony.

IRIS: A symphony of squawking little big-eyed frogs is not music to my ears.

MARIA: Iris, coquies are not frogs. (*Victor enters with another one of Maria's bags.*)

VICTOR: Look Norma, she looks exactly like Olga. The exact same face.

NORMA: Hm!

VICTOR: How's Olga?

MARIA: Mami's fine . . . she's doing really well.

VICTOR: Very good.

MARIA: She's good, and papi's good too . . . everybody's good . . . um . . . um . . . Is Tío Manolo feeling better?

VICTOR: No mama, he is muy sick.

MARIA: (*Speaking in incorrect Spanish.*) Mami digaba that Manolo has been sick.

IRIS: (*Correcting her.*) Dijo! Said!

MARIA: What? ¿Qué?

IRIS: Mami "said" . . . that Manolo is sick . . .

MARIA: Spanish is so confusing. I confuse the verbs. I want to learn Spanish very well. I studied it in the university, but I need more practice.

VICTOR: That's wonderful. You should learn your language. And you speak it well for an American.

MARIA: (*Norma has been standing upstage, away from them, staring at them.*) I can't believe I'm here in Puerto Rico. This place is more beautiful than I ever imagined. Oh . . . I forgot I have gifts for everyone.

NORMA: Save the gifts for tomorrow. You will sleep in the room next to Iris' . . . she will show you. Pues . . . let's go to sleep Victor.

MARIA: Bendición Tía y Tío.

NORMA AND VICTOR: Que la Virgen le acompañe. (*Norma exits without hugging Maria. Victor hugs Maria. Maria and Iris remain staring at each other.*)

MARIA: It feels great to be with my people. I want to see everything on the island, not only the buildings . . . (*Looking for the word in Spanish.*)

IRIS: Edificios. I speak English.

MARIA: Good you can help me . . . I want to get close to the land, I want to bond with Puerto Rican soil.

IRIS: You'll bond with Puerto Rico by tomorrow morning, when the mosquitos discover new meat, boom you're bonded.

MARIA: When the plane was descending I saw San Juan . . . the lights looked like stars in the universe. It was beautiful. Oh, here I have something for you. (*Maria goes into her bag and give Iris her gift.*)

IRIS: Hmmm. It smells good.

NORMA: (*Off-stage*) Iris, go to sleep!

IRIS: I'm coming . . . I don't want to hear my mother's voice.

MARIA: Yeah . . . Buenas noches Iris!

IRIS: Thanks a lot . . . Good night! (*Iris exits. Maria takes a deep breath.*)

MARIA: I love it here . . . No in Spanish . . . Me encanta estar aquí.

END OF SCENE 1

Scene 2

The next morning (December 28). Maria has made coffee. The radio is on.

MARIA: GOOD MORNING!

VICTOR: Maria, I like the hankerchiefs you gave me . . . Gracias, they are too nice, I can't blow my nose in them.

MARIA: You're welcome . . . no, no, de nada. (*Maria takes her coffee and looks out into the audience.*) Isn't there supposed to be a brook out there?

VICTOR: That brook dried out years ago. Iris was a little girl.

(*Norma enters.*)

NORMA: Look Victor, I got some yerba buena for Manolo. Doña Fela made the tea for me.

MARIA: Bendición Tía!

NORMA: Que la Virgen te acompañe. Maria please turn off the radio! (*Maria turns it off quickly.*)

MARIA: I made some coffee.

NORMA: I know you were being helpful, but this is my kitchen.

MARIA: I didn't mean any harm. (*Victor gets up.*)

VICTOR: Don't worry mija. Gracias por el café. I am going into town now to buy the part my truck needs.

NORMA: I told you to get one of those new Mitsubishi trucks last year . . . but you don't listen to me.

VICTOR: I'd rather shoot myself. The truck will work with that part. See you later. (*Victor exits. PAUSE.*)

NORMA: I don't like people cooking in my kitchen. Please, Maria, this morning you took too long in the shower. I know people from New York are used to wasting everything, but water costs money here, . . . and no music playing in the house.

MARIA: Okay Tía, I'm sorry. (*Maria picks up a gift from the table.*) I have your gift here.

NORMA: Not now. I have to give Manolo his tea.

MARIA: I'll bring him his tea.

NORMA: He's not up for visits.

MARIA: I want to . . . cheer him up.

NORMA: ¿Animarlo?

MARIA: Yes, and I also wanted to give him the gift I brought for him. It's always nice to have visitors when you're sick. If he doesn't want me to stay, I'll leave. I promise.

NORMA: Make sure he drinks the tea.

MARIA: Okay.

NORMA: Don't stay there too long.

MARIA: Yes tía. (*Maria exits with the tea and his gift.*)

END OF SCENE 2

Scene 3

Lights up on the marquesina. Manolo's room is still dark. Maria enters with the tea and the gift hanging from her arm in a shopping bag. Manolo, who is in bed, looks up.

MANOLO: Come in. (*Maria enters but the room is still dark. Manolo sits up with difficulty.*) Olga . . . Olga . . .

MARIA: No Tío Manolo, it's me Maria, Olga's daughter.

MANOLO: Turn on the light. (*Maria turns it on. Manolo sits up with difficulty. Maria sees a great many theatre posters, the Comedy and Tragedy masks African style, shelves of records and an old record player, empty rum bottle underneath his bed, clothes everywhere and books on the floor.*) Maria? You look exactly like your mother. You're all grown up.

MARIA: Yes. I'm twenty-two years old . . . How do you feel?

MANOLO: I feel like a piece of crap, but now that I see your beautiful face, I am happy.

MARIA: Here is your tea, and I have a gift for you.

MANOLO: Give me the gift.

MARIA: You have to drink your tea first. That's what Tía said.

MANOLO: Nah . . . What did you bring me? . . . Tell me . . .

MARIA: . . . Okay . . .

MARIA: (*Manolo tries to open the gift but his hands are a bit stiff. Maria helps him open the gift.*) Here.

MANOLO: Thank you. (*Manolo holds up two albums.*) Beethoven and La Lupe . . . my favorites.

MARIA: Mami knew you would like them.

MANOLO: How is my sister and the man who kidnapped her to New York?

MARIA: My mother and father are doing well . . . they send their love. Your tea . . .

MANOLO: Yuch . . . how about some big, fat, juicy pork chops?

MARIA: There's no way Tía Norma will make you pork chops. Come on. Tía let me come here on the guarantee that you would drink your tea.

MANOLO: You can drink it and tell Norma I did. (*Maria shakes her head no and raises the cup to Manolo's lips. He refuses to open his mouth.*) I'm not a baby.

MARIA: You're acting like a baby. Men always act like babies when they're sick.

MANOLO: I'm not sick, I'm dying.

MARIA: You shouldn't say that.

MANOLO: Why not, it's true. We all have to die.

MARIA: Well you're alive now, drink your tea. (*Manolo lets Maria put the cup to his mouth. He drinks the tea.*)

MANOLO: No more . . . YA!

MARIA: Did you see all of those plays?

MANOLO: Some . . . I performed in others.

MARIA: As an actor? I don't believe you.

MANOLO: Don't believe me.

MARIA: What about *Hamlet*?

MANOLO: That one I saw.

MARIA: *La vida es sueño?*

MANOLO: I did lights for that one.

MARIA: *Don Juan Tenorio?*

MANOLO: I did the props.

MARIA: You told me you were an actor!

MANOLO: You didn't point to the play I was in.

MARIA: Which one?

MANOLO: . . . *Romeo and Juliet.*

MARIA: What part?!

MANOLO: Romeo of course.

MARIA: No way! I bet you only know "Romeo, Romeo, where art thou Romeo . . ."

MANOLO: "O Romeo, Romeo, whereFORE art thou Romeo?" (*Maria realizes he's not kidding.*)

MARIA: "Deny thy father and refuse thy name; or if thou wilt not be but sworn my love, And I'll no longer be a Capulet . . ."

MANOLO: "What's in a name? That which we call a rose / By any other name would smell as sweet . . ."

MARIA: You really played Romeo?

MANOLO: For one night. I was the understudy, and I cleaned the stage and fixed the costumes . . . but one night Romeo got sick. Everyone said I was the best Romeo they had ever seen. Then the company ran out of business and I was back on the sugarcane field . . . You'd make a great Juliet.

MARIA: I played Juliet once.

MANOLO: Are you an actress?

MARIA: I did a couple of plays in college. You don't believe me?

MANOLO: Then you are an actress.

MARIA: I wanted to study theatre, but mami says it's not a stable life.

MANOLO: So you studied something stable?

MARIA: I double-majored in business and Puerto Rican studies, I really loved my Puerto Rican studies classes.

MANOLO: (*Laughs out loud.*) Puerto Rican studies . . . what crap!!

MARIA: I wanted to learn about my culture, there's nothing wrong with that?

MANOLO: You speak Spanish pretty good for a gringa.

MARIAL: I'm not a gringa!

MANOLO: Oh, okay, sorry, mira, go over there, a shoe box, take it out. (*Maria does so.*) I bet you didn't study this in Puerto Rican Studies. (*Maria opens the box.*)

MARIA: A güiro . . . Do you know how to play it?

MANOLO: . . . Of course I know how to play it!

MARIA: Play something.

MANOLO: The last time I played it was a long time ago. I don't know if I can. Here, you play it. Take the pick and scrape the side. (*Maria tries to play the güiro.*) AH NO! Stop, stop . . . give it back to me. (*Manolo plays a short rhythm. When he gets the rhythm, he stops playing and squeezes his wrists and tries again.*)

MARIA: Ah . . . that's excellent.

MANOLO: I used to play better . . . you just have to know the rhythm. I love playing it. I made this one.

MARIA: Teach me how to play it.

MANOLO: Not now mija. I'm a little tired.

MARIA: Okay. (*She gets up to leave.*)

MANOLO: Thank you for the gifts Maria.

MARIA: If you need anything I'll bring it to you.

(*Maria exits and as lights fade on Manolo's room, the playing of a güiro is heard.*)

END OF SCENE 3

Scene 4

Iris enters. She's dressed very well.

NORMA: What smells so good?

IRIS: The perfume Tía sent to me.

NORMA: Oh . . .

IRIS: Mami, did you open the gift that Tía Olga sent you?

NORMA: Uh . . . I haven't had any time . . .

IRIS: Help me with my hair.

(*Norma fixes Iris' hair. Maria reenters.*)

NORMA: Did he drink the tea?

MARIA: Yes tía.

NORMA: How is he feeling?

MARIA: He's weak, but he looks good. You look great. Where are you going?

IRIS: I have a job interview.

MARIA: Think positive . . . um . . . feeling good, positivo, you'll get the job.

IRIS: This is my third interview for a pharmaceutical company in two weeks.

NORMA: Don't worry, you'll get something.

IRIS: When? There's got to be some company somewhere on this island that can hire me.

MARIA: Why would you want to work for a pharmaceutical company? They pollute the environment.

IRIS: They pay a lot of money. You know this is not New York, where there are jobs everywhere.

MARIA: It's very difficult to find jobs in New York. (*Maria is scratching her arms.*)

IRIS: You bonded with Puerto Rico already!

MARIA: Hm?

IRIS: The mosquitos branded you like one of Don Pepe's cows!

MARIA: I wasn't bitten, I see it more like an initiation into the tribe. Mami sent a rosary for Abuela. I want to hang it on her headstone.

NORMA: We can't go there. Your mother moved mami to Rincón, which is four hours away, on the other side of the island. Didn't your mother tell you that?

MARIA: (*Taking out a map.*) Yeah, but the island is small. We can drive straight across to Rincon.

IRIS: It looks like you can cross the island, but you have to pass through the cordillera, which means hours spent climbing mountains, then going down the mountains, and on and on . . . or you can go around the mountains, but it takes just as long. Going to abuela's grave is a whole day adventure that begins at dawn.

MARIA: I have so many plans for my visit and I wanted to begin with abuela's grave . . . I want to experience my patria and abuela's part of my history. From there to El Morro . . . and all of Old San Juan—I want to see El Parque de las Palomas, the Pablo Casals Museum, and of course I want to see Cataño. Then the ENTIRE ISLAND.

NORMA: Maria, we're not on vacation.

MARIA: Um . . . I was thinking Iris and I could visit these places . . . and you're not working right now . . .

IRIS: Maria, remember my job interview in San Juan . . .

MARIA: Tomorrow? Nice island drive . . . Two cousins driving on the coast, smelling the ocean, checking out Puerto Rican men . . .

NORMA: She has a boyfriend.

IRIS: He doesn't own me, the problem is that I only have Ricardo's car until tonight. He lent it to me to go pick you up and for my job interview today.

MARIA: Okay . . . I can go with you to your job interview and then we can go to El Morro and walk around Old San Juan.

IRIS: I'm really not in the mood to see things I didn't like the first time I saw them. AND I can't think about seeing Puerto Rico now, I'm very nervous about the interview, if I don't get this job . . . I can't handle another rejection.

MARIA: I'll help you do breathing exercises. Try this. (*Maria takes deep breaths. Iris gives her a sarcastic look.*) To help you relax . . .

IRIS: Okay forget about the breathing exercises . . . A trip to San Juan might be good for you . . .

MARIA: Please Iris . . . please, please . . . I'm only going to be here two weeks . . . we only have the car today, we can see San Juan . . .

NORMA: Iris, take her to San Juan.

IRIS: Okay, okay, okay I'll do it.

MARIA: Thank you!! Thank you!!

IRIS: Fine. (*Maria puts on her jacket with the Puerto Rican flag on it.*)

IRIS: Take that off.

MARIA: It's my favorite jacket.

IRIS: I'm not walking around San Juan with you and that jacket.

MARIA: Nobody is even going to notice it . . . Trust me!

IRIS: We're all Puerto Rican in this island—we don't have to advertise it.

MARIA: Okay, okay . . . (*Maria takes off her jacket.*) I'm ready. Got my camera.

IRIS: Bendición mami.

MARIA: Bendición tía.

NORMA: Que la virgen te acompañe. (*Maria and Iris exit.*)

END OF SCENE 4

Scene 5

Iris and Maria enter and find Norma.

IRIS: My feet are killing me! We walked all over Old San Juan. And we had to stop every five seconds to take another picture of a Puerto Rican moment . . .

MARIA: Don't complain, you had a great time.

IRIS: She took pictures of El Morro, facing the water, then facing inland; all the Taino statues in the museum. Even a picture of the dump, La Perla. You know your niece wanted me to go into one of those jail cells and put my hands in the irons and pose for her stupid camera. I told her forget it! Then she went in there and started to act like she was being tortured and I had to take a picture of her. A natural picture. I almost left her in the jail!

(*Beethoven's Ninth Symphony, "Ode to Joy," fourth movement is heard.*)

IRIS: What's that?

MARIA: I think it's Beethoven.

IRIS: From where? . . . (*She listens for a second.*) Mami, it's coming from Manolo's room.

NORMA: Really? (*She listens.*) I don't believe it.

MARIA: Oh I like Beethoven . . . Look tía, I bought a miniature figure of a coquí. (*The music continues for a beat.*)

IRIS: Mami do you know ésta loca here gave up a trip to Europe to see this puny island?

MARIA: Mami and papi wanted me to see Europe. They felt a trip to Europe would make me a well-rounded person . . . How do you say it?

IRIS: Una persona más completa . . .

MARIA: Yes, exactly . . . I felt it was more important to visit my country. Connect with my ancestors . . . my grandmother, my great-grandmother . . . my family . . .

IRIS: Ancestors.

MARIA: Mami is always talking about Puerto Rico and I wanted to see it for myself. I have the rest of my life to see the world, which I intend to see. I was dreaming about Puerto Rico for a long time . . . El Morro was more than I expected. I felt a true sense of history. While I was walking around in El Morro, I had this feeling of . . . of . . . peace. As my feet touched the stones, it felt right . . . I was hypnotized by the sound of the waves slamming against the fort's walls . . . I realized then that I came home . . . The sound of the coquis, the smell of nature, my one-day sunburn . . .

IRIS: The mosquitos.

MARIA: Even the mosquitos bite . . . my little signs of welcome . . . so right here . . . I can't go back to New York. This is my home. I'm staying in Puerto Rico.

(*Norma and Iris stare at each other.*)

IRIS: You have a life in New York.

MARIA: I don't have anything there. I mean, I have mami and papi, but I could visit them.

IRIS: How about your boyfriend?

MARIA: . . . We broke up a month ago.

IRIS: Don't you have a job in New York?

MARIA: I'll quit and look for a job here.

IRIS: Wake up from the dream Maria, I can't even get a job here. My name's on every waiting list from here to the San Juan area.

MARIA: I'll try . . . we'll try together . . . we'll both look for jobs.

IRIS: Great, more competition . . . What if it takes you two or three years?

MARIA: I have faith that it won't.

NORMA: What is your mother going to say about this?

MARIA: . . . Mami will understand . . .

NORMA: I'm not sure about that . . . and the interview, Iris?

IRIS: They liked me, I'm very educated, but I have to wait for an opening . . . the same as always. I have a Bachelor's degree and a teaching license and I can't get a job. Unless I want to work in a factory, which according to the paper pays very well.

MARIA: The job situation is the same in New York . . . although you'd have better luck in New York, there's a shortage of qualified bilingual teachers in the public schools. You'd get a job immediately.

NORMA: Iris, you don't have to go all the way to New York to find a job.

IRIS: How's the money?

MARIA: Pretty good, $35,000 a year starting salary, better than in private schools.

IRIS: What? That's great.

NORMA: Iris, it's very, very expensive to live in New York.

IRIS: It's very expensive to live in Puerto Rico.

NORMA: People in New York live like animals.

IRIS: Mami, people driving on the highway here act like animals.

NORMA: New York is also overcrowded and full of drugs.

IRIS: So is San Juan.

NORMA: But not where we live, and it's very cold in New York.

IRIS: I'd love to see snow sometime in my life.

MARIA: You can just imagine it Iris.

NORMA: When you marry Ricardo he won't let you go to New York.

IRIS: As long as we have jobs here, otherwise we become the New Puerto Rican migrants looking for work . . . and he doesn't give me permission to do things. I do what I want to do.

MARIA: Just like when mami left looking for work.

NORMA: Your mother didn't leave to find work, she left because that's the way she is. Because she wanted to do it.

MONCHI: (*Off-stage*) Buenos días.

(*There's a knock at the door. Monchi enters.*)

NORMA: Buenos días Monchi.

MONCHI: Buenos días. I have some plátanos, ñames, and grapefruits for you.

NORMA: Gracias Monchi.

IRIS: Oye, Dr. Jíbarito, what are you doing here? Aren't you supposed to be collecting worms?

MONCHI: Buenos días cousin-in-law.

IRIS: You're not my cousin-in-law yet.

MONCHI: When you marry Ricardo, you are going to be the most beautiful cousin in the family.

IRIS: I can't believe you're related to Ricardo.

NORMA: Have some coffee Monchi.

MONCHI: Muchas gracias, Señora Burgos. Too bad your daughter is not as good a hostess as you are.

IRIS: Oh excuse me, Maria I want you to meet El último jíbaro, Monchi. Monchi this is my cousin Miss Puerto Rico.

MARIA: Hi Monchi . . . ignore my cousin, my name is Maria.

MONCHI: Nobody listens to Iris . . . I'm Ramón, but everybody calls me Monchi. (*She picks up a grapefruit.*)

IRIS: He's strange like you. He got this scholarship to study engineering but he became a farmer—a high-class hick, with an agricultural degree.

MARIA: Iris, living off the land is noble.

IRIS: I like my food the gringo way, cut and in plastic or in cans.

MARIA: Hmm . . . these grapefruits smell so good. Puerto Rico is perfect, the mountains, the coquies and my people.

MONCHI: Are you here on vacation?

MARIA: Yes and no . . . I want to discover my roots.

IRIS: You wanna a root, here's a root. (*Iris hands Maria a ñame.*)

MARIA: Thanks Iris.

MONCHI: Oye, mind your business.

IRIS: ¡Ahórcate! (*"Choke yourself!"*) (*Monchi pretends to choke himself.*)

NORMA: Ave Maria, how's business Monchi?

MONCHI: Good, too good, I can't keep up. During Christmas I expected to sell alot, but I'm behind in my work. If I'm delivering, I'm not gathering; if I'm gathering, I'm not planting . . . How's Manolo doing?

NORMA: The same.

IRIS: Maria, Monchi owns his own farm. Oooo!!

MARIA: I think it's great that you own your own farm.

IRIS: Miss Puerto Rico is defending Doctor Jíbarito.

(*Victor enters.*)

NORMA: What happened? You came back early.

VICTOR: Carmelo no me pudo conseguir la pieza. It's not the right part for the truck . . . Monchi how are you?

MONCHI: Good. How are you?

VICTOR: Muy bien. Did you meet my beautiful niece?

MONCHI: Si, ahora mismo. Victor if you need anything you can use my Volki.

IRIS: Forget it!

VICTOR: Gracias Monchi, maybe another day.

MARIA: What's a Volki?

IRIS: Monchi's car of death, with no breaks.

MONCHI: I have an old Volkswagen I use to take my verduras around. I'm saving for a truck.

VICTOR: Don't worry Monchi, when my truck is working you can use it.

IRIS: Don't hold your breath Monchi.

MONCHI: Gracias, Victor.

MARIA: It can't be that bad if it's working.

MONCHI: It takes me where I need to go.

MARIA: Maybe he can take us to Rincón . . .

NORMA: NO! (*Everyone looks at Norma.*) Monchi just said he was very busy and the car can't make it there and back.

MONCHI: The Volki has never gone that far . . . but . . . I'm so busy now.

IRIS: I know, Maria why don't you help our jíbarito?

MARIA: . . . That's a fantastic idea.

IRIS: Por favor Maria! I was just kidding.

MARIA: Working on a farm is a great way to learn about the land.

MONCHI: You can't spend your vacation picking plátanos.

MARIA: Why not? I insist . . . really . . . you need the help and I'm offering . . . I want to do it . . . that way you'll have some free time.

MONCHI: . . . I do need the help . . . uhm . . . okay . . .

MARIA: Perfect.

MONCHI: Thanks . . . tomorrow morning at dawn.

MARIA: I'll be there.

MONCHI: Adios . . . I have to go into town.

VICTOR: Adiós Monchi, cójelo suave Ramon.

MONCHI: Take care.

NORMA: Saludos a tu familia Monchi.

(*Monchi exits.*)

IRIS: Now you'll really touch Puerto Rican land.

MARIA: I'll see the process of nature at work. How exciting!

END OF SCENE 5

Scene 6

Maria is up late in the evening speaking to her mother on the phone.

MARIA: Mami I'll find a job here . . . I'll mail in my resignation . . . I don't have to give them two weeks notice. Believe me, they won't miss me at all . . . If he doesn't give me a reference I'll live . . . What do you mean I can't live here anyway . . . you can't tell me that, I'm twenty-two years old . . . I can do whatever I want!! Mom, mom, mami, let me speak, (*Maria holds the phone away from her.*) Mami, are you finished? You're not even giving me a chance to . . . okay, okay, because I love it here, I love Puerto Rico, do you understand that? I want to live my life in Puerto Rico, mom . . . mom you're always talking about how much you love Puerto Rico, your childhood, climbing trees . . . It's not different for you. Your love for Puerto Rico is more than memories . . . Well then I want my memories to be Puerto Rican memories . . . mom . . . you never listen to me . . . mom . . . okay mom, I have to go. Long distance is expensive, bye . . . What? Yes everybody loved the gifts . . . Tía Norma . . . yes I gave her the gift . . . I don't know if she opened it . . . she didn't say anything to me. Okay . . . bye. (*Maria hangs up and she's very angry and depressed.*) ARGH!!

END OF SCENE 6

Scene 7

Monchi and Maria enter. It is very early morning in the morning.

MONCHI: Okay . . . now pick the yucca, and put them in the sack. I'll get the yautía . . .

(*There is one sack half full.*)

MARIA: Which is yucca?

MONCHI: This brown vegetable, it's really a root . . . you see it looks like it has hair on it.

MARIA: Okay . . . I brought some coffee. Do you want some?

MONCHI: Not now, we have only two hours to get the yucca, yautía, and the plátanos, and the gandules, no forget those . . . I have enough. We have to bring all this to the pueblo and deliver them to the stores that made orders.

MONCHI: (*Monchi works very quickly, but Maria picks up one yucca at a time. She also picks up the yucca with only two fingers.*) I have more sacks when you've filled that one.

MARIA: Okay. (*Maria is trying to pull up a yucca, very daintily and it won't come out. Monchi sees how Maria is working, he laughs.*)

MARIA: What's so funny?

MONCHI: The yucca is not going to bite you.

MARIA: Don't make fun of me. It won't come out.

MONCHI: You have to stick your hand in the Earth and pull up the root. The yucca isn't going to jump in the sack by itself. (*Monchi grabs her hand and plunges both of their hands into the dirt. PAUSE. Maria freezes. They look at each other.*) Your hands are going to get dirty.

MARIA: I'm not afraid of dirt.

MONCHI: Good . . . and you . . . have to work faster, we don't have a lot of time. (*They go back to working. Maria finally fills a sack. She tries to pick it up. It's very heavy.*) I got it.

MARIA: No, I can do it. I said I would help you.

MONCHI: Okay . . . bring it to the Volki. (*Maria tries to pick it up again but she can't. Monchi picks up the sack.*) It's okay, I'll take this. You keep getting the yucca and I'll get the plátanos now. (*Monchi exits with the sack.*)

MARIA: (*Extremely exhausted.*) Whatever you say.

MONCHI: (*Off-stage.*) Oh carajo!

MARIA: What happened?

MONCHI: They're yellow! (*Monchi reenters.*)

MARIA: What are?

MONCHI: The plátanos. The plátanos are yellow. Damnit! Carajo! I can't sell them like that.

MARIA: People like ripe plátanos.

MONCHI: Not for pasteles, people want green ones to make pasteles or acapurrías. What a waste!

MARIA: Don't you have more green ones?

MONCHI: Yeah, up the hill. There's not time now to get them . . . That's it, I'm ruined!

MARIA: How can this ruin you? You have so much to sell.

MONCHI: In two or three days all of the plátanos will be yellow, then I won't be able to sell them unless I get people to help me pick them, but I won't because nobody wants to work on a farm.

MARIA: I'm helping you.

MONCHI: It's not enough . . . Maria I have two cousins that were laid off and I offered to PAY them to work for me and they refuse to do it.

MARIA: Some people are not cut out for farming.

MONCHI: I can't even get people to pick up the vegetables themselves for free. They could be starving and they'd rather buy two plátanos for a dollar in the supermarket . . . I can't believe I didn't see the plátanos ripening. (*He sits on the ground.*)

MARIA: Want some coffee now?

MONCHI: Sure. (*Maria pours coffee, they sit down and drink.*) I'm sorry I blew up.

MARIA: I understand . . . you must feel overwhelmed.

MONCHI: I didn't realize that running a farm would be so hard . . .

MARIA: It's so quiet.

MONCHI: . . . Listen . . .

MARIA: What?

MONCHI: Hear that?

MARIA: No . . . what is it? . . . what . . .

MONCHI: Sh . . . it's a lizard running up a tree . . . Ah this is my favorite time of the day. It's very pure.

MARIA: . . . I feel so calm right now, tired but calm. I grew up in front of an El train. It came out of the tunnel and ran right by our apartment in the projects. The whole apartment shook every time the train passed . . . I'd love to live in a place like this.

MONCHI: New York seems to be an interesting place.

MARIA: Yeah . . . there's alot to do but you can get lost sometimes. You're always walking on asphalt and the buildings block the sun.

MONCHI: The mountains block the sun.

MARIA: It's not the same thing . . . Here you can see things grow right before your eyes.

MONCHI: Everything grows here. The land is so fertile. You plant a seed and boom, it's already growing the next day . . . I'm going to tell you a secret . . . Three of my buddies from school and myself decided to buy back Puerto Rico.

MARIA: What?

MONCHI: We're buying back Puerto Rico. It's more like a corporation but instead of buying stocks, we're buying acres of land . . . I'm in the east. One is in the north, another in the south and one in the west. We'll keep buying land until we meet in the middle of the island. I already have two and a half acres but it's a hard idea to sell to people. My friend in the south already has ten investors.

MARIA: . . . I'd like to buy some land . . . when I can afford to.

MONCHI: The more of us that buy the land, the sooner we'll get Puerto Rico back. To grow and sell our own food, that's our goal.

MARIA: Until then, I suggest you guys get help or you won't make it to the middle of the island alive. AH!!

MONCHI: What happened?

MARIA: Something's in my hair. AH!!

MONCHI: Stay still!

MARIA: It's scratching me!! AH!!

MONCHI: 'Perate.

MARIA: Get it off . . . AH!

MONCHI: There I got it.

MARIA: AH! . . . What was it?

MONCHI: A lizard, you scared it.

MARIA: I scared it?! It was digging into my head Monchi.

MONCHI: Yeah, I can see your brain through the big hole in your head.
MARIA: Very funny. (*Monchi caresses her hair.*)
MONCHI: You have beautiful hair.
MARIA: Thanks. (*Maria moves away from him.*)
MONCHI: Sorry . . . you're seeing somebody, right?
MARIA: . . . No . . . I . . . not anymore.
MONCHI: But you still think of him, right?
MARIA: I don't want to go through that again.
MONCHI: This guy sounds like a big mamao ("*jerk*"). I bet he works in an office. (*Maria laughs.*)
He pushes paper right! I knew it, he has soft hands . . . see my hands, filthy, hard, and calloused. I have a man's hands . . . these hands do real work for a living.
MARIA: So do mine. My hands are dirty too.
MONCHI: (*Touching her hands.*) Those are the prettiest, dirtiest hands I've ever seen.
MARIA: Want more coffee?
MONCH: Yeah. (*Maria pours coffee.*)
MARIA: What about you?
MONCHI: What?
MARIA: Do you have a girlfriend?
MONCHI: How many women do you know want to go out with a farmer?
MARIA: Why not? You're a great guy!
MONCHI: I'd be a real great guy if I'd become an engineer. Everybody thinks I'm crazy. Nobody believed that I gave up a great future to do this. The only people that supported me were Manolo and Norma.
MARIA: Norma? My tía Norma?
MONCHI: She understood my love of seeing things grow.
MARIA: I can understand Manolo, but Norma . . .
MONCHI: I used to help her with her flower garden. She taught me alot.
MARIA: She doesn't show much affection in the house.
MONCHI: That's the way she is. But she takes care of Manolo and she paid for Iris's school. She's your aunt, but she's also a stranger to you . . . it takes time to get to know someone . . . (*He looks at his watch.*) Come on, we have to get to the pueblo. (*They grab the sacks and exit.*)
END OF SCENE 7

Scene 8

Later that evening. Maria enters Manolo's room from her long day with Monchi. She is walking slowly and in pain.

MANOLO: What happened to you?
MARIA: I'm in love.
MANOLO: With Monchi? I knew it.

MARIA: NO! With my beloved island . . .

MANOLO: Oh? Siéntate. (*She walks, with great difficulty to the chair.*)

MARIA: I was packing gifts from the Earth. (*She sits down.*) AH!! Beautiful jewels brought forth from the greatest of Mothers, Mother Earth.

MANOLO: Vaya regalito. (*"Go precious gift."*)

MARIA: Everyday I feel closer to my home. I know for certain this is where I belong.

MANOLO: Planting yucca?

MARIA: I'm trying to be serious! AH! My whole body's in pain.

MANOLO: You only worked one day.

MARIA: Even the muscles behind my ears are sore.

MANOLO: You need a hot bath.

MARIA: Ah . . . I can't move . . . I really found Puerto Rico today.

MANOLO: Where? I've been looking for it for a long time and I haven't found it.

MARIA: In the ground, in the dirt, in the yucca . . . there's something spiritual about collecting food that you are going to feed people with . . . Oh, oh, you know Tío Victor gave me a rabbit . . . beautiful, grey, with green eyes. I named her Stella. What a wonderful day. I'm going to help Monchi tomorrow.

MANOLO: I think it's because you like him.

MARIA: NO! . . . I don't hate him. I just don't like him like that.

MANOLO: If I were a girl, I'd go out with Monchi.

MARIA: You're not his type.

MANOLO: At least you won't starve to death.

MARIA: I don't want to go out with anyone for a very long time.

MANOLO: AH!! Somebody broke your heart.

MARIA: That's in my past, I don't want to talk about that.

MANOLO: That means your heart was really broken, abaratao, torn apart, aplastao!!

MARIA: Drop it!! I told you that's all part of my past. . . I glued my heart back together. Today I was reborn in Puerto Rico. My life from now on goes forward.

MANOLO: You can't forget things that happened to you.

MARIA: Yes I can . . . I just did . . . See? (*She snaps her fingers.*) I'm the new improved Maria.

MANOLO: Those things you want to forget made you who you are. All those things brought you to this point right here today.

MARIA: (*She is visibly upset. PAUSE.*) The new and improved Maria doesn't get angry at the past anymore. (*Manolo stares at her.*) I told you my past is my past! . . . Damnit!

MANOLO: Um, hm . . .

MARIA: Stop looking at me . . . ARGH . . . we did *Romeo and Juliet* together in school, okay!

MANOLO: Who?

MARIA: The guy!

MANOLO: Who?

MARIA: The guy, the guy . . . THE GUY, you know the broken heart, the guy . . .

MANOLO: Hm, the guy. Did he play Romeo?

MARIA: NO! He played Tybalt.

MANOLO: At least he gets killed!

MARIA: I was madly in love with "the guy"—he was Sicilian. He told his family I was Sicilian because they were racists. AND I went along with it like a big pendeja!

MANOLO: "Love Be Blind, cannot hit the mark!"

MARIA: Blind, deaf and dumb. He said I didn't look like the other Puerto Ricans, but I didn't look Sicilian enough . . . then he broke up with me because he needed space!!

MANOLO: Then why don't you just date Puerto Rican guys?

MARIA: Because the Puerto Rican guys I know date Barbie dolls. Peter . . .

MANOLO: Who?

MARIA: The guy, he looked Puerto Rican and he could dance a mean salsa.

MANOLO: You went out with him because he looked Puerto Rican and he went out with you because you didn't look Puerto Rican . . . ¡qúe reguero! Sorry Maria . . . you cannot hide the rice and beans in those eyes! I don't know how he missed them.

MARIA: Sometimes I feel Puerto Rican and sometimes I don't. These last couple of days I have felt so connected to being Puerto Rican . . . I've never felt this before . . . It's all so confusing in New York . . . Mami and papi never taught me Spanish. They kept me sheltered in private schools. They wanted me to be American, to succeed. I'm glad I went to those schools but I don't have any roots, a tree can not live without roots . . .

MANOLO: Nobody can take your roots away from you. Even the smallest plants have roots.

MARIA: Not me. I'm rootless like when a yucca is plucked from the Earth leaving its root behind.

MANOLO: Now you're a yucca, coño you're really confused.

MARIA: If I were a yucca everyone would know who or what I was. Then I'd have no problems.

MANOLO: You should find a vegetable psychiatrist.

MARIA: Very funny Manolo . . . I don't know my history . . . I need to know where my place is.

MANOLO: There's no doubt that you are related to us, you act, I act; we are a dramatic family, everyone has talent, except Inez, she's my second cousin, I think it's second or maybe third, but she has the worst voice on Earth . . . the priest stopped her from singing in church because he said she scared the hell out of the holy spirit . . .

MARIA: That's not a very nice priest.

MANOLO: He was so nice that he didn't throw her out of church. Inez's voice was so bad that she scared the coquies and the lizards away from the house. (*Maria laughs.*) I never let her sing with me. Norma did used to sing with me, . . . she has a beautiful voice.

MARIA: Norma?

MANOLO: She sings real good. She was in a jíbaro band. Some guy came by one day and wanted her to make a record. Your grandmother said no.

MARIA: Mami is like Abuela. She loves to say no to everything.

MANOLO: Like Norma.

MARIA: Ooh listen to the coquies . . .

MANOLO: You like them?

MARIA: They make a wonderful sound. Love should be like this sound, calm, soothing, peaceful.

MANOLO: Do you understand what they're saying?

MARIA: I hear them.

MANOLO: No, no, listen closely . . . They're singing a song. Let's go outside.

MARIA: You can't go outside.

MANOLO: Come on. (*Manolo struggles to get up.*) I want to get fresh air . . . I feel good today . . . I want to hear the coquí song under the stars . . . (*He stands up.*)

MARIA: Slowly, slowly . . . (*Maria helps him.*)

MANOLO: Allí está. Listen carefully for their song. (*The folkloric music plays, as they exit Manolo's room. Maria helps him walk.*)

MANOLO: SH! . . . The song is very soft and powerful at the same time.

MARIA: My yoga teacher said Puerto Rico is a power vortex. It could be from the coquis.

MANOLO: Sh! Listen. (*Maria watches as Manolo gets into the song of the coqui. Norma enters and watches them for a beat. She is in shock.*)

NORMA: Manolo . . . Manolo . . .

MANOLO: Norma, mi amor, come listen to the song of the coquis.

NORMA: (*Very angry and confused.*) Manolo . . . how did you get outside of the room?

MANOLO: I walked.

NORMA: Don't . . . lie . . . to . . . me Manolo . . . Maria did you do this?

MARIA: Tía, I swear he got up on his own.

NORMA: (*Getting upset.*) He's been stuck in a bed for five years . . . and TODAY he decides to stand up . . . (*Manolo finds difficulty balancing himself. Maria helps him.*) Cuidao . . . Oh my God . . . (*Norma grabs his arm.*)

MANOLO: I'm fine . . . You see . . . Maybe those teas are working . . .

NORMA: . . . Maybe . . . Let's go inside now.

MANOLO: I haven't been outside in a long time. (*Norma helps Manolo back into his room. Maria also goes to help. Norma stops her.*) Maria, you have to listen very carefully for their song.

(*Norma and Maria exit the marquesina. The coqui song is heard as the lights fade.*)

END OF SCENE 8

Scene 9

It is New Year's Eve and the whole family is preparing a special meal.

MARIA: Something smells good.

NORMA: Victor is a great cook.

IRIS: Maria, look who's here! (*Monchi enters.*)

NORMA AND VICTOR: Felicidades Monchi!

MONCHI: Felicidades!

MARIA: Hi Monchi . . .

MONCHI: Hi . . . (*He kisses Iris on the cheek.*)

IRIS: What was that for?

MONCHI: Greetings from my cousin.

IRIS: You don't have to do me any favors . . . I'll see him in the casino later on tonight . . . why was he invited?

NORMA: Because he's family.

MARIA: Something smells really good. (*Victor brings over a plate from the stove to the table.*)

NORMA: Victor made this special for you Maria. His favorite dish.

VICTOR: Your rabbit . . .

MARIA: My rabbit . . . (*PAUSE.*) Stella . . . This is Stella?!

VICTOR: In my special sauce.

IRIS: I love the rabbit papi makes.

NORMA: Victor you outdid yourself.

MARIA: You cooked Stella AH!!!! I just fed her this morning. (*Maria moves away from the table and starts crying.*)

NORMA: Victor cooked it for you as a gift.

VICTOR: Mija, you don't like rabbit?

MARIA: Yes, but I can't eat Stella. She was my pet. You gave her to me.

VICTOR: No, I did give it to you, but to cook her. I should have told you.

MARIA: Yes tío.

NORMA: She doesn't know, she's not from here.

VICTOR: I'm sorry nena, you don't have to eat it.

MARIA: No, I'm sorry tío. Thank you.

(*Manolo enters singing the Christmas song, "El Camello del Melchior" ("Melchior's Camel") to Norma.*)

MANOLO: Coño, something smells good . . . smells like rabbit . . . give me a leg.

NORMA: Manolo, what are you doing outside of the room?

MANOLO: I want to celebrate the New Year. And I'm hungry, I could eat a bull, but I'll settle for rabbit.

NORMA: No señor, no solid food for you. You're not breaking your diet. Were you drinking?

MANOLO: No . . . I'm high . . . (*He laughs.*) . . . I'm high on life. It's a wonderful thing.

NORMA: You're not supposed to be on your feet!

VICTOR: Norma, just sit him down.

MANOLO: Oye Victor, "El camello de Melchior está baratao . . ." (*"Melchior's camel is broken."*)

(*Manolo continues singing the song.*)

VICTOR: Manolo . . . Norma I didn't believe you when you said Manolo could walk . . .

IRIS: Tío's cured! (*They try to help him walk straight.*)

MANOLO: I love life. Life is beautiful Norma . . . Feel it around you . . . Monchi, hombre if my niece doesn't go out with you I will.

MONCHI: Thanks for the offer . . .

NORMA: Victor help me bring him downstairs.

VICTOR: Norma, he's getting better, he's walking.

NORMA: I don't care what he's doing, walking, standing, jodiendo, he belongs downstairs!

VICTOR: Norma, it's New Year's, let him stay.

NORMA: Can't you see what is happening to him?

IRIS: Mami, he's getting better.

NORMA: We don't know that!! The doctor is the one that says he's getting better.

VICTOR: Norma this is a party!

NORMA: I know we're having a party but he belongs downstairs. Let's go Manolo.

MANOLO: No. I am going to celebrate the New Year!! (*Norma tries to bring him downstairs. Manolo resists. He is surprisingly strong. Victor, Iris, Maria, and Monchi do not approach Manolo but encircle him just in case he falls.*)

MANOLO: I gave you life. (*To Iris.*) I am the reason why you are alive.

IRIS: I thought Mami gave birth to me.

MANOLO: It was I that introduced your father and mother, smarty pants. Remember Victor, we working on the caña. Where's Maria, mira gringa . . .

MARIA: Don't call me that!!

MANOLO: Sorry . . . you take pictures of the sugar cane. That is the really Puerto Rico. Sing, sing something Norma. (*Manolo tries to sing and dance.*) Norma, vente, "El Camello de Melchior."

NORMA: Manolo leave me alone, stop it!

MANOLO: I'm sorry, you're still beautiful. (*To Iris.*) Dance with me.

IRIS: I don't dance with old men.

MANOLO: The wind is older and it still blows.

IRIS: Mami, it's almost 12:00 . . .

MANOLO: ¡FELIZ AÑO NUEVO!

IRIS: Not yet tío.

EVERYONE: 10-9-8-7-6-5-4-3-2-1 (*Manolo counts but he is not in sync with everyone else.*) ¡¡FELIZ AÑO NUEVO!! (*Manolo has put his head down on the table.*)

VICTOR: Let's bring him to his room.

NORMA: This would not have happened if he was downstairs . . . Manolo get up.

MANOLO: Hm . . . Ya?

NORMA: Get up! You have to go downstairs . . . Coño if I found out he drank something . . . (*Norma and Victor pick him up.*)

MANOLO: Hm . . ."Melchior's camel passed the inspection." Victor, Victor . . .

VICTOR: Vámonos Manolo . . . (*They are exiting.*)

MANOLO: Victor, Victor.

VICTOR: What?

MANOLO: Tell Norma to sing . . . I want to hear Norma sing.

NORMA: Forget about singing, you have to go downstairs. (*Norma and Victor have him, he trips and Iris, Maria, and Monchi run to help.*)

IRIS: I got him . . . it's okay . . .

MARIA: You sure?

IRIS: Yeah.

NORMA: Buenas noches Monchi.

VICTOR: Felicidades hombre.

MONCHI: Buenas noches.

IRIS: Good night, my cousin, the jíbaro, and MARIA . . . (*Victor, Norma, Manolo, and Iris exit.*)

MARIA: My cousin isn't very discreet.

MONCHI: Then she wouldn't be Iris. (*PAUSE. They stand very awkwardly next to each other.*) It's unbelievable, Manolo has gotten better since you've been here.

MARIA: Yeah . . .

MONCHI: Happy New Year. (*He approaches Maria.*)

MARIA: Happy New Year. (*He tries to kiss Maria, but she backs away. They don't know what to say to each other.*)

MONCHI: I have to go now.

MARIA: Yeah . . .

MONCHI: Good night.

MARIA: Good night. (*Monchi exits then he turns back.*)

MONCHI: Are you still going to help me tomorrow?

MARIA: Of course . . . I'll see you at 5:00 A.M. sharp.

MONCHI: Looking forward to it. (*Monchi exits.*)

END OF SCENE 9

Scene 10

A figure enters dragging a huge sack of plátanos. She is struggling, she also has on long pants, long-sleeved shirt, a hat, a scarf, sunglasses, work gloves, and work boots. Halfway into the marquesina she falls on her butt.

IRIS: Ah! Carajo! (*She kicks the plátanos. She removes her hat and scarf. It is Iris. Monchi enters, also carrying two sacks of plátanos on his shoulders.*) This farming jíbaro thing stinks.

MONCHI: You're looking for a job, I have one for you.

IRIS: "Job?!" Hah! Monchi this is not a real job with opportunities.

MONCHI: Oh yes it is. The pay is good.

IRIS: I'm not going to be a professional jíbaro thank you . . . but I wasn't made to work the land . . .

(*Iris takes off her gloves.*)

IRIS: See! I broke a nail!

MONCHI: So you prefer a factory that pollutes the land, water and air?

IRIS: Don't get all righteous on me . . . I prefer the classroom!

MONCHI: You'll always have a job, people need food every day. (*Norma enters.*)

NORMA: Ah, Dios mío, Monchi, this is wonderful. We have more than enough to make the pasteles. (*Maria enters the kitchen. She's in a floral dress. She's looking for Norma or Iris. She hears voices coming from the marquesina and goes downstairs.*) What do you think of one dollar a pastel?

MONCHI: Perfect. (*Norma takes money out of her pocket.*)

NORMA: Here.

MONCHI: Don't worry about it.

NORMA: MONCHI . . . toma . . . (*She places the money in his hands.*) Iris, we have to bring the plátanos upstairs.

IRIS: Mami I can't move.

NORMA: We have to grind the plátanos. (*Iris tries to get up as Maria enters.*)

MARIA: Hi Monchi.

MONCHI: Hi Maria.

MARIA: Iris thank you for the dress. Did tío finish fixing the truck?

IRIS: Just because he said he found the part doesn't mean the truck is going to work. Maria, that truck hasn't worked for years . . .

NORMA: The last trip that truck made was to take Olga to the airport.

MARIA: I trust tío. (*Iris and Norma roll their eyes to each other.*)

MONCHI: I can't believe you got an interview so fast.

MARIA: The job is for the Hato Rey office of the American company I'm going to work for in New York. I hope I get it, then I can move down here immediately.

IRIS: Monchi has a position available in his company . . . since you love the land so much . . .

MARIA: Ha, ha . . . (*The sound of an engine starting is heard.*) Yes!! Thank God! (*Norma, Iris, Maria, and Monchi begin to run outside, when the engine dies.*) But he said he found the part!

IRIS: Maria, papi can say what he wants, the truck is ready for burial. (*Victor enters.*)

VICTOR: I'm going to kill Carmelo, the part he gave me is a piece of junk, now the puntera truck doesn't work . . . I'm sorry Maria, and Carmelo just left, he could have taken you. I'm sorry.

NORMA: No interview today.

MONCHI: I'll take you . . . I finished my errands.

MARIA: . . . Thanks Monchi. (*Manolo enters dressed in a nice guayabera [Caribbean-style dress shirt]. He is walking much better and is healthier.*)

MANOLO: Buenos días todo el mundo.

VICTOR: Manolo . . .

IRIS: Tío, you're really looking good.

MONCHI: We have to warn the world that Don Manolo is back.

NORMA: Manolo . . . get back into bed.

MANOLO: Nah . . . I feel great . . .

NORMA: Why are you dressed up?

MANOLO: I am going to Hato Rey with my niece.

NORMA: You're not going anywhere.

MANOLO: I am wearing my new guayabera, and I shaved, so I am going out . . . Norma you worry too much . . . I haven't been to town in years and after my niece gets the job we will go for a drive around San Juan, Cataño, Loiza Aldea, where Yüisa lives. I want to see my favorite cacique, Taina chief of El Yunque . . . she loves me just as much as Atabey.

IRIS: Good luck in Monchi's death box.

MONCHI: Atabey is with us.

NORMA: You're not going anywhere!!

MANOLO: Of course I am. Let's go.

NORMA: Manolo wait! . . . It's been a long time since you've gone out.

MANOLO: I know Norma, it's been a long time, and I have alot to do. Let's go. (*Maria, Monchi, and Manolo exit.*)

VICTOR: Don't worry Norma, he's getting better . . . (*Lights fade.*)

END OF SCENE 10

END OF ACT ONE

ACT TWO

Scene 1

It is several hours later. Norma and Iris are grinding plátanos in the kitchen.

IRIS: . . . Do you think she'll get the job?

NORMA: She studied business.

IRIS: Ricardo studied business and he got laid off . . . yet la gringa comes here and gets the job she wants.

NORMA: She's just like your Tía Olga . . . Olga wanted to go to New York, she went. She didn't care about how the family had to deal with your grandfather's death. That didn't stop her.

IRIS: Mami, she left for economic reasons.

NORMA: It's true, we were poor, but we survived. She didn't have to go to New York.

IRIS: I am sure Tía didn't want to abandon her family to go to a strange country.

NORMA: As soon as she had the chance to leave Puerto Rico, she left. We needed her here, NOT in New York. She never thought about what the family needed. When your abuela died, Olga wanted to bury her in Rincón, where her family is from. I wanted to bury her near our house. Ah Dios mío, ¿para qúe fue eso? Olga called crying, she said Abuela wanted to be with her family in Rincón, not here. I told her to mind her business, since she lives over there in New York.

IRIS: Mami, maybe that's what Abuela wanted.

NORMA: So you think that Olga, who lives in another part of the world, knew what Abuela wanted better than me?

IRIS: I'm just saying that it's logical that she wanted to be buried with the rest of her family.

NORMA: I'm also her family.

IRIS: I'm not saying that. I understand Abuela's desire to be with her brothers and sisters.

NORMA: So I was wrong?

IRIS: No, mami, I . . .

NORMA: Your Tía Olga thought the same thing. She came for the funeral and with all of her money had her moved to Rincon. I'll never forgive her. I was so mad at her I didn't let her step foot in this house. And then she gets mad at me.

IRIS: I don't blame her. This is the family house.

NORMA: Olga doesn't think that. She told me that this house is hers, she paid for it with the money she made working in New York and that if she wanted to she'd throw us out and then sell the house.

IRIS: She can't do that. Abuela put in her will that the house can't be sold, only passed down through the family.

NORMA: Olga doesn't understand family . . . She paid for the house, but I built it with my own sweat and blood. I told her to go to hell and that as soon as I can I will pay her back every single penny she sent to us! Olga thinks I'm stupid.

IRIS: Mami, Tía Olga is not that way.

NORMA: You don't know her the way I do. And now Maria. She wants to go to the cemetery to see Abuela, knowing that it will annoy me . . . and all these pictures she's taking of the house are not to show her friends how beautiful Puerto Rico is . . . they're for Olga, who wants to come back to Puerto Rico and live in the house . . . she's going to have a fight on her hands. I'm NOT leaving!!

(*The slam of a car door is heard. Maria enters crying.*)

MARIA: Iris, thank you for the use of your dress, I'll give it back to you as soon as I clean it.

IRIS: Don't worry about it.

(*Maria exits. Manolo and Monchi enter.*)

NORMA: Manolo, what happened?

MANOLO: Ay Dios mío! She's a mess.

IRIS: What happened?!

MANOLO: The guy who interviewed her told her she can't work there because she's not a Puerto Rican national. ¡¿Para qué fue eso?! She left the office crying. Monchi and I took her to the beach to cheer her up. She wouldn't get out of the car.

IRIS: I told her it wasn't easy to get a job in Puerto Rico.

(*Maria reenters with her jacket with the Puerto Rican flag.*)

MANOLO: Sh!

MARIA: Iris, I promise I'll clean your dress.

MANOLO: Maria don't let people tell you who you are!

MARIA: He said I wasn't a Puerto Rican.

IRIS: But you are American.

MARIA: You see? (*She throws her jacket on the floor.*) Here's the flag of your country!!

MANOLO: She's Puerto Rican.

IRIS: Tío Manolo, she's American!

MARIA: In New York City I was hired as the token Puerto Rican!

IRIS: You were born and raised in America, so you're American.

MARIA: You're born and raised in an American colony. Does that make you a gringa?!

IRIS: I was born here in Puerto Rico! And your first language is English, you are AMERICAN!

MANOLO: Speaking Spanish doesn't make you Puerto Rican.

MARIA: I'm not accepted in America . . . There is no place for me!! I am a foreigner in my place of birth. I am exotic, I am from the island, I'm an immigrant who's taking American jobs away from the Americans, I am a welfare burden on America!!! A Spic!

IRIS: If your mother had moved to France, and if you were raised there speaking only French, you would be French.

MANOLO: If a cat gives birth in an oven, what is born, kitten or bread?

IRIS: Who cares? We're not talking about cats or bread!

MANOLO: Divide and conquer . . . united we stand, divided we fall . . . you're helping the colonial powers that be keep us apart. All Puerto Ricans all over the world have to stick together to keep our culture alive.

IRIS: Then we should accept every gringo as a Puerto Rican?!

MARIA: Stop calling me a gringa . . . can't you get that through your head, jíbara?!

IRIS: Jíbara?! Jíbaro is that plátanos boyfriend of yours.

MARIA: I'm Puerto Rican enough to be dumped by Peter.

IRIS: Who?

MANOLO: The defunct boyfriend.

MARIA: Who dumped me because I am Puerto Rican, not a gringa. First, I'm rejected by Peter, then by my own people.

IRIS: I'm only saying the truth.

MANOLO: The truth is that she's Puerto Rican. She really wants to know about Puerto Rico, most people in Puerto Rico don't care about Puerto Rico.

IRIS: Just because somebody read a book on Puerto Rico doesn't mean that they're

Puerto Rican . . . but she comes down here thinking that she can just stake her claim in Puerto Rico like all the rest of the Americans.

MANOLO: She does have a claim to a part of this island.

IRIS: Not on my island.

MARIA: I came down here to bond with my island, my people, my family . . . I never expected that they would stab me in the back.

IRIS: You can't expect to abandon Puerto Rico and then take it back when you want.

MARIA: I didn't abandon Puerto Rico.

IRIS: Your family left Puerto Rico.

MARIA: My parents left Puerto Rico to find work . . . believe me they didn't want to leave Puerto Rico.

NORMA: When they left the island, they gave up the rights to the island.

MANOLO: If that became a law for everyone that left Puerto Rico to find work, there would be no Puerto Rico left! Puerto Ricans were taken all over the world to work, hasta Hawaii. Those people had kids, and they had kids who are still Puerto Rican.

IRIS: No they're not! They have no connection to Puerto Rico.

MARIA: God forbid those Hawaiian–Puerto Ricans should want a connection with Puerto Rico . . . they'll be kicked right in their ass.

IRIS: OH, how beautiful you speak . . . if you live in New York, with a great job, why do you want to be here?

MARIA: Because this is a part of who I am.

MANOLO: Iris, what are you protecting? You don't care about Puerto Rican culture. You only buy American things, clothes, food; you don't want to take her around, "I saw it before . . . it's boring . . ." So you think our culture is boring. She loves our culture, the history, the music . . . she looking for her roots, you can not say NO to her!

IRIS: Ah no, (*to Maria.*) NO!!

MARIA: Well, YES!

MANOLO: Maria doesn't have to be born in Puerto Rico to be Puerto Rican. She will always be BORICUA. Discussion over.

IRIS: Well you're wrong.

MARIA: If I'm not Puerto Rican then we're not family and I'm the unwelcome guest in a stranger's house.

IRIS: You said it, I didn't!

MANOLO: You (*to Maria*) belong here, the house is for the whole family.

IRIS: Manolo, please, this has nothing with the house.

MANOLO: Of course it does, Maria has every right to be in this house, to be in Puerto Rico, just like Olga.

NORMA: Olga will never step foot in my house!

MANOLO: Without Olga there would be no house.

NORMA: We built it.

MANOLO: With her money.

NORMA: Our blood and sweat built this house! The floor has our blood in it, these walls have our pain and suffering in them. Olga doesn't know anything about pain and suffering.

MARIA: Mami and papi's money is all blood and sweat . . . you think they had it easy, they worked 12 hours a day, two jobs. New York isn't for lazy people.

MANOLO: Mami left this house to the whole family, the whole family Norma!

NORMA: Don't raise your voice in my house, now go downstairs.

MANOLO: I'll leave, not because you threw me out, but because I am pissed off!! (*Manolo exits.*)

(*Lights fade.*)

END OF SCENE 1

Scene 2

It is very late that evening. Victor sneaks into Manolo's room.

MANOLO: You didn't bring me anything?

VICTOR: Since you're not dying, I didn't bring you beer.

MANOLO: Hermano, the whole world is dying.

VICTOR: I know that, but at least you don't have a foot in a box.

MANOLO: You really didn't bring me anything? (*Victor takes out a bottle of maví.*)

MANOLO: AH! Maví. (*Victor takes out some plastic glasses and he pours the maví. They toast.*)

VICTOR AND MANOLO: ¡Salud!

MANOLO: ¡Qúe bueno! The drink of the caciques. I haven't had maví in a long time.

(*Manolo drinks.*)

VICTOR: Enjoy it!

MANOLO: That was the worst thing about being sick, not consuming the things I loved . . . orders from General Norma.

VICTOR: Except the beer . . . I sacrifice everything for a great friend.

MANOLO: You're a saint . . . the daring chances you took for me right under the general's nose . . . if she only knew . . .

VICTOR: We would have known if she knew, believe me . . .

MANOLO: That wife of yours . . .

VICTOR: Your sister. Pues, you know how Norma is . . . she will not take that idea out of her head that Olga wants the house. And Iris and Maria are not talking to each other. La pobre, Maria didn't even eat dinner.

MANOLO: Some vacation Maria had. She'll never come back.

(*Manolo takes great pleasure in drinking his maví. Maria enters. She hears some noise coming from Manolo's room and she listens for a bit. Maria knocks.*)

MARIA: Manolo . . . Manolo . . . Tío . . .

MANOLO: (*Whispering to Victor*) It's only Maria. Yes?

MARIA: Hi, were you sleeping?

MANOLO: No. Come in.

MARIA: . . . I'll leave as soon as you get sleepy. (*Maria enters.*)

MARIA: Tío Victor! ¿Qúe haces aquí?

VICTOR: Like they say in New York, I am hangiando with your tío.

MARIA: I'm sorry to interrupt your hangiando but . . . (*She starts to cry.*) I really need to talk to somebody . . . I don't want to be alone.

MANOLO: I think you should try to get some rest tonight.

MARIA: Because I am leaving tomorrow.

VICTOR: ¿Qúe?

MARIA: I'm leaving this place tomorrow.

MANOLO: Damn.

MARIA: It's true, by 6:00 P.M. tomorrow night I will be on flight 601 going back to New York City.

MANOLO: How can you leave like that?

MARIA: Easy. I called for reservations.

MANOLO: What did your mother say?

MARIA: . . . Nothing . . . she said she knew I wouldn't find a job here and that she'd pick me up from the airport.

VICTOR: I can't believe you want to leave. Don't let Norma and Iris push you out . . . it's not personal.

MARIA: Of course it's personal, they attacked me. I hate it here. It's too hot, too humid, and too many bugs.

VICTOR: You love the mosquitos.

MARIA: They keep biting me. I thought they'd stop biting after they get used to me, but they come for more. Damn vampires.

MANOLO: You have sweet blood.

MARIA: I think they bite me so I can leave. The mosquitos are the true defenders against invaders. I guess they don't think I'm Puerto Rican either . . . the people in the job don't think I'm Puerto Rican, my OWN family doesn't think I'm Puerto Rican. You know what, I'm not Puerto Rican! I can't even hear the coqui's song.

MANOLO: You were touched by Puerto Rico today. You'll never be the same.

MARIA: I was slapped by Puerto Rico.

MANOLO: Babies are slapped when they're born. You were born today.

MARIA: One birth a lifetime is sufficient.

MANOLO: You're born hundreds of times in a lifetime. Everytime you have an experience you're born.

MARIA: How many times do I have to be slapped?

MANOLO: For you it might be more than a million.

MARIA: Oh great!

VICTOR: Listen to your tío, he knows what he's talking about.

MANOLO: Oye, mind your business.

VICTOR: Maria is also my niece and I want to help her.

MANOLO: But I'm giving her advice now.

VICTOR: And I can't say anything?

MANOLO: When I'm speaking, NO!

MARIA: I thought you were best friends. (*She laughs.*)

MANOLO: Some best friend, he marries my sister.

VICTOR: You introduced us.

MANOLO: For that I am sorry hermano. I was losing my mind.

VICTOR: Ah Manolo, Norma, she was so beautiful . . . when Manolo and I worked on the sugar cane fields, she would come everyday and bring Manolo and his father la fiambrera . . .

MARIA: ¿Qué?

VICTOR: Steel pots with food . . . After working really hard all morning under the sun, dead tired; to see Norma walking toward the caña, with her long hair blowing in the wind, as if she was coming from the sun . . . she left me speechless.

MANOLO: Ave Maria . . . that's why I had to introduce him to Norma, if not I had to listen to Victor talk about Norma ALL DAY LONG! Then Victor got worse when she started bringing him mangoes from our tree. ¡Olvídate!

VICTOR: And the best thing was when she sang to me . . . as if the angels were singing to me.

MANOLO: I had to live with angels, and stars, the moon, the sunrays, and the light of my life . . . I had to hear the worse poetry I ever heard in my life . . . Sorry, Victor.

VICTOR: Look who's talking? At least I fell in love with a beautiful woman.

MANOLO: Don't start.

VICTOR: Maria, your uncle always liked the ugly ones . . .

MANOLO: Victor!

VICTOR: Much older . . .

MANOLO: Victor, don't exaggerate . . . Maria he doesn't remember anything, old age you know.

VICTOR: I remember that your specialty was widows.

MARIA: Oh no! That's horrible.

MANOLO: I can't believe you would sink so low as to cheapen what beauty I brought to those women's lives.

VICTOR: Ugly . . . ¡Feísimas! (*Maria laughs.*)

MANOLO: Oye . . . that's not nice to say about human beings . . ."Beauty is in the eye of the beholder . . ." Anyway they were lonely, someone had to give them love. I'M AN ARTIST.

VICTOR: Now you will really know your tío.

MARIA: How much older were they?

VICTOR: By twenty or thirty years.

MARIA: They could have been your mother.

VICTOR: Grandmother.

MANOLO: I can't help it if they fell in love with me . . .

MARIA: You could have said NO.

MANOLO: And break their hearts . . . NEVER. Besides older women are faithful. They never leave their men.

VICTOR: Mierda! They all threw you out! (*Maria continues to laugh.*)

MARIA: You never married any of these women?

MANOLO: There was a woman I almost married . . . she was only five years older than me . . .

MARIA: And?

MANOLO: I wasn't her type: stable, practical and faithful . . . She was jealous of my intimate relationship with Atabey. Anyway I loved her too much to torture her with being married to me . . . (*PAUSE.*) But my hermano found the great love of his life. I was very pleased when they started going out; it was only a matter of time before the magic wore off and fighting would begin.

MARIA: I think it's nice to hear about people who really love each other.

VICTOR: We didn't go out immediately. We were friends first. She came to talk to me when her mother did not let her sing with that group. Norma was destroyed . . . She thought no one understood her.

MANOLO: Your mother (*to Maria*) and I told her to go sing with the group anyway, but she didn't want to disobey mami.

VICTOR: But she continued to sing . . . to me . . . I was very lucky she fell in love with me. She doesn't sing anymore.

MARIA: Well, Norma was slapped by that experience, I don't see how she was reborn.

VICTOR: Norma had the desire and the talent, but her fear stopped her.

MARIA: I'm not scared of being Puerto Rican.

MANOLO: Why are you running back to New York . . . You can't be afraid to be slapped!

MARIA: You might like being slapped but I don't.

MANOLO: That's why you're going to work in the insurance company forever instead of chasing your dreams of acting.

MARIA: You didn't follow your dreams, you gave up on them.

MANOLO: I tried to . . . You don't know how tough it was for a country boy to leave his house in the mountains to go to La Perla Theatre in Ponce to become an actor. I had to give up my job at the caña. Mami and papi were upset, we needed the money. My father told me "if you leave, don't come back." ¿Te acuerdas Victor?

VICTOR: Ah sí.

MANOLO: He threw me out of the house.

VICTOR: He stayed with me. Then INDIO . . .

MANOLO: INDIO . . . I always think of him. There was an old man INDIO, who I used to give fruits to . . . He was a wise man, a philosopher . . . I told him what happened to me and he told me something very profound: "if you want fish, you'll have to get your rear end wet."

MARIA: What?

MANOLO: To get anything in life you have to stop living life so safely. That's when I went to Ponce. When *Romeo and Juliet* went to San Juan, my father died and I had to go back home.

MARIA: I'm sorry . . . Life gets in the way of chasing dreams.

MANOLO: I did chase my dreams . . . it was just cut short.

MARIA: I really could use a drink.

MANOLO: I have maví . . . the caciques loved it.

MARIA: I'm not Puerto Rican, I can't drink that. I need a gringo drink.

MANOLO: Stop talking all that garbage.

MARIA: I'm leaving Puerto Rico forever.

MANOLO: Before you leave try some maví.

MARIA: Uh . . . okay I like it, give me more . . .

VICTOR: Ah she likes it!

MARIA: Nobody cares about the history of Puerto Rico here . . . or about seeing the beautiful things.

MANOLO: Being Puerto Rican is not about seeing places. Tourists do that.

MARIA: . . . Now I'm a tourist! Adios Boriquen! (*Maria gulps down the maví.*)

MANOLO: NO! . . . you are and will always be Puerto Rican!

MARIA: So I'm a Puerto Rican tourist in Puerto Rico . . . All I wanted to do was touch my land, hear the sounds, see the sunset, be a part of Puerto Rico. It's not that much to ask for. I'm more confused NOW than when I was in New York. I used to feel Puerto Rican in New York. Now I realize that I am NOBODY wherever I go.

VICTOR: No, no, mija, yo te acepto. I know you're Puerto Rican.

MARIA: It doesn't matter anymore, I am nothing everywhere, no roots, no home.

MANOLO: Tomorrow we take you to Abuela's grave so that you can leave her the rosary on her tomb.

VICTOR: We have to leave very early.

MARIA: We don't have a car.

VICTOR: I can ask Carmelo to lend us his truck.

MANOLO: No . . . I want Monchi to take us.

VICTOR: In that Volki? We all don't fit in there.

MANOLO: You cannot come with us.

VICTOR: Why not?

MANOLO: You have to protect us from Norma.

VICTOR: Thank you for a wonderful job.

MANOLO: If we are going to get Maria to the cemetery, it has to be like this. Tomorrow morning I'll get Monchi and we leave before dawn.

MARIA: Are you sure?

MANOLO: Of course I am . . . Get up early and don't let anyone see you leave.

MARIA: I don't think anyone will care . . . believe me. (*Maria exits. Lights shift.*)

END OF SCENE 2

Scene 3

Very early the next morning. Maria sneaks into the marquesina with a rosary. She checks her watch. Norma enters.

NORMA: Maria.

(*Maria is startled.*)

MARIA: Tía Norma?

NORMA: What happened?

MARIA: Nothing, you just scared me. (*She hides the rosary behind her back.*)

NORMA: What are you doing up so early?

MARIA: . . . I couldn't sleep . . .

NORMA: So you got all dressed up and came down to the marquesina.

MARIA: I . . . needed to get some fresh air.

NORMA: Maybe if you try going to sleep now, after you received some fresh air, you will sleep.

MARIA: I, I . . . um, um . . . I'm wide awake now. You know when you wake up, you're up for the whole day . . . Besides it's my last day in Puerto Rico. I just want to absorb everything.

(*Victor enters with coffee.*)

VICTOR: I prepared you some coffee . . . coño Norma . . . What a surprise!

NORMA: Victor, Buenos días . . . you're up early.

VICTOR: Carmelo and me, are going . . . to . . . pick up some new tools . . . for . . . for our garage.

NORMA: What time is Carmelo going to be here?

VICTOR: Very soon. (*A car is heard pulling up. The Volki makes a screeching sound as it brakes.*)

NORMA: I imagine that's Carmelo.

VICTOR: Sí . . . Okay we'll see you later, bye. (*Victor walks out with Maria, pulling her arm.*)

NORMA: Maria is going with you?

VICTOR: Since it's her last day, I want to show her the garage so she can see it. (*Monchi enters.*)

MONCHI: Maria let's go. We have to . . . leave . . . Norma!

VICTOR: Monchi . . . good morning. How are you?

MONCHI: Victor . . . Norma, Good morning. What a surprise!

NORMA: Yes, there are many surprises this morning.

MONCHI: Yeah. (*Manolo enters, rushing.*)

MANOLO: I said, as soon as you hear the car pull up . . . Norma!

NORMA: Manolo, what a surprise!

MANOLO: Definitely!

NORMA: You couldn't sleep, and you're waiting for Carmelo . . . Monchi, you SHOULD be on your farm and Manolo should be in bed, where he belongs. But instead everybody's here. Well? . . .

MANOLO: Norma, you win first prize if you guess right here on SUPER SÁBADO! (*Norma does not laugh.*)

MARIA: It's okay, I'll tell her . . . Tío Manolo uhm, has agreed to take me to see Abuela's grave.

NORMA: Behind my back.

MARIA: We all know how you feel about that, and since I'm leaving tonight, it's only fair that I have a chance to pay my respects.

NORMA: You're sneaking around and you're talking about being fair?!

MANOLO: It's not a big deal Norma.

NORMA: Of course it's a big deal!

MANOLO: She wants to see her grandmother and I'm going to take her. Let's go.

VICTOR: Maria, here's some coffee. (*He hands Maria the coffee.*)

MANOLO: Monchi, Maria, vámonos. We don't have time to waste. (*Manolo exits. Maria and Monchi PAUSE for a beat. Then they exit. A car starting, then driving off is heard. Norma and Victor are left alone.*)

NORMA: Is Carmelo coming over, Victor?

VICTOR: Later on.

NORMA: Why are you against me?

VICTOR: Norma, por favor, she just wants to see the grave of her grandmother.

NORMA: You're supposed to support me, but instead you made her coffee for the trip.

VICTOR: This has nothing to do with you.

NORMA: You're right, this is about how you're joining the family to hurt me.

VICTOR: Norma, listen to this . . . I think it's right that Maria should go to Abuela's grave.

NORMA: Who are you to give permission to go to the cemetery?

VICTOR: You're not the owner of the cemetery. People can visit their family whenever they want.

NORMA: It's easy for you to say, your mother is buried in this town. You can see her whenever you want.

VICTOR: Norma, I can take you to see your mother whenever you want.

NORMA: You don't understand, I want the grave near me.

VICTOR: It's not near you Norma. And you just have to understand that and accept it.

NORMA: Stay out of my family business.

VICTOR: This is my family too.

NORMA: You're only part of this family because of me, and I'm telling you to stay out of our business.

VICTOR: I am sick and tired of you yelling about the "house" and the "grave." . . . Cut the shit already!

NORMA: This shit is the only thing I have left. Olga took mami away from me, she's not getting my house . . .

VICTOR: I'm tired of you saying that this house is yours. I helped build this house. Norma, I am so tired of all your pity and complaints . . . You're making me hate the house. I hope it blows up.

NORMA: That would be the last straw. You want to destroy my family . . . I know you were giving alcohol to my brother. I can't believe you gave a dying man beer.

VICTOR: Yes, he was dying, so it didn't matter if he drank beer, tea, or medicine. He should enjoy his last drink . . . since he got better I stopped bringing him beer.

NORMA: So the beer cured him?

VICTOR: The important thing is that he's better.

NORMA: Oh what a miracle! One day he's dying, the next day he's running around like a kid.

VICTOR: I can't believe you're upset because he's better.

NORMA: Don't tell me he's better, you're not a doctor. You're a mechanic. If Manolo was a car then I would believe you, but he's a human being.

VICTOR: He's walking, he's eating after being stuck in a bed for five years. That's proof enough for me.

NORMA: I need more proof than you do, Mister Doctor, the doctor who quit school in fourth grade; the doctor who worked on the sugarcane fields, the doctor who's a mechanic who can't even fix his own truck, who has a garage with no customers.

(*PAUSE. Victor is stunned and hurt. He storms out of the marquesina.*)

NORMA: Victor, Victor . . . (*Norma is left standing alone as lights fade.*)

END OF SCENE 3

Scene 4

Several hours later. Maria enters the cemetery first. She has the rosary.

MANOLO: (*Offstage*) I don't think it's this way.

MARIA: She's nearby I know it . . .

MANOLO: (*Offstage*) 'Perate Maria, wait for us.

MARIA: She's right here . . . I sense it . . . (*Looking around.*) Here. (*She looks at the gravestone.*)

MANOLO: I haven't been here in so long I forgot where . . .

MARIA: FELICIDAD SANTOS COFRESÍ. (*Manolo and Monchi catch up.*) Manolo this is Abuela.

MANOLO: (*Looking at the gravestone*) This is my mother.

(*PAUSE. They all look at the grave.*)

MARIA: . . . (*Whispering*) . . . Wow . . . I remember her braiding my hair when I was little. I always looked forward to her visits during the summer. She always brought us something—mangoes, quenepas, pasteles . . . and she'd tell us about Puerto Rico. I really missed her when she got sick and stopped coming to New York . . . Mami keeps it beautiful. I like the flowers. (*She touches the stone.*) The woman who gave birth to my mother is here. If it wasn't for her I wouldn't be alive. The woman in here carried you in her womb for nine months.

MANOLO: Eight months. I was premature.

MARIA: . . . Jodón . . . but you were inside of her. And now you're here.

MANOLO: One day you're here, then you're gone. But she's here, she's not just dust. She's in me, she's in you. She still lives in us.

MONCHI: It's like she never died.

(*Manolo over to the adjacent tomb.*)

MANOLO: Come over here Maria. (*Maria goes over to him. Monchi follows.*) Read the name.

MARIA: "EMILIA COFRESÍ TORRES."

MANOLO: My grandmother.

MARIA: She's buried next to her mother . . . That's why abuela wanted to be in Rincón.

MANOLO: And that's why Norma wants her to be near her.

MARIA: I can understand that.

MANOLO: Her whole family is here, her father, her brothers and sisters, aunts and uncles . . . We are like these beads on this rosary. We will always be connected, it doesn't matter where we are.

MARIA: (*Manolo gives rosary to Maria. She goes over to Abuela's gravestone and places the large rosary in front of it. She kisses gravestone.*) Bendición Abuela.

MANOLO: Maria, I want to show you something else . . . Monchi ven aca. (*Maria and Monchi walk over to a plot of land with no gravestone.*) Look.

MARIA: ¿Qué?

MANOLO: This is where I will be buried.

MONCHI: Manolo.

MARIA: Stop talking like that.

MANOLO: Maria, we're all going to die one day.

MARIA: I know preparing for it is kind of morbid.

MANOLO: Abuela checked out this area way before she died. She bought all these plots so her family can stay together.

MARIA: Does mami know about this?

MANOLO: Of course she does, she'll probably be over there by the shade. She hates the sun. Norma we will put her far away! (*Maria laughs.*)

MANOLO: Where do you want to be?

MARIA: I can barely manage my life, I won't even try managing my death.

MANOLO: Good to be prepared.

MARIA: You don't have to worry about that anymore.

MANOLO: Whether I die today, tomorrow, next year, it doesn't matter. I like my spot . . . Monchi, you're almost family, you wanna spot?

MONCHI: . . . Okay, but I want a spot next to Maria . . . The Earth is amazing isn't it. It gives forth food, fruit and flowers . . . life . . .

MANOLO: Then it takes us back when we die.

MARIA: Yeah . . . in New York it's difficult to think about Mother Earth.

MANOLO: When I am buried here I am going to be part of the Earth. And the first apple tree in Puerto Rico will grow out of me. (*They all laugh.*)

MARIA: When I have my children I'm going to bring them here.

MANOLO: I want to bring you some place.

MARIA: Where?

MANOLO: Let's go. How's your Volki doing?

MONCHI: I think it'll be okay.

MANOLO: Vámonos.

MARIA: But where?

MANOLO: Come on. (*Manolo hurries off and Maria and Monchi follow. Light fade.*)

END OF SCENE 4

Scene 5

Lights up on El Yunque—the rainforest. Maria, Monchi, and Manolo enter. Maria looks around in wonder.

MANOLO: Atabey, I'm sorry I haven't come here for a long time . . . I've been sick, una jodienda, but I'm better now.

MARIA: I can't believe I'm in El Yunque. (*Thunder and lightning are heard.*) Oh no, it's going to rain.

MANOLO: It's Atabey.

MONCHI: Yeah . . .

MANOLO: She's greeting us. (*Thunder and lightning get louder. The sound of rain is heard. Maria looks around for signs of rain.*)

MARIA: Let's leave before the storm gets worse.

MANOLO: NO! Atabey is welcoming you. She never welcomes anyone on their first visit, except for me of course.

MARIA: She's welcoming me? (*Thunder and lightning get louder.*)

MANOLO: Yeah . . .

(*PAUSE. The sound of rain becomes louder. Maria begins to be immersed in DRY rain. She feels herself getting wet, but Monchi and Manolo don't get wet.*)

MARIA: The water is so warm . . . (*Maria releases her ponytail and lets the water run through her hair. She's enjoying the DRY rain falling on her face.*)

MANOLO: She opened the door.

(*Maria bathes in this water. She savors it as it goes down her face, then neck, chest, stomach, waist . . . she slowly sinks down to the ground as the water goes down her legs . . . She lays on the ground. PAUSE. The thunder and lightning subside.*)

MANOLO: My turn to commune with Atabey. You wanna come Monchi? Atabey can turn herself into four women; one for you and three for me.

MONCHI: No, just tell her to send water to my farm . . . (*Manolo takes off his clothes. He exits off-stage. There is a PAUSE for several beats before Maria wakes up.*)

MARIA: Hmm . . .

MONCHI: It feels strange . . .

MARIA: A little. (*Maria seems to come out of a trance.*) But I am not wet.

MONCHI: That's how it is. You look different . . . You're glowing.

MARIA: I feel different . . . I feel so high and lightheaded . . . it feels so good . . . It's beautiful here. It's so quiet. Where's Manolo?

MONCHI: He went to see Atabey.

MARIA: You can't hear anything, the chickens or coquis . . .

MONCHI: We're pretty high up.

MARIA: I do hear a waterfall.

MONCHI: First time here and Atabey took you in. She knows you're special. (*Maria closes her eyes and concentrates on the waterfall.*) I felt the same way you felt . . . although I first came here as a kid, 'this' didn't happen until I came with Manolo—the second time—I was never the same after that.

MARIA: In what way?

MONCHI: Stronger . . . Less afraid.

MARIA: I also feel strong . . . I feel whole.

MONCHI: After that experience I knew I could start a farm. I never looked back.

MARIA: And you did it . . . But . . . what if you're hit by a hurricane?

MONCHI: I have nothing to worry about if they're from the East.

MARIA: Why?

MONCHI: El Yunque protects me.

MARIA: How?

MONCHI: She won't let the hurricane pass. She uses her body to shield the rest of the island from danger.

MARIA: What if the hurricane comes from the West?

MONCHI : I'm screwed . . . (*They laugh.*) Those things are inevitable; mosquitos, storms, the government . . . the food will grow again . . . I'm going to miss you, even though I didn't get to know you that well.

MARIA: Me too . . . you were very kind to me. Thanks for the use of the Volki.

MONCHI: My pleasure. Thank you for helping me on the farm.

MARIA: I had a great time and I learned alot.

MONCHI: Good . . . I have to be honest, I don't want you to leave.

MARIA: Monchi I can't promise you anything.

MONCHI: You're still in love with that guy, right?

MARIA: . . . No . . .

MONCHI: That didn't sound like a No.

MARIA: It's definitely a NO. He loved someone else that looked like me, seemed like me, but she wasn't me. I feel like I wasted all this . . . I don't know . . . all this love from my heart, and now my heart is dead.

MONCHI: Where there is death there was life. (*PAUSE. Monchi kisses Maria very gently on the lips. He pulls away from her and then kisses her again. They continue kissing as Manolo walks in dripping wet from his swim—his communion with Atabey.*)

MANOLO: ¡Qúe lindo!

(*Monchi and Maria quickly separate.*)

MANOLO: Mira, Atabey will bless the both of you.

MARIA: Manolo are you alright?

MANOLO: Of course, I saw my love. She forgave me for not seeing her for many years. And she accepted my niece with love.

MONCHI: Manolo, put your clothes on.

MANOLO: Ay no! I feel younger than I've ever been . . . Atabey set my spirit free. I can go home a free man. (*PAUSE. Manolo hears the coqui song.*)

MANOLO: Do you hear anything Maria?

MARIA: Not a thing . . . I feel an amazing sense of inner peace.

MANOLO: Just listen Maria, listen. (*They all seem to meditate and sink in the calm of the Yunque as lights fade.*)

END OF SCENE 5

Scene 6

Later that evening. Maria's suitcases are packed in the kitchen.

NORMA: Where is Maria? Look how late it is!

(*Maria and Manolo enter the marquesina.*)

NORMA: Where the hell have you been?

MANOLO: We went to see the antecedents.

NORMA: I know that. Look at the time. Do you know what time it is, Maria?

MARIA: I don't know, maybe um . . .

NORMA: It's 6:45. (*Maria does NOT react.*) Weren't you supposed to be on a flight going to New York City at 6:00 P.M.?

MARIA: Oh my God, I totally forgot.

NORMA: You forgot?! Or you didn't care.

MANOLO: We both forgot.

MARIA: Tía, I swear, the day went by so quickly, we lost track of time.

NORMA: We've been waiting for you all day . . . I even packed your bags for you, and you decided to stay all day in a cemetery.

MARIA: That's not what happened.

MANOLO: We went to receive Atabey's blessing for Maria.

NORMA: AH, ¿a dónde?

MANOLO: We went to her altar, en El Yunque.

NORMA: El Yunque?! Are you crazy taking him there? Do you know how sick he is?

MARIA: He's cured.

NORMA: He could get pneumonia.

MARIA: He doesn't belong locked up. Look what happened to him when he came out of his room, fresh air, sunshine . . . he came back to life.

MANOLO: I'm like the Phoenix, I rose out of the ashes.

NORMA: That Phoenix didn't fill his belly with alcohol and that Phoenix didn't spend five years in a bed. You went to El Yunque because you wanted to go Maria.

MANOLO: I wanted to go to El Yunque and give my niece a gift before she left Puerto Rico.

NORMA: It's this girl here . . . (*To Maria.*) You don't follow rules, you expect a chauffeur, you put on music, you leave a mess everywhere, you take Manolo out of his room and drag him to Rincón and El Yunque. You get everything you want . . . You're just like your mother. She wanted to leave Puerto Rico, she left . . . I know what you're up to . . . You want to get a job here so that you can keep an eye on the house for Olga, before she comes here and takes it.

MARIA: If mami wanted the house she would be here already.

NORMA: Why does she want pictures of the house?

MARIA: She wants the pictures to see the house, Puerto Rico . . . that's all. To see Puerto Rico. She misses it very much.

NORMA: If she misses Puerto Rico so much, why doesn't she move back home?!

MARIA: You just said you didn't want her here.

NORMA: . . . I mean . . . I wanted to take care of my mother's tomb, but Olga prefers a stranger to do that.

MANOLO: I don't know why you don't accept mami's wishes. Thank you for ruining a beautiful day. (*Manolo storms into his rooms in the marquesina.*)

NORMA: Get out of here!

(*Iris enters.*)

IRIS: Mami we should finish the pasteles.

NORMA: Don't tell me what we should do . . . When are you off to New York City?

IRIS: I'm not moving to New York.

NORMA: I thought you were going there to get a teaching job.

IRIS: It was just talk. And I don't want to live in a strange country.

NORMA: Just go to New York with your cousin and enjoy yourself. Don't bother with the pasteles. I don't need your help.

IRIS: Fine.

(*Iris exits. Norma is left alone then Victor enters.*)

NORMA: Victor.

VICTOR: Has it been that bad?

NORMA: What?

VICTOR: Your life. You make it seem like your life is so horrible . . . That means I'm horrible because you share your life with me, I'm ALSO your family.

NORMA: I never said that.

VICTOR: You should hear yourself. You're always complaining about being stuck with the family and everybody else getting what they want . . . I'm sorry you didn't become a singer or go to New York, BUT so what if we stayed behind . . . we have a beautiful daughter and a beautiful home. We've had a pretty good healthy life. You complain about what you don't have, BUT you're so blind to what you do have . . .

(*Norma doesn't respond.*) Look around you Norma, you have love . . . Everyone in this house loves you very much. And you won't take their love because you feel the world has been terrible to you. If you don't accept people's love, one day they're going to stop giving it.

(*PAUSE. Victor exits. Lights fade as Norma starts to cry at the table.*)

END OF SCENE 6

Scene 7

Later that evening. Manolo and Maria are in front of his room in the marquesina. They are listening to the coquies.

MANOLO: It's a beautiful night, like the calm after the storm.

MARIA: The coquies are singing very pretty tonight. (*The coqui song is heard. Manolo is the only one who hears it. He hums along.*)

MARIA: But I still don't hear the song.

MANOLO: You will.

MARIA: I'll be in cold New York City soon . . . I feel ready to go back . . . Can't say my vacation wasn't interesting.

MANOLO: I'm going to miss you.

MARIA: Me too . . . I have something to show you . . . Look . . . (*Maria shows Manolo a shoebox full of grass.*)

MARIA: I got my box of grass for the Three Kings and their camels.

MANOLO: Very nice. (*He inspects it.*) Put it in front of my room. The three kings never miss it.

(*Maria does so and finds Manolo's güiro.*)

MARIA: Look what I found . . . (*She shows Manolo the güiro.*) My only regret is that I didn't experience a parranda.

MANOLO: ¡Ah parrandas! . . . They were great. Mami was a great cook. Everyone came to our house for mami's pernil, arroz con gandules, pasteles, and your mother, she made the best arroz con dulce.

MARIA: She still does.

MANOLO: Hmmm . . . and of course everyone wanted to hear me play the güiro and Norma sing. She sang Bombas like no one else could . . . she sang aguinaldos, coplas, boleros . . . The whole pueblo stayed at our house all night . . ."Que no, que no, que no me voy de aquí hasta por la mañana . . ." "I will not go until the morning." It sounds better in Spanish. (*Iris enters carrying a bag of pasteles.*)

IRIS: I thought Mami was here . . . (*Iris begins to exit.*)

MARIA: Iris, can I talk to you for a second? Yes, there is, alot more. I didn't come here to hurt anybody nor to be hurt . . . I've been taught to hate myself for not knowing who I am because I grew up in the United States, and you've been taught to feel complete, to feel better than me because you grew up on the island—well I don't buy that argument anymore, I'm changing it. The way I see it you're either part of the problem or you're part of the solution. There are many things that separate us and there are many more that unite us. If you're choosing the one that separates us then you're part of the problem. I'm choosing the one that unites us . . . if you ever come to New York, whether it's to visit or look for a job, whatever, I'll give you a place to stay. (*Iris hesitates to speak.*)

IRIS: . . . WE are family, and that is very important to me, even with the fights . . . Blood is thicker than . . . than . . . geography. You shouldn't go to New York angry about a fight that's about neither here nor there. And you know, even though you're a Gringa, you're still Puerto Rican.

MANOLO: How are the pasteles doing?

IRIS: I finished wrapping them.

MANOLO: I would really love some of those great pasteles.

MARIA: Me too.

IRIS: But mami said we're selling them.

MANOLO: We have to try them out first . . .

IRIS: They were actually pretty fun to make.

MARIA: I love pasteles. Every Christmas mami makes pasteles. It's my favorite part of Christmas.

IRIS: I hate Christmas.

MARIA: Oh no! Christmas is my favorite time of year.

IRIS: Since Abuela died, Christmas in my house is dead.

MARIA: Let's have a parranda!

IRIS: I don't think so. Especially after what just happened with mami.

MANOLO: Let's do it! (*Manolo grabs the güiro.*) Come on, Maria, sing bombas with me.

MARIA: I don't know any bombas.

MANOLO: Iris does.

IRIS: That was a long time ago.

MANOLO: You love to sing the bombas.

IRIS: ¿Tú estás loco? . . . although I loved the one you used to sing about the lemon.

MANOLO: "Oye lo que te voy a decir." ("*Listen to what I'm going to tell you.*") "Ayer pasé por tu casa; me tiraste un limón; el sumo me dio en los ojos, y el golpe en el corazón." ("*Yesterday I passed by your house; you threw a lemon at me; the juice/zest hit me in my eye and the pain in my heart.*")

IRIS: BOMBA! You're supposed to say that after every verse.

MARIA: Okay, BOMBA.

MANOLO: Louder.

MARIA: BOMBA!

IRIS: You got it. (*Manolo stops playing the güiro.*)

IRIS: What happened?

MARIA: Play something. (*He gets up to hug them both. They stare at him very strangely.*)

MANOLO: My two nieces, you're going to be okay. I am proud to be your uncle.

IRIS: Just one bomba did this to him. I'm afraid to sing another one.

MARIA: Let's go for it. (*Norma appears, but she doesn't interrupt.*)

MANOLO: "Oye lo que te voy a decir . . . Ayer pasé por tu casa; y me ladraron los perros; me doble a cojer una piedra, y se me cagaron los dedos." (*"Yesterday I passed by your house; the dogs barked at me; I bent down to pick up a rock and I got dog poop on my fingers."*)

MARIA AND IRIS: BOMBA!

EVERYONE: BOMBA! (*They laugh. Monchi enters.*)

MONCHI: Buenas noches, felicidades.

EVERYONE: Buenas . . . Monchi . . .

MANOLO: Monchi, come, we're throwing a parranda. Canta una bomba.

IRIS: Ah Monchi doesn't know any.

MONCHI: "Oye lo que te voy a decir . . . En el patio de mi casa, hay una mata de rosa y un letrero que dice el que no besa no goza." (*"In the patio of my house; there is a rose bush and a sign that says—if you don't kiss; you don't have a good time."*)

EVERYONE: BOMBA!

MANOLO: "Oye lo que te voy a decir . . . Decirme que soy viejo, es cosa que *no* me inca, pero todavía tumbo caña y te yerbo cualquier finca . . ." (*"To call me old, doesn't bother me at all, but I can still cut sugar cane and harvest any field/farm . . ."*)

EVERYONE: BOMBA!

NORMA: "Oye lo que te voy a decir . . . Ni por bonita dichosa . . ." (*"Not only for beautiful good fortune . . ."*)

IRIS: Mami . . .

(*They freeze.*)

MARIA: Tía.

NORMA: No, no, quédate . . . Sigan . . . (*PAUSE. She walks over to Manolo and kisses his head.*) "Ni por fea desgraciado . . ." (*"Nor for the ugly breaks in life . . ."*)

NORMA AND MANOLO: "que la suerte de cada qual, Dios se la tiene guardado." (*"that the luck of every one, is reserved by God."*)

MARIA, IRIS: BOMBA!

EVERYONE: "La Bomba hay que rica es, le sube el ritmo por los pies, por los pies, Mulato traiga tu trigueno, por, que baila bomba, bomba puertorriqueno." BOMBA! (*"La Bomba, how wonderful it is, the rhythm rises from your feet, mulatto bring your mulata, to dance the bomba, the Puerto Rican Bomba."*)

MANOLO: Norma, bienvenidos a la parranda de Manolo!

NORMA: Muchas gracias. It's like returning to the family.

MANOLO: Somebody's missing from the parranda.

(*Norma nods yes.*)

NORMA: Verdad, where's Victor? He's not home yet?

MANOLO: Forget about Victor, I'm talking about Olga.

NORMA: . . . Yeah . . . I really do miss her . . . I think about when we used to swim in the quebradilla . . . Olga jumped from the highest rock and dived into the water. I wasn't as brave as Olga . . .

MANOLO: Give her a call.

NORMA: (*Nods yes and caressing Maria's hair.*) Yes . . . You look so much like her . . . and you are just like your mother; Ah Maria . . . I'm sorry to all of you . . . I know I didn't treat you very good.

MARIA: Tía I know I wasn't an easy person either.

NORMA: You belong here with your family in Puerto Rico. And you can stay as long as you want to . . .

MARIA: Gracias. (*Maria and Norma hug.*)

NORMA: Oye play something . . ."Oye lo que te voy a decir. Ayer me dijiste que hoy, hoy me dices que mañana, y mañana me dirás se me quitaron la gana . . ." ("*Yesterday you told me today, today you tell me tomorrow and tomorrow you'll tell me that you are no longer in the mood . . .*")

MANOLO, MARIA AND IRIS: BOMBA!

MANOLO: Maria, your turn. (*Manolo hands Maria the güiro.*)

MARIA: I don't know how.

MANOLO: Come on Maria, play something for me . . . you're ready.

NORMA: Go on Maria, don't be afraid.

MARIA: Okay.

MARIA: (*Maria starts playing the güiro for a couple of beats. Manolo disappears Upstage. Then she hears the coqui song that Manolo only heard.*) Manolo I hear something . . . (*She stops singing the bomba. She hums the coqui song.*)

IRIS: What happened?

MARIA: The coquies. I hear it . . . I hear the song . . .

NORMA: You hear it.

MARIA: Yes.

NORMA: That's good. I hear it too. (*The sound of a truck starting is heard.*)

NORMA: Victor!

IRIS: The truck?!

MARIA: It started.

IRIS: I can't believe that piece of junk is working.

NORMA: Victor said it was going to work. (*The engine sounds real strong. Maria exits.*)

MARIA: Manolo, isn't it great that Victor's truck is working? . . . Let's go outside . . . Manolo . . . Manolo . . . (*Manolo doesn't answer.*) Manolo . . . Are you okay? Tía, . . . Manolo . . . Oh My God . . . tía . . . Manolo come on . . . Manolo wake up . . . TÍA . . . TÍA . . .

(*Maria reenters.*)

NORMA: Maria ¿qué pasó?

MARIA: Manolo . . .

NORMA: Manolo . . . Manolo . . . Ah Dios mío . . . Victor!! (*They all exit.*)

END OF SCENE 7

Scene 8

It is the middle of the night, approaching early morning January Sixth, the Epiphany. Norma is sitting alone in the kitchen. She breaks down touching Manolo's guiro.

NORMA: Manolo . . . I remember when you made your first one . . . I can't believe you just died, you were getting better . . . Oh no . . . I can't do this again. First papi, then mami, now you . . . I don't have anybody left . . . Oh Manolo, I am so sorry for fighting with you . . . What am I going to do without you?! . . . (*She sings the melody of the coquies.*) After all these years . . . tonight we sang together for the first time in so long and you die, coño, . . . I'm afraid . . . I'm afraid of being alone . . . Don't say that . . . I am alone . . . I can't call Olga . . . It's too late she won't listen . . . Manolo I can't . . . (*She takes out the gift that Olga had sent to her and opens it.*) Ah Olga . . . (*She holds up an old photograph of their family.*) Look, she sent an old picture of the family. You were already a teenager here, and I was still a girl, holding your hand . . . um and the house, it doesn't look so bad, strong and solid. Look how Manolo stands, straight and proud . . . Manolo . . . Mama and Papa, their life was so difficult, but they loved each other . . . (*PAUSE. She picks up the phone and dials.*) Hello, Olga, . . . it's Norma. I woke you up, right? I'm sorry I'm calling so late but . . . No . . . no . . . no . . . Maria is okay . . . She's beautiful . . . She's grown up to be a wonderful woman. You did a good job with her . . . No she didn't swim in the quebradilla, it dried up . . . yeah it's only mud . . . It's Manolo, . . . Olga he died tonight . . . (*Norma breaks down.*) I am not sure what happened. He was getting better and then he died, just like that . . . I'm okay . . . Mami was sick for so long and we knew she was going to die, but he was getting better Olga . . . and then that's it, he's gone. No, we're going to have him in the house . . . OF COURSE you can come here . . . you stay in OUR house. I really want you to . . . You do . . . We have alot to talk about, and I'm, I'm sorry Olga for everything. No you don't have to be sorry, . . . okay, okay you're sorry too. You'll come tomorrow. Let me know what time, and we'll pick you up. No, I don't need anything, thanks. You just come here . . . okay . . . and thank you for the photograph, it's beautiful . . . bye . . . oh Olga, I love you. Thanks. Bye.

(*Norma sits at the table for a few beats. Then she goes to Manolo's room to put the güiro in there. She finds Maria humming the coquí song. The coquí song is also heard.*)

MARIA: Tía, I really thought he was getting better.

NORMA: That's what we all wanted. Maria, I called your mother.

MARIA: You did? Is everything okay?

NORMA: Yes . . . she's coming tomorrow.

MARIA: I wish Manolo didn't have to die for her to come, but I'm glad she's coming.

NORMA: Me too . . . but I'm happy she's coming anyway. Just like I am happy that you came here. (*Norma and Maria hug very hard.*)

MARIA: Gracias tía.

NORMA: The things that Manolo knew how to do. (*She stands up and puts the güiro on bed. She also shows Maria the photograph.*) Look, Manolo's birthday. Your mother sent me this picture. Buenas noches.

MARIA: Bendición Tía.

NORMA: Que la Virgen te acompañe. (*Norma exits.*)

MARIA: Oh . . . I know you're here . . . I feel it. (*A light appears on Maria's face and darts all over the room. It is Manolo's spirit. She holds güiro.*)

MARIA: . . . I'm really going to miss you. Thank you for everything . . . for helping me understand. I know by now you probably found Atabey. Heaven is really an interesting place now . . . (*She puts güiro on bed.*) Well good night Manolo. (*Maria exits Manolo's room and closes the door and the light darts out and focuses on a shoe box as she exits out. She almost trips on it. She pulls another güiro out of the box. Maria kisses the güiro. She plays a rhythm on the güiro and sings the coqui song.*) Gracias, Tío.

(*The lights fade slowly as the coqui song gets louder.*)

END OF PLAY

Notes

1. Biographical information provided by the playwright, e-mail to the editors, July 10 and 11, 2007, and additional correspondence on October 24, 2010 and October 26, 2010.

2. Stephanie Goodman, review of *Celia: The Life and Music of Celia Cruz,* by Carmen Rivera, *New York Times,* September 7, 2007, B23.

3. D. J. R. Bruckner, "Theatre in Review: A Bit of the Ridiculous In a Search for Her Roots 'La Gringa' Repertorio Español," *New York Times,* March 7, 1996.

4. Susan Jones and David Richard Jones, study guide for *La Gringa,* www.repertorio.org, accessed August 10, 2007.

CHAPTER 11

Widening the Repertoire

Migdalia Cruz's *Another Part of the House* (1997)

Migdalia Cruz, by permission of the photographer, Diana Solis.

The Playwright/La Dramaturga

Migdalia Cruz was born in the Bronx, New York, November 8, 1958, and was raised there.[1] Her mother was born in Cabo Rojo, Puerto Rico, and her father in San Sebastián, Puerto Rico. She graduated magna cum laude in 1980 with a Bachelor of Fine Arts degree in playwriting from Lake Erie College, Painesville, Ohio, and received her Master of Fine Arts degree in playwriting from Columbia University, New York, in 1984.

Migdalia's theatre experience is vast. Her work has been produced across the United States and abroad at various venues, including Mabou Mines, Classic Stage Company, Playwrights Horizons, INTAR (International Arts Relations) Theatre, Brooklyn Academy of Music, New York Shakespeare Festival's Festival Latino, and Theater for the New City. Regional stages include Latino Chicago Theater Company, Teatro Vista (Chicago), Houston Grand Opera, American Repertory Theater (Cambridge), Cleveland Public Theatre, and Cornerstone Theater Company (Los Angeles), among others. Her work has also been produced internationally at the National Theater of Greece (Athens), Foro Sor Juana Inés de la Cruz/Centro Cultural Helénico (Mexico City), the Old Red Lion (London, England), Vancouver Players (Vancouver, B.C.), Théâtre d'Aujourd hui (Montreal), and the Ateneo Puertorriqueño (P.R.).[2]

Migdalia has been nurtured by Maria Irene Fornes's Playwrights' Laboratory at INTAR, Royal Court Theatre/New Dramatists Exchange 1994 (London), Steppenwolf Theatre's New Plays Lab'96 (Chicago), Bay Area Playwrights' Festival 1994, Festival Latino 1993 at Teatro Misión (San Francisco), the Sundance Institute, Midwest PlayLabs, Mark Taper Forum's New Play Festival, Omaha Magic Theatre, Songs from Coconut Hill Theater Festival 2005, and South Coast Rep's HPP 2004. Her extensive body of written work includes over thirty plays, among them *Salt, Fur, Miriam's Flowers, Lucy Loves Me, Dreams of Home, Telling Tales, ¡CHE-CHE-CHE!, Latins in La-La Land, Cigarettes and Moby-Dick, Lolita de Lares,* and *Running for Blood: No. 3* (a radio play). She wrote book and lyrics for the musicals *Rushing Waters, Welcome Back to Salamanca,* and *When Galaxy Six and the Bronx Collide;* the libretto for an opera, *Street Sense*; and lyrics and monologues for *Frida: The Story of Frida Kahlo.*

Migdalia's plays and monologues have been published widely. She has taught playwriting at the University of Iowa Playwrights Workshop, New York University's Tisch School of the Arts, Princeton University, and Amherst College. She has guest lectured at Yale University, Wesleyan University, Mount Holyoke College, and Columbia University. In addition, her work has been commissioned by Mabou Mines, New York Shakespeare Festival's Public Theater, Crossroads Theatre, Steppenwolf Theatre, Latino Chicago Theater Company, Arena Stage, Playwrights Horizons, WNYC radio, Ballet Hispanico, DUO Theater, and INTAR. Cruz's work has resulted in numerous awards. She received a 1996 Kennedy Center's Fund for New American Plays Award for *Another Part of the House.* Her play *The Have-Little* was the runner-up for the 1991 Susan Smith Blackburn Prize, and *Salt* was a 1997 runner-up. She received a Connecticut Commission on the Arts grant for playwriting in 1994, and a Massachusetts Cultural Council Grant in 2005. At Classic Stage Company, she was a 1994 Pew Charitable Trust/Theatre Communications Group national artist-in-residence. She was a 1997–98 Sackler Fellow at Connecticut Rep/University of Connecticut, a 1991 and 1995 NEA Playwriting Fellow, a 1988 McKnight Fellow, and she is an alumna of New Dramatists.

Most recently, Migdalia's *El Grito del Bronx* was workshopped by Teatro Vista at the Goodman Theatre's Festival Latino (August 2006) and at NYU's hotINK Festival in January 2007. Teatro Vista in Illinois produced *Another Part of the House* (September 2006), Ateneo Puertorriqueño produced *Fur/Pelaje* in April 2007, *Telling Tales* was produced by the Riot Act Theater in Jackson, Wyoming, in May 2007, the Bronx part of *Song for New York: What Women Do While Men Sit Knitting* was produced by Mabou Mines in New York in September 2007, *Fur* was produced by the University of Wyoming at Laramie in October 2007, and Monarch Theater Company in New York produced *Dreams of Home,* also in October 2007. She is currently adapting the Roman text of Petronius's anti-Nero *Satyricon* to George W. Bush's America. The world premiere of *El Grito del Bronx* was held in July 2009 at the Goodman's Owen Theatre.

Migdalia, who has been writing professionally since 1985, continues to expand her current repertoire of more than three dozen plays, screenplays, and librettos. This prolific and productive playwright, whose work is continuously in demand, is arguably one of the most important Latina dramatists working in the United States today.

About the Play/Sobre la Obra

Migdalia Cruz's work completes the repertory provided here, and it is fitting that this final entry illustrates the work that has been done in adapting the classics. Cruz has chosen to rework the legendary *La casa de Bernarda Alba* (*The House of Bernarda Alba*) by Federico García Lorca into a story with the point of view of Maria Josefa, Bernarda's mother, who appears insane but may be suffering from dementia and old age. Locked in her room, she lives in a household of eight women, including her daughter, five granddaughters, and a live-in housekeeper. Maria Josefa, along with her granddaughters, is secretly in love with the mysterious and forbidden Pepe el Romano. She plots with Adela, the youngest of the daughters, to escape the tyranny of the mother, and the results are tragic.

In his review of the play, D. J. R. Bruckner observed that "The ancient Maria Josefa . . . is a devastating force of subversion, exposing the emptiness of her daughter's repressive regime and enticing her granddaughters into shattering sexual fantasies. The jealousies, hatreds and desires these arouse, including a lesbian liaison between two sisters, are palpable, and passionately portrayed."[3] Produced at Classic Stage Company in New York, the play was "praised for its glimpse of a 'desperate world' seething to life in this production, 'enticing us as irresistibly as Pepe el Romano beckons the daughters of Bernarda Alba' in this 'magic-tinged tragedy.'"[4] While the play is powerful, it is Cruz's ability to get at the soul or spirit of the women that makes the play so powerful, evoking sentiments in the vein of *el ánimo del ser humano* (the human soul) that is so often associated with García Lorca's writing. Given the heart-wrenching experiences she has already brought to the stage, it is entirely fitting that Cruz would choose this particular classic of the Spanish repertory in this exploration of the tragedy of these women's lives.

Artistic Vision/Punto de Vista Artístico

ECR & CRC: Briefly describe your theatre experience.

MC: I have written professionally for twenty-two years and lived for forty-eight, so it's difficult to be brief. So, I'll start with the first time I got paid for doing it. My first professional production was in 1985, in an evening of one-acts devised by my teacher and mentor Maria Irene Fornes, called "The Box Plays." Irene asked each of the students in her playwrights' laboratory at INTAR to write a short play that would take place literally in a box. From that moment on, I knew I was a playwright.

When I came to know myself to be a storyteller, came much earlier. At the age of six, I wrote my first puppet show—a political satire about the Ku Klux Klan (made of facial tissues) and Black people (made of Spaulding rubber balls). The balls bounced back and the tissues burned.

It was my first morality play—very medieval. Then, at the age of eight, my best friend was raped and murdered and thrown off the roof of our building. I wrote a story about it, an essay or collection of feelings, a kind of diary entry that would help me express my emotions and record the events. That is when my real writer's voice appeared for the first time, I think. It was in Irene's workshop that I revisited this piece of writing and it became a monologue called "Sand," which is included in the play *Telling Tales* and led to the play *The Have-Little*.

I studied with Maria Irene Fornes as a member of INTAR's Hispanic-Playwrights-in-Residence Laboratory from 1984 to 1989, and in 1991. This was the place where I learned to listen to my own voice, develop it, and to always tell the truth. I decided to become a playwright when I met Irene Fornes and she terrorized and inspired me to tell the truth about who I was and where I came from because it was a story that needed to be told as I could tell it. She helped me to believe not only in my work, but also, and more importantly, in my history. After two degrees in playwriting, I still did not know who I was or who I could be. Then I studied with Irene Fornes and finally became Migdalia.

ECR & CRC: How did you decide to write and/or perform?

MC: As I said earlier, I wrote my first play—a puppet show about civil rights—when I was six years old and I think I wrote it because as a Puerto Rican girl growing up in the South Bronx during the violent and heartbreaking times of the civil rights movement in America, I felt I needed to show that I knew about current events so that things would change rather than repeat. Somehow I knew that the key for me to understanding the tumult of those times was by making these little shows. No one came to see them. They were in my living room, performed mainly for my father, but in my mind, the message was out in the air as soon as a puppet spoke it—through me, of course. Perhaps it made it easier for me to understand what was happening all around me and how "good" people could win one day. "Good" people mainly win in fairy tales, so I invented my own. It was a way for me to cope with the violence I grew up with all around me, in my neighborhood, my school, and my country. And which country was that? Where exactly was home? Not Puerto Rico. Not the United States. The Country of the Bronx was my territory. The only place I can truly call home.

ECR & CRC: Why do you write what you do?

MC: Because it is what I know. Or perhaps what I imagine I know. For each play, the inspiration has been different. Mostly, I smell my characters first. Then I see them. Then they begin to speak. For *Another Part of the House* I smelled Florida Water cologne. The grandmother, Maria Josefa, slathered it on—her daughter, Bernarda, hated the smell, while Maria Josefa thought it was an aphrodisiac. So I smelled her first and then I could enter her world. She was the first one who came to me. Bernarda smelled of camphor.

I wrote *Another Part of the House* when I was given a commission from Classic Stage Company to adapt a classic. I then remembered that ten years earlier a director I had worked with on one of my earliest plays, *Telling Tales*, told me that I should adapt Federico García Lorca's *La casa de Bernarda Alba* because my characters seemed spiritually connected with García Lorca's—whose obsessions were similar to mine—about sexual repression and desire, search for freedom and for country, longing for acceptance and understanding, messed up by Catholicism and the inherent heterosexual patriarchy of Spain and Latin America. So I thought about it. I read this masterpiece and surprisingly, I did, with all due humility and respect, find parallels and finally, I found a way to make the characters my own. That's when I could smell them. I also thought about writing the secrets I felt he could not have written from the inside of a woman's character. I felt my play could be an echo of his, a response to his call. That was when I felt I could proceed and write my own version using his structure as my sturdy and well-formed skeleton without disgracing his work or mine.

ECR & CRC: Who do you write for and what audience are you trying to reach?

MC: I write to peel my own skin. My ideal audience is connected to its own emotions so it can have a visceral reaction to my work. With *Another Part of the House,* I suspected I would be able to reach a wider audience, the kind that would more easily follow a classically structured journey as compared to my usual nonlinear, emotionally structured work. But I also hoped that once I got that audience there with the promise of a genteel evening in the theater, that I would be able to grab their jugulars and have them like it. And ask for more.

Production History/Palabras Dramatúrgicas

The final draft of *Another Part of the House* was completed on February 27, 1997, and was copyrighted by the author in 1997. The play was commissioned by Classic Stage Company through the Pew Charitable Trust/Theatre Communications Group National-Artist-in-Residency Program. It was a winner of the 1996 Kennedy Center's Fund for New American Plays. The World Premiere production opened on March 4, 1997, and closed April 6, 1997, at Classic Stage Company, 136 East 13th Street, New York, NY 10003.

Artistic director: David Esbjornson
Executive director: Mary Esbjornson
Directed by David Esbjornson
Dramaturg: Morgan Jenness
Set design: Chris Müller
Costumes: Michael Krass
Lighting: Kenneth Posner
Sound: John Kilgore
Production stage manager: Amy Patricia Stern
General manager: Jason Loewith
Casting director: Judy Dennis

Featuring the following Actors' Equity cast, in alphabetical order:

Doris DiFarnecio as Poncia
Sara Erde as Adela
Kadina Halliday as Magdalena
Mercedes Herrero as Angustias
Seth Kanor as Pepe El Romano

Paula Pizzi as Martirio
Irma St. Paule as Maria Josefa
Adriana Sevan as Amelia
Patricia Triana as Bernarda

Subsequent productions: Vancouver Players (Vancouver, B.C.), Sonoma State University (Calif.), Ohio University, University of North Texas, Teatro Vista (Chicago).

Midwest premiere: Teatro Vista in Chicago, opened September 2006, under the artistic direction of Edwin Torres, direction of Cecilie Keenan, and featuring (in alphabetical order): Charin Alvarez, Rachel Cerda, Laura Crotte, Ilana Faust, Adrian Gonzalez, Sandra Marquez, Lily Mojekwu, Julia Neary, Tanya Saracho, and Juan F. Villa.

Contact Information

 For performance rights or for the rights to reproduce this play in any form please contact Ms. Peregrine Whittlesey, Peregrine Whittlesey Agency, 279 Central Park West (CPW), New York, NY 10024, 212-787-1802, pwwagy@aol.com.

ANOTHER PART OF THE HOUSE

Inspired by *La casa de Bernarda Alba* by Federico García Lorca

> Do you hear the silence? Well, there's a storm brewing in every room.
> The day it bursts, we'll all be swept away!
> —Poncia from *La casa de Bernarda Alba*

Selections from Lorca's *The Maiden, The Mariner, and the Student,* and also *The Romancero Gitano* and *Poema del Cante Jondo* poetry collections are used in this play.

* * *

For David & Morgan & Peregrine . . .

* * *

The Names in Bernarda Alba and their traditional meanings:

ADELA—"noble" or "of noble rank and good cheer"
AMELIA—"industrious or laboring one"
ANGUSTIAS—"anguished one"
MAGDALENA—"elevated, magnificent, a tower"
MARTIRIO—"martyred one"
BERNARDA—"brave as a bear" or "warrior"
PEPE—"the supplanter"

MARIA—"bitter or bitterness" / JOSEFA—"he shall add, the increaser." This person will add to their learning by experience . . .
PONCIA—"the bridge"

* * *

Cast of Characters

MARIA JOSEFA—BERNARDA's mother, 80. The lively one.
BERNARDA ALBA—MARIA JOSEFA's daughter, 60. The oppressive one.
PONCIA—An Afro-Cuban maid of 50, more than a servant to BERNARDA.
ADELA—MARIA JOSEFA's youngest granddaughter, 20. The hopeful one.
AMELIA—MARIA JOSEFA's granddaughter, 27. The frightened, caring one.
ANGUSTIAS—MARIA JOSEFA's oldest granddaughter, a half-sister to all the other daughters of BERNARDA, 39. The sickly one.
MAGDALENA—MARIA JOSEFA's granddaughter, 30. The political and pious one. Realistic and pessimistic.
MARTIRIO—MARIA JOSEFA's other granddaughter, 24. The martyred one.
PEPE EL ROMANO—A lamb who is mistaken for a handsome young man of 24. The shameless one.

Time

A morning in February, an afternoon in April, and a night in June 1895.

Place

A modest farmhouse and corral in a small town, Santa Clara, in the province of Las Villas, in Cuba. The inside walls are white and thick, the rooms airless and still, except in MARIA JOSEFA's bedroom, where a window is always open and there is sometimes a breeze. The exterior is the color of sunburned wheat. It is dry and hot.

Note: Everyone dresses in black, except for MARIA JOSEFA, who wears white. Born in 1898, García Lorca completed *La casa de Bernarda Alba* in June of 1936. In August of 1936, he was assassinated by Franco's Falangist Civil Guard, never having seen his play produced.

ACT ONE

One morning, just before dawn.
In the darkness, we hear the sound of bells tolling and women crying.

THE VOICE OF BERNARDA ALBA: (*An urgent, hissing whisper; to herself*) I silence myself . . . only Jesus weeps before God.
THE VOICE OF MARIA JOSEFA: Wicked! More than wicked!
THE VOICE OF PONCIA: A tongue like a knife!

(*At the church, we see the daughters of BERNARDA ALBA leading a funeral procession by Don Antonio's coffin. As the DAUGHTERS enter holding candles, they kneel.*)

BERNARDA: ¡Alabado sea Dios! (*Blessed be God!*)

THE DAUGHTERS: Sea por siempre bendito y alabado. (*Forever blessed and holy.*)

BERNARDA: ¡Descansa en paz con la santa compaña de cabecera! (*Rest in peace, with the souls of the departed watching over you.*)

THE DAUGHTERS: ¡Alabado sea Dios! (*Blessed be God!*)

BERNARDA: Con el ángel San Miguel y su espada justiciera. (*With Saint Michael the Archangel and his sword of justice.*)

THE DAUGHTERS: ¡Descansa en paz! (*Rest in peace!*)

BERNARDA: Con la llave que todo lo abre y la mano que todo lo cierra. (*With the key that opens all and the hand that closes all.*)

THE DAUGHTERS: ¡Descansa en paz! (*Rest in peace!*)

BERNARDA: Con los bienaventurados y las lucecitas del campo. (*With the blessed saints and the little lights of the fields.*)

THE DAUGHTERS: ¡Descansa en paz! (*Rest in peace!*)

BERNARDA: Con nuestra santa caridad y las almas de tierra y mar. (*With our holy charity and the souls of the earth and the sea.*)

THE DAUGHTERS: ¡Descansa en paz! (*Rest in peace!*)

BERNARDA: Concede el reposo a tu siervo Antonio María Benavides y dale la corona de tu santa gloria. (*Grant repose to your servant Antonio María Benavides and give him the crown of your sacred glory.*)

ALL: Amén.

BERNARDA: Requiem aeternam donat eis domine.

ALL: Et luz perpetua luce ab eis.

(*AMELIA is holding up MAGDALENA, who is near fainting and is wailing about the death of her father, Don Antonio.*)

MAGDALENA: Why did he have to die, Amelia?! Why not her?! He's the only one who ever loved us.

AMELIA: Sssh, sssh, ssh, Magdalena. We can't question God. It was his time, his time for rest. And freedom. Sssh, sssh, ssh. You still have me. (*We hear the sound of the crashing sea and seagulls, but only MAGDALENA hears them. MAGDALENA screams, then faints.*)

(*To her other sisters*) Help me!

BERNARDA ALBA: (*Entering and rushing forward to AMELIA & MAGDALENA*) Magdalena! Behave yourself! Everyone is watching us. Fainting is vulgar—for guajiros. In good families, fainting is only allowed in your heart. (*To AMELIA.*) Keep her quiet, Amelia.

AMELIA: Yes, Mother.

MAGDALENA: (*Fearfully; to AMELIA who continues to comfort her*) Didn't you hear them?! The seagulls calling . . . when they come to the mountains, it means something . . .

(*ADELA, MARTIRIO, and ANGUSTIAS watch PEPE EL ROMANO who strums a guitar with no strings, but the sound we hear is of a Bach cantata on guitar. Lights up dimly on MARIA JOSEFA dancing to the cantata—we see only her flowing white gown, not her face. MARTIRIO follows ADELA closely and pokes her when she sees that ADELA is watching PEPE EL ROMANO.*)

ADELA: What?!

MARTIRIO: What? Your eyes are what . . . and who you look at with them and what you think when you do. I know what you think when you do, Adela.

ADELA: You're the one who always watches me, Martirio. Don't you have better things to do? I didn't chase your little boyfriend away. You scared him off yourself. Poor Martirio . . . Always standing by the window waiting for him to return to you . . . We'll have blood fall instead of rain before that will ever happen.

(*MARTIRIO slaps ADELA, who moves away from her. ANGUSTIAS comes up to MARTIRIO.*)

ANGUSTIAS: Pepe's beautiful, isn't he?

MARTIRIO: They all seem beautiful—once you've buried one . . . or one buries you.

ANGUSTIAS: You're too pretty to be so bitter.

MARTIRIO: And you're too ugly to be my sister.

(*ANGUSTIAS walks quickly away from MARTIRIO.*)

BERNARDA ALBA: (*Hissing*) Sssh! All this chatter at a funeral is too much.

(*Lights cross to the dining room, where PONCIA, who is crying quietly, chops the head off a small, finch-sized bird on the banquet table for Don Antonio's post-funeral reception.*)

PONCIA: (*Singing to herself; comforting herself*)

"Little birds make sweeter soups, when set free from little coops.
And pounded well into a sauce, thickened by tears and lovers' loss."

(*The lights cross to MARIA JOSEFA, a once elegant woman of 80, who is picking one of the two locks on her bedroom door. She is dressed for a wedding: A flowing white dress, beautiful jewelry. Flowers in her hair. She speaks to PEPE the SHEEP, who is resting beside her. PEPE is also decorated with a wreath of flowers.*)

MARIA JOSEFA: Don't worry, my love. We'll be out soon. Out on the edge of the sea. We will marry there because by the sea there's nothing to keep us from our love. No horrible daughter or trembling maids to run from. Just my love and the waves to envelop us, comfort us by following our rhythms. So much comfort.

PONCIA: Good-bye, Evaristo. Such a mess, but all your parts, all mixed together, will be luscious. I wonder why we only eat this well at funerals? Weddings aren't nearly so appetizing.

MARIA JOSEFA: (*Rattling the door in frustration and shouting through it.*) Bernarda!

PONCIA: (*Speaking conspiratorially to the bird she's just killed.*) She's a crafty one. Could have been a locksmith—if women were allowed such work. Her fingers work a bolt from the inside out. From the inside out, she can open any door. That's why I change the locks every few days. It keeps us both busy. Listen . . . (*We hear the* *sound of MARIA JOSEFA's bedroom door rattling and being pounded more aggressively.*) See what I mean? That sound's as familiar as a death rattle caught in an old man's throat.

MARIA JOSEFA: (*She gives up on the door and sits beside the lamb.*) She is not a comfort. My daughter is a tumor. A boil. A sore that is growing over this house. I have medicine for it though. Don't you worry. It won't get us, Pepe. We have the falling night—that's our time. (*PEPE moves to her lap and begins to suckle from her breast.*) Oh, Pepe, that's just what I needed—my breasts get so full for you. They say I have no milk in these dried-up old things, but they don't know because they never tasted my dryness. In eighty years, my nipples have only grown harder and smoother—like young boys watching horses mate—up and with full attention. Sucking is its own lullaby. (*PEPE makes love to her and as she reaches climax she shouts.*) Release me! Release me! Release me! Release me!

PONCIA: She can call all she wants, but no one in this house listens. Except me. I enjoy the sound of her despair. It reminds me of myself. (*Pouring blood from the bird into a pitcher of water on the banquet table.*) Mmmm! This will be delicious added to the sugar cane water. And the sores it will heal . . . What do you think, little bird? Hard to think with no head, I suppose . . . And even harder to keep things cool in this place, but the sugar water always stays cool. I wonder why? Maybe it just doesn't stay around long enough. Sweet things disappear here.

MARIA JOSEFA: (*From inside her room*) Release me, Poncia! You know how to do it.

PONCIA: It's your daughter who wants you dead, Doña Maria—not me. But she's too good a Christian to steal your breath.

MARIA JOSEFA: (*From inside her room*) Such a nice man, Don Antonio was. I don't know why he ever married her. It's like marrying a sharp stone that cuts when you caress it. But you know of his caresses, don't you, Poncia? La Poncia, the faithful slave. I have a clear view of the corral from my window . . . and I hear *all* the animals inside . . .

PONCIA: You're never getting out of that room, Doña Maria, so what does it matter what you hear?!

MARIA JOSEFA: (*From inside her room*) You disappeared a few years back . . . Where'd you go, Poncia? I missed you so. Gone almost a year. She beats me more when you're not around.

PONCIA: I take your blows for you. Isn't that enough to buy your silence? Maybe if you were quieter, she'd let you out now and then. Wouldn't you like that?

MARIA JOSEFA: Bernarda!! Bernarda!!

PONCIA: She can't hear you.

MARIA JOSEFA: Lucky for you, Poncia, that I believe in love, so I would never give you away. Yes . . . pure, physical love, like the creatures of the sea have. Sometimes I think it's shame that keeps me in this room. How could I have given birth to such a monster? I should have had her in the ocean and given her to those sea creatures. Would they have made a meal out of her or made her their queen? Then the sea would have the smell of stillness . . . Is your child still alive, Poncia? Maybe you should drown it. But dark, little babies don't drown as well as white ones, do they? They know how to survive.

PONCIA: (*Making the sign of the cross*) Yes, we do.

MARIA JOSEFA: (*Singing in the same sort of sing-songy tune as PONCIA's little bird song*)

> "Virgin white, coffee brown, or the blackest midnight blue?
> What color baby did La Poncia give birth to?"

With Don Antonio's Creole white and your mother's African brown—anything could appear . . .

PONCIA: Why am I everyone's dog in this house?

(*Lights cross to BERNARDA at the threshold to the house.*)

BERNARDA: (*To herself*) A moment alone. To breathe. Everyone watches me. Wants something from me. But I can't hear them. Not today. Today words have no meaning.

(*MARTIRIO enters behind her.*)

BERNARDA & MARTIRIO: No one understands sadness better than I.

(*BERNARDA freezes as MARTIRIO continues.*)

MARTIRIO: But no one cares what I feel. My feelings are the pounding lead of the Sun's heat. I feel a fever in my heart.

(*ANGUSTIAS enters behind her.*)

MARTIRIO & ANGUSTIAS: It's never been hotter.

(*MARTIRIO freezes as ANGUSTIAS continues.*)

ANGUSTIAS: But Pepe brings a breeze with him. His sweat is like honey, stronger even than the scent of death. Don Antonio shouldn't have been left in the Sun for so long.

(*ADELA enters behind her.*)

ANGUSTIAS & ADELA: A smile was melted onto his face. (*ANGUSTIAS freezes as ADELA continues.*)

ADELA: I never saw my father smile like that before. A full, swollen smile. He must have held his breath when he saw Saint Michael coming for him. Took all the air in the village with him.

(*AMELIA enters, still supporting MAGDALENA.*)

ADELA & MAGDALENA: I can't breathe.

(*ADELA freezes.*)

AMELIA: Once we're alone, you'll feel better.

MAGDALENA: Somehow, I doubt that.

(*Lights come up on the Alba family entering the house, BERNARDA, followed by MARTIRIO, ANGUSTIAS, ADELA, and finally AMELIA, holding a fainted MAGDALENA.*)

BERNARDA: Can't you keep some silence in this house, Poncia!? I could hear my mother squawking from the church steps. Get some water for Magdalena.

AMELIA: The poor thing! I would be afraid to faint, I think, in front of all those people.

BERNARDA: All those people will have nothing bad to say about us. Magdalena just loved her father more than most. There's nothing wrong with that.

(*PONCIA gives MAGDALENA some water. She revives but begins to cry.*)

AMELIA: Sssh, Magdalena. Sssh. You should get some rest.

BERNARDA: Stop crying or I'll chain you under your bed until you stop.

MAGDALENA: I don't care if you do! Why should I care? Papi was the only one who cared about me.

ANGUSTIAS: I loved him too. Perhaps not as much as Magdalena—he was my stepfather after all. But still I shed a tear for him even though I really didn't have to. And it made me sick to be in that church with his body like that.

BERNARDA: Like what?

ANGUSTIAS: Dead and exposed. It's not good for me to see such things. The doctors said I must be careful—especially if I want children—

BERNARDA: Children?! There'll be no talk of children until we hear of a wedding. It's just the heat that makes you ill. The Sun is like lead today. My clothes are heavy with it. (*To ADELA.*) Get me a fan, Adela. Before I faint too.

ANGUSTIAS: I hurt my wrist using that fan of grandma's. She must have arms like a bull.

BERNARDA: (*Striking ANGUSTIAS with her cane*) Don't talk about your grandmother like that. (*ADELA enters holding a cardboard fan decorated with red and green flowers and hands it to BERNARDA who hurls it to the floor.*) What kind of fan is that for a widow!? Those cheap church fans are not for people like us. Show some respect for your father and get me a black one. Don't you girls know anything?

ADELA: I'm sorry, Mami. I'll find you another one.

MARTIRIO: (*Handing BERNARDA her black fan*) Here. I don't need it. It's not so hot to me.

BERNARDA: You'll have to find another one soon because it will just keep getting hotter here.

ANGUSTIAS: I can lend you one of mine, Martirio. I have two because this is the second father I lost and—

BERNARDA: Angustias, please! Please! All of you, just listen. For once, my daughters, be quiet and listen. The coming years will not be easy, but they are necessary. We must maintain our dignity and our—(*Pause; as we hear MARIA JOSEFA laughing from behind her door.*) Following the tradition of my father and his father before him, we'll have eight years of mourning in this house. (*The DAUGHTERS react with stunned gasps and exclamations. BERNARDA silences them by rapping the floor with her cane.*) ENOUGH! Also, the windows and doors must be shut tightly so that the sins of the primitive world do not enter—(*pause; as we hear MARIA JOSEFA rattling the locks on her door*)—and pollute the purity of our mourning. Remember that there is important work for you to do in that time: You will busy yourselves sewing your trousseaux. Remember we are descended from the Alba family of Andalucia where young women of your station still follow tradition. We are nothing without it. God bless us all. (*With a rap of her cane, she summons PONCIA.*) Poncia, help me sort out Don Antonio's clothes, God rest his soul. I told Padre Francisco I would bring them to the church tonight. So many people need things. Oh—but just his old things, mind you. All the men left in this town couldn't wear my husband's finery—it would just spoil them. Poor people look ridiculous in good clothes. We'll burn all his newer things.

(*BERNARDA exits and PONCIA follows her. There is a moment of stunned silence.*)

MAGDALENA: This isn't possible . . .

AMELIA: Yes! How could she burn father's clothes?!

MAGDALENA: Father's clothes?! Who cares about that?! Eight years, Amelia?!

MARTIRIO: What is she so afraid of?

ADELA: We're to be prisoners in our own home!

ANGUSTIAS: The longer a woman wears mourning black, the smaller the chances of her loved one coming back.

MARTIRIO: Keep quiet, Angustias! Do you ever have thoughts of your own or do you only repeat simple countryfolk sayings?!

ANGUSTIAS: But there's truth to it, I think. That's why Mother's so afraid. I'm not afraid of that. I'd wear the brightest colors so he'd be sure to find me.

MAGDALENA: It's a curse to be a woman in a place like this.

ADELA: Like a spell made from a dried-up old tree.

MARTIRIO: What does it matter, sisters?! This spell's already been broken. Angustias was chatting with Pepe El Romano at the funeral.

ANGUSTIAS: No, I wasn't.

ADELA: I saw you too, Angustias.

ANGUSTIAS: What's the harm in a chat? A little conversation on a very sad day.

AMELIA: Yes. What's the difference? He's nothing special. She was watching all the men at the funeral.

BERNARDA: (*From offstage*) SILENCE! You demons! In church, one looks at no man but the priest, and at him only because he wears skirts! They're demons, Poncia.

(*PONCIA enters.*)

PONCIA: There will be no more talk of men in this house today! Do you understand?! Go to your rooms, all of you! And leave your mother in peace.

(*BERNARDA and PONCIA's shouting makes everyone fall silent. MAGDALENA goes to her room as MARTIRIO, AMELIA and ANGUSTIAS follow, but ADELA sneaks out the front door. PONCIA returns to BERNARDA's bedroom.*)

PONCIA: You were a little harsh, don't you think?

BERNARDA: Don't tell me what I was. You serve me. You don't lecture me.

PONCIA: Of course. Forgive me. (*An awkward silence.*) Did you hear about Paca la Roseta? Some men tied her husband to a tree so they could have their way with her.

BERNARDA: Why would I care about that at a time like this!?

PONCIA: I thought you would like knowing that your prediction came true—she went with them willingly too, the whore. You were right about her, Bernarda. A common slut.

BERNARDA: Yes. I'm not surprised. And please don't forget the "Doña."

PONCIA: Yes, Doña Bernarda.

(*Lights cross to ANGUSTIAS, MAGDALENA, AMELIA, & MARTIRIO listening at BERNARDA's bedroom door.*)

MARTIRIO: That Paca La Roseta wasn't content with just one man. I wonder how many there were . . .

MAGDALENA: At least she made a strong choice. She saw what she wanted and had it.

ANGUSTIAS: Followed her desires . . .

AMELIA: You see what could happen! How disgusting! They used her. Why would any woman want that?! (*MAGDALENA, MARTIRIO, & ANGUSTIAS look at AMELIA.*) I mean, that way. So savage. I'd rather be alone than be an animal.

MARTIRIO: It's much safer, but so boring.

ANGUSTIAS: I agree. I want to taste something before I leave this earth.

MAGDALENA: And when will that be, Angustias? By the time we get out of this house, we'll probably have lost our sense of taste.

AMELIA: Oh, that doesn't happen, Lena. Some of the best cooks are quite old. (*Her sisters stare at her in disbelief.*) Well, aren't they?

(*Lights cross back to BERNARDA & PONCIA.*)

BERNARDA ALBA: I'll have to let Padre Francisco know about Paca. That's the only solution to such sinning—public exposure. Everybody goes to church. (*PONCIA and BERNARDA smile as co-conspirators do.*) Except for your mother, of course. That black, thieving whore never dared step foot in one. That's why I found you—

PONCIA: Outside the church doors. I know the story, Doña Bernarda.

BERNARDA: You were a lovely child. You looked a lot like me—only darker. I thought it was like the story of the baby Moses found in the rushes by the Pharaoh's sister. I could take you into my house and you could live a decent life.

PONCIA: Yes. I feel just like the baby Moses some days.

BERNARDA: Such modesty, Poncia. I meant *I* was like the Pharaoh's sister.

PONCIA: I know what you meant.

BERNARDA: I've always kept your secret, haven't I?

PONCIA: Yes. And I *all* of yours.

(*Lights cross back to ANGUSTIAS, MAGDALENA, AMELIA, & MARTIRIO still listening at BERNARDA's bedroom door.*)

MARTIRIO: I think La Poncia has more secrets than she's willing to reveal.

What would it take, I wonder, to make her talk . . .

AMELIA: She's a wounded bird. Anyone can see that.

MARTIRIO: Can they? Are you an expert on birds, Amelia?

AMELIA: No. And I don't need to be to tell when they're in pain, Martirio.

MARTIRIO: Tweet-tweet. Do you feel sorry for all animals or just birds?

MAGDALENA: Quiet! Do you want Poncia to come out and interrogate us, good little soldier that she is?!

ANGUSTIAS: I wonder what sort of secrets mother could have? I can't imagine . . .

MAGDALENA: Whatever they are—I'm sure they're not as interesting as Paca's. Let's go to our rooms and wait for the Sun to come *all* the way up before we have any more intellectual conversations, sisters. That would be a very good thing.

(*The lights cross to MARIA JOSEFA crawling to her bedroom door, attempting to pry the hinges off the door with her teeth.*)

MARIA JOSEFA: A black cloth gets pulled over my face on days like today and I can't see through it. This cloth reminds me how alone I am. No one can get inside here with me—in my head. Bernarda pretends to—but she can't, not at all. I erase a little bit of it each day, so that even if she does figure out how to break in here—she won't find it all out. She won't be able to. It'll be gone. She'll only ever have a small piece of my story. There's no one to trust.

(*Lights cross to ADELA, in the courtyard outside MARIA JOSEFA's window, pulling wild flowers out of the ground and stomping on them. MARIA JOSEFA moves to watch ADELA from her bedroom window, and calls down to her.*)

MARIA JOSEFA: You are not much of a gardener, Adela.

ADELA: You remember my name!

MARIA JOSEFA: Of course. It never changed, did it?

ADELA: No, but mother said you couldn't remember anything anymore. That's why—

MARIA JOSEFA: She keeps me a prisoner? How old are you now? Twenty?

ADELA: Yes. Exactly. Today's my—

MARIA JOSEFA: Old enough to know that your mother lies.

ADELA: She's keeping us all prisoners now. For eight years! I won't stay shut-up here for that long.

MARIA JOSEFA: Leave then. I would, if I was you.

ADELA: I don't know where to go.

MARIA JOSEFA: Oh . . . I could show you, if you help me escape.

ADELA: But how?

MARIA JOSEFA: Some rope. A ladder. A stack of chairs. Many pillows piled high beneath my window. Something I can get down with—or on—or through. Something I can use to escape this place. Aren't you a thief?

ADELA: No, grandma. I'm just Adela.

MARIA JOSEFA: I know. But you have the eyes of a thief. Those eyes are quick to envy. They burn green. Green is your fire, little one. I know that color. My eyes were green once too.

ADELA: I don't understand you. Were you always like this?

MARIA JOSEFA: I'm smarter now than I used to be. Used to be I trusted your mother. No more. She's just a common jailer. But you know that already, don't you?

ADELA: I don't know what I know.

MARIA JOSEFA: (*Gesturing ADELA closer*) Ah hah! You're a beauty . . . You look equally good in daylight as in moonlight. That's rare in a woman, I think. So much exactly who you are. So much like me.

ADELA: You don't know anything about me.

MARIA JOSEFA: Don't I? I'm old but not deaf. I hear everything from up here. From up here, I can hear the flowers thinking. "When will it rain again? When will I bloom?" They talk all the time. I used to be able to lie down among them and hear the most glorious things. Flowers know how to make good conversation. I heard them screaming when you were killing them.

ADELA: I didn't mean to kill them. We don't deserve to have beautiful things near this house. They're happier now, sent back to the earth.

MARIA JOSEFA: Perhaps. That's an attractive thought—back to the earth. Starting again. I think about that all the time now . . .

ADELA: Starting new . . . Oh, Abuela, I like this! Talking to you like this. Me outside and you inside. It feels delicious. But I don't know why.

MARIA JOSEFA: It's forbidden. Such things are always the most delicious. Have you met my husband?

ADELA: Grandpa died many—

MARIA JOSEFA: My fiancé I mean. We're to be married in the spring, because that's his birthday. He's sentimental that way. I'm a February child myself. Is that why you're here? To wish me a happy birthday?

ADELA: Is it your birthday too? Happy birthday, Grandma.

MARIA JOSEFA: Everyone forgets. I've had so many birthdays. And they always make me cry. I don't know why. I know that once I began to cry on my birthday, it seemed the most natural thing. Like breathing—except it comes in gasps. That's after many years of birthdays, of course.

ADELA: It's mine too.

MARIA JOSEFA: Is it really?! Are you in love also?

ADELA: No. Not yet.

MARIA JOSEFA: You better hurry. Looks fade fast. I mean, I'm one of the lucky ones. I still have a spark, but most others are not so fortunate.

ADELA: Now, I have to wait eight years.

MARIA JOSEFA: Oh, my dear! You could be dead by then—I mean inside. If you don't get your juices stirred up soon, they'll turn to dust. So you never . . .

ADELA: (*Shocked*) No, Abuela! What are you saying?!

MARIA JOSEFA: I'm saying a little poke would be good for you. It always served me well in hard times.

ADELA: Even when you weren't even married?

MARIA JOSEFA: Marriage is about money. But sex is about nature. Can't control that.

ADELA: What about love?

MARIA JOSEFA: Ah!! That's about hope. Isn't that right, Pepe?

ADELA: Pepe? Is someone there with you?

MARIA JOSEFA: Just a lamb. This old girl gets cold at night and needs a warm animal lying beside her. You should try it. But it would be so much better if we could do it on the beach. I can't think about the beach too much—it makes me cry.

ADELA: Don't be sad. I'll try to help you.

MARIA JOSEFA: Find the keys, Adela. Find them and steal them and set me free. What a nice gift that would be . . .

ADELA: Poncia sleeps with those keys in her panties.

MARIA JOSEFA: Hmmm . . . That could make them hard to get. Unless you grew very close to her. Maybe you can grow close to her and slowly work up to taking the keys. It could work. It's never been tried before, I'm sure. Who would want to go through her pantaloons? Not me—but you, you're young. You can do anything.

ADELA: Yes, Grandma. I have a gift for you.

MARIA JOSEFA: It's not another black shawl, is it?? I mean they are all lovely, but I have about twelve of them now and it's not so cold since I'm in the house almost all the time and—

ADELA: It's a—a song.

MARIA JOSEFA: Oh.

ADELA: (*She sings Lorca's "Zorongo Gitano" [Gypsy Zorongo].*)
"Las manos de mi cariño te están bordando una capa
con agremán de alhelies y con esclavinas de agua.
Cuando fuiste novio mío por la primavera blanca,
los cascos de tu caballo cuatro sollozos de plata.
La luna es un pozo chico, las flores no valen nada;
lo que valen son tus brazos cuando de noche me abrazas."
[*The hands of my beloved are embroidering you a cape,*
edged with wall flowers and bangles of water.
When you were my sweetheart in the white spring,
the hooves of your horse were four sobs of silver.
The moon is a small well, flowers are worth nothing;
what are worthwhile are your arms when they hold me at night.]

MARIA JOSEFA: That's so true, child. But what do you know about lovers' arms around you?

Come back when you've learned something.

(*MARIA JOSEFA retreats from the window and sits on the floor facing PEPE the SHEEP.*)

ADELA: Grandma? Grandma! (*Lights go down on MARIA JOSEFA.*) No one ever wants to hear my songs . . . I think I was born at the wrong time. I should have been born at a time when love poems flourished—like abuela. I think abuela understands about love. Maybe she's the reason I should stay here . . . (*Playfully*) I'm falling in love with you, Grandma. Can you hear me? We do have the same eyes . . .

(*The sound of a Bach cantata pulls ADELA away from her grandmother's window and to the stable. ADELA sees the shadow of PEPE EL ROMANO. He turns and beckons to her. She moves to join him, slowly stripping off bits of her mourning clothes as she does so.*)

(*Lights cross to MAGDALENA & AMELIA in their bedroom. There is an altar to José Martí in their bedroom which is MAGDALENA's. His pamphlets and manifestos are stacked up and tied with ribbons. MAGDALENA is counting her money which she pulls out of a pile of loose pamphlets; AMELIA is sorting her jewelry according to its value.*)

MAGDALENA: I've got two hundred. How about you?

AMELIA: These pearls are worth about fifty and those earrings abuela gave me must be worth about the same.

MAGDALENA: That's all?

AMELIA: Yes.

MAGDALENA: That won't take us very far.

AMELIA: No. But it's nice to know we have a little something in case of an emergency.

MAGDALENA: This *is* an emergency, Amelia! She's trying to suffocate us.

AMELIA: It's not that bad. Only eight years. What can happen in eight years?

MAGDALENA: Everything. The world is changing. We could get jobs. We could work in the fields, side-by-side with men from other places.

AMELIA: I thought you didn't like men.

MAGDALENA: I like their jobs though. Their wages. It's all going to pass us by, Amelia. There's still much work to be done before Cuba is her own country. If we could save enough money, we could even go fight with the forces in Oriente. Then we could meet . . . him.

AMELIA: Him?

MAGDALENA: Martí. They say he's coming soon to lead us. I can feel him getting closer. I can feel it in my fingertips. Sometimes I wake up in a fever and I know he's held my hand. He's the only one who can lead us.

AMELIA: To where? The brothels?!

MAGDALENA: Don't be ridiculous!

AMELIA: What else do men think we're good for? Anyway, we could never travel that far unchaperoned.

MAGDALENA: It's only the other side of the island, Amelia. Maybe he'll even take us to New York. That's where he does all his best writing—right in the face of the monster.

AMELIA: But New York, Lena?! Why would anyone want to go there? They have no churches—not decent ones. Streets filled with people filled with desires. And they live like sheep—black and white—all so close—the houses all so close, they can hear each other breathe. I don't want other people's breath on me like that.

MAGDALENA: You don't want anything that's fun.

AMELIA: That's not true. I want to be like you. You're fun.

MAGDALENA: Yes. I'm a riot. I should just go anyway. Even if I have to go alone.

AMELIA: Don't say that. It scares me.

MAGDALENA: Maybe you should fall in love, Amelia. I'm just your sister. One of several. Can't you attach yourself to one of them? They're all much nicer than I am.

AMELIA: That's true. But it's you who I love—the most I mean. You saved me from the river that time—

MAGDALENA: Yes, well. I didn't know I would have to keep saving you. (*AMELIA looks hurt.*) Oh, come on. Those looks won't work on me anymore. When are you going to start thinking about what's truly important? What's sacred? (*Quoting Martí's "Poetry Is Sacred"*) "A poem is something sacred. Let no one take it for anything except itself. Let no one force it to his will, as slaves are forced with tear-filled eyes—"

AMELIA: He also wrote, (*quoting Martí's "Simple Lyrics"*) "She gave the forgetful one a fragrant pillow; he came back married; she died of love." Without you, Lena, I would die.

MAGDALENA: Don't.

AMELIA: Did Martí say who would watch over you? Who'd keep you warm at night? Is that discussed in one of your books?! You wouldn't know what to do without me.

MAGDALENA: Maybe not. But I'd like to find that out for myself.

AMELIA: You don't mean that. You know we need each other. I'll go anywhere you want. But we just have to agree on a place.

MAGDALENA: What if, by some miracle, I want something that you don't?

AMELIA: That wouldn't happen. We're blessed with each other.

MAGDALENA: Blessed?! I think there's a curse on us. Some witch turned our feet to lead and sits by the sea laughing at us. I can hear her cackle in the morning. It sounds like seagulls calling. "Here we are at the sea," they say, "here we are and here you aren't."

AMELIA: You exaggerate too much, Lena. Anyway, the world is bound to last more than eight years. There's a lot we can learn by ourselves in this house.

MAGDALENA: Like what? Like who we want to be when we grow up? Who in this house do you want to be like? Our crazy mother or our crazier still grandmother?

(*Long pause, as AMELIA truly considers this.*)

AMELIA: So, there's no one to be like. It's the same in all families.

MAGDALENA: All families don't wear black all the time and keep the windows tightly closed. Our family is special.

AMELIA: Traditional.

MAGDALENA: Mad. But I guess it could be worse. I could be in love.

AMELIA: What a thought! You?

MAGDALENA: It's not impossible.

AMELIA: I know, but it's not feasible. Not for you—or for me. We took a vow.

MAGDALENA: Yes, but that was a long time ago.

AMELIA: Have your feelings changed?

MAGDALENA: No.

AMELIA: Change scares me.

MAGDALENA: Everything scares you. Come here. (*AMELIA goes to her and they hug each other.*) Martí has the soul of a woman. His books—his words. They're soft yet strong. Every bone in his face points to his soul. (*Stroking AMELIA's face.*) Just like your face, Amelia . . . that's why I love him so much. (*Continuing to caress AMELIA.*) It would be so much nicer to do this somewhere else.

AMELIA: (*Unbuttoning MAGDALENA's top to reveal one of her breasts*) Do you think there's a breeze outside? I bet there's a breeze. (*As lights fade, AMELIA moves her lips gently across MAGDALENA's nipple and then rests her head gently on her breast, as MAGDALENA closes her eyes and sighs.*)

(*Lights cross to ANGUSTIAS & MARTIRIO's bedroom. ANGUSTIAS powders her face and speaks to her reflection in a mirror, as we hear Lorca's "La Tarara" in the background, sung by men working in the field outside her window.*)

MALE VOICES: (*Offstage*)

"Tiene me Tarara un vestido verde lleno de volantes que el aire los mueve.
La Tarara sí, la Tarara no, la Tarara, niña de mi corazón."
[*My Tarara has a green dress covered with frills that are blown by the air.*
Tarara yes, Tarara no, Tarara, girl of my heart.]

ANGUSTIAS: I know I'm not the prettiest woman . . . but powder helps. Powder makes the sunlight more forgiving. I can have skin as white as the moon now. Any man would be seduced by that moon. (*Pause; MARTIRIO enters quietly and watches her.*) I'll speak to him only at night. Then he'll see my true self—with no sisterly distractions. There are far too many of them. But there's only one, Angustias. I used to hate my name, because I thought it meant I had to suffer. But now I can choose my own anguish. The money came just in time.

MARTIRIO: It's ironic, isn't it? That my father had to die, so that you could get your father's money. Strange.

ANGUSTIAS: Don Antonio guarded my dowry very well. I never expected he would do less, Martirio. He was a noble man.

MARTIRIO: I wasn't accusing you of anything.

ANGUSTIAS: Anyway, you don't need it like I do.

MARTIRIO: What do you mean?

ANGUSTIAS: I mean, I must leave this house as soon as possible. It's beginning to fall in on me like a house of cards. Have you noticed the new cracks in the walls? They are all pointing toward that portrait of me in the dining room. It means something. I think it's a sign from God.

MARTIRIO: You're not serious?

ANGUSTIAS: Perfectly.

MARTIRIO: Well, if that's what you want. If you think a man will help you get out of this mess, then God bless you. I hope you find him. Even with a dowry, men are getting harder and harder to find.

ANGUSTIAS: I think I found him, Martirio.

MARTIRIO: Angustias! What do you mean? You found somebody at my father's funeral?! That's incredible and probably immoral.

ANGUSTIAS: Pepe El Romano is both. I think I'm in love!

MARTIRIO: He's too handsome for you. He'll just leave you. A plain man is what you need.

ANGUSTIAS: I'll decide what I need, thank you.

MARTIRIO: I hope you can. Some of us are blinded—by beauty.

(*We hear the Harvesters sing again. MARTIRIO, then ANGUSTIAS slowly move to watch the MEN from the window. In another part of the house, at another window, MAGDALENA & AMELIA also move to listen to the MEN.*)

MALE VOICES:

"Ay, Tarara loca mueve la cintura para los muchachos de las aceitunas.
La Tarara sí, la Tarara no, la Tarara, niña de mi corazón."
[*Oh, crazy Tarara moves her waist for the boys who pick olives.
Tarara yes, Tarara no, Tarara, girl of my heart.*]

MARTIRIO: (*Singing, with the male voices faintly in the background like they are moving away from the house.*)

"No llores Tarara ni tú tengas pena—
[*Don't cry Tarara, and don't be sad—*]

ANGUSTIAS: (*Singing*)

—que tú irás al cielo por santa y por buena.
[*—for you'll go to heaven for being good and a saint.*]

MARTIRIO & ANGUSTIAS:

La Tarara sí, la Tarara no, la Tarara, niña de mi corazón."
[*Tarara yes, Tarara no, Tarara, girl of my heart.*]

AMELIA: Workers are always so happy.

MAGDALENA: Are they?

(*Lights cross to BERNARDA kneeling in front of a photograph of Don Antonio.*)

BERNARDA: I've been hoping all morning for a word alone with you, Antonio. (*Long pause.*) And the truly sad thing is that I have nothing to say.

(*Lights cross to MARIA JOSEFA tying a piece of her bedsheet around PEPE and the other end to the doorknob.*)

MARIA JOSEFA: Depression is not the best emotion to have when you need to escape. It gets in the way. Look at Anne Boleyn. Very depressive. But with three tits I'd be depressed too. Although you'd love that, wouldn't you, Pepe? If I had three. But so unbalanced. Ready? One, and two, and three! (*MARIA JOSEFA slaps PEPE on his back and PEPE tears off, breaking the door open.*) Everything just takes time, Pepe. And the right kind of tools. (*She goes running out into the living room where BERNARDA, PONCIA, and ANGUSTIAS sit. PONCIA jumps up and tries to restrain her.*)

BERNARDA: (*Lashing out at PONCIA with her cane*) Didn't you lock her in?

PONCIA: She must have broken the door!

BERNARDA: Can't you do anything right?! You people are like animals!

(*PONCIA begins to drag MARIA JOSEFA back to her room. ADELA, AMELIA, MARTIRIO & MAGDALENA enter, watching in amazement as their grandmother speaks.*)

MARIA JOSEFA: I want to get away from here! Bernarda! To get married at the edge of the sea, at the edge of the sea! Don't you understand that I'm not meant to be dry like you. I need a man. And I don't kill mine off like you do.

BERNARDA: Be quiet, Mother!

MARIA JOSEFA: No more men with any money in this town—not that anyone would marry you anyway. He'd find no pleasure with you—that's for certain. But me, ah, that's different. I know how to hold a man. It's like this. (*She grabs PONCIA in a passionate embrace.*) And then you say to him—

PONCIA: Help me, Doña Bernarda!

BERNARDA: Mother, you must stop this!

MARIA JOSEFA: You say, "I love you sweetness. Every bit of you. If I could make a meal of you, I would."

PONCIA: Oh, dear God! Let go of me!

MARIA JOSEFA: "I would start with your ears—firm, hard meat. A lot to chew on. Then your eyes so I could see inside your heart. Slowly I would feast on each gentle fold. Slowly, I would let my lips meet yours in a kiss of gardenias in the moonlight."

(*As she is about to kiss PONCIA, MARIA JOSEFA sees PEPE the SHEEP walk through the room, past the women. They all are aware of the presence of something, but only MARIA JOSEFA, ADELA & BERNARDA can see him. MARIA JOSEFA and ADELA are mesmerized. BERNARDA is terrified. The door opens as if the wind blew it open and PEPE disappears through it. MARIA JOSEFA sighs, as the lights fade on them.*)

End of ACT ONE

ACT TWO

Two months later.

An afternoon.

The lights come up on the adjoining bedrooms of AMELIA, MAGDALENA, MARTIRIO & ANGUSTIAS. They are busy embroidering their initials into the bedsheets they have just finished hemming. ANGUSTIAS has too much powder on her face. She looks almost like a clown.

MARTIRIO: I don't know why we continue to do this. No one in this house will ever marry.

AMELIA: But look at Angustias. She's finally engaged.

MAGDALENA: To that wicked Pepe El Romano. I don't know why mother allows it. And so soon after father's funeral. It's disgusting.

ANGUSTIAS: Because she loves me. And he was so sweet when he asked her—mother didn't even tap her cane once. She just nodded and said "When?" Anyway, I'm the oldest, so I have to get married first. Pepe is so handsome, isn't he?

MARTIRIO: Stop saying that! You're becoming an echo.

MAGDALENA: All men look alike to me.

AMELIA: Me too. They scare me. I hope I never get married.

MARTIRIO: You don't have to worry about that.

ANGUSTIAS: Why are you always so unpleasant? Maybe a man would do you some good. It's given me a taste for heaven. I'm very lucky to have Pepe.

(*The lights cross to MARIA JOSEFA dancing a danzón with PEPE.*)

MARIA JOSEFA: Who taught you how to dance, Pepe? Your feet are like lead. Lift. Lift. That's it. Make your body a fine piece of white lace. Let your breath flow through the holes in that lace like a butterfly taking its first bright breath. That's more like it. Yes.

(*ADELA, who wears an emerald green dress, enters in a rush, through MARIA JOSEFA's window.*)

ADELA: (*Rushing to grab MARIA JOSEFA and hug her tightly*) You make me so happy.

(*ADELA begins to cry.*)

MARIA JOSEFA: Oh my dear! That's more like delirious. Why are you crying?

ADELA: I just—feel so different now.

MARIA JOSEFA: So it finally happened. (*An aside.*) No wonder Pepe wanted to learn how to dance.

ADELA: Does it show? I know I should be ashamed, but instead it's like I have an ocean swimming inside me. So full.

MARIA JOSEFA: Tell me everything. How did it start?

ADELA: I was brushing the horses and he came to me and asked if he could help, so I gave him a brush. And he began to brush *my* hair as I brushed the horses.

MARIA JOSEFA: Is that it?

ADELA: Yes. The first time. Then after that he touched every part of me.

MARIA JOSEFA: How many times have there been?

ADELA: Almost every day—for the past three weeks.

MARIA JOSEFA: And in the corral too. That's a good place for it. Hay is very exciting. Was he gentle?

ADELA: Not exactly. He stomped and whinnied—just like the horses. I thought he would rip me in half at first. But I wanted to be torn like that—with him inside me.

MARIA JOSEFA: Sounds good. So what's wrong?

ADELA: He asked Angustias to marry him.

MARIA JOSEFA: You can't let guilt separate you from your heart. Families of women are always like this. We all lust for each other's man, it's a natural result of years of repression. Endure the lust. It's our nature.

ADELA: I think I'm beginning to understand nature now.

MARIA JOSEFA: Nature lasts longer than sisters. (*Pause.*) Of course, *you* could almost be my sister . . . we're so much alike. Maybe you should call me Maria Josefa. It's more dignified. I never think of myself as a grandmother.

ADELA: Yes, Maria Josefa. My dearest sister. Can you teach me to be like you? I want to meet this man's passions.

MARIA JOSEFA: Do you love this man more than you love your own family?

ADELA: I think I do.

MARIA JOSEFA: Think? You must be sure. There's so much to lose.

ADELA: I don't know what you mean.

MARIA JOSEFA: I mean, you're going to have to leave this house and not ever come back.

ADELA: I don't want to go without you.

MARIA JOSEFA: Then we'll have to make a plan, Adela. You and me. We could get out of this house. And someone could actually have some love in this family. I've waited all my life to see that.

ADELA: Mother said you tried to kill yourself once.

MARIA JOSEFA: Liar! I tried it twice. Almost got to the bottom of the well that one time. But that's something for old ladies to know—not beautiful young girls. You have to stop thinking about me. It'll drive you crazy. It does me.

ADELA: Do you think I'm crazy, Abuela?

MARIA JOSEFA: Well . . . no. Not enough to worry about anyway.

ADELA: But I have all these feelings I'm not supposed to have. And I let these things happen.

MARIA JOSEFA: Things have to happen, child. That's the nature of—things. I once did what you're doing, and I was never the same after that. No matter how many people I was surrounded by, I was alone. You have to be ready . . . Women who follow their nature are always alone.

ADELA: Is that why you never got married again? I'm sure you had a lot of suitors.

MARIA JOSEFA: Once, yes. And every now and then I see a man, and I don't know what comes over me . . . That man who sells lace was here today. He had such a lovely head of hair. That's all I saw of him, of course, from up here. But still such a nice view . . . Oh, the ideas it gave me, child. I got La Poncia to buy a full roll of his lace. That much lace could reach from the earth to the sky. Can you imagine the beauty of that? (*Pause.*) With that lace, I could take any man I wanted, wrap him up and drag him out into the sugar cane and make a sweet tooth with him.

ADELA: I have a sweet tooth too now. So does Pepe.

MARIA JOSEFA: Oh, I know. But when it starts to hurt, don't look at your own reflection, especially in deep water.

(*Lights cross back to the sewing circle.*)

MARTIRIO: So where's our Adela this afternoon? She usually goes out at night.

MAGDALENA: Oh, I saw her go out to the barn to show off the dress I made her.

AMELIA: You made her a dress?? But—but who's there to see it?

MAGDALENA: The chickens. (*The SISTERS laugh.*) Yes. You can laugh but it really disturbed me. She put on that beautiful green dress which I helped her embroider and said, "Magdalena, I'm going to show all my friends what a wonderful sister I have." And out the door she went and then I heard her calling, "Chickens! Come out and see my new dress! Here, chickens!" That girl is really acting strangely these days . . .

AMELIA: Oh, but she's always been like that. She always got along with the animals better than with us. I can almost understand it.

MARTIRIO: Can you?

AMELIA: Yes. I mean, the animals are so gentle. They don't shout at you or judge you. And as long as you feed them, they always love you. There's something beautiful about that, I think.

MARTIRIO: You're as pathetic as she is.

AMELIA: It's not pathetic to be romantic. To have hope.

MAGDALENA: Yes, Martirio. You should try it. Maybe you'd be happier.

ANGUSTIAS: Will you help me put my wedding lace on my sheets, Magdalena? You're the best at it.

MAGDALENA: Of course. I don't have anything else to do, do I?

ANGUSTIAS: Don't be like this, sisters. Wish me well. For once in your lives, wish me well. I can't help it that I was born first. But once I'm out of the house, then the rest of you are free to find your—

MARTIRIO: Thank you, Angustias. You are a saint who is saving us all. I don't know why I didn't see it before.

MAGDALENA: Maybe talking to chickens isn't so bad, after all.

MARTIRIO: What do you mean?

ANGUSTIAS: Yes, what *do* you mean?

MAGDALENA: I mean, my sisters are an unpleasant and disagreeable bunch. I wouldn't talk to you either, if I didn't have to.

MARTIRIO: And you're such a ray of sunshine, is that it?

MAGDALENA: Compared to you—yes.

(*MARTIRIO jumps on MAGDALENA pummeling her with her fists. MAGDALENA easily restrains her.*)

AMELIA: Careful with the needles!

MAGDALENA: (*Shoving MARTIRIO onto the floor*) You're pitiful, Martirio.

ANGUSTIAS: Calm down, both of you! You'll ruin my bedsheets.

(*MAGDALENA & MARTIRIO both jump on ANGUSTIAS, ripping one of her bedsheets.*)

AMELIA: We were almost done with that one too!

(*PONCIA enters and pulls the girls apart.*)

PONCIA: Stop it! You're behaving like wild beasts. Oh, dear, it's only been two months. I can just imagine how you'll be in eight years.

(*ANGUSTIAS is crying over her torn bedsheet, fingering the ripped embroidery.*)

ANGUSTIAS: And the "A" was almost done.

MAGDALENA: I'm sorry, Angustias.

MARTIRIO: Me, too.

AMELIA: If mother sees this ruined sheet, she'll kill us.

PONCIA: She won't. I'll pick up another at the market today. So, is someone going to tell me what happened? (*No response.*) That's alright. I bet I can guess. Everyone is just anxious about Angustias' engagement. The first one to leave always breaks everyone's heart.

ANGUSTIAS: Were you married once, Poncia?

PONCIA: No. But I was in love.

MARTIRIO: When was that? You never leave this house.

PONCIA: I left it enough to meet him.

AMELIA: Why didn't you marry him?

PONCIA: He died before—we could get married, even though he proposed.

ANGUSTIAS: How did he do it? I only ask because Pepe was so shy.

MAGDALENA: He's never struck me as the shy type.

MARTIRIO: Me neither.

ANGUSTIAS: Well, he is. He could barely get it out of his mouth—he was so nervous.

MARTIRIO: What did he say?

ANGUSTIAS: He said, "Isn't it time—for you to be married?" And I said, "Yes."

AMELIA: That doesn't sound very romantic.

ANGUSTIAS: It was to me. He was holding his stomach, and stuttering, and shifting from one foot to another. He was so . . .

MARTIRIO: Nauseated?

ANGUSTIAS: Anxious. Was it the same for you, Poncia?

PONCIA: Not exactly. My man was . . . forceful in his proposal.

MARTIRIO: I don't believe you. You would have gone a long time ago if that were true.

PONCIA: You don't know everything about me, Martirio. I'm not so easy to hear behind closed doors.

MARTIRIO: I don't know what you mean.

MAGDALENA: Never mind her, Poncia. Tell us about your proposal.

ANGUSTIAS: Yes! What did he say?

PONCIA: He didn't "say" anything. He just grabbed me and—

ANGUSTIAS, MAGDALENA & AMELIA: And what??

PONCIA: —he took me on a graveled mountain road . . . my virgin's blood staining those painful little stones pink.

MARTIRIO: That's disgusting!

MAGDALENA: How liberating! And no one found out?

PONCIA: No. Not until today.

AMELIA: Which stones are those? Are they the ones to the right of the church? By the well?

(*PONCIA nods "Yes"; all the girls except MARTIRIO gasp a little.*)

MARTIRIO: This is quite a story . . . too bad your man is dead so we can't get his side.

PONCIA: You don't need to ask him a thing. I still have the marks on my back to prove it. When I hear gravel crunching beneath my feet, I think of him.

(*The girls laugh.*)

ANGUSTIAS: So he proposed right then and there?

PONCIA: No, first he kissed the blood off the hem of my dress, then he took me over to the church steps and we stood there and he pledged his love to me forever.

(*ANGUSTIAS & AMELIA sigh romantically.*)

MAGDALENA: Why didn't you go to the priest?

PONCIA: Because he was already promised to someone else. It was going to take time for us to be together. So he sent me gifts instead.

MARTIRIO: What kind of gifts?

PONCIA: Birds. Young bright finches. They have such a sweet song. He sent me thirty of them over the years . . . The first twenty-nine were female. Then he sent me this little son-of-a-bitch. When any female laid an egg, he would peck her to death.

MAGDALENA: Jealousy's an ugly thing.

MARTIRIO: Why didn't you separate them?

PONCIA: I believe in the nature of things. And this seemed to me the way of finches. Anyway, each dead bird reminded me that I couldn't be with him. I couldn't mourn our love so I had funerals—for the birds. One day, I took that evil bird to my kitchen and chopped off his head. And made a nice broth with his blood. He was tasty.

MARTIRIO: You're making this up.

PONCIA: No. Those broths are good for healing wounds. Your grandmother taught me all about that.

ANGUSTIAS: How did your lover die?

PONCIA: I don't like to remember . . . but that was the day I killed Evaristo. That was the bird's name.

AMELIA: What a good name for a bird! Evaristo . . .

MARTIRIO: You would know.

AMELIA: Yes, I would, Martirio. There are some things I do know something about.

MARTIRIO: ¡Brava!

MAGDALENA: Don't you dare—

PONCIA: Come on, Angustias. Let's wash your face.

MARTIRIO: Yes. All your powder's come off. I'll help too. You're so complex, Poncia. I never would have guessed.

(*PONCIA shoots a disapproving look at MARTIRIO, then smiles at ANGUSTIAS and leads her out of the room with MARTIRIO following closely behind.*)

(*MAGDALENA & AMELIA look at each other and smile.*)

AMELIA: Did you finish it?

MAGDALENA: Yes. It's been hiding under the bed this whole time. (*MAGDALENA pulls out a puppet theater she built from pieces of the corral.*)

AMELIA: It's beautiful! It looks just like the corral.

MAGDALENA: It's supposed to. I'm amazed Poncia didn't find it.

AMELIA: Look! (*She pulls out two puppets she has made from pieces of their trousseaux bedsheets.*) And I can use these fancy pieces of Angustias' sheet to make a curtain for the stage. These are better than any trousseau. Mother would hate us, if she knew.

MAGDALENA: She hates us anyway.

AMELIA: I don't care anymore. Let's start.

(*As they prepare their theater, a light also comes up on BERNARDA, kneeling in front of Don Antonio's photo. BERNARDA has her head in her hands and is still searching for words. Lights fade on her and come up on MAGDALENA & AMELIA. they step behind the puppet theater, lighting candles as footlights for the tiny stage. There is a piece of white lace as a backdrop for the puppets, painted like a tropical paradise scene—palm trees, ocean, etc. AMELIA & MAGDALENA's heads show over the top of the theater. They perform parts from Lorca's* The Maiden, the Mariner, and the Student.)

MAGDALENA & AMELIA: (*Simultaneously*) Leave me to my embroidery.

AMELIA: That's my part.

MAGDALENA: Oh. You're the maiden?

AMELIA: Yes, of course. I have the sweeter voice. You play the mariner.

MAGDALENA: Alright then. Go ahead.

AMELIA: (*In her Maiden's voice*) Leave me to my embroidery. My pillowcases do not have my initials on them and this makes me very afraid. What girl in the world doesn't have her clothes marked?

MAGDALENA: (*In her Mariner's voice*) What is your name?

AMELIA: I embroider my clothes with all the letters of the alphabet, so that the man who will be with me may call me anything he wishes.

MAGDALENA: Then you are a shameless creature . . . Perfect for a man at sea.

AMELIA: Yes. A or B or C or D. Just what man will stay with me? Mariner begins with "M," Student with "S"—So what letter will make me confess?

MAGDALENA: (*In her Mariner's voice; with another puppet.*) I.

AMELIA: You?

MAGDALENA: A boat is such a paltry thing without you there to make it beautiful.

AMELIA: I'll fill it with embroidered lace—if my mother allows me.

MAGDALENA: Stand up so that I can see you.

AMELIA: Here I am.

MAGDALENA: What beautiful thighs you have.

AMELIA: I've ridden a bicycle ever since I was a child.

MAGDALENA: And I a dolphin.

AMELIA: You, too, are beautiful.

MAGDALENA: When I'm naked. (*AMELIA kisses MAGDALENA passionately, as the puppets also kiss. MAGDALENA pulls away as AMELIA begins to undo her shirt.*) It's too hot for that.

AMELIA: But it was nice wasn't it? When I kissed you. Let's do that part again.

MAGDALENA: No. It's not—in the script.

AMELIA: I know.

MAGDALENA: We shouldn't keep doing this.

AMELIA: I don't want to stop. (*She picks up her puppet and starts a different puppet show.*) I worship you. I adore you.

MAGDALENA: (*Picking up her puppet and playing along*) Please, don't.

AMELIA: Let me walk across the sea with you, Mariner. Braid your hair into mine.

MAGDALENA: My hair's not as long as yours.

AMELIA: That doesn't matter. We'll grow together. Weave ourselves into one.

MAGDALENA: I want my own hair, and my own life, Amelia. (*Dropping the puppet.*) Please don't do this.

AMELIA: (*Dropping her puppet*) You lied. You said it was forever. We didn't say it on the church steps but it was like we did.

MAGDALENA: Aren't we closed in enough without being chained to each other? (*AMELIA runs out crying.*) You're crying because it's the truth. People fall in love because they're bored. And they need to be swallowed up by someone else so they can forget themselves. I don't want to stop remembering. That's when you start talking to the chickens . . .

(*MAGDALENA puts away the theater and the puppets.*)

(*Lights cross to ADELA, wearing a beautiful, emerald green dress, in the barn talking to the chickens.*)

ADELA: Hello, my friends! Don't you love this dress? Green is my color. "Verde que te quiero verde." Abuela was right. I have to be careful how I dress now. He doesn't like me in black. "The mother of my children will never wear black," he told me. Do you think he'll like this dress? I want to wear only beautiful things for him. He got engaged only so he could come to the house and see me. Poor Angustias. She doesn't know who he really loves. Poncia thought it was my time of the month, but I bled from love with him.

(*As she twirls around showing off the dress, we hear a voice-over of PEPE reciting Lorca's poem "Romance Sonámbulo" in English, as he enters playing the guitar.*)

PEPE EL ROMANO: (*Voice-over*)

["Green, how I love you green. Green wind. Green branches.
The horse on the mountain. and the ship on the sea—
With their shadows on her waist, she dreams on her balcony.
Green flesh, hair of green, her eyes a cold silver stare.
Green, how I love you green.
Under the gypsy moon—all eyes gaze at her there
but they cannot be seen."]

ADELA: (*Singing*)

"Verde que te quiero verde. Verde Viento. Verde ramas.
El barco sobre la mar y el caballo en la montaña.
Con la sombra en la cintura ella sueña en su baranda,
verde carne, pelo verde, con ojos de fría plata.
Verde que te quiero verde. Bajo la luna gitana, las cosas la están mirando
y ella no puede mirarlas."

(*AMELIA enters, her eyes still full of tears.*)

AMELIA: Why are you always in here?! Don't you have other places to go in this house?

ADELA: This isn't the house—that's why I like it. What do you care?

AMELIA: You're not supposed to be wearing that dress. Mother would be very upset to see you in it.

ADELA: I'm not wearing it to upset her, Amelia. Why are *you* so upset?

AMELIA: I bought that material. Magdalena said that green doesn't suit me, so she made the dress for you. But it doesn't suit you either. Green's a really bad color. It doesn't suit anyone's skin. You look like death in it.

ADELA: This doesn't sound like you, Amelia.

AMELIA: How do you know what I sound like? You never listen to me. Everyone in this house thinks I'm stupid, but I'm not. I'm just the sensible one. And I'm so tired of it! (*She picks up some dirt and flings it at ADELA, stunning her.*) You see?! I can be as tough as any one of you. I just choose not to be. I just choose to remember who I am, where I come from, and what is the proper and kind way to be. Yes. That's it. I'm the only one who still believes in God. A merciful God. An understanding God. Who knows all and sees—all . . . (*ADELA kisses AMELIA sweetly and exits. Long pause as she looks around the dark corral, then suddenly throws herself into a pile of hay and sobs.*) I know it's a sin, but, dear God, I want to wear green too!

(*We hear the sound of PEPE's guitar playing as lights cross to PONCIA polishing furniture. AMELIA moves to join her.*)

AMELIA: Why doesn't this furniture stay clean, tita? No one ever comes to dirty it.

(*BERNARDA eavesdrops on them from the shadows.*)

PONCIA: It's amazing, isn't it? How much dust covers things that don't move. And why are you calling me your tita again. You haven't called me that for years.

AMELIA: I guess I forgive you.

PONCIA: Forgive me? What for?

AMELIA: You know. The time you went away.

PONCIA: You were the only one who missed me—you and your grandmother. She likes to use me as a shield.

AMELIA: You're good at that.

PONCIA: (*Touching her face gently*) You're a sweet thing, Amelia. I was the saddest about your growing up. Now there's a little angel, I always said.

AMELIA: I'm not an angel, tita.

PONCIA: Well, you're the only one of your sisters who ever helped me clean—that's as close to an angel as I'll see in this house.

AMELIA: Do you think I could take some extra sausages—for Magdalena? She hardly touched her dinner and she's too fragile not to eat.

PONCIA: No one gets "extras" in this house. I think your mother counts her possessions in her sleep. And I am always at the top of that list.

AMELIA: You're wrong about that. You're a godsend to her. I heard her praying once. And she—mentioned you.

PONCIA: Did she? Maybe she was praying that I would go away.

AMELIA: Never. How did you get to be such friends with her? She's so . . . and you're—not.

PONCIA: How do you know I'm not?

(*BERNARDA rubs a nightgown into the ground, soiling it.*)

AMELIA: I'm not either. But Magdalena is. I wish I knew what she wanted—so I could give it to her.

PONCIA: When are you going to get what you want? You love your sister so much, Amelia, that you forget to take care of yourself.

(*BERNARDA enters holding the soiled nightgown.*)

BERNARDA: (*Flinging the nightgown in PONCIA's face*) What is this?! Can't you do the simplest things—like washing, right? Did you think I wouldn't notice?!

AMELIA: Mother, you never wear that nightdress. And anyway, she was probably just tired. You just ask for too much from simple people. (*Trying to protect PONCIA.*) Go do the wash, Poncia.

BERNARDA: (*Yelling at AMELIA*) Since when are you telling my servants what to do?! Go to your room, Amelia.

(*AMELIA exits.*)

PONCIA: It's not the nightdress, is it?

BERNARDA: How dare you speak to my daughters like you were a member of this family! You are not a relative, you are a servant. A servant that owes me her life. Do you understand?

PONCIA: Always have.

BERNARDA: I want you to do your work—alone. If you need help, maybe it's time for us to get a new servant. One who can work hard, without complaining.

PONCIA: I never complain.

BERNARDA: My daughters are too—fragile to do housework. Housework ruins your skin. All that going in and out of the house. Getting the water, feeding the animals. Too much Sun. They have to protect their skin—keep it white—or no one will marry them—no one worthy. You'll ruin her if you make her into a common housekeeper! What are you thinking, Poncia!?

PONCIA: What are *you* thinking, Doña Bernarda?

BERNARDA: What were you talking to Amelia about?

PONCIA: Nothing really. She just likes to clean, I think.

BERNARDA: No one likes to clean, Poncia. She comes and talks to you—never to me. I'm her mother. It's me who can tell her about the world. I want to tell her.

PONCIA: Maybe you should let her know that.

BERNARDA: Why do my daughters hate me?

PONCIA: I have no idea. Your sweet, gentle nature, perhaps?

BERNARDA: Why are you the only one who tells me the truth?

PONCIA: Because I have to.

BERNARDA: I'm so tired, Poncia.

PONCIA: Rest then.

BERNARDA: No. I mean of this. This life. Why don't girls know how to behave any more? I always knew. I knew my mother didn't want me, but I knew how to make myself indispensable to her. I knew she yearned for order and I gave that to her. Well, maybe now that Angustias finally has an offer, maybe the rest will—But I hear things at night. Seagulls don't fly as far as this village—yet still I hear them calling. It's like all the animals are restless. Those horses are making all kinds of strange noises. What's happening, Poncia?

PONCIA: Do you really want to know?

BERNARDA: Yes—no. Tell me anyway. (*Long pause.*) It's my mother stirring up Adela, isn't it?! Why won't she just die? It would be so much easier.

PONCIA: You don't mean that.

BERNARDA: What would you know about what I mean?

PONCIA: I know everything. That's the job you gave me.

BERNARDA: And you do it well. Everyone in the village is afraid of your tongue.

PONCIA: That's nothing I ever wanted. I better go wash that nightdress.

(*PONCIA picks up the nightdress and exits.*)

BERNARDA: I have to do something about my mother. She's pulling my house down into the grave with her. I won't have it. Not again. (*BERNARDA crosses to the portrait of Don Antonio and speaks to it.*) I—never loved you, Antonio. That was my secret. But you knew it. I endured every child—every child a female. A torture. Because I knew what I had to teach them and give them so that they could turn out better than I ever could. A boy would have been so much easier. You can ignore them. But girls have to be trained to keep their legs together. Without the training they become whores or servants or worse—poor. So poor that they can't stop begging for everything they get. Only begging keeps those kind of girls alive. No one in this family will ever beg. And that's my doing, husband. Mine! Where were you in this? Where were you ever? I wish I could cry for your dead soul, but I can't Antonio. For the first time in many years, I can finally hear myself speak. Because your desire isn't drowning me, filling every pore in my skin with wetness. Being alone now is like a desert, and I feed on that sand that keeps you out of me. Stay away, Antonio. I'll wear black forever if you'll just stay away—from me and from my daughters. Everything you taught them could kill them. I have to undo you from us all. (*BERNARDA takes down Don Antonio's portrait and exits with it under her arm.*) Maybe I'll bury you.

(*Lights up on ADELA looking in a mirror, as BERNARDA exits.*)

BERNARDA & ADELA: Maybe it's too late.

ADELA: This can't be . . . What will I do?

(*Light up on AMELIA picking up the puppet pieces.*)

ADELA & AMELIA: I have to tell someone.

AMELIA: Lena's trying to get away. But she's so delicate.

(*Light up on MARTIRIO playing with ANGUSTIAS' makeup.*)

AMELIA & MARTIRIO: It could kill her.

MARTIRIO: Angustias is fooling herself, if she thinks a virile, pretty man like Pepe will ever love her. With all that white powder she puts on, she'll be invisible next to him.

(*Light up on ANGUSTIAS looking out the window dreamily.*)

MARTIRIO & ANGUSTIAS: That'll show her.

ANGUSTIAS: Martirio thinks Pepe just wants my dowry. But she's wrong. He gave me a kiss today. Slow and deliberate . . .

(*Light up on MAGDALENA washing her face.*)

ANGUSTIAS & MAGDALENA: It was a dangerous kiss.

MAGDALENA: She tasted like fear this time . . . tasted like me.

(*From offstage, the sounds of a violent crowd breaking glass and throwing stones. A woman sobbing. The loudest voice is that of BERNARDA ALBA.*)

BERNARDA: (*Offstage*) Whore! Feed her the coals. Let the dogs eat her like the flesh of her dead sinner child! (*BERNARDA enters to get her daughters.*) Come see this, all of you! This is what I warned you about!

(*They all go to the open front door and look out in horror as BERNARDA continues to relish the scene. ADELA slowly joins them. As she watches, she begins quietly to cry as her hand comes up to her stomach protectively.*)

BERNARDA: Stick them inside her! Right where that devil's baby came through! That will teach her.

AMELIA: What did she do?

BERNARDA: Let her be an example to all young ladies!

MAGDALENA: The poor thing! What's that they threw on her now?

PONCIA: A baby. Her baby—that she murdered! It was born without a father so she buried it under some rocks. Don René's dogs uncovered it this morning. That's how the whole thing started.

(*ADELA exits unnoticed.*)

BERNARDA: The whole thing started when she was born a whore. Look at her! Look at how she pleads now! Too late, little garbage! You see! You see what happens to women with no respect!

MAGDALENA: Respect! Is it respectful to kill her?! This is torture. You have to stop them, Mother!

BERNARDA: Stop them? If I weren't in mourning I'd be right there with them . . . teaching her a lesson.

MAGDALENA: She won't live to show what she learned, will she?!

(*BERNARDA strikes MAGDALENA to the floor with her cane. AMELIA runs to MAGDALENA's side.*)

AMELIA: Hit me too! It won't change anything!

(*The lights cross to MARIA JOSEFA's bedroom. ADELA stands with her back to the window as MARIA JOSEFA looks out the window at the stoning.*)

ADELA: I saw the blood and then I ran to tell you. Is it true that God took her and her baby because she wasn't married? Doesn't God have better things to do?

MARIA JOSEFA: I don't know. But you don't have to believe in God to know that there are evil people. Stoning a poor girl! (*ADELA gasps. MARIA JOSEFA turns to ADELA and holds her.*) Calm down now, little one. Calm down.

(*Lights cross back to the other WOMEN.*)

BERNARDA: Let her suffer. She's an abomination on the village. God wants her punished! God wants her dead!

(*Suddenly there is silence as the sky gets very dark.*)

PONCIA: Looks like a storm is coming. What a relief! Maybe this heat will leave us alone for awhile. Rainwater is good for washing away women's blood.

BERNARDA: More quaint country sayings?! Why don't you tell these girls the truth?! You have no understanding of what could really happen to them, do you? You don't know because you have no morality. You people never do. You think praying to some heathen beads will save you.

PONCIA: It's time for us all to get inside.

(*BERNARDA strikes PONCIA.*)

ANGUSTIAS: Don't hurt anyone else, Mother. Poncia did nothing wrong.

BERNARDA: You defend her too, Angustias? Why?! She's never cared about you.

ANGUSTIAS: I know. No one has. (*Pause.*) But now there's Pepe.

(*Lights up to include ADELA & MARIA JOSEFA. MARIA JOSEFA is gently rocking ADELA while she sings a lullaby. Her song goes under the action of the other WOMEN watching the stoning. Both areas, MARIA JOSEFA's bedroom and the threshold to the front door, now stay lit.*)

MARIA JOSEFA: (*Sings softly to ADELA as she rocks her*)

"Fig trees are like young girls filled with unborn babies.
Young girls filled with babies wish their shapes were figs."

BERNARDA: Look at her, calling to Jesus now. "In your mercy, please help me, Sweet Jesus." Do you hear it?! (*Striking her cane on the ground to get a response.*) Do you?!

AMELIA: Yes, Mother.

BERNARDA: And the rest of you? ANSWER ME!!

ANGUSTIAS & MARTIRIO: Yes, Mother.

MAGDALENA: (*Standing to face her mother*) I don't hear a thing.

BERNARDA: Listen! It'll remind you of the vengeance of the Lord, Magdalena.

PONCIA: Why are you doing this, Doña Bernarda? These girls don't need to see such horrors.

(*PONCIA, AMELIA, MAGDALENA, & ANGUSTIAS move away from the front door into the house. BERNARDA stops MARTIRIO.*)

BERNARDA: You see, Martirio. This is what I saved you from.

MARTIRIO: What are you talking about?

BERNARDA: That boyfriend of yours didn't want a wife. He wanted to come to you at night and use your beauty until it became a shadow.

MARTIRIO: Oh. You—saved my life, Mother.

MARIA JOSEFA: (*Listening*) It will be over soon. She's stopped crying—peace finally—I want a peace like that.

MARTIRIO: (*To herself*) So *she* sent him away . . . at least I know now that he tried.

BERNARDA: (*Struggling to see over people's heads*) Where are all the people coming from? There must be two hundred of them.

MARTIRIO: You could see more from my bedroom window. I'll go with you.

BERNARDA: Yes, Martirio. You're so much like me. We need to stay together.

MARTIRIO: We will, Mother. We will.

(*BERNARDA & MARTIRIO go to the window for a better view.*)

ADELA: If I stay here, I'll turn into a fig tree. Not a woman anymore—just something to sit under and enjoy its shade.

(*PONCIA & the other DAUGHTERS come in and close the door in stunned silence.*)

MARIA JOSEFA: I'll think of something.

AMELIA: Where's Adela?

ANGUSTIAS: She was just here.

MAGDALENA: Good for her. She didn't have to put up with mother's ravings.

(*A final scream from the stoned woman. ADELA stifles a scream when she realizes the woman is dead. BERNARDA & MARTIRIO at the window.*)

BERNARDA: She's finally dead. God rest her pitiful soul! (*The sound of thunder.*) He's really taking her, Martirio. Do you hear Him coming? That's what thunder means—God is traveling to Earth to save someone.

(*The sound of thunder.*)

MARTIRIO: Yes, Mother. I hear him. (*A whisper.*) Every time I close my eyes, I hear him.

End of ACT TWO

ACT THREE

Two months later. One night.

Lights come up on ANGUSTIAS' bedroom. The last light of day is fading, but it is a gray, rainy day. She is trying on her wedding dress and MARTIRIO is pinning it for a hem. They are working in candlelight.

ANGUSTIAS: It's beautiful, isn't it? This is the finest lace he had.

MARTIRIO: Yes. That old man smells of mucous and foul tobacco, but his lace is the best.

ANGUSTIAS: Isn't it strange how that happens?

MARTIRIO: How what happens?

ANGUSTIAS: How something so beautiful can come from something so . . . unattractive.

MARTIRIO: (*Looking her up and down*) Yes. This is going to be a lovely wedding dress.

ANGUSTIAS: Will you be my maid of honor, Martirio?

MARTIRIO: (*Pricking her finger on a needle*) Ouch! Me?? Why me?

ANGUSTIAS: (*Making the sign of the cross*) Oh, no!! You didn't get any blood on my dress, did you?

MARTIRIO: Just a drop—on the inside hem. No one will ever see it. It's only blood.

ANGUSTIAS: That's good. Anyway, will you stand beside me? You were the only one who always told me the truth. I want to be a better sister to you. I know your heart is still broken.

MARTIRIO: My heart is fine. There. I'll finish hemming it tomorrow.

ANGUSTIAS: Will you? It would make me very happy.

MARTIRIO: (*Slightly flattered*) If it means that much to you—Do I have any choice?

ANGUSTIAS: You have a lot of anger. It makes me scared for you.

MARTIRIO: Don't be. In seven years, I'll probably be a nun.

ANGUSTIAS: You?! I can't imagine that.

MARTIRIO: Why not?

ANGUSTIAS: I suppose . . . if it's what you want. But you're so pretty. Pretty nuns always upset me. What a waste. To hide all that.

MARTIRIO: Yes. I'll go into the darkest jungles and save some unsuspecting natives. It's the perfect job for me, really.

ANGUSTIAS: I'll go change, and then will you help me plan the reception?

MARTIRIO: Of course.

(*A strong gust of wind suddenly blows open a window. The candles go out. The WOMEN light matches and relight the candles.*)

ANGUSTIAS: This storm is getting worse. Why won't it stop raining? Do you think it will rain on my wedding day? That's bad luck, isn't it?

MARTIRIO: I wouldn't know. (*ANGUSTIAS exits.*) Mother did save my life—but what for? I never wanted to be saved; I wanted to explode.

(*AMELIA enters.*)

AMELIA: Have you seen—

MARTIRIO: Magdalena's cleaning the sewing machines.

AMELIA: How did you know who—

MARTIRIO: Just a guess. (*AMELIA exits. MARTIRIO begins snooping through ANGUSTIAS' things, opens her jewelry box, and pulls out a green gemmed necklace.*) Maybe she'll give me this necklace. It looks good against my skin. And she won't need it where she's going. Once she leaves this house, she'll never need to wear another pretty thing. She'll just be a wife—waiting and waiting for him to come home—he won't if he's smart. He'll wait until she's sound asleep before he ever crawls in next to her and smells her longing. I wanted to take that needle and sew the dress on to her dusty skin. If only that little drop of my blood could spread over her dress and stain her forever. Never take that dress off, Angustias—it's the only memory you'll ever have.

(*Lights cross to ANGUSTIAS taking off her dress and carefully hanging it up.*)

ANGUSTIAS: Even I look good in this dress. I'll shine like a star. For once, everyone will see me . . . (*She gently kisses the hem of the dress and exits.*)

(*Lights cross to ADELA, alone in a pool of light.*)

ADELA: I'm not a girl anymore. And I don't like it. I hear things now, in my sleep—like that woman screaming. And other things that sound like my mother crying. She cries for me but I don't know why. I wake in a sweat. A cold wetness that keeps me from sleep. Dear God, what's wrong with me? (*Pause.*) Abuela and I must leave here tonight. Please, sweet Jesus, lead us to the sea!

(*Lights cross to BERNARDA & PONCIA, in BERNARDA's bedroom. PONCIA massages BERNARDA's head.*)

BERNARDA: Who taught you such a soothing touch? My fingers don't know how to move like that. You steal the pain right out of me . . .

(*Lights cross to MAGDALENA cleaning the sewing machines. Her hands are covered in grease.*)

MAGDALENA: I love the smell of grease. It's the smell of small things grinding against big ones to make them run. Every time I take this machine apart, I learn something. Today I learned how the needle must be placed against this cold metal plate—and that's what keeps it running properly. Reminds me how things work. Nothing important moves without grease. (*Pause.*) I'm finally alone.

(*AMELIA enters, out of breath.*)

AMELIA: There you are!

MAGDALENA: Here I am.

AMELIA: Why—why are you avoiding me?

MAGDALENA: I just like being alone every now and then.

AMELIA: No. You're definitely avoiding me.

MAGDALENA: Don't you have something else to do? Help Angustias. She needs a lot of help.

AMELIA: Martirio is helping her.

MAGDALENA: That's unusual.

AMELIA: Can I help you?

MAGDALENA: No.

AMELIA: I can clean the bobbins.

MAGDALENA: They don't need to be cleaned.

AMELIA: Then I can rethread the needles.

MAGDALENA: Not until I'm done.

AMELIA: Can I just watch you work? I'll be quiet. (*She moves to a far corner of the room.*)

MAGDALENA: (*With a resigned sigh*) Sewing machines are incredible inventions. They can make long, boring tasks, shorter. (*AMELIA moves closer.*) Of course, some things will always take an eternity. (*Pause.*) Why can't you leave me alone, Amelia?

AMELIA: Because I love you.

MAGDALENA: Could you love me less? Could you love me without suffocating me?
I can't breathe when you're near me.

AMELIA: Stop it! You know you don't mean that.

MAGDALENA: YOU STOP IT, AMELIA! You're killing me!

AMELIA: That's not possible, sweetest Lena. You know that's not possible.

MAGDALENA: Get out of this room and hide for a while, Amelia. Hide because if I find you, I'll kill you—just to get released from your eyes. You have no spine. (*Mimicking her.*) "Yes, mother. No, mother." You make me sick sometimes.

AMELIA: You're just overtired. Come to bed. I'll rub your back.

MAGDALENA: This is the only thing that relaxes me anymore. I've taken this machine apart about sixty times now.

AMELIA: Maybe you need a new machine.

(*AMELIA smiles. We hear the sound of the horses stomping and whinnying.*)

MAGDALENA: If I close my eyes, will you disappear?

(*MAGDALENA closes her eyes. AMELIA watches her in silence.*)

AMELIA: You're silly.

MAGDALENA: And what are you?! Just a shadow. I refuse to love a shadow. You know I'll only ever love El Maestro—

AMELIA: He's dead, Magdalena. Didn't you hear? Your noble prince is dead. Shot three times, as he was riding into battle . . . about two weeks ago. I was sure you had heard about it.

MAGDALENA: What are you saying?!

AMELIA: Martí is dead. (*Pause.*) I'll wait in the bedroom for you then. Don't be long.

(*AMELIA exits. MAGDALENA breaks her sewing machine against the wall, as the lights cross to MARIA JOSEFA's bedroom. MARIA JOSEFA is asleep in a chair. BERNARDA comes up behind her, watches her for a moment in silence, then notices the white lace she has draped around her torso. She slowly picks up that piece of lace and drapes it across her own torso—the same way MARIA JOSEFA had it draped. For a moment she pretends to be her mother, doing a slight twirl, her eyes filled with MARIA JOSEFA's joy for a moment, then she loses her balance slightly.*)

BERNARDA: When I try to move like you, I always stumble. (*Pause.*) What goes on in that head of yours when you're asleep? Watching your silence is waiting for a volcano to erupt. Even in your sleep. You're planning something. I know it. (*Pause.*) So innocent now. I should have let you go a long time ago. But it wouldn't have been the proper thing to do—let your mother die—if you could stop it. Though it's what you always said you wanted. (*Pause.*) It would be the merciful thing . . . like when evil women cry to be released from their pain—you've been so quiet since that happened. Maybe . . . now would be a good time. No pain in sleep.

(*BERNARDA moves to touch MARIA JOSEFA who is awakened by the baa of the SHEEP, so BERNARDA stops.*)

MARIA JOSEFA: (*Sniffing the air*) Oh. It's you. What do you want now? (*Noticing the lace.*) Didn't have the nerve to do it, did you? What a pity! I would have welcomed it! So what are you still here for? You didn't do what you came to do so go.

BERNARDA: How about a visit? Just a visit with my mother. It's been a long time since we've been alone together.

MARIA JOSEFA: Alone together? We're always alone together—it's just more unbearable when we're in the same room, Bernarda. What are you going to do with that lace now? It's mine, but I suppose you'll take it—a souvenir of another battle lost. Why not? You have everything else.

BERNARDA: I want you to stop talking to Adela. You fill her up with foolish ideas. She's a sensitive girl. You know we must be careful with her.

MARIA JOSEFA: Yes. I know. I know how to care for precious things. Adela is a brilliant jewel sprung straight from the earth, and you'll turn her into dust. If you really cared about her, you'd set her free.

BERNARDA: You are alive still because I took care of you. How many times did you try to throw yourself down the well?

MARIA JOSEFA: I'm one short of my goal.

BERNARDA: I should have let you drown. What were you always looking for in there?

MARIA JOSEFA: Something human.

BERNARDA: Yes. And now you have your lamb. I'm glad you found something to love finally. I always thought that one day, you would turn to me with love in your eyes. But I could never be a lamb.

MARIA JOSEFA: No . . . I gave birth to a leopard. Your smell shamed me. I heard you in my dreams . . . before you were even born. You were always talking to me—never let me sleep, always expected something. I'd look at my belly and see your fingers clawing the inside of my stomach. You'd claw from the point nearest my breasts, move them vertically down the center of my stomach, and when you reached the end, you would poke with each one of your fingers—one at a time into my skin—clawing and poking until I couldn't stand it anymore. My tears always calmed you down. My child liked to make her mother suffer right from the beginning. I should have killed you, but the priest wouldn't let me. How could I give birth to something that couldn't dance—wouldn't play? I never wanted to know you.

BERNARDA: That's why I had to fight for my life from the very beginning. Every second—even in my sleep I'm fighting. I have the same dream over and over. I dream that you hand me a silver comb and you say, "Here. Open me up. Here. Erase the dried-salt stench of men out of my hair. Take my secret out of me and swallow it whole." In my dreams, I start to choke. I wake up choking. You don't have to share your secrets with me or with Adela. Those are things that could kill her.

MARIA JOSEFA: What are you afraid of?

BERNARDA: Maybe I am the disease you always said I was.

MARIA JOSEFA: But you have a chance to change that now, and, finally, stop being so afraid. Let Adela go. It's not too late for her. She and I could leave right now—start again. There's so much I haven't taught her.

BERNARDA: Why won't you understand that those are things Adela doesn't need to know?! For Godssake, leave her alone before you turn her into a viper like you. Let her live a young girl's life—

MARIA JOSEFA: You call this living?! Trapped on a mountain with six shriveled-up shrews? Adela's the only one worthy of my blood.

BERNARDA: Your blood?! Do you know how much I hate your blood?! Adela doesn't need lessons from a woman who had to sleep with her daughter's husband.

MARIA JOSEFA: Only the first one. And I didn't have to. I just had nothing else to do. (*BERNARDA pulls MARIA JOSEFA's hair, pulling her head back.*) Bite me, leopard! But if you bite me, tear my whole head off or I'll come back to life. That's the only way, Bernarda.

(*BERNARDA lets go of MARIA JOSEFA.*)

BERNARDA: I know, damn you! If your poison didn't run through my veins, you'd be dead by now. Leave Adela alone, Mother. Leave her alone or you'll have the sound of my footsteps nailed into your head. I'll just keep coming back. And you know I can always find you.

MARIA JOSEFA: Yes . . . Unlike most of us who go in many different directions, you are a forward-moving creature. You're like time. That's the scariest thing about you. Go away, tick-tock clock. Go away.

(*BERNARDA exits slowly. When she gets to the door she suddenly turns back and takes the piece of lace with her out the door, locking it tightly behind her.*)

MARIA JOSEFA: The more she marches forward, the further back I feel myself. Deeper and deeper into a dark, blank place. A place without music—without Adela.

ADELA : (*From outside the window, ADELA calls up to MARIA JOSEFA.*) Abuela! Abuela! ¿Ha visto a Pepe?

(*MARIA JOSEFA moves to the window.*)

MARIA JOSEFA: Our time is running out, Adela. Your mother knows about our plans.

ADELA: So we have to do something soon. Maybe tonight.

MARIA JOSEFA: But what?! She watches me all the time. I could never leave the house without feeling her eyes on me.

ADELA: Don't give up, Abuela.

MARIA JOSEFA: I'm trying not to . . . I do have a plan. But I don't know if—

ADELA: Don't worry! It will work. And if it doesn't, I have a plan too.

MARIA JOSEFA: You do?!

ADELA: My plan is simple. We just pack our bags and go.

MARIA JOSEFA: What about Pepe?

ADELA: If he loves me, he'll come with us.

MARIA JOSEFA: Will he? There's only one thing I believe in any more. The earth—I respect it and talk to it every chance I get. I spread my hair on the ground and let the sharp blades of grass part it and comb it with memories. Sometimes I wish the earth would just swallow me and birth me again into a spring garden. That's all I think about anymore.

ADELA: Don't talk like this, Abuela. I wouldn't know what to do without you. The earth likes it when we walk on her. Then she knows she's alive—by the sound of our footsteps—especially when we dance!

MARIA JOSEFA: There's danger in the future, Adela. You must leave here soon . . .

ADELA: *We* must leave here soon. I won't go without you.

MARIA JOSEFA: We'll see . . . I can't run as fast as you any more. Anyway, your freedom seems like my own. But it could be dangerous. Are you sure that's what you want?

ADELA: Why are you saying this now? Has mother scared you into this? Don't let her. (*As she exits.*) I know what I'm doing.

MARIA JOSEFA: That's what I used to think. (*MARIA JOSEFA strokes PEPE in silence for a moment. Then he transforms into PEPE the MAN.*) Pepe, my star-filled evening sky, the sooner you go, the easier it'll be . . . for all of us. You smell like the earth now too.

(*PEPE kisses MARIA JOSEFA passionately and then slowly disappears. MARIA JOSEFA sits alone for a moment holding the remnants of his skin, as the lights fade.*)

(*Lights cross to ANGUSTIAS, AMELIA, MAGDALENA, & MARTIRIO in the middle of an argument. They are all dressed in nightclothes and are lit by candlelight.*)

ANGUSTIAS: Who took it?! Tell me now! I know one of you jealous animals stole it and I want it back! Right now! Tell me!

(*PONCIA enters.*)

PONCIA: What's this? You should all be in bed.

MARTIRIO: Angustias is having a fit. I hear brides-to-be can get like that.

PONCIA: Yes. Calm down, Angustias. It's bad for your health to get so excited.

AMELIA: Who would steal your photo anyway?! You probably just misplaced it.

(*ADELA enters through the front door.*)

ANGUSTIAS: (*Grabbing ADELA and shaking her*) Was it you? I know it was you! I saw you looking at him.

PONCIA: Will someone tell me what this is all about?

MARTIRIO: Someone took her beloved's picture from under her pillow. Are you afraid you might forget what he looked like?

(*MAGDALENA begins to cry, thinking about Martí.*)

MAGDALENA: El Maestro . . . (*AMELIA moves to comfort MAGDALENA, but is rebuffed.*) Don't you dare touch me!!

ANGUSTIAS: Give it back to me!

ADELA: I don't have any photo. I've never even seen it.

(*BERNARDA enters.*)

BERNARDA: Can't one night go by in peace at this house?

PONCIA: Someone took Angustias' picture of Pepe.

BERNARDA: Who would do that? Surely you've misplace—

ANGUSTIAS: I know it was taken.

BERNARDA: Search their rooms, Poncia. Otherwise we'll get no sleep tonight. (*PONCIA exits to search the rooms. The OTHERS wait in an uncomfortable silence. Trying to be a concerned mother.*) So . . . how are your wedding plans coming, Angustias?

(*ANGUSTIAS bursts into tears.*)

MAGDALENA: Dear God, let this night be over. (*Falls to her knees and begins to say the rosary. AMELIA immediately follows suit.*) Can't I even pray alone, Amelia?!

BERNARDA: Maybe we should all pray.

(*BERNARDA drops to her knees, but then notices ADELA, MARTIRIO, and ANGUSTIAS still standing. She raps them on the feet with her cane and they too fall to their knees. PONCIA rushes back in.*)

PONCIA: I found it. Well, part of it anyway.

ANGUSTIAS: (*Looking at ADELA and grabbing the framed photo*) Where? I'll strangle whoever took it!

PONCIA: Well . . .

BERNARDA: Tell us, Poncia.

PONCIA: (*With surprise*) Under Martirio's bed.

MARTIRIO: Just a joke, sister. I thought brides had a sense of humor.

BERNARDA: (*Striking MARTIRIO with her cane; MARTIRIO just laughs*) Why would you do such a thing?! You were supposed to be my clever, sensible daughter—the one I could be proud of!

PONCIA: Don't hit the girl, Doña Bernarda. She meant no harm. Did you?

MARTIRIO: No. No harm.

ANGUSTIAS: (*Looking closely at the photo*) Is this another joke?! Where's his photo?

(*All the women gather to look at the photo.*)

BERNARDA: I don't believe it.

MAGDALENA: Grandmother's everywhere, isn't she?

AMELIA: How did her picture get in that frame?

MARTIRIO: That wasn't my doing. Last time I saw it, he was still in there.

ADELA: Grandmother must have him.

PONCIA: She's sound asleep. I just checked. We'll get your photo back to you in the morning, Angustias. Don't worry.

BERNARDA: Can we all go back to sleep now? Bring me some milk, Poncia. My headache came back.

(*BERNARDA exits to her bedroom and closes the door. The women all exchange a look, slowly move to their respective bedrooms, and close the doors. ADELA quietly opens hers and comes out furtively, hugging her shawl around her. MARTIRIO opens her door and moves to follow ADELA, but then sees PONCIA start after ADELA, and retreats back into her room, but listens at the door.*)

ADELA: (*Furtively pulling out the photo of PEPE*) You're mine now.

PONCIA: (*In a whisper*) Where do you think you're going?

ADELA: (*Quickly hiding the photo in her shawl*) Nowhere. Just outside. To get some air.

PONCIA: Give it up, Adela. You'll find another man. But your sister never will.

ADELA: It's me he loves, Poncia.

PONCIA: That's why you have to stop this. Love like this can only end badly. You're too young to know that, but I know it. I once loved a man so fiercely that I drove him away. I loved him like the night loves the moon. I loved and I waited and he married someone else. Someone with more money. Don't do that. Keep your pride, girl. That could be all you have left.

ADELA: What good is pride, Poncia? When you want to wake with the smell of him inside you? When you lose your own smell because you're so filled with his? Pride can't kiss you at night. Or taste away your tears.

(*MARIA JOSEFA enters dressed as BERNARDA. ADELA and PONCIA follow her.*)

ADELA: This will never work, Abuela. She knows you're not her.

MARIA JOSEFA: This will help us get past the monster. That's all we need. To get past her and out that front door.

PONCIA: That's not a very good disguise, Doña Maria.

MARIA JOSEFA: Sssh! Keep my secret too, Poncia. I'm the one who found you, not her.

ADELA: What are you saying, Abuela?

PONCIA: She's delirious, as usual. Go back to bed, Doña Maria. Let me help you.

MARIA JOSEFA: Keep those hands off me, you dog. Do you lick her face at night too?

PONCIA: Something horrible's about to happen.

ADELA: What happens if you get out? Will you forget about me?

MARIA JOSEFA: Of course not. That's why I chose this particular dress. There's space for you under my skirts.

ADELA: No, Abuela. Go back to your room, before you hurt yourself.

MARIA JOSEFA: Come on, girl! What are you waiting for now? Pepe will never save you.

ADELA: (*Sadly*) Yes, Abuela. Let me tie your shawl. This is how she wears hers. (*She ties MARIA JOSEFA's shawl tightly at the waist, like BERNARDA wears hers as PONCIA looks on in silence.*) There. You look a lot like her now.

MARIA JOSEFA: Good! Alright then. Just slip under here. Don't worry. There's plenty of room.

ADELA: (*Touching her stomach*) For both of us?

MARIA JOSEFA: Of course. But promise me, we won't name her Bernarda.

ADELA: Never! I promise.

(*ADELA gets under MARIA JOSEFA's skirts.*)

PONCIA: She'll punish you both, Doña Maria. And I don't think I can stop her this time.

MARIA JOSEFA: Ssssh! You can come too, if you want. We'll need a good cook where we're going.

(*MARIA JOSEFA walks furtively towards the front door, but is stopped by BERNARDA who enters from her bedroom.*)

BERNARDA: Who is that?

MARIA JOSEFA: Who do you want it to be?

BERNARDA: What are you doing in my clothes?!

MARIA JOSEFA: They're my clothes.

BERNARDA: Who are you trying to fool?!

MARIA JOSEFA: Who's listening?

BERNARDA: Take off my clothes!

MARIA JOSEFA: You take off *my* clothes! It's all mine. Everything you have. Mine.

BERNARDA: You're not going out there. I don't need the neighbors gossiping about you—again.

MARIA JOSEFA: That was years ago.

BERNARDA: Go back upstairs, Mother. Go to your room so I don't have to kill you. (*With her back to them.*) And you come out from under those skirts, Adela. You're not going anywhere.

(*BERNARDA exits to her bedroom. ADELA comes out from under her skirts as MARIA JOSEFA goes slowly to her own bedroom with PONCIA guiding her.*)

MARIA JOSEFA: I was just trying to help the girl, but nothing will work, will it, Poncia?

PONCIA: No, Doña Maria. Nothing. Don Antonio is the lucky one.

(*ANGUSTIAS enters dressed in ADELA's shawl. ADELA sees her and follows closely behind her.*)

ADELA: Where do you think you're going dressed like that? My father gave me that shawl. No one wears it but me.

ANGUSTIAS: But it goes perfect with my mood tonight. I think I'm going to let Pepe have me tonight.

ADELA: What are you saying?

ANGUSTIAS: I want to sleep with him, Adela. I want to feel him over me and beneath and behind me. Everywhere. I can't wait any longer. It's hard to be a virgin in the summer. Everything smells like sex in the heat. Everything has a vapor rising over it. Please don't tell anyone. I just couldn't keep it to myself. And I know you know how to keep a secret, little sister.

ADELA: That shawl won't help you. He still will never love you, no matter how he touches you.

ANGUSTIAS: I know he won't, Adela. I wake up every day and feel blessed that he would even walk with me. But I need to feel something else—and he's a man so—he won't mind, giving this old virgin the thrill of her life. And I won't mind tasting every minute. Be happy for me. Don't look so worried.

ADELA: (*Beginning to cry*) He can't love you, Angustias. If you get pregnant, it will kill you. I heard Poncia talk about how weak you are.

ANGUSTIAS: If I die giving birth, I would be glad for those few moments before when I felt a thrashing life inside me. To feel that . . . It doesn't even seem like dying. (*Moves to comfort ADELA.*) Don't be so sad. I'm still ugly, old Angustias who everyone talks about behind her back and no one used to love. But Pepe will learn to love me. I'll teach him.

ADELA: Please take off my shawl.

ANGUSTIAS: I'll bring it back to your bedroom. If Pepe comes, tell him I'll be right down.

ADELA: Yes, alright.

(*ANGUSTIAS exits and ADELA moves to the front door and looks out for PEPE, then decides to return to her room. The lights cross to BERNARDA and PONCIA in BERNARDA's bedroom.*)

BERNARDA: My mother gets crazier every second she still breathes. I'm glad Martirio was just joking. This house has too many secrets already.

PONCIA: You believed that?

BERNARDA: Of course. Go to sleep, Poncia.

PONCIA: No. I will not go to sleep, Bernarda.

BERNARDA: What is it now? I don't have any room in my brain for town gossip.

PONCIA: Even tales from your own house?

BERNARDA: What are you talking about?

PONCIA: Adela is in love with Pepe El Romano.

BERNARDA: Don't be silly, Poncia. He's going to marry her sister. That's the end of that story. Go to sleep.

PONCIA: You're killing them. All of them. You give them no freedom and no love. And then you wonder why they don't love you. When are you going to open your eyes and see something that matters?! Something more than just the airs you put on and show for the village folk at church?! Something horrible is going to happen in your house, Bernarda, and you are the only one who can stop it.

BERNARDA: I will not hear any more of this. Do you understand? No more. You were always proud—even as a child. But I thought I taught you not to be, ever since the day I found you—

PONCIA: Maria Josefa found me.

BERNARDA: So you believe the rantings of my mother now? Maybe it is time for you to leave my house. Find another family to destroy with your willfulness.

PONCIA: I can't leave now. This is the only family I have ever known. Others might be even more frightening. I don't now what else there is.

BERNARDA: Then go to sleep.

(*PONCIA moves to her bedmat at the foot of BERNARDA's bed and moves to lie down.*)

PONCIA: One day, I'd like my own bed.

BERNARDA: One day, you shall have it. Goodnight, little Moses.

PONCIA: Goodnight, Pharaoh's sister.

(*The lights cross to AMELIA furtively burning MAGDALENA's Martí books.*)

AMELIA: There. Like my tita taught me. You have to burn sense into people sometimes. She doesn't need any more reminders of this man around her. Too many ideas can be confusing. Good-bye, Martí. You *were* a good poet . . . God rest your soul.

(*The lights cross to ADELA, who enters the living room dressed in only a sheer white nightgown. She looks furtively from side to side and disappears through the door to the corral. The sound of a horse rearing and bucking against the corral walls. MARTIRIO enters through another door and stands, waiting in anguish, at the center of the stage. She, too, is in her nightgown, but wears a black shawl with the ends tucked tightly at her waist. MARIA JOSEFA enters holding the remnants of PEPE the LAMB. The horse sounds segue into the sounds of human lovemaking. MARIA JOSEFA and MARTIRIO both speak but do not hear each other.*)

MARTIRIO: She won't get away with this. I'll see to that.

MARIA JOSEFA: Is there anything sweeter than the sound of love?

(*MARTIRIO & MARIA JOSEFA both close their eyes for a moment—filling themselves with the sound.*)

MARTIRIO: (*Spitting*) My sister's an animal! Oh! (*Listening more closely.*) What's she doing now? Whore! How can Pepe stand to touch someone so unclean?! You can't tell the horse from the man on this kind of night. On this kind of night they become one—like some strange creature yearning for the comfort of a woman's moist bed. Why you sister? Why not me?

(*MARIA JOSEFA startles MARTIRIO.*)

MARIA JOSEFA: You should open *all* the windows. Then you'd hear more.

MARTIRIO: Grandmother, what are you doing awake?

MARIA JOSEFA: Just listening. Like you. You look familiar. Do I know you?

MARTIRIO: How did you get out of your room?

MARIA JOSEFA: Poncia forgot to lock me in. Who are you?

MARTIRIO: Go to bed.

MARIA JOSEFA: You're Martirio, now I see you. Martirio, face of a martyr. And when are you going to have a child? I've had this one.

MARTIRIO: Where did you get those rags?

MARIA JOSEFA: Isn't he beautiful? (*Confidentially.*) I know he's a lamb, but why can't a lamb be a child? It's better to have a lamb than to have nothing. They have the sweetest eyes—hard to hide love in those eyes . . . not like some others. (*A bit louder; tauntingly.*) Bernarda, face of a leopard; Pepe, face of a lamb.

MARTIRIO: Don't talk so loud in the darkness. Then the devil hears you.

MARIA JOSEFA: (*Shouting*) Bernarda—Face of a leopard. Martirio—Face of a martyr. Ovejita—Baa-baa-baa, baa, baa, baa.

MARTIRIO: Quiet, be quiet! Come on. Go to bed. (*She pushes MARIA JOSEFA roughly, scaring her.*)

MARIA JOSEFA: Don't try to hurt me! It won't help you get what you want. You'll never have another man, Martirio. You scare them away with your face full of longing. Not like Adela, who draws them to her like bees are drawn to sweet, warm nectar.

MARTIRIO: Enough! (*She slaps MARIA JOSEFA who begins to cry.*) You see?! You see what happens if you don't sleep? Please go back to your room. It's the only safe place.

MARIA JOSEFA: Then that's where you should go, you little witch! They kept me locked up all these years when it should have been you left to rot and die.

MARTIRIO: (*Pulling the lamb remnants out of MARIA JOSEFA's hands*) Stupid, meddling, old lady! In love with some tattered pieces of nothing! (*Throwing the pieces into the air.*) There. Now your child is dead. Go to your room, Grandmother—and mourn him.

MARIA JOSEFA: NO! (*MARIA JOSEFA begins picking up the pieces frantically and clutching them to her. When she's gathered all the remnants, she slowly begins to ascend the stairs, gently weeping and singing sadly.*)

"Ovejita, child of my own.
Come with me to the kingdom of the sea.
The little ant is at your throne,
In a hut made of coral—where is home?"

(*MARTIRIO moves towards the corral and calls for ADELA.*)

MARTIRIO: (*Quietly*) Adela! (*Moving closer to the corral door.*) Adela!

(*ADELA runs out of the corral, her nightgown off her shoulders, her hair loose and flowing. MARTIRIO blocks her path.*)

MARTIRIO: Finally, you emerge. A wet mare. What's this on your stomach? And this?

ADELA: (*Slapping her hands away*) Don't!!

(*MARTIRIO pushes up ADELA's nightdress and wrestles with her, trying to get her hands inside ADELA.*)

ADELA: NO!! Stop it!!

MARTIRIO: That's what you should have said to Pepe. Now everyone will know.

ADELA: I don't care who knows, Martirio. I have nothing left to hide. I know I can't hide my love for him. It shines out of me like morning light. Pepe's my sunrise. Tell mother that when you tell her the rest. Tell her things she won't ever understand.

MARTIRIO: Could we truly be sisters? Sharing blood with you is a disease. I want you out of me, Adela. I want you out of this house. But you have no other place to go, do you?! Just like all the rest of us—Except of course for Angustias . . . she'll have a home with Pepe once they're married. Once she's married she'll go away with him and you'll never see him again. What will you do then?

ADELA: Wait.

(*ADELA runs back into the house with MARTIRIO in close pursuit. As ADELA exits the other sisters enter, one by one.*)

MARTIRIO: Where are you going now?! There's no hiding from it anymore!

(*PEPE EL ROMANO enters running from the corral. He encounters each sister as he races around trying to escape. The last sister he encounters is ANGUSTIAS. Then he exits back toward the corral.*)

(*The horses stomp and whinny loudly. BERNARDA ALBA enters.*)

BERNARDA: Something is killing the horses! Poncia! Get my gun.

PONCIA: No. If you're going to shoot at something, get it yourself.

(*PONCIA exits the house.*)

BERNARDA: Martirio!

MARTIRIO: (*Handing BERNARDA the gun*) Here it is, mother! Hurry! He'll get away!

BERNARDA: Who?

MARTIRIO: Pepe. He's been defiling Adela, ruining the whole family. We can't let him do that any longer.

(*BERNARDA ALBA walks outside. She carries the gun.*)

BERNARDA: (*Calling into the dark corral*) Come out! I know you're in there! (*She fires a warning shot. PEPE the MAN comes running out and away from BERNARDA. She fires her gun at him. He runs out of sight. She runs after him until she falls.*) Pepe! Run, you coward! You piece of dirt! You piece of nothing! You came with Satan and left your rotting stench on my house. Adela!! Where are you??

(*ADELA enters carrying a suitcase, but still dressed in her nightgown. She moves to where MARTIRIO stands barring the door.*)

MARTIRIO: I hope you're happy now, Adela. Mother has killed him.

ADELA: You're lying!

MARTIRIO: I never lie—not about death anyway. And here we were getting ready for a wedding and now it's just another funeral. Poor Angustias!

(*Lights cross to MARIA JOSEFA's bedroom. She is dressed in ANGUSTIAS' wedding gown.*)

MARIA JOSEFA: I'm so tired . . . (*PEPE enters.*) Oh, Pepe! You came back for one last kiss, didn't you? You know how bored I get dressing up for myself. I like a man's eyes on me. I like that dark eyelash caress that opens secret doors. (*PEPE kisses MARIA JOSEFA passionately.*) Feed me? You're like seaweed—salty and nourishing. Kiss the hem of my dress. Take my dress in your mouth and leave your spit there for me to drink from and remember. (*MARIA JOSEFA touches his lips gently.*) It was lips like yours which destroyed civilization. It's like witchcraft what you do. (*Taking PEPE's face in her hands.*) Don't look so worried, my love! It's just time. (*MARIA JOSEFA dances in her bedroom with a long piece of mesh lace with PEPE helping her. She winds the lace around every piece of furniture, every window, every door jam—like an elegant spider spinning a human-sized web. When everything is covered, she slowly begins to wind herself in the remaining lace—like into a cocoon.*) White is a comfort. White is nothing. To be wrapped in nothing is comforting. When wrapping, wrap in white.

(*We hear the sound of thunder. ADELA enters, still dressed in her nightgown, still carrying her suitcase.*)

ADELA: Abuela! Come! It's raining so hard now, she'll never be able to find us! It's time for us to go! (*Seeing that MARIA JOSEFA is dead and beginning to weep.*) ABUELA! Don't leave me here. We were almost free . . . (*Slowly, ADELA pulls herself away from MARIA JOSEFA and moves to the window.*) Don't go too far, Abuela. I would hate to lose you.

(*ADELA disappears out the window. It closes down hard like a wind followed her out.*)

(*Lights cross to BERNARDA, rocking furiously on her knees as the others, PONCIA, MARTIRIO, ANGUSTIAS, AMELIA & MAGDALENA crowd around her in the living room.*)

BERNARDA: Where is Adela?! Did you see them outside? If she ran off with him, I'll kill them both. I swear I will. How could she do this to me? I don't know how . . .

(*The lights cross to ADELA pulling a wooden chair behind her into the corral. ADELA begins to speak softly.*)

ADELA: I imagined myself an old woman, lying on a feather bed, my head propped up by the many pillows sewn for me by my many grandchildren. I take my last breath smelling the baby sweat from their little fingers. Then I smile.

(*ADELA hangs herself. We hear the sound of thunder. PONCIA, AMELIA, MAGDALENA, ANGUSTIAS, and MARTIRIO crowd the door of the corral behind BERNARDA. They all carry lanterns. Their light fills the corral and we see ADELA hanging from the rafters of the corral, her white nightgown soaked in blood. Everyone gasps. PONCIA makes the sign of the cross. MAGDALENA begins to cry and AMELIA moves to comfort her. ANGUSTIAS is silent and stunned. MARTIRIO begins to laugh.*)

MARTIRIO: It's a joke! Of course, it is! Adela, get down! Adela!

PONCIA: Stop it, Martirio. Laugh at the dead and lose your tongue.

ANGUSTIAS: (*Begins to scream*) No!!

AMELIA: There's so much blood! Why is there so much blood?

MAGDALENA: She killed her baby too. Just like that woman. Dear God, why are you letting this happen?!

BERNARDA: Silence! Silence in this house! (*To PONCIA.*) You go inside and bring my mother. She should see this. It's her doing.

PONCIA: (*As she exits*) What should I tell the neighbors this time, Doña Bernarda?

BERNARDA: There's nothing to tell. My daughter died a virgin. That's all they need to know. No weeping in public. Weep only when you're alone. Be silent! Everyone! Silence!

(*Each Woman speaks her inner thought.*)

BERNARDA & AMELIA: No one was to leave the house.

AMELIA: But Magdalena's in my arms again . . .

AMELIA & MAGDALENA: Is this what freedom brings?

MAGDALENA: How dare you be the one to escape!

MAGDALENA & ANGUSTIAS: It should have been me . . .

ANGUSTIAS: At least she got a taste of love—

ANGUSTIAS & MARTIRIO: Maybe I could have stopped this.

MARTIRIO: But this is what mother wanted. She knew what might happen. She always knew.

(*PONCIA enters quickly holding a piece of blood-stained white lace, and breaks the spell on the others.*)

PONCIA: Doña Bernarda?

BERNARDA: How dare you bother me now?!

PONCIA: I'm sorry, but—She's dead. Your mother.

(*The DAUGHTERS are stunned into total silence.*)

BERNARDA: No! It's not possible . . . Can't you hear me? I said, Silence. Why can't I have silence? (*Silence.*) WHY CAN I STILL HEAR YOU?!

(*BERNARDA begins to shake. PONCIA, MAGDALENA, ANGUSTIAS, MARTIRIO & AMELIA go to her. They freeze, standing there, staring in silence at the silhouette of ADELA's hanging body.*)

EPILOGUE

MARIA JOSEFA & ADELA appear, floating above them. They are in DON ANTONIO's coffin, like it is a sailing vessel. They sit in silence for a moment. MARIA JOSEFA finally breaks the silence.

MARIA JOSEFA: I told you it was dangerous . . . Next time, maybe we won't have to lose ourselves to be together.

ADELA: We don't make the same journey twice. I'm sure of that. (*Pause.*) Do you think we'll join father soon?

MARIA JOSEFA: No, I'm afraid not. Men and women don't go to the same place.

ADELA: Why not?

MARIA JOSEFA: We're supposed to *rest* now.

ADELA: (*ADELA laughs and begins to sing Lorca's "Romance pascual de los pelegrinitos" [Easter Ballad of the Little Pilgrims].*)

"Hacia Roma caminan dos pelegrinos, a que los case el Papa, mamita,
porque son primos, niña bonita, porque son primos, niña."
[*"Towards Rome are walking two little pilgrims, for the Pope to marry them, mother,
because they are cousins, my pretty girl, because they are cousins, my girl."*]
(*MARIA JOSEFA joins her in singing.*)

ADELA & MARIA JOSEFA: "Le ha preguntado el Papa cómo se llaman. Él le dice que Pepe, mamita, y ella que Adela, niña bonita, y ella que Adela, niña."

[*"The Pope asks them what their names are. He says Pepe, mother,
and she says Adela, my pretty girl, and she says Adela, my girl."*]

ADELA: "Las campanas de Roma ya repicaron porque los pelegrinos, mamita,
ya se han casado, niña bonita, ya se han casado, niña."
[*"The bells of Rome are already ringing, because the little pilgrims, mother,
have gotten married, my pretty girl, have gotten married, my girl."*]

MARIA JOSEFA: It's good to be outside again. I was getting tired of my view. For a view it's always best to go to different parts of the house. I'm somebody different in every room.

ADELA: Me too. (*Pointing.*) Look! A shooting star!

MARIA JOSEFA: If you open your mouth wide and stick out your tongue, you can catch pieces of it and roll them in your mouth. That's a taste of a new beginning. One filled with light.

MARIA JOSEFA & ADELA: One filled with us.

(*They open their mouths and close their eyes as stars fall all around them. PEPE the MAN crosses in front of them as the lights fade.*)

END OF PLAY

Notes

1. Biographical information courtesy of playwright. See also Elizabeth C. Ramírez, *Chicanas/Latinas in American Theatre: A History of Performance* (Bloomington: Indiana University Press, 2000), 131–34.

2. Press kit for Migdalia Cruz, January 2007, and correspondence from the playwright, March 16, 2009.

3. D. J. R. Bruckner, review, "In Performance: Not the Sort of Household That Inspires Return Visitors: 'Another Part of the House,'" *New York Times,* March 25, 1997, available at http://theater2.nytimes.com/mem/theater/treview.html (accessed January 28, 2007).

4. Elizabeth C. Ramírez, *Chicanas/Latinas in American Theatre: A History of Performance* (Bloomington: Indiana University Press, 2000), 134, quoting Alisa Solomon, "House and Home," theater review, *Village Voice,* March 25, 1997, 101.

PART VI

Commentary on Latina Theatre in the United States

The final two chapters are commentaries provided by two leading spokeswomen in the United States about the work of Latinas and women of color. Kathy Perkins and Caridad Svich each expound their views on the state of Latina theatre in the United States. Since they are practicing professionals in the field of playwriting (Caridad) and criticism (Kathy), their global views on all aspects of performance make these contributions of the highest order. Through them and the countless women they have mentored, influenced, and worked with, we can widen our scope even more in disseminating *la voz latina,* and we remain grateful for their closing remarks.

This collection of playtexts furthers the contributions of Latina performance in the annals of theatre history. The playwrights' voices are among many others who have renewed Latinas' and Latinos' sense of community by connecting and reconnecting history and culture, thus insuring the continuation of Latina and Latino dramatic expression. Fortunately, the twenty-first century continues to give rise to many exceptionally gifted Latina and Latino playwrights, ensuring the continuation of what is already a long performance legacy on the U.S. stage.

CHAPTER 12

Contributions by Women of Color

Kathy Perkins

I make an annual ritual of going through the October issue of *American Theatre* magazine to see what women playwrights of color are being produced. This issue announces the seasons of over 250 theatres throughout the United States, listing the names of plays, playwrights, and directors. Looking primarily at mainstream and "anchor" institutions, I count nearly 1,300 plays (excluding certain Shakespeare companies, puppet theatres, and racially specific theatres). For the 2008–9 season, among those 1,300 plays I discovered fewer than thirty written by African American women; over half by just five playwrights and produced by theatres evidently unwilling to take risks to broaden the voices being presented. The number of works by Latinas and Asian Americans was even smaller; almost no Native Americans were represented. The 2009–10 season fared even worse for women of color.

I hear my critics saying "but Lynn Nottage just won the 2009 Pulitzer Prize for *Ruined,* which means women of color are really gaining recognition." Well, yes and no. While I was thrilled that Nottage became the second African American woman to win the coveted prize, my joy was muted by the fact that too many women of color continue to work in isolation and in near anonymity. Plays written by women of color receive countless workshops, but very few full productions. To prove my point, the 1st National Meeting of Women of Color Writing Drama specifically convened in September 2008 in Chicago, to address this issue of invisibility. The conference was born from the Black Women Playwrights Group (BWPG), a national organization that, as noted at its website, "has been a growth place for everyone from the very young writers to those who have been nationally recognized. The work comes from the communal, and yet diverse, understanding of being Black and female in America." With this first national conference, BWPG extended "the nurturing sphere to include *all* women of color writing plays and scripts." In the announcement of the event, Karen L. B. Evans, president and founder of the BWPG, was "really excited by the vision of BWPG operating nationally in its two capacities—as a 'grass roots' organization, meeting up with women writers at whatever point they are in their careers—and also being able to advocate nationally for works written by women of color." Evans pointed out "that since Lorraine Hansberry's *Raisin in the Sun* only three Black women have been produced on Broadway," and although Broadway recognized Latina playwright Quiara Hudes with a 2008 Tony Award for *In the Heights,* it has still never produced a play by an Asian American woman." In a letter Evans sent to the individual members of BWPG, she especially urged these Black women to attend, telling them: "Everyone knows we are woefully underrepresented in theater, film, and television. As a result, we become rather rare, amorphous creatures in the minds of not only the public, but also those who are producing theater, film, and television." As she added, "We are not rare. . . . This is your chance to speak loudly and clearly and say, 'This is who we are, this is what we think, and we are here. We are all here.'"[1]

Approximately a hundred practitioners attended the Chicago meeting, with mostly African American women although some Latinas and Asian Americans also participated. The women realized that this conference was the beginning of an important dialogue, using the meeting as a way to share ideas and provide support. The topic continues to be at the forefront of discussion and concern both regionally and nationally, including forums at the Black Theatre Festival, Latino Theatre Festival (Chicago), the recent Theatre Communications Group (TCG) Conference, and other venues. I had the opportunity to speak on a panel at the TCG Conference titled "Are You Looking for Me? Diversifying Creative Teams," and Professor Sandra Richards (Northwestern University) and I brought this concern before an even larger audience in our 2010 article, "Contemporary Women Playwrights."[2]

Works by women of color make important contributions to the breadth and diversity of American culture. The women are there but simply need to be heard. In 1996 Roberta Uno and I coedited *Contemporary Plays by Women of Color,* a collection of plays representing a diversity of voices. We were amazed at the number of plays written at the time, but not enough were being produced, particularly in our mainstream institutions. Fortunately, today women of color are unwilling to wait for the call from mainstream theatres to have their work produced, and they are taking charge through one-woman shows, such as Brenda Wong Aoki and several of the women discussed in this collection. Many women have started their own companies to address the lack of opportunities available to most female playwrights of color. The Chicago-based Teatra Luna, founded in 2000, is one such theatre that has attracted a large audience. According to their website: "We came together because we realized that the stories and experiences of Latina/Hispana women were undervalued and underrepresented not only on the Chicago stage, but beyond. . . . We were also concerned that the few parts written for Latina women often went to non-Latina actresses. We felt that we had to do something. Our answer was Teatro Luna, Chicago's first and only all-Latina Theater."[3] Another example is the Asian American playwright and director who created her own company, the Young Jean Lee's Theatre Company, in order to write and direct her own plays. This Obie award–winning experimental playwright-director Young Jean Lee, like Teatra Luna, has attracted large audiences nationally and internationally with such works as *The Shipment* and *Songs of the Dragons Flying to Heaven,* which focus on racial relationships and stereotypes.

I am hopeful that in this exciting age of change, where we have witnessed the election of an African American president for the first time in our nation's history, where we have a Latina now serving on the U.S. Supreme Court, and where we are seeing more and more women of color being appointed and elected to positions of power, we will soon see a greater impact of these women spread to the larger theatre community. Given this climate, I see this anthology as a much-needed work, especially given the fact that Latinas/Latinos are the fastest-growing minority in the United States. I am grateful to the contributors and the editors for bringing us this new collection. We need to hear different voices. We simply must see the work by women of color on our stages.

Notes

1. Conference announcement for the lst National Meeting for Women of Color Writing Drama, at http://www.blackwomenplaywrights.org/revamped_site/conference_2008.asp, accessed November 1, 2010; and Letter to members of the Black Women Playwrights' Group, at http://www.blackwomenplaywrights.org/revamped_site/survey.asp, accessed July 24, 2010.

2. Sandra Richards and Kathy Perkins, "Contemporary Women Playwrights," *Theatre Journal* 62, no. 4 (December 2010).

3. See Teatro Luna, Chicago, http://www.teatroluna.org/hist.html, accessed November 5, 2010.

CHAPTER 13

NoPassport: Dreaming the Americas

Caridad Svich

We're all travelers now: cyborgs expert at multitasking and multitracking our lives. We move through multiple time zones in virtual spaces that has become a substitute for the real, and time-travel imaginatively through different historical epochs while we become more and more alienated from the chaos of our present. We let ourselves pretend we live in a sober culture. Our soberness is smoke-free, faith-based, and news-cropped to suit our immediate needs. In the shadow of globalization, we are so intoxicated by our soberness that global climate change can be deemed either a reality or a leftist-leaning political construct depending on your point of view, although scientific indicators point consistently to the former. The 2001 invasion of Afghanistan and the 2003 invasion of Iraq were either 'necessary' inventions or bungled combat operations, depending on your point of view. Yet casualties continue to mount. Coffins are filled.

Terminally jetlagged, we suffer the traveler's condition but live like tourists. Our dislocations free us from responsibility and let us entertain the hysteria but not the pain of the immigrant, the exiled and the displaced. We comfortably speak in the assumed "We" to include all, but is it a habitual verbal posture, a sign of arrogance, or a true desire to include and really see who We are? Authenticity is furiously traced to bloodlines down to the bone to validate works of art and life. Yet, fiction—the imagined imaginary—may contain perhaps the most authentic expressions of selves because of and not due to the stories that can be told outside our own bodies, skins, and genders.

Race is debated, constructed, and erased, despite the persistent racism that exists in this country and around the world. Class is a floating signifier that refuses to be stared at head-on because the romance of a classless society is too seductive to let go of. Talk is diminished to action in much of our art. An emphasis is placed on speech devoid of too much history, and unburdened by reference. Speak a language that everyone can understand is the test screening and writing-by-committee approach. The fear of being misunderstood is so great that our mainstream talk is reduced to a steady stream of flattened consonants and vowels democratized to the point of anonymity. The being that is inside the language is a pure sign as easily read as culturally conditioned traffic signals. Yet our streets and neighborhoods and countryside are tricked out with words and phrases and defiantly irreducible historical talk barely listened to or caught by our wily all channels all the time satellite and wireless services. In the age of commercialized hip-hop and ersatz salsa, barrio babies are asked and feel often required to sell their language to the ad machine, the dream machine that produces conglomerate-in-the-making pop artists and singers who embrace beige-r and blonder versions of themselves to fit the global market.

Indigenous voices, meanwhile, tend to be routinely dismissed, marginalized, or worse: ignored. North, Central, and South America and the Latino/a cultures of the Caribbean rise in wary fits and starts as political leaders inspire hope and tension. Morales's uneasy grasp of Bolivia, Chavez's bullying but charismatic hold on Venezuela, Lula da Silva's poised but difficult path in crime-ridden Brazil and all the recent changes in the politics of *el Sur* do not in and of themselves change the daily trouble of lives led by itinerant farmers, refugees, and day laborers, who are constantly shortchanged by the inequities of corruption and greed effected by top-down and middle-middle graft. The case of the women of Juárez has been closed by Mexican authorities, violating the memory of the lives of all the women who have been killed along the border. Resilient, fragile Cuba finds itself at a potential crossroads, and a young generation is increasingly squeezed by a dollar economy that is forcing them and their grandparents into a market mentality: a mindset of Nike, Adidas, and Juicy Couture desire that threatens the spiritual ecosystem of the island's fragile infrastructure. And Spain—maligned, fetishized, flamenco-ized Spain—is constantly taken to task for its bloody conquests and colonizations centuries ago, while England, France, and the United States are given the very short end of the memory grievance stick. Consistently erased Spain—the land of Lorca and Almodóvar, but dare we know anyone else before, between, and after?—is Europe's "hidden" (as in not in the news) immigrant sanctuary, as citizens of Bolivia, Colombia, Ecuador, and El Salvador find *albergue* (refuge or shelter) in Madrid and Barcelona. Spain is being remade through Latin American eyes. What new languages will arise in ten years' time? And will we be too virtually jetlagged to really listen?

In this mobile culture where everything we experience must fit into the palm of our hand, myopia is paramount. We're so in touch that we can't really see the person sitting next to us on the bus or subway car. In the big city lived small, even in the supposed small of the Midwest, the digital close-up view is preferred to the full-on gaze of our fellow citizen. The culture of Us and Them increases as the political climate keeps our country divided in conveniently reliable patches of red and blue, and keeps the world out there a mass of targets that can be struck through the computer screen. More and more memorials are erected to sustain and contain our collective grief. We tour memorials and monuments as if they were tourist attractions, checking one after another off of our list of dutiful spiritual cleansing, divesting ourselves in the process of fear and empathetic recognition.

It is fear, in effect, that holds us as culture hostage. The orange and amber and yellow alerts contrast with the very real immediate fear of collapse and ruin possible at every nonmarketable turn. The fear of not being understood absolutely and clearly without question or ambiguity. The fear of being too elitist or too lowbrow. The fear of theatrical intimacy in favor of distanced spectacle and pageantry. The fear of being too serious, and the fear of being too frivolous. We live in fear of losing the audience. So, we test-market, research, and do national surveys to figure out how we can bring the audience back to the noncommercial theatre, which has stolen away proportionally only the same mere fraction it has always done with its steady diet of splashy, and sometimes extraordinarily minimalist, musicals and the occasional play or two.

Plays, you see, those strange, aberrant beings are the constant topic of symposiums, neo boho, freak-folk coffee klatches, earnest campfire rabble-rousing on university campuses, and utopian-spirited conferences. What is happening to the American play? Where is the American play? What are we going to do about the American play now that all those Brits are coming here and not only telling us their stories but our own stories back to us? In the endless questioning and debate, the point often missed about the American play is, well, its Americanness. How often do we see plays from Canada in the United States? How often from Central and South America? How often from the Caribbean? And how often stories written from the perspectives of not only North and South, but the hemisphere itself? And who gets to tell the stories?

In the state of play discussion, the author is usually the starting point. But what happens when, say, an Australian writer wants to tell a story about Buenos Aires? Or an Anglo native of Virginia wants to write about Cubans in Miami? Questions of validity rear their ugly head around the ownership of stories. As writers, the chief responsibility we have is to tell a story that moves us as compellingly and artfully as we can. Of course, the dicey politics of co-opting another person's history and experience enters in. But if we limit ourselves to only telling a prescribed story about where we grew up and how and where we live now, then the provincial mindset that often predicates and keeps the business but sometimes offends the art of what we do in the theatre will flourish. Our theater too much of the time lives in transitive verb farces, gerundial comedies, and capitalized dramas wrested from the topical hall of mirrors we choose not to see past and through. Neat stories about neat people doing crazily cozily neat things sit unwell with the larger American task of speaking to the many politicized and depoliticized bodies that live and perform in the Americas. As writers and practitioners working with verbal, visual, and physical text, we have a moral duty to write inside and outside our sex, skin, class, and age. The pain of exile and migration is not only told through the on-site interview but also the imagined transcription of an encounter that took place one hundred years before you were born. Future stories, past stories, and present stories are alive in the invisibly visible traces of our many intercultural illuminations. Our American theatre can tell its U.S. stories, but it should pay heed to not only the stories of the rich and highly educated, but also the stories of the poor, working class, and vanishing middle class.

In this big ol' country that traces its sound to broken steps on prairie grass and the mannered mysteries of backwoods songs, speak the stories out loud of how an oil rig in Iraq dictates the life of a checkout clerk in Oklahoma *and* a field worker in Venezuela.

Speak out the story of a non-Gothic southern farm family teaching its children to sing a Guatemalan song learned from a *bracero* who's been working their land for ten years. Speak a quiet story of how legislated terror keeps dirty wars alive and the heritage of nations captive in an endless cycle of erasure. In American theater, a border story can take place not only in California, Arizona, or Texas, but also within a three-block radius in a Philadelphia neighborhood. A Latina story can exist in a bayou where not a word of Spanish or Spanglish is spoken. A straight story can be told queer. If we dream our American theater as big as it truly is and really listen and let others listen to the many stories that inhabit this hemisphere, then our stages will not beg for art. Rather, it will be plentiful in nonstreamlined, non-ready-made, perhaps not immediately understood languages that will make our theater and our daily talk as spiritually rich as it truly is.

The choices we have as artists and presenters are vast. As vast as desire itself. If we can brace ourselves to stare good, long, and hard at the chaos, tragedy, and farce in which we live, then we will truly be travelers in our increasingly mobile world. But it's up to us if we want to continue to live in the bordered spaces that govern the divide between US and Them, or take the glorious and perhaps confounding risk of living and making art without a passport.

Note

Caridad Svich is a U.S. Latina playwright, translator, lyricist, and editor whose works include *12 Ophelias, Alchemy of Desire/Dead-Man's Blues, Any Place But Here, Fugitive Pieces,* and *Iphigenia . . . A Rave Fable.* She is an alumna playwright of New Dramatists, a founder of NoPassport Theatre Alliance & Press, an associate editor of *Contemporary Theatre Review,* and a contributing editor of *TheatreForum.* She has edited several books on theatre and performance published by TCG, Smith & Kraus, BackStage Books, and Manchester University Press. She holds a Master of Fine Arts from the University of California, San Diego.

ELIZABETH C. RAMÍREZ is the fine arts specialist administrator with the Edgewood Independent School District of San Antonio, Texas, and the author of *Chicanas/Latinas on the American Stage: A History of Performance.*

CATHERINE CASIANO has assisted Elizabeth C. Ramírez with numerous dramaturgical projects and is an attorney practicing family and criminal law with indigent Latina/Latino populations in San Antonio.

The University of Illinois Press
is a founding member of the
Association of University Presses.

University of Illinois Press
1325 South Oak Street
Champaign, IL 61820-6903
www.press.uillinois.edu